15–

IN THE NAME OF WAR

IN THE NAME OF WAR

Judicial Review and the War Powers since 1918

CHRISTOPHER N. MAY

HARVARD UNIVERSITY PRESS

*Cambridge, Massachusetts,
and London, England*
1989

Copyright © 1989 by the President and Fellows of Harvard College
All rights reserved
Printed in the United States of America
10 9 8 7 6 5 4 3 2 1

This book is printed on acid-free paper, and its binding materials
have been chosen for strength and durability.

Library of Congress Cataloging-in-Publication Data
May, Christopher N.
  In the name of war : judicial review and the war powers since 1918/
Christopher N. May.
    p. cm.
  Bibliography: p.
  Includes index.
  ISBN 0-674-44549-X (alk. paper)
  1. Judicial review—United States—History. 2. War and emergency
powers—United States—History. 3. World War, 1914–1918—Law
and legislation—United States. 4. United States—Politics and govern-
ment—1913–1921. I. Title.
KF4575.M39 1987
342.73'052—dc19   88-9444
[347.30252]   CIP

For Barbara

Preface

This is a story about the birth of a principle. Before World War I the Supreme Court—with one short-lived exception—refused to pass on the validity of laws adopted under the war powers of the Constitution. As a result, by simply invoking its emergency authority the government could ignore the Constitution with impunity. In December 1919 the justices suddenly announced that they were abandoning this century-old practice of nonintervention; by 1924 it was firmly established that even war measures were subject to judicial review. The explanation for this dramatic turnabout lies in the rich and fascinating history of the late Progressive Era. The economic, social, and political forces which led the government to persist in using its war powers despite the signing of the armistice were in the end responsible for enhancing the role of the Constitution in periods of national emergency.

The idea for this book grew out of a National Endowment for the Humanities seminar taught by the late Robert M. Cover in New Haven during the summer of 1980. Bob's interest and enthusiasm were instrumental in my decision to undertake this study.

I am deeply grateful to those who assisted me along the way. The scholars upon whose work I have drawn are cited with appreciation in the notes. I am particularly indebted to Allan P. Ides and Daniel L.

Stewart, who reviewed successive drafts of the manuscript and offered many valuable suggestions. Arthur N. Frakt read parts of the manuscript and, as dean, aided the project in every possible way. Frederick J. Lower, Jr., gave me the benefit of his good counsel on numerous occasions. Albert R. Sonntag helped to clarify my understanding of Progressivism. The errors that remain are my own.

I would also like to thank R. Michael McReynolds, Alohoa P. South, and Steven D. Tilley of the National Archives and Records Service; James H. Hutson and his staff at the Library of Congress Manuscript Division; Mrs. James H. Chadbourn of the Harvard Law School Library; Richard H. Engeman of the University of Washington Library; Marty Lacey of the Stanford University Library; and William J. Vollmar of the Anheuser-Busch Companies, Inc.

The following persons and institutions graciously extended permission to quote from materials under their control: Paul A. Freund; the Harvard Law School Library; the Library of Congress; the Princeton University Press; Tracy Strong; the University of California Library, Los Angeles; and the Yale University Library.

Ruth Palmer typed and retyped the entire manuscript, always with care and good humor. I am also indebted to Frederica Sedgwick and Karen Verdugo of the Loyola Law School Library, and to Pam Buckles, Erlinda Tupas, and John Harflinger, who provided secretarial assistance. Aida D. Donald of Harvard University Press was a most helpful and encouraging editor.

In addition to an NEH summer fellowship, financial support for this book came from the James P. Bradley Chair in Constitutional Law at Loyola Law School.

Above all I wish to thank Barbara, my wife, whose patience and understanding saw me through the hard times. Without her this book could not have been written.

C.N.M.

Contents

1 ~   The War Powers at the Armistice:
      Where the Will Meets the Way   *1*

2 ~   Experiments in Socialism:
      Federal Control of the Rails and the Wires   *26*

3 ~   Wartime Prohibition:
      "A Freakish Legislative Child"   *60*

4 ~   The High Cost of Living:
      Recipe for Revolution   *94*

5 ~   The War on Radicalism:
      Prosecuting the American Heretic   *133*

6 ~   Censorship and the "Cowed Mind":
      Perpetuating the Aura of Repression   *162*

7 ~   Judicial Review:
      Its Hour Come Round at Last   *191*

8 ~   The Tug-of-War over Rent Control:
      A Futile Exercise in Defiance   *223*

9 ~   Preserving the Legacy:
      The Timing of Judicial Intervention   *254*

      Notes   *279*
      Index   *359*

IN THE NAME OF WAR

~ 1 ~

The War Powers at the Armistice:
Where the Will Meets the Way

With the signing of the armistice on November 11, 1918, the United States passed into a twilight zone. The country's nineteen-month involvement in World War I was over; yet, because the Senate would not ratify the Versailles Treaty with its League of Nations provisions, the legal state of war persisted. In July 1921 Congress approved a joint resolution terminating the conflict, but there were serious doubts as to the adequacy of this procedure. It was not until November 1921, when new treaties were ratified and proclaimed, that the war finally came to a formal and unequivocal end.[1]

During this three-year period of neither war nor peace the federal government drew upon the full panoply of its war powers. The measures undertaken included operating the country's rail and communications systems; seizing the cable companies; imposing nationwide prohibition; regulating consumer prices; taking civil and criminal action against strikers; prosecuting radicals; censoring the press; and establishing rent control in the District of Columbia.

Though each of these endeavors was clothed in war powers garb, none bore any genuine connection to the war. Despite the transparency of this pretext, the federal judiciary initially refused to question the constitutionality of these statutes, adhering to the long-standing position that war powers legislation is not subject to judicial review.

As the pattern of abuse continued, the Supreme Court began to reassess this stance, eventually abandoning it entirely.

The Courts and the Progressive Movement

The government's use of the war powers after the armistice was closely tied to the Progressive movement. This largely middle-class reform effort was a variant of the Populist crusade of the 1890s. It sought to rescue America from a moral, economic, and political decay which seemed to threaten the future of democracy. Opportunity had been drastically curtailed by the rise of the trusts, while many of the nation's workers lived in a state of virtual poverty. At the same time efforts to cure these evils were severely hampered by the fact that the government seemingly had become the pawn of corporations and the rich.[2]

Despite their perception of widespread malaise, the Progressives were deeply optimistic. Propelled by a strong sense of idealism, they believed that the country's problems were the result of moral deterioration, economic injustice, and disregard for the law. Appealing to a strong sense of individual responsibility and personal guilt, they sought to expose the nation's ills to a public whose conscience had been aroused. Once the muckrakers had done their work, reforms might be enacted. For this program to succeed, however, it was necessary to repair the machinery of government so that politics was no longer the domain of special interests.

At the state and municipal levels Progressivism manifested itself in such political innovations as home rule, city manager government, direct primaries, initiative and referendum devices, recall of public officials, and the civil service. Among its numerous substantive reforms were child labor laws, wage and hour legislation, workers' compensation systems, corporate income and inheritance taxes, and public ownership of various utilities.

Many of the issues the Progressives sought to address defied solution at the local level, causing reformers to look more and more to the national government. As Eric Goldman noted:

The problem with which the reformers were most concerned, the large corporation, did not yield to state action. Time after time progressives battled a law through a legislature only to have a court rule that it violated the state constitution . . . Worse yet, state social legislation was being thrown out almost as fast as it was passed . . . In the early 1900's, much more than in the Populist era, reform eyes were focusing on Washington. The trend was so marked that . . . some progressive writers were even arguing that the state had no place "in our governmental system."

The Interstate Commerce Act of 1887 and the Sherman Antitrust Act passed three years later heralded the new approach, which became even more pronounced after the turn of the century.[3]

For a time Progressives were divided over the issue of centralization. Advanced reformers such as Herbert Croly, Walter Lippmann, and Walter Weyl urged that federal authority be greatly expanded. Their ideas found expression in Theodore Roosevelt's call for a New Nationalism. Though Woodrow Wilson initially favored a more limited role for government, it was clear by 1916 that these differences were more imaginary than real. In implementing his New Freedom program Wilson secured passage of most of the principal reforms advocated by Roosevelt's Progressive party.[4]

The Progressive emphasis on a powerful national government was matched by a belief in aggressive leadership on the part of the executive branch. Despite the dangers inherent in such a scheme, a resolute president could effect positive change without the delay, shortsightedness, and compromise that distinguish the legislative process. Croly argued that the liberal statesman should "proclaim, and . . . assert his own leadership" over "the many 'plain people,' " thereby "creating his own following." Under the benign direction of a strong executive, reformers hoped to save the middle class from its own stupidity—a stupidity which might otherwise result in anarchy and revolution.[5]

This ameliorative aspect of Progressivism had deep preservationist roots. Much of the reform fervor stemmed from a conviction that unless America rapidly transformed itself, democracy was imperiled. Richard Hofstadter observed of these reformers, "On one side they feared the power of the plutocracy, on the other the poverty and restlessness of the masses." Nearly all Progressives dreaded the prospect of class warfare, including Croly, Weyl, Lippmann, and Roosevelt; and in the 1912 campaign Wilson cautioned that without basic change turmoil might ensue. He later described his political philosophy as that of seeking "sober and practical legislative reforms which shall remove the chief provocations of revolution." These views were shared by Louis Brandeis, who had helped to shape the New Freedom. In 1905 Brandeis declared, "The greatest factors making for communism, socialism, or anarchy among a free people, are the excesses of capital." The future Supreme Court justice told the Commercial Club of Boston that "true conservatism necessarily involves progress" and suggested, "We shall inevitably be swept farther toward socialism unless we curb the excesses of our financial magnates."[6]

One of the most formidable obstacles to reform was the nation's judiciary. In the three decades before the armistice federal and state courts pitted themselves against Populist and Progressive programs. Much of the story can be told in numbers. In the 97 years from 1789 through 1885 the Supreme Court invalidated only 18 acts of Congress and 111 state laws. From 1886 to 1918—a period only a third as long—23 federal statutes and 174 local measures were overturned. Of the latter more than 90 were struck down between 1910 and 1918.[7]

The state court picture was sketchier but far more striking. An analysis of ten states reveals that from 1900 to 1918 over 400 statutes were held to violate either the state or federal Constitution. In New York local courts invalidated nearly 300 laws between 1861 and 1905, of which more than half were overturned after 1890. Before 1900 New York judges agreed with the constitutional challenge in fewer than 25 percent of the cases, whereas between 1901 and 1905 such claims succeeded more than 44 percent of the time. A composite study of all state and federal courts in the United States disclosed that in the six-year period from 1903 through 1908 some 400 statutes were invalidated.[8]

Of the state and federal laws overturned by the U.S. Supreme Court only a handful involved social and economic reforms. Yet because of their visibility and importance, these cases became bench marks of judicial action. Among the measures held unconstitutional by the high court between 1905 and 1918 were a New York statute regulating the number of hours bakers could be employed; a federal law barring interstate railroads from discriminating against union members; a Kansas ban against "yellow dog contracts" which barred workers from joining a union; and a federal law regulating the use of child labor.[9]

When one looks below the Supreme Court level, the judiciary's anti-Progressive bias becomes even more visible. The Department of Labor found that between 1890 and 1922 federal and state courts declared more than three hundred pieces of labor legislation unconstitutional; nearly two-thirds of these cases were decided after 1900. Most of the decisions involved state legislation held invalid by the highest court of the state, often based on the federal Constitution. Because such decisions were not reviewable by the Supreme Court at this time, reactionary state judges exercised an absolute veto over local reform efforts.[10]

In their assault on state and federal legislation courts often relied on vague and open-textured clauses of the Constitution, the meaning of which was clear only to judges. The due process clauses of the Fifth and Fourteenth Amendments were used to protect certain judicially defined liberties against "unreasonable" government interference. From the standpoint of the Progressives the most significant of these natural liberties was freedom of contract. Of the four Supreme Court rulings just noted, three concluded that the legislation in question impaired the liberty of employers and employees to bargain freely. Courts invoked other equally indefinite constitutional provisions, including the due process clause as it pertained to property, the equal protection clause, and the dormant commerce clause.[11]

Through a mechanistic application of abstract legal principles courts became the stronghold of laissez-faire. Their decisions frequently reflected the Social Darwinistic belief that all facets of human evolution are governed by laws beyond man's control. They saw any attempt to regulate the struggle for existence as not only futile and misguided but often illegal as well. There was considerable merit to the charge, leveled by Justice Oliver Wendell Holmes in 1905, that the Constitution had come to embody the "economic theory" of "Herbert Spencer's Social Statics."[12]

The Scholarly Assault on Judicial Review

Judicial opposition to Progressivism deprived millions of men, women, and children of the benefits of reform legislation and increased the danger of social unrest. Moreover, a growing public antipathy toward the courts threatened them as an independent branch of government. In an effort to ease the crisis liberal thinkers began to reexamine the foundations of judicial review. As one writer explained in 1914, "Socialists and Progressives are waging a relentless war on ... the veto power of American courts as 'one of the most cruel and ruthless checks upon democracy permitted by any civilized people.' " The campaign proceeded on several fronts. At a philosophical level scholars rejected the idea that higher principles of law could be invoked to restrain the will of the people. Historians sought to undermine the moral authority of the Constitution by showing that the Framers had protected their own selfish interests. Finally, the legitimacy of the judiciary's self-proclaimed right to overturn action of the political branches was again called into question. This combined offensive provided strong support for the popular movement to curtail the power of the courts.[13]

The doctrine of judicial review was an apparent anomaly in a nation founded on democratic principles. For nearly a century this "anti-majoritarian difficulty" had been resolved by the notion that judges did not make law but merely discerned preexisting rules, which were applied to the case at hand. Even when the courts interpreted the Constitution, their role was portrayed as one of neutrally ascertaining whatever "necessary meanings" were logically present in the clause in question. Law in this sense was a "brooding omnipresence in the sky," and judges, rather than acting as legislators, were akin to astronomers who "declared" that which already existed. As Roscoe Pound said in 1910, "Eighteenth century jurists conceived that certain principles were inherent in nature. . . and that these principles were discoverable *a priori*. They held that it was the business of the jurist to discover these principles, and, when discovered, to deduce a system therefrom and test all actual rules thereby. Such is even now the orthodox method in our constitutional law."[14]

This conception of judicial review, however, was being challenged by advanced thinkers. While Social Darwinism had "brought to the iron chain of ideas protecting the status quo all the added strength and modernity of steel," it also provided the key to unlock that chain. If all things were in fact products of their environment, then it followed that the beliefs and institutions which were dominant at any particular historical moment were but temporary victors in a process of evolution. As such they could lay no greater claim to validity than those arrangements which eventually would succeed them. Rather than simply wait for change to occur, individuals might shape that transformation by experimenting with the environment, perhaps accelerating the arrival of a better social and economic order. In contrast to the grim inevitability of laissez-faire, Pragmatism emerged as a profoundly optimistic creed and stimulated progress in all areas of human endeavor. Its influence was such that by 1912 "Pragmatism was already a national password."[15]

As William James explained in 1907, this philosophy rested on the premise that "the truth of an idea is not a stagnant property inherent in it. Truth *happens* to an idea. It *becomes* true, is *made* true by events." Concepts have value only as "instruments of action," and "true" thoughts are those which prove helpful in attaining a goal. "You can say of [such an idea] either that 'it is useful because it is true' or that 'it is true because it is useful.' Both these phrases mean exactly the same thing." James articulated in philosophical terms what others were discovering in history, economics, political science, and religion. The participants in this "revolt against formalism" rejected the notion of an abstract and immutable truth in favor of a knowledge linked to the protean world of fact and experience.[16]

Legal pragmatists—or "pragmatic instrumentalists," as Robert Summers describes them—spurned the idea of law as a system of logical deductions. Pound complained that "after philosophical, political, economic and sociological thought have given up the eighteenth-century law of nature, it is still the premise of the American lawyer." He declared that "the revolution which has taken place in other sciences in this regard must take place and is taking place in jurisprudence also." As Holmes wrote in 1881, "The life of the law has not been logic: it has been experience. The felt necessities of the time, the prevalent moral and political theories, intuitions of public policy, avowed or unconscious, even the prejudices which judges share with their fellow-men, have had a good deal more to do than the syllogism in determining the rules by which men should be governed."[17]

Once law was seen as a human fabric, it was possible to abandon the fiction that judges perform merely a declaratory function. Instrumentalists argued that judges were as much engaged in lawmaking as were legislators. In the area of constitutional law, courts often interpreted opaque provisions whose content could not be ascertained solely through historical research or logical deduction. Contrary to the orthodox explanation of judicial review, when judges gave meaning to such cryptic phrases as *liberty, due process,* and *equal protection,* they were in fact creating law no less than when they announced a new rule of tort liability. To the extent that courts invoked these clauses to block reform measures, they were in effect using the Constitution to shield the status quo from changes which they "as legislators might think . . . injudicious."[18]

Scholars mounted a relentless attack on the formalistic conception

of judicial review. In 1909 Walter Dodd asserted that "courts have
... invaded the field of public policy and are quick to declare unconstitutional almost any laws of which they disapprove." Ernst Freund
echoed the sentiment, observing that "unwise legislation" was
"treated by the courts as unconstitutional." In *Social Reform and the
Constitution* Frank Goodnow charged that through judicial construction of the Bill of Rights natural law served as "the basis of the
American constitutional system" at a time when "most students regard the postulation of fundamental political principles of universal
application as ... 'mere useless opprobrious theory.' " Pound believed that "it is not what the Legislature desires, but what the courts
regard as juridically permissible that in the end becomes law. Statutes
give way before the settled habits of legal thinking which we call the
common law."[19]

In bringing attention to the reality of judicial lawmaking, instrumentalists did not claim that this was a function that courts must
somehow avoid. Their focus was rather on the values which should
inform the process. They disagreed with the practice of interpreting
law mainly with an eye to preserving its internal harmony and co-
herence. Since law was a device for attaining practical ends, the goal
ought instead to be the realization of society's wants. Roscoe Pound
thus stressed the need for "pragmatism as a philosophy of law; for the
adjustment of principles and doctrines to the human condition they
are to govern rather than to assumed first principles; for putting the
human factor in the central place and relegating logic to its true
position as an instrument." J. Allen Smith urged that "laws, institutions and systems of government ... be judged in relation to the ends
which they have in view. They are good or bad according as they are
well or poorly adapted to social needs." Walter Lippmann suggested
that if judges had "made law that dealt with modern necessities," the
"revolt against the judiciary" would not have occurred. This perception of law as a tool for fulfilling society's needs harmonized perfectly
with the ameliorative side of Progressivism. Had reformers "articulated a theory of law, it almost certainly would have been instrumentalist and pragmatic."[20]

The same approach was to be employed in reading the Constitution. Holmes thought that "the 14th Amendment is perverted when it
is held to prevent the natural outcome of a dominant opinion." Pound
and Goodnow believed that judges should construe the charter cre-
atively to uphold measures necessary for human progress. These views

were endorsed by Woodrow Wilson in his 1912 presidential campaign. "All that progressives ask," he said, "is permission—in an era when 'development,' 'evolution,' is the scientific word—to interpret the Constitution according to the Darwinian principle; all they ask is recognition of the fact that a nation is a living thing and not a machine."[21]

This insistence that the Constitution be read in accord with democratically defined values threatened those provisions which imposed limits on the majoritarian process. The Bill of Rights and the principle that the federal government was one of limited, enumerated powers were at odds with a philosophy whose implicit premise is that the end justifies the means. This basic incompatibility between legal pragmatism and constitutionalism is suggested by Holmes's famous remark that "free speech stands no differently than freedom from vaccination"; while "the occasions would be rarer when you cared enough to stop it," he said, "if for any reason you did care enough you wouldn't care a damn for the suggestion that you . . . might be wrong." Though Holmes later changed his view of free speech, the attitude he expressed in 1918 typified the instrumentalist belief that the majority should ordinarily not be restrained.[22]

The idea that a century-and-a-quarter-old charter could control the fate of later generations was further undermined by the work of several leading historians. A contemporary writer noted that most Americans viewed the Constitution with "almost superstitious reverence," considering it "the last word which can be said as to the proper form of government—a form believed to be suited to all times and conditions." In the decade before the war two books appeared which portrayed it as an attempt by the rich to protect their own interests. J. Allen Smith's *Spirit of American Government* was published in 1907 and achieved great notoriety in Progressive circles. Its thesis was that the "wealthy and conservative classes," in order to curb the effects of the American Revolution, had "posed as the friends of democracy," and through "political sophistry" persuaded the people to adopt "a form of government the avowed object of which was to limit their power." The dilemma facing reformers, Smith said, was that "we are trying to make an undemocratic Constitution the vehicle of democratic rule. Our Constitution embodies the political philosophy of the eighteenth century, not that of to-day. It was framed for one purpose while we are trying to use it for another." The problem was compounded by the fact that this anachronistic document was rigidly enforced by the judiciary. Smith denounced the Supreme Court as an embodiment of the "monarchial principle" and "the old medieval doctrine that the King can do no wrong."[23]

Six years later Charles Beard wrote an even more damning critique. In his *Economic Interpretation of the Constitution* Beard analyzed the financial position of each delegate to the Philadelphia convention and concluded that the Framers "were, with a few exceptions, immediately, directly, and personally interested in, and derived economic advantages from, the establishment of the new system." The Constitution, he said, "was essentially an economic document based upon the concept that the fundamental private rights of property are anterior to government and morally beyond the reach of popular majorities."   The effect was to strip the Constitution of its veil of sanctity, revealing an arrangement through which the upper classes sought to preserve their position of dominance. Beard later denied any intention "of forwarding the interests of the Progressive party," but the book was quickly seized upon by reformers. *La Follette's Magazine* declared: "The time has come when . . . the Constitution, which has ever been the retreat of privilege, must be changed. When we once realize that this was a human document, written by men acting in many cases under human impulses, we shall have achieved the initial attitude necessary to change it. Professor Beard's book . . . will do more than any other volume to set us right."[24]

The judiciary's entrenched opposition to social legislation reignited the controversy over whether *Marbury v. Madison* had been correctly decided. The power of review which John Marshall there proclaimed for the Court was nowhere alluded to in the Constitution. While the matter previously had been the subject of controversy, the new debate was more intense than ever before. A year before his *Economic Interpretation* appeared, Beard published a work seeking to demonstrate that *Marbury* was consistent with the Framers' intent. Shortly thereafter influential writings by Edward Corwin and Horace Davis cast fresh doubt on the matter and suggested that the doctrine was one of pure judicial usurpation.[25]

Popular Efforts to Curb the Courts

The scholarly assault on judicial review fueled public discontent. In 1905 Pound noted with alarm that "there is a growing popular dissatisfaction with our legal system" and "a feeling that it prevents everything and does nothing." A few years later, Jane Addams observed that "the one symptom among working-men which most definitely indicates a class feeling is a growing distrust of the integrity of the courts, the belief that the present judge has been a corporation attorney, that his sympathies and experience and his whole view of life is on the corporation side." In 1914 one writer reported that "judges imbued with eighteenth-century natural law notions . . . are frequently held up to ridicule and condemnation."[26]

Like many liberal intellectuals Pound was committed to reform, but with preservationist concerns. He feared that the decisions striking down Progressive legislation might have caused irreparable "injury to the courts and to the public regard . . . for constitutional law in particular." He warned that unless the judiciary were to "compromise" by striking "a more even balance between individualism and socialism," the people might say, " 'Have we not reason, as well as our courts?' " Pound later cautioned that law "must not become so completely artificial that the public is led to regard it as wholly arbitrary. No institution can stand upon such a basis to-day."[27]

Few scholarly critics went beyond recommending that the courts practice self-restraint. Pound thought that the solution lay in teaching judges to respond to the needs of society. Holmes hoped that by recognizing the legislative nature of the judicial process, courts would function less dogmatically. And in a seminal essay published in 1893 James Bradley Thayer urged return to a "rule of administration" under which the legislature's reading of the Constitution would be accepted unless the lawmakers "have not merely made a mistake, but have made a very clear one—so clear that it is not open to rational question."[28]

In popular circles, however, dissatisfaction with judicial review led to a sweeping array of proposals for basic institutional reform. The bulk of these demands came after 1910. They continued through 1924, when Senator Robert La Follette of Wisconsin made the courts a major issue in his bid for the presidency. The most radical of these schemes called for stripping courts of the power to declare acts of Congress unconstitutional. Proposals to this effect were introduced in Congress after 1910. In 1919 the plan was endorsed by the American Federation of Labor (AFL).[29]

Slightly less extreme, but enjoying wider support, were suggestions that the legislature or the electorate be permitted to override a ruling of unconstitutionality. A plank supporting this use of the referendum device was included in Theodore Roosevelt's 1912 Progressive party platform. Colorado amended its constitution to incorporate such a mechanism, but it was struck down by the state supreme court on the basis of the U.S. Constitution and principles of natural law. From 1922 to 1924 La Follette stumped for an amendment allowing Congress to override the judiciary by simply repassing any law held unconstitutional. As a third-party candidate La Follette won 17 percent of the popular vote in 1924; many who supported him were said to have been "influenced by his stand in opposition to judicial supremacy."[30]

Also indicative of the public's mood were efforts to make it more difficult for courts to overturn statutes. Between 1912 and 1920 the constitutions of Ohio, North Dakota, and Nebraska were amended to require concurrence of all but one or two judges before a law could be declared invalid. From 1912 through 1923 more than a dozen such proposals were introduced in Congress.[31]

Another set of reforms involved the selection and tenure of judges. The Populist party had called for direct election of all federal judges, but the idea did not attract attention until a decade later. Between 1911 and 1920 there were frequent proposals to elect federal judges or limit their term of office. In 1924 La Follette combined these ideas by urging the election of federal judges to fixed terms of not more than ten years. Provisions allowing recall of judges were approved in California, Oregon, Nevada, Kansas, and Arizona. Schemes for removing federal judges by congressional resolution or popular referendum were introduced periodically after 1911. And in 1919 the AFL came up with the novel solution of urging Congress "to impeach all judges from office who may hereafter exercise governmental functions and authority not *expressly* delegated to them."[32]

To reduce the ability of state courts to veto legislation on federal constitutional grounds, the judicial code was amended in 1914, making such decisions reviewable by the Supreme Court. It was also proposed, but without success, that lower federal courts be barred from declaring state enactments unconstitutional.[33]

A final means of limiting the impact of judicial review involved efforts to streamline the process of constitutional amendment. The 1912 Progressive party platform promised "a more easy and expeditious method of amending the Federal Constitution." In the ensuing years a variety of measures was submitted to Congress. In 1924 Senator La Follette campaigned for a system under which amendments could be proposed by a majority vote of Congress or by ten states, with ratification to be deemed complete upon approval by a majority of states.[34]

Though none of the schemes for restricting federal judicial power was approved, the sheer number of the proposals and the fact that many were adopted at the state level reveal the depth of public disenchantment with the courts. Many people no longer accepted the legitimacy of judicial review. In their eyes judges had no business invoking logical abstractions distilled from an ancient Constitution to thwart the needs of twentieth-century America. Charles Grove Haines believed that the situation was already critical in 1914: "If a growing popular sentiment which will brook no restrictions to the rule of the people in the end prevails, judicial supremacy will eventually give way to legislative omnipotence and unrestricted popular rule such as prevails in European countries." This atmosphere of frustration and hostility, which had been building since well before the war, could not help but affect the government's willingness to make use of the war powers in the period after the armistice.[35]

The War with a Silver Lining

The debate surrounding judicial review, and the reform movement which had inspired it, came to a halt when the United States entered the war against Germany in April 1917. For the next year and a half the nation's energies were devoted to making the world safe for democracy. With the armistice in November 1918, however, there came a resurgence of interest in the Progressive agenda. The war had imbued reformers with a fresh sense of purpose and a belief that "the outmoded institutions, arrangements, and habits of the nineteenth century would at last be swept away." Will Durant voiced a common hope that "the sufferings of war are the birth pains of a world-wide social rebirth." He and other liberals were buoyed by the Russian Revolution and by the rise of the British Labour party, which had adopted socialism as its guiding principle. Reconstruction conferences were held in cities across the country. Among the measures proposed were a continuation of wartime controls over industry; government ownership of the railroads, telephone, and telegraph; federal regulation of prices; national health insurance; eradication of the slums; and greater rights for organized labor.[36]

The impetus for reform lasted nearly a year before it succumbed to the hysteria of the Red Scare. The Progressive imagination had long been haunted by the specter of revolution, and the wave of strikes, riots, and bombings that shook the nation during 1919 threatened to transform that nightmare into reality. Stanley Shapiro noted that "Wilsonian liberals, the conservative men of the progressive movement, were frightened by events which seemed to run too fast for them." In their fear they responded in ways that revealed the darker, preservationist side of the reform movement. Besides prosecuting radicals and censoring the leftist press, the government turned against the workers and small businessmen who had once been the focus of liberal concern.[37]

The war aided the Progressives in a number of respects. For one thing it led to a tremendous expansion of the federal government, which "was compelled . . . to call upon, take over, direct, or control almost every element of the life of the people, industrial, commercial, scientific, and educational, to the end that all these activities might be brought to bear directly upon the prosecution of the war." A vast array of committees, councils, boards, and corporations was established to coordinate these endeavors, many of which remained in place following the armistice. Between 1915 and 1919 the federal budget increased twenty-fivefold. People became accustomed to expect national solutions for problems which, a few years earlier, might have been regarded as matters of purely local concern. Public ownership, prohibition, and price control were among the reforms which benefited after the armistice from the enhanced stature of the federal government.[38]

These wartime bodies also provided an ideal setting for practicing the style of management advocated by Croly and exercised by Wilson even before 1917. Agency heads often

fashioned the administrative machinery they needed as they went along, or they modified the existing organization beyond the recognition of the authors of its being . . . Sometimes the new or modified machinery and the combinations of existing agencies were later legalized by acts of Congress or otherwise, but whether they were or not made little difference to the busy men who were engrossed in the fascinating job of getting things done.

Employing a pragmatic approach to the exercise of power, executive personnel geared their conduct to the task at hand, often paying little heed to questions of delegation or authority.[39]

The significance of this phenomenon was magnified by the lack of any real presidential leadership during the last twenty-seven months of Wilson's term in office. Except for one nine-day visit to Washington, the president was out of the country continuously from early December 1918 until July 1919. Before embarking for the Paris peace conference Wilson assured the country: "I shall not be inaccessible. The cables and the wireless will render me available for any counsel or service you may desire of me, and I shall be . . . constantly in touch with the weighty matters of domestic policy with which we shall have to deal." Yet he was unable to remain abreast of affairs. According to the *Washington Post*, "The President found this was impossible very soon after he established himself in Paris. And when he returned to Washington last July he frankly admitted that he was not acquainted with conditions at home and would have to seek further advice." He spent July and August in the capital lobbying for the treaty. In September he left on a tour of the West, where he hoped to generate popular support for ratification. On this trip the president suffered a stroke which left him partially paralyzed. For the next seven months he lived in virtual seclusion. Department heads were unable to speak with him, and any communication they had with the White House was with the First Lady.[40]

In the absence of central guidance cabinet members came to wield enormous authority. This was especially true of Attorney General A. Mitchell Palmer and Postmaster General Albert S. Burleson, both of whom had exercised broad discretion in their wartime service with the Wilson administration. Executive officials were at times able to achieve their aims without additional help from Congress. This resulted from the fact that many of the war laws were effective until peace was formally proclaimed. By using statutes already on the books at the time of the armistice, the government was able to test the Progressive concept of public control over the rail and wire systems. Existing law also served, however, as the basis for suppressing labor and curbing civil liberty—schemes not found on the reform agenda but resorted to during the Red Scare of 1919 and 1920.[41]

Some of the Progressive goals could be attained only with the aid of new legislation. In these cases the three years of being technically at war allowed the government to assert far greater domestic control than would have been possible under its peacetime powers. Federal authority to regulate interstate commerce was extraordinarily limited at this time. It did not extend to such areas as manufacturing, mining, or agriculture, all of which were deemed to fall within the exclusive domain of the states. There were even significant aspects of the rail industry that Congress could not reach, and its ability to prohibit the shipment of goods was confined to items themselves injurious to commerce. The taxation clause held some promise, for a 1904 Supreme Court decision had implied that the government might indirectly regulate local affairs by taxing them at prohibitive rates. Yet the device was an uncertain one, and when Congress employed it in 1919 in an attempt to discourage child labor, the tax was held unconstitutional.[42]

The war powers offered a much more attractive umbrella. After the armistice Congress relied on this source of authority to adopt a number of Progressive reform measures, including outlawing the manufacture and sale of alcoholic beverages, making profiteering a crime, and establishing rent control for the District of Columbia. In light of contemporary impatience with both the judiciary and the Constitution, it is hardly surprising that the government was willing to invoke its war powers in settings having little if anything to do with the emergency. This conduct was further encouraged by a belief that the courts would not interfere with measures enacted in the name of war.

The Great Temptation

The notion that the war powers were exempt from judicial scrutiny had a long and distinguished lineage. In *The Federalist Papers* Alexander Hamilton wrote, "The idea of restraining the legislative authority in the means of providing for the national defense is one of those refinements which owe their origin to a zeal for liberty more ardent than enlightened." Half a century later former President John Quincy Adams, then a member of the House of Representatives, declared that while the "peace power is limited by . . . the constitution . . . the war power is limited only by the laws and usages of nations. The power is . . . constitutional, but it breaks down every barrier so anxiously erected for the protection of liberty, of property, and of life." The great justice and commentator Joseph Story likewise felt that "to oppose constitutional barriers to the impulse of self-preservation" would be "vain" and "utterly preposterous."[43]

Its record through 1917 suggests that the Supreme Court accepted the Hamilton-Story view. Prior to World War I the justices decided some two dozen appeals involving the validity of war measures. Most of the suits dealt with unilateral conduct of the executive branch, unsupported by an act of Congress. Of the eight cases in which the government was found to have acted unconstitutionally only one involved a legislative exercise of the war powers, and it was overruled the next year. History suggested that while the Court could examine action taken by the president alone, review was inappropriate if he or his subordinates had operated pursuant to statute.[44]

That the judiciary would not scrutinize war legislation was also supported by the language of the Court's opinions. In some instances where the president was held to have violated the Constitution, the justices indicated that the outcome would have been different had Congress approved the action. Even more telling were the cases upholding war legislation against constitutional attack. Such challenges could take several forms. It was sometimes urged that the war powers could not be employed because a crisis no longer existed; this durational argument might relate to the date when a law was either passed or enforced. Second, a litigant could argue that a measure bore no reasonable relationship to the war emergency. Finally, a law otherwise within the scope of the war powers might be alleged to violate the Bill of Rights. The pre-1918 decisions suggested that none of these avenues was likely to succeed.[45]

Durational challenges to executive action prevailed in several instances, but never where an act of Congress was involved. The Court sustained a number of war powers laws adopted long after the war was over without discussing the longevity issue. In *Stewart v. Kahn* (1871), the only case to address the question, it upheld a measure extending the statute of limitations on suits brought against residents of the Confederacy after the Civil War. Justice Noah Swayne stated for a unanimous Court, "The power is not limited to victories in the field and the dispersion of the insurgent forces. It carries with it inherently the power to guard against the immediate renewal of the conflict, and to remedy the evils which have arisen from its rise and progress." He promptly added, however, that any limits on Congress's authority are not for judicial cognizance but rest "wholly in the discretion of those to whom the substantial powers involved are confided by the Constitution." Should Congress make too extended a use of the war powers, the only check appeared to be the president, who might cite the lack of emergency as grounds for vetoing or refusing to enforce the law in question.[46]

The same dichotomy existed with respect to the second type of challenge to the war powers. Where the executive had proceeded on its own, the judiciary displayed a remarkable willingness to analyze the relationship between its conduct and the war emergency. In *Mitchell v. Harmony* (1852) the Court held that a U.S. Army colonel who, pursuant to orders, had seized private property on the field of battle was liable to the owner where his action was not warranted by the circumstances. The justices rejected appellant's claim that when "troops are employed in an expedition into the enemy's country, . . . the commanding officer must necessarily be intrusted with some discretionary power as to the measures he should adopt; and if he acts honestly, and to the best of his judgment, the law will protect him." Instead, wrote Chief Justice Roger Taney for the majority, "the emergency must be shown to exist before the taking can be justified . . . [H]e must show by proof the nature and character of the emergency, such as he had reasonable grounds to believe it to be, and it is then for a jury to say, whether it was so pressing as not to admit of delay."[47]

By contrast, the judiciary was extremely tolerant of Congress's efforts both during and after a war. The classic formulation appeared in *McCulloch v. Maryland* (1819), where the Court upheld the constitutionality of the Bank of the United States as "necessary and proper" to the legislative power "to declare and conduct a war; and to raise and support armies and navies." In that decision John Marshall declared: "Let the end be legitimate, let it be within the scope of the constitution, and all means which are appropriate, which are plainly adapted to that end, which are not prohibited, but consist with the letter and spirit of the constitution, are constitutional." Five years earlier Marshall had suggested that when Congress invokes its war powers, the choice of means "depends on political considerations" entirely beyond the purview of the courts.[48]

The sole exception to this deferential approach came in *Hepburn v. Griswold* (1870). The Court there struck down the Legal Tender Act adopted during the Civil War, rejecting the claim that it was "an appropriate and plainly adapted means for carrying on war." But in overruling *Hepburn* a year later the Court returned to its familiar standard, stating, "The degree of the necessity for any congressional enactment, or the relative degree of its appropriateness, if it have any appropriateness, is for consideration in Congress, not here." The majority expressly rejected a requirement "that the relationship between the means and the end shall be direct and immediate."[49]

The cases dealing with Bill of Rights challenges to the war powers likewise distinguished between executive and legislative conduct. Any question concerning review of presidential action was put to rest in *Ex parte Milligan* (1866), which found that President Lincoln had unconstitutionally permitted the military trial of civilians. The government urged that in the absence of restrictions imposed by Congress, the president is "sole judge of the exigencies, necessities, and duties of the occasion, their extent and duration," and that "during the war, his powers must be without limit." The Court unanimously disagreed, proclaiming, "The Constitution of the United States is a law for rulers and people, equally in war and in peace . . . No doctrine, involving more pernicious consequences, was ever invented by the wit of man than that any of its provisions can be suspended during any of the great exigencies of government."[50]

It appeared that the Court might recognize a similar principle as governing the war powers of Congress. In a dictum in *Milligan* five justices said that the outcome would have been no different had there been a statute authorizing martial law, for "Congress could grant no such power" stripping persons of their constitutional rights. Chief Justice Salmon P. Chase and three of his brethren disagreed, stating that Congress's war power "is not at all affected by the fifth or any other amendment."[51]

The issue which split the Court in *Milligan* resurfaced five years later in *Miller v. United States* (1871). There six members of the Court indicated that they now accepted Chase's view. The case upheld the validity of the Confiscation Acts, which allowed *ex parte* seizure of property belonging to those suspected of disloyalty. In a plurality opinion for four members of the Court Justice William Strong said that because the statutes "are an exercise of the war powers of the government, it is clear they are not affected by the . . . fifth and sixth amendments . . . Upon the exercise of these powers no restrictions are imposed." In a dissenting opinion Stephen Field and Nathan Clifford likewise agreed that "the war powers of the government have no express limitation in the Constitution, and the only limitation to which their exercise is subject is the law of nations." *Miller* thus unequivocally repudiated the notion that Congress's war powers are constrained by the Bill of Rights.[52]

It was generally accepted at the time of World War I that laws enacted under the war powers are immune from judicial scrutiny. In 1917 former Supreme Court Justice Charles Evans Hughes told the American Bar Association that Congress's war powers are "plenary," and he agreed with Hamilton that upon them "no constitutional shackles can wisely be imposed." Hughes added that these powers are not "impaired by any later provisions of the constitution or by any one of the amendments." Henry Fletcher reached the same conclusion in an article which was circulated widely in 1918. The legislature, he said, "is the sole judge of the imminence of the danger; it is a political and not a judicial question; the power existing, the courts cannot inquire whether the facts justify its exercise either in the actual theater of war or in places remote from the field of action." Moreover, said Fletcher, Congress was free to proceed "in ways which in peace time would be a deprival of liberty and property without due process." The *Columbia Law Review* reluctantly agreed that the same principles applied during a technical period of war following the armistice: "Once given the legal state of war, the determination of whether the exigency is in fact such as to justify a particular war measure is for the legislature and executive only. A flagrant abuse of this power by the executive without the authority of Congress will be interfered with by the courts, but there seems to be no case where the judiciary has presumed to limit the power of Congress to enact war measures." Similar views were expressed by a host of other scholars.[53]

Members of Congress, many of whom were lawyers, were familiar with the pattern of the Court's war powers decisions. James Lewis of Illinois explained to the Senate in 1917 that "the Constitution, at this particular time, is more or less suspended." The Court in *Milligan* (1866), he said, had delivered "a splendid juridical oration" concerning constitutional rights in wartime, but in *Miller* (1871) it had "completely ignored that doctrine" in upholding a congressional exercise of the war powers. Representative Courtney Hamlin of Missouri quoted *Miller*'s statement that "upon the exercise of these powers no restrictions are imposed," suggesting it was proof that the Court would not invalidate laws adopted under the war powers. Georgia's Thomas Hardwick told his Senate colleagues in June 1917, "You can violate the Constitution of the United States as much as you please and as often as your conscience will let you; there is no remedy for that, unless our Supreme Court will pluck up a little additional courage; there is . . . no redress for that except in the forum of conscience and morals."[54]

The thrust of the Court's rulings was also noted within the executive branch. A month after the armistice Mitchell Palmer delivered an address to the Bar Association of the City of New York describing his continuing work as Alien Property Custodian. Palmer complained that lawyers were resisting his efforts to take over enemy property to an extent unknown during the war. The future attorney general warned that "until the peace terms are finally signed," the war powers remained in effect and were not subject to judicial review: "Of that emergency and the measures necessary to meet it, the Congress is the sole judge in the field of legislation and the commander-in-chief in the field of action. The Fifth Amendment to the Constitution does not operate against the exercise of the war power." Palmer declared, "The courts are shut to suitors who would obstruct the Executive in the prosecution of the war."[55]

The expectation that the judiciary would turn a blind eye toward war powers legislation proved irresistible to the political branches. In invoking this authority after the armistice Congress and the executive branch were generally indifferent to the constitutionality of their actions. Mention of these issues was typically limited to protests from a handful of senators or representatives, who were either ignored or denounced as obstructionists. Those who opposed a particular bill on constitutional grounds often supported other war powers schemes without objection. While this insensitivity was inspired by a confidence that the courts would not intervene, it also reflected the widespread opposition to judicial review and an instrumentalist tendency to treat constitutional questions in purely judicial terms. If, as most pragmatists believed, "provisions limiting the kinds of laws Congress . . . could validly create merely meant whatever the highest courts said they meant," then a measure was legitimate until it was overturned. On this view neither Congress nor the executive had to assess the propriety of its conduct, for judges in effect had a monopoly in such matters.[56]

Constitutional Questions: The Risks of Abdication

The notion that constitutional issues are exclusively for the judiciary flew in the face of established legal doctrine. Article VI of the Constitution states that "Senators and Representatives . . . and all executive and judicial Officers . . . of the United States . . . shall be bound by Oath . . . to support this Constitution." It was traditionally thought that each branch of government is under a separate obligation to evaluate the constitutionality of its actions. This tripartite theory was endorsed by Thomas Jefferson, John Marshall, Joseph

Story, and virtually every other leading student of the Constitution in the eighteenth and nineteenth centuries. While these men differed on the extent to which courts might oversee the coordinate branches, "all agreed on a duty in members of Congress to scrutinize the Constitution for clear evidence of granted power." As Story wrote in his *Commentaries:*

> The constitution, contemplating the grant of limited powers, and distributing them among various functionaries, . . . it is of necessity, that such functionaries must, in the first instance, decide upon the constitutionality of the exercise of such power . . . If, for instance, the president is required to do any act, he is not only authorized, but required, to decide for himself, whether, consistently with his constitutional duties, he can do the act. So, if a proposition be before congress, every member of the legislative body is bound to examine and decide for himself, whether the bill or resolution is within the constitutional reach of the legislative powers confided to congress.[57]

Donald Morgan suggests that the demise of the tripartite theory began in the mid-1930s. Yet it was in the wake of the 1918 armistice that the theory suffered its first major setbacks. One might argue that the failure of Congress and the executive to examine their actions at this time did not involve an abdication of duty since the Supreme Court, by declaring war laws immune from constitutional restraint, had thereby assured their validity. There are a number of difficulties with this position. To the extent that the Court's decisions may be read as holding simply that the constitutionality of war measures involves a political question to be resolved by the political branches rather than by the judiciary, the responsibility of those branches remained fully intact. Moreover, even if such laws were wholly exempt from Bill of Rights limitations, Congress and the executive would retain a good faith obligation to assure that exercise of the war powers was genuinely related to the national defense. It was the lack of any such connection which characterized many of the actions taken at the end of World War I.[58]

A failure by Congress or the executive to evaluate the constitutionality of its conduct could have grave and enduring consequences. For one thing, the measure in question might never be subjected to judicial review, in which case the political branches would be the sole guarantors of its validity. This was especially true of war powers legislation, where judges had historically deferred to Congress. Even if the Court were to hold such matters to be judicially cognizable, as it eventually did, constraints built into the judicial process may render the courts unable to redress a failure by the other branches to perform their duty. For this reason "decisions not striking down laws do not always mean that the laws are constitutional."[59]

The Framers recognized that courts must resolve issues of constitutionality on a less demanding basis than Congress or the president. James Wilson urged the Constitutional Convention that judges should therefore be included in a Council of Revision. "It had been said, that the judges, as expositors of the laws, would have an opportunity of defending their constitutional rights . . . [B]ut this power of the judges did not go far enough. Laws may be unjust, may be unwise, may be dangerous, may be destructive, and yet may not be so unconstitutional as to justify the judges in refusing to give them effect." Chief Justice Marshall observed that "the judiciary cannot, as the legislature may, avoid a measure because it approaches the confines of the constitution." Courts patrol the far end of the validity spectrum; short of that point only the political branches may reject a measure whose constitutionality is suspect.[60]

Judge Thomas M. Cooley expounded this principle to generations of law students, noting that "cases must sometimes occur when a court should refrain from declaring a statute unconstitutional, because not clearly satisfied that it is so, when if the judges were to act as legislators upon the question of its enactment, they ought with the same views to withhold their assent, from grave doubts upon that subject." The reason for this, he said, is that "the duty is different in the two cases, and presumptions may control in one which do not exist in the other." The judiciary will ordinarily assume that a measure is constitutional, for "the legislature, which was first required to pass upon the question, acting, as they must be deemed to have acted, with integrity, and with a just desire to keep within the restrictions laid by the constitution upon their action, have adjudged that it is so." Cooley emphasized, however, that such deference is dependent on a reciprocal duty by lawmakers to "abstain from adopting such action if not fully assured of their authority to do so." This arrangement, through which judicial moderation is balanced by legislative self-restraint, is a fragile and unstable one. Should lawmakers not take their obligation seriously, and "in cases of doubt . . . [allow] themselves to lean in favor of the action they desired to accomplish, the foundation for [judicial deference] would be altogether taken away."[61]

By the time James Bradley Thayer wrote a generation later, the scheme was badly in need of repair, though the fault did not lie entirely with the legislative branch. According to Thayer judges had lost sight of the principle that laws should not be invalidated unless "unconstitutional beyond a reasonable doubt." By "too promptly and easily proceed[ing] to set aside legislative acts," the judiciary had encouraged lawmakers to "shed the consideration of constitutional restraints . . . turning that subject over to the courts." The dilemma was that to the extent judges did honor the traditional canon of deference, the risks of abdication by the political branches became that much greater.[62]

Such a default occurred after the 1918 armistice, when the war powers were used to pursue ends having no genuine nexus with the war. If Congress and the executive had taken their obligations seriously, these measures would almost certainly not have been adopted. Yet once they were promulgated, the prospects for effective judicial review were poor. Not only would the legislation benefit from the presumption of constitutionality but, if the Court followed its customary practice, the war powers disguise would also serve as a complete shield against judicial scrutiny.

Had one of Marshall's dicta taken root, the situation might have been less critical. In 1819 the chief justice stated for a unanimous Court that "should Congress, under the pretext of executing its powers, pass laws for the accomplishment of objects not entrusted to the government; it would become the painful duty of this tribunal . . . to say that such an act was not the law of the land." Mainly owing to the practical difficulties of making such a determination, the Court in later years generally refused to inquire into the purposes behind a statute, except in cases of forbidden discrimination.[63]

Because of this institutional reluctance to probe legislative motives judges could be put in the artificial position of having to accept at face value ostensible war measures which the public knew to be a sham. On these occasions, to paraphrase a 1953 opinion by Justice Felix Frankfurter, the Court had to "shut its eyes to what is obviously . . . an attempt to control conduct which the Constitution left to the responsibility of the States, merely because Congress wrapped the legislation in the verbal cellophane of a [war] measure." Under such circumstances the challenged action would have to be upheld if it bore any conceivable relation to a war emergency, despite the fact that Congress or the executive might have had quite different goals in mind. In 1904 the Supreme Court acknowledged that our constitutional system is particularly vulnerable to this type of deception: "If a lawful power may be exerted for an unlawful purpose, and thus by abusing the power it may be made to accomplish a result not intended by the Constitution, all limitations of power must disappear, and the grave function lodged in the judiciary, to confine all the departments within the authority conferred by the Constitution, will be of no avail." Yet, said the Court, "where a wrong motive or purpose has impelled to the exertion of the power," the remedy lies not with the courts "but in the people."[64]

The post-1918 misuse of the war powers violated basic principles of federalism, enabling the government to invade a domain the Constitution reserved to the states. In some cases, the purported war measures also caused serious harm to the rights of individuals. Even those whose liberty and property interests were not directly infringed on may have been injured by the spectacle of authority being exercised under patently false pretenses. These abuses also posed dangers for a judiciary which was institutionally blind to schemes others could see. As James Bradley Thayer remarked, if "legislatures are . . . faithless to their trust" while "judges . . . confess the limits of their own power," courts may lose respect, owing to the impression that they are "turning out but a broken reed."[65]

Between 1919 and 1924 the Supreme Court responded to the continuing misuse of the war powers by eventually abandoning its attitude of total forbearance toward war legislation. While the judiciary still refused to examine the motives behind a purported war law, it would review the measure to make certain that a war emergency existed, that the law was genuinely related to it, and that the Bill of Rights had not been violated. The impetus for this dramatic transformation came primarily from conservative justices, who saw peacetime use of war powers as a threat to states' rights and to private property. In this respect the decision to review congressional exercises of the war powers was consistent with the Court's contemporary practice of closely scrutinizing social and economic legislation. Yet the precedent had a richer legacy, for the principle that war measures are subject to judicial review has since been invoked to protect political and civil rights. The abuse of the war powers after the 1918 armistice thus paradoxically helped strengthen the fabric of the American Constitution.

~ 2 ~

Experiments in Socialism:
Federal Control of the Rails
and the Wires

During World War I the government invoked the war powers to take possession of the country's railroad, telephone, and telegraph systems; after the armistice the cable lines were seized. Control of these systems, which continued well into 1919, was widely regarded as a prelude to nationalization.

Public ownership was a major item on the Populist and Progressive agendas. In the two decades before the war this reform made great strides locally, with a sharp rise in the number of municipally owned enterprises, including gas, water, and electric companies. Though the pace was much slower at the federal level, between 1910 and 1914 the government entered the postal savings and parcel post businesses and decided to build its own rail and communications networks in the Alaska Territory. Progressive writers urged more sweeping reforms, and in 1914 the *New York Times* observed that there was a strong "movement for Government ownership of railways, as well as telegraphs."[1]

The ability to extend public ownership on a national basis was quite limited. Socialistic schemes might be undertaken in Alaska or the District of Columbia where Congress had plenary legislative authority. Parcel post and postal savings also presented special cases, for they were supported by the clause permitting Congress to establish a postal system. Beyond this, the going became difficult. The government could not condemn private property except through its enumerated powers. The commerce clause, which authorized federal regulation of interstate commerce, might have allowed a takeover of interstate utilities, but it could not reach the thousands of firms operating entirely within a single state. Some argued that the wire systems could be seized under the postal power, but the suggestion was at best a shaky one.[2]

The situation changed dramatically when war was declared on Germany. This not only increased the need for federal control of certain key industries but also provided a temporary means of realizing nationalization. For advocates of government ownership the war afforded a unique opportunity to demonstrate the advantages of state socialism. If the experiment was a success, the country might be willing to take whatever steps were necessary to make the scheme a permanent one.

As part of its preparedness efforts Congress in 1916 authorized the president "in time of war" to assume control over all transportation systems, including companies not involved in interstate commerce. Even before the United States became engaged in hostilities, increased demand generated by the European war placed a heavy strain on American railways. The country's entry into the war only made matters worse. In December 1917 President Wilson, exercising the authority given him by Congress, seized all of the country's rail and water transportation systems except municipal streetcar lines. Three months later Congress adopted the Federal Control Act, ratifying the takeover and establishing guidelines for federal operation.[3]

Congress was aware that this wartime action might constitute a first step toward government ownership. The 1918 Control Act acknowledged the experimental quality of the undertaking and declared that "nothing herein is to be construed as expressing or prejudicing the future policy of the Federal Government concerning the ownership, control, or regulation of carriers." The act permitted the president to operate the railroads up to twenty-one months after the proclamation of peace. In explaining this provision the Senate report noted: "It may be that the nation will be unwilling to return to the conditions obtaining before the assumption of Federal control. Legislation may be demanded radically changing the relation of the Government to the railroads." It is understandable why some doubted that the railways would ever be returned to private hands.[4]

Nor is it surprising that Congress had serious concerns as to the constitutionality of a war powers measure which was to continue nearly two years beyond the formal declaration of peace. In an attempt to obviate these difficulties the Federal Control Act provided that a railroad's acceptance of benefits under the statute constituted a waiver of any objections which might otherwise lie against it.[5]

Sylvester Konenkamp's Script for Wire Control

The December 1917 seizure of the railways offered a precedent which was soon applied to the nation's wire systems. The catalyst for the takeover was a threatened strike at the country's two major telegraph companies, Western Union and Postal-Telegraph. The planned walkout was the culmination of a long and unsuccessful effort by the Commercial Telegraphers Union of America (CTUA) to organize the industry. Since 1907, when it was badly beaten in an eighty-nine-day strike, this AFL affiliate entertained the idea of seeking nationalization of the wires. The telegraphers believed they would fare better with the government than in private nonunion shops, where their income had fallen steadily.[6]

Under the leadership of Sylvester Konenkamp the CTUA launched a new organization drive in January 1918. It hoped that because of the war the government would intervene if the companies refused to recognize the union. This tactic had recently worked on the West Coast, where Pacific Telephone & Telegraph accepted collective bargaining after a federal mediator recommended that the company be taken over by the government. The CTUA also hoped to benefit from the labor policies issued by the president in April 1918, to be implemented by the War Labor Board. These, which included the "right to organize," provided that "employers should not discharge workers for membership in trade unions."[7]

The campaign to organize Western Union and Postal-Telegraph was bitterly resisted. Both firms continued their practice of firing those who joined the CTUA. The War Labor Board took up the case in May 1918. Though it had no enforcement power, the reputation of its co-chairmen, William Howard Taft and Frank P. Walsh, helped assure public support. In a ruling prepared by Taft and Walsh the board ordered that all telegraphers discharged for union affiliation be reinstated. The employers, however, were not required to recognize or deal with the union, and if an impasse occurred, the CTUA was to petition the board rather than strike. Despite the modesty of the decision, the companies rejected it. The CTUA responded by threatening to walk out unless the companies were seized by the government. The AFL urged President Wilson to nationalize the wires for the duration of the war "and as long thereafter as may be deemed advisable."[8]

In mid-June the president intervened by asking all parties to accept the Labor Board's decision. Clarence Mackay, the head of Postal-Telegraph, agreed at once, but Newcomb Carlton of Western Union refused, declaring that he would rather have federal control than see his company unionized. On June 30 the CTUA played its last card, announcing that it would strike Western Union on July 8 unless the company reinstated eight hundred workers and accepted the Taft-Walsh ruling. Despite Konenkamp's claim that the walkout would affect 96 percent of Western Union's employees, Carlton remained indifferent, for he had taken pains to eliminate all suspected CTUA members from the company's employ.[9]

Had the union proceeded to strike, the result would almost certainly have been a disaster. The CTUA, however, was counting on the government to avert a showdown. Nor had Konenkamp left matters to chance. Before the drive began he informed friendly members of the administration "what our programme would be." In January 1918 Congressman James Aswell of Louisiana introduced a resolution authorizing the president "to take possession of the electrical agencies of communication to meet certain military exigencies." According to Konenkamp, this measure was "left to lie as a sleeper until needed"; but the groundwork for future federal intervention had been carefully laid.[10]

After the rebuff by Western Union the president and his cabinet decided to seek additional authority from Congress. The administration's bill, introduced by Representative Aswell on June 27, allowed the president to seize the telegraph, telephone, cable, and radio companies "if in his discretion it is deemed desirable, in order to insure their continuous operation ... or for other military or public reasons." In contrast to Aswell's earlier resolution, a takeover need not be required by the war or limited to its duration.[11]

While the rumored strike was the catalyst for this bill, the administration was not deluded as to the effect of a work stoppage. Before the cabinet met, Secretary of Labor William Wilson advised the president that the CTUA "has not been strong numerically or otherwise" and that "there would be no general walkout." It was possible that "in a number of important centers" a strike might "seriously interfere with telegraphic communication," yet there was no reason to fear the dire consequences predicted by the union. The government's sudden interest in wire control had little to do with a possible walkout. Instead it reflected the fact that many of the president's closest advisers adhered to a neo-Populist belief in public ownership. The CTUA plan worked not because the union was taken seriously but because its plea for federal operation fell on sympathetic ears.[12]

When Konenkamp told the administration of the impending membership drive, he contacted the secretary of labor and the postmaster general, both longtime advocates of nationalization. William Wilson, a former coal miner and a founder of the United Mine Workers union, had participated in several AFL conventions calling for federal ownership of the coal mines, railroads, and wire systems. Albert Sidney Burleson was a former congressman from Texas with strong Populist leanings. Upon becoming postmaster general in 1913 he began a secret study of the feasibility of taking over the wires. His first annual report declared that "the Post Office should have control over all means of the communication of intelligence," a recommendation which was repeated in each of his subsequent reports. Burleson also urged immediate seizure of the wires in Alaska, Hawaii, Puerto Rico, and the District of Columbia as a "valuable experimental demonstration for the Postal Service looking to the administration eventually of a complete National Service." Burleson helped draft the second wire control bill introduced by Representative Aswell.[13]

Other cabinet officials were equally receptive to the idea. Secretary of War Newton Baker had actively promoted public ownership while serving as mayor of Cleveland. Navy Secretary Josephus Daniels, who favored seizure of the country's radio stations and railways, was responsible for construction of a federal armor plate factory. In supporting the Aswell Resolution Daniels urged permanent government control of all means of communication. William G. McAdoo, who served as secretary of the treasury and Director General of Railroads, favored creation of a federally operated central bank, and advised that the United States enter the shipping business. McAdoo later sought to prolong national control of the railroads in order to improve the experiment's chance of success. Franklin K. Lane, secretary of the interior, helped persuade Congress to build a federal railroad in Alaska.[14]

At least six members of the cabinet were thus hospitable to the principle of government ownership. To their number must be added another highly influential White House figure—Joseph P. Tumulty, Wilson's private secretary. In a memorandum entitled "The Revolt of the Underdog," prepared in January 1918, Tumulty urged the president that it was time for the government to take a new approach toward business: "We must no longer attempt to regulate. We must control, own and operate those instrumentalities which have to do with the ownership and control of the basic needs of our life." A short time later Tumulty sent Wilson a copy of the British Labour party platform calling for nationalization of the means of production, describing it as "the most mature and carefully formulated programme ever put forth by a responsible political party." Tumulty likewise urged Democrats in his home state of New Jersey to "stand for the ownership of all public utilities."[15]

Woodrow Wilson had himself flirted with public ownership. In *The State*, published in 1889, he argued that "natural monopolies" such as the railroads and telegraph should normally be controlled by regulation, but he added that direct administration might in some cases prove necessary. Over the next two decades, as the Socialist party grew in strength, Wilson's public utterances became more conservative. Yet within a month of entering the White House he wrote privately to Burleson: "For a long time I have thought that the government ought to own the telegraph lines of the country and combine the telegraph with the post office. How have you been thinking in the matter?" It was in response to this query that the postmaster general began secretly to explore the possibility of such a takeover.[16]

Perhaps as a result of Tumulty's prompting the president took a renewed interest in government ownership. In January 1918 he suggested that the United States should go into the housing business to prevent Washington's landlords from exploiting the wartime shortage of dwellings. A few months later, while drafting the Democratic party platform for Indiana, he urged the inclusion of a plank favoring nationalization of a broad range of industries. Wilson's adviser Colonel Edward M. House and Joseph Tumulty feared, however, that direct endorsement of government ownership would prove too divisive; they suggested, "We ought to use the War as a Laboratory . . . for the trying out of these ideas and *after 1918* we can go to the country, standing for the permanency of those instrumentalities whose use in the War has been demonstrated to be practicable and helpful."[17]

Here lay the key to the wire control venture. The debate on the Indiana platform occurred shortly before the administration asked Congress for authority to seize the telegraph and telephone lines. In seeking this power the president and his advisers apparently hoped to conduct an experiment that might result in nationalization. This would explain why the measure exceeded in both scope and duration any conceivable emergency posed by the threatened telegraphers' strike. Wilson nearly admitted as much to Senator Morris Sheppard of Texas shortly before the Aswell Resolution was introduced. When Sheppard proposed allowing wire control only if required by the war, the president replied: "I wish that the authority might be less restricted. There are reasons why we should control the telegraph systems of the country which are not immediately connected with the conduct of the war, and I feel that there would be the same advantage in possessing a general authority to take over the telegraph lines as there proved to be in the authority to take over the railroads."[18]

The CTUA's demand for seizure of the telegraph thus met no resistance from the administration. More surprising was the fact that it was not opposed by the wire companies. This may have been due partly to the speed with which the resolution was adopted, clearing Congress in barely two weeks. Only four witnesses testified, three of them members of the cabinet. The fourth was Newcomb Carlton, who said that Western Union had no objection, assuming its shareholders were adequately compensated. Postal-Telegraph remained silent, perhaps from a belief that because no strike had been called against the company, it would not be taken over.[19]

American Telephone and Telegraph may have operated under a similar assumption. Ever since the Justice Department forced the company to divest itself of Western Union in 1913, AT&T had engaged exclusively in the telephone business. Since there was no threat of a telephone strike, it perhaps viewed the Aswell Resolution with indifference. When the industry was later seized, AT&T's president, Theodore Vail, was said to be taken aback. For a number of reasons, however, the company welcomed federal control. The Bell System was losing money in many parts of the country. Nationalization accompanied by a guaranteed return to investors would afford a much-needed subsidy. It might also permit Vail to attain his dream of consolidating the wires into "one nation-wide system, under single control." He and Burleson saw eye to eye on this matter, disagreeing only on whether the monopoly should be run by AT&T or the Post Office. Once the wires were seized, Vail promised to cooperate in what he called a "golden opportunity" to bring about an "affiliation of telephone and telegraph service of the various competing companies."[20]

Western Union probably shared many of these attitudes toward federal control, for Newcomb Carlton was a Vail protégé and a former AT&T vice president. Moreover, the company had been widely criticized for defying the War Labor Board and President Wilson. While there was no doubt that Western Union could defeat a strike by the CTUA, the company's intransigence compared unfavorably with its rival's patriotic response. Takeover of the company would avert a walkout without necessarily allowing the union to get its foot in the door. Carlton told members of Congress that he had no problem with government control as long as "unionizing the telegraph companies" was not part of the package. This condition may have sounded absurd, for the anticipated seizure stemmed from his refusal to grant the CTUA this right. Yet Western Union had good reason to believe that federal control would not help the union.[21]

It was expected that in the event of a takeover the wires would be administered by a man whose opposition to organized labor was at least as strong as Newcomb Carlton's. Postmaster General Burleson had strenuously resisted efforts by the postal employees to unionize, even though federal law guaranteed them this right. When quizzed by a House committee on his attitude toward such activity by the telegraphers, he replied, "They should not be affiliated with any outside organization." Burleson thus agreed with Western Union that while workers might be allowed to form a company union, they could not join the CTUA.[22]

The telegraphers were aware of the risks they were taking and vowed to "fight control by Burleson." One AFL delegate, noting the dismal treatment of postal employees, recommended that federal intervention "be accompanied by guarantees that the workers would have the right to organize." Labor's fears may have been eased by Burleson's assurances that he would be a "model" and "generous employer," that working conditions would improve, and that telegraphers could expect a 15 to 30 percent pay hike. It was also hoped that his antiunionism would be held in check by the war labor policy favoring the right to organize. In the end the CTUA was prepared to gamble. As a union spokesperson put it, "We are willing to take a chance with the Government—anything would be better than the intolerable conditions under the present policy of the company."[23]

A Dubious Congress Acquiesces

The telegraphers, the companies, and the administration—each for its own reasons—agreed as to the desirability of federal control. All that was left was for Congress to provide the requisite authority. Wilson and his advisers lobbied for the Aswell Resolution as necessary for the war. Yet despite efforts by Baker, Daniels, Burleson, and the president himself, Congress remained skeptical to the end. The measure was approved in the face of widespread belief that it was merely a subterfuge for nationalizing the wires.

In a letter to the House Interstate Commerce Committee dated June 28, 1918, the postmaster general warned that the impending telegraph strike could have "consequences prejudicial to our military preparations and other public activities that might prove serious or disastrous." He "urge[d] passage of the resolution, in order that the President may act, if necessary, to safeguard the interests of the country during the prosecution of the war." Wilson told Congress that he "endorse[d] entirely" the views set forth by Burleson. Yet Secretaries Baker and Daniels made no mention of the strike in their letters to the committee. Congressman Aswell also downplayed the walkout, suggesting that federal control was needed to release telegraphers for war work. From this discord it was unclear why wire control was thought necessary. Nor was it clear whether the authority would be invoked immediately or only in the event of a future emergency. As the *New York Times* reported, "The exact intention of the Administration could not be definitely learned."[24]

When Baker, Daniels, and Burleson appeared before the House committee, they were pressed as to the reason for the administration's request. Although the secretary of war agreed that no current military necessity compelled seizure of the land lines, he urged passage of the resolution as a precautionary measure. The navy secretary conceded that the threatened strike had nothing to do with the matter but voiced his belief that the government should manage the wire systems on a permanent basis. Only the postmaster general sought to tie the Aswell Resolution to the impending walkout, declaring that "it would be disastrous," and that "the mere suggestion of a strike ought to move us all with the desire to take whatever steps may be necessary to prevent it or provide against its effects." While Burleson disclaimed any intent to advance his "pet policy" of government ownership, he acknowledged that once the telegraph and telephone were seized, "the probability is that they never will be returned to private control." [25]

This testimony reinforced suspicions as to the administration's true designs. Even if the postmaster general's strike concerns were well founded, the Aswell Resolution was not limited to the telegraph, nor was it confined to wartime. A House amendment prohibited control from extending beyond the proclamation of peace. Those defending the resolution promised that it would be invoked only "should it become necessary in the prosecution of the war," but not everyone was convinced of this. Kansas Representative Philip Campbell doubted that the telegraphers would strike; he called the bill "the pretext of . . . a war measure to force Government ownership." Another Republican, J. Hampton Moore of Pennsylvania, noted that while the president's authority had been restricted to wartime, he was not compelled to exercise it merely for "war purposes." Moore also feared that federal control might be used to aid some companies at the expense of others. The House nevertheless approved the measure on Friday, July 5, three days before the walkout was to begin, by a margin of 222 to 4.[26]

President Wilson asked for swift Senate action on the wire bill, citing the Western Union strike set for Monday. Warning that such a disturbance "might at a critical time be of the most serious consequence," Wilson added: "I have found one of the great telegraphic companies quite unwilling to do what every other great service of the country has done in responding to the suggestions of the Government, and it has become absolutely necessary that the Government should have control while the war lasts." By the time the Senate convened on Monday, July 8, the walkout had been canceled. The administration appears to have secured this reprieve, however, by promising the union that the telegraph would be seized. The president therefore continued to press for the Aswell Resolution, while the CTUA declared that the strike would be reinstated if the measure were not approved.[27]

The Senate Interstate Commerce Committee originally planned to conduct several weeks of hearings on the wire control bill, but when this threatened to delay a summer recess, the plan was altered. At a one-hour meeting on July 8 the committee voted to dispense with hearings and reported the measure without recommendation. In its haste the body failed to obtain a quorum, and the Senate rejected its report. When the committee met again the next day, Newcomb Carlton happened to stop by; his was the only testimony heard. The committee acceded to the administration's request for wire control authority without making any determination of its own as to the need for this legislation.[28]

In the Senate as in the House, the Aswell Resolution was repeatedly identified as a war powers measure. While the House had been moved by fear of a telegraph strike, the Senate dismissed the specter as illusory. Senator Frank Kellogg, a Minnesota Republican, charged that the "call for a strike upon the Western Union line was a bluff" which had been canceled after only fifty-six of the company's forty thousand telegraphers agreed to walk out. Wisconsin Republican Irvine Lenroot concurred, saying that "the President was ill advised as to that threat . . . and the consequences that might follow if the attempt were made to carry it out."[29]

Supporters of the resolution conceded that there was no present need to seize the wires. According to Democratic Senator Oscar Underwood it was a matter of giving the executive "discretion to take them over if a war necessity arises in the future." Senator Lenroot was confident that if Wilson were given such authority, "he will exercise it only because of military exigencies." The president, he declared, would not "abuse the discretion" by seizing the wires "upon the threat of any strike by anybody."[30]

Some were more skeptical of the administration's aims, particularly since Burleson and others in the cabinet were known to be advocates of public control. Senator James Wadsworth, a New York Republican, found an aura of "mystery surrounding . . . this joint resolution," since no one could "point out the emergency now confronting the country which would make the taking over of these utilities necessary, nor the emergency which might confront the country in the future." Like many others in the Senate Illinois Republican Lawrence Sherman feared that the wires would "be taken under the guise of war necessities and used thereafter as an argument when the war ends to continue the plan of Government ownership and operation." James Reed, a Missouri Democrat, expected that "without waiting for any new emergency to arise, the powers under this joint resolution will be exercised [and] the telephone and telegraph lines will be taken over."[31]

The Senate was under no illusions concerning the wire control bill.

As Warren G. Harding, an Ohio Republican, remarked, "No one pretends to believe that it is not designed . . . to initiate Government ownership." Though sympathetic toward nationalizing the wires, the future president objected to the attempt "to establish a change in policy in the name of war." Despite these doubts as to the need for the measure, few were willing to confront the president. In addition, some members of Congress supported the idea of federal control. The result was that on July 13 the Senate passed the Aswell Resolution by a vote of 46 to 16.[32]

Seizing the Land Lines and Ocean Cables

Even before the bill became law, rumors circulated that the wires were about to be seized; later reports said that they would soon be in the hands of the Post Office. Amidst this uncertainty a telephone company in Indiana wrote President Wilson: "If it is your intention to take over such small companies . . . we trust you will place them in charge of Mr. McAdoo rather than Postmaster General Burleson. We are afraid of Mr. Burleson and we are not afraid of Mr. McAdoo." The Madison Telephone Company was quickly disappointed. On July 22, 1918, Wilson announced that effective August 1 the post-master general would assume control over "each and every telegraph and telephone system" in the United States. The administration had wished to seize the marine cables as well, but the plan was dropped when complications arose overseas.[33]

Reaction to the takeover was generally positive. The AFL expressed delight at a development it had been urging for years. Thomas Lamont of J. P. Morgan and Co. was equally pleased, noting that federal operation would provide more stable earnings for investors. William Jennings Bryan, who congratulated Burleson on his "new honor," assumed like many others that the systems would never be returned to their owners.[34]

Having seized the wires, the government was at a loss as to what to do with them. Company managers were told to continue "in the usual and ordinary course," and were assured that "no changes will be made until after the most careful consideration of all the facts." Most orders issued in the first four months of federal operation were trivial in scope. They included setting a service-connection fee and requiring prior approval for rate increases, as well as a rule that employees give two weeks' notice before resigning; a directive barring the discharge of workers for union membership was never enforced. The failure to take any significant action following the takeover undermined the claim that the step was dictated by war concerns. There were numerous signs, however, that federal control was intended as the first step toward nationalizing these systems.[35]

Immediately after the seizure Burleson created a Wire Control Board; two of its three members had assisted with the secret 1913 study which recommended federal operation or acquisition of the wires. Most of the government's prearmistice wire activity was preparatory in nature, dealing not with the companies' current needs but with their future unification. Burleson had frankly warned that federal control would lead to "coordination and consolidation of competing systems wherever possible." A committee was named to consider linking telegraph offices with postal branch stations, and the Post Office studied the possibility of combining the telephone lines into a single system built around AT&T. Another committee helped bring about the voluntary merger of thirty-four telephone companies.[36]

The postmaster general acknowledged that some of his actions were aimed at "development of a national system of telegraph and telephones," whereas an order such as the connection fee he described as "a war measure" to reduce demand. As he later explained, the period of federal control proved too short to achieve the basic reorganization he had contemplated: "When these properties were taken over on August 1, 1918, it was generally assumed that they would be in the possession of the Government for at least three years, one additional year of war, one year before the proclamation of peace, and one allowed for adjustment and settlement should Congress at the close of the war require the return of the properties." Instead hostilities ended less than four months after the wires were seized. This mistaken estimate concerning the length of the war, he said, was "responsible for some of the projects set on foot under the direction of the Postmaster General."[37]

Though he may have misjudged the timing of the armistice, Burleson, by his own calculations, had two more years in which to pave the way for nationalization. He was not about to abandon the quest merely because the truce had come early. Indeed the termination of hostilities had just the opposite effect: the period of study abruptly ended, and the experiment began in earnest.

Five days after the armistice the government took possession of the cables linking the United States with Europe, South America, and

Asia. The proclamation placing these systems in Burleson's hands was dated November 2 but did not appear until two weeks later. The impression at least was that peace had caught the Post Office by surprise, and that in order to defend the takeover as a war measure the date had been, as one senator bluntly put it, "falsified." Repeated denials by the administration were of no avail. Five months after the event the *New York Times* wrote, "There has never been any satisfactory explanation of why the order, somewhat furtively promulgated on November 16, was dated November 2—before the armistice. The public has had its suspicions which have not been dispelled."[38]

Though it remained unclear at the time, the proclamation was in fact signed on November 2; the delay in issuing it resulted from Burleson's attempt to proceed without alerting the cabinet. He had decided to seize the cables in mid-October, when a truce was being discussed with Germany. The postmaster general perhaps anticipated the criticism which would be unleashed if the takeover did not occur before hostilities had ended. After consulting Vail and Carlton, he forwarded a draft proclamation directly to the president, bypassing the State Department and the Justice Department; Burleson urged that "for many reasons I think immediate action should be taken." The president signed the order and forwarded it to the State Department to be promulgated.[39]

Secretary of State Robert Lansing was surprised by the proclamation. Rather than issue it, he wrote Wilson, repeating the objections he had raised when the matter had been considered and dropped several months earlier. Lansing noted that the Central and South American countries had the right to cancel the U.S. cable concessions should the government become directly involved in their operation. He also questioned the fairness of Burleson's having consulted only Western Union and AT&T.[40]

The president was sufficiently troubled by Lansing's letter to seek a response from the postmaster general. Burleson replied on November 12, a day after the armistice, urging that

necessities of the hour and of the future require that the cable properties should be taken over ... The controlling thought in combining the cable systems is to bring the United States into the most effective cable communication with ... the Eastern and the Western hemispheres at this important period. To seize the advantages now offered requires foresight and courage and may involve remote risks which are fully justified by the manifest advantages of such an important system of cable communication.

He did not explain what the "necessities of the hour" were. The action was not said to be required by the peace conference or any other specific reason. Instead it appears that Burleson and Wilson sought to take last-minute advantage of a wartime statute to accomplish a scheme both had favored for years. On November 13 the White House ordered the State Department to issue the proclamation. It appeared three days later, buried on page four of the *Official U.S. Bulletin.*[41]

Not long thereafter the administration took the position that a proclamation is not effective until it is promulgated; by this definition the cable seizure came after the armistice. Yet even if it were deemed to have occurred on the date of the president's signature, the government did not move to take control of these properties until a week after the armistice. In an attempt to justify the seizure the postmaster general cited a recent breakdown of the Western Union cables. The explanation was unpersuasive, for the incident happened after the proclamation had been signed. Clarence Mackay of the Commercial Cable Company rejected Burleson's explanation and charged that the true reason for the takeover was "incipient Government ownership."[42]

The editor and publisher Herman Henry Kohlsaat was also unconvinced. He wrote Wilson that "Burleson's *explanation* does not *explain*. If there is some good reason for it *you* personally should issue a statement." Kohlsaat believed that "taking over the cables *at this time*" was sure to "breed suspicion." While the president replied that such public distrust was "too contemptible to be worthy of notice," he was in fact troubled by it. The day he answered Kohlsaat, Wilson advised A. Mitchell Palmer not to add further to the list of "enemies" whose property was subject to confiscation by the Alien Property Custodian, explaining that "misapprehensions . . . would arise if we seemed to be taking advantage of the technical continuation of the war . . . The misunderstandings which have arisen in connection with the taking over of the cables will illustrate the misinterpretations which can be put upon action taken at this time." The misconceptions would grow worse in the days ahead.[43]

The seizure was denounced throughout the country, even by newspapers ordinarily supportive of the administration. The progressive *St. Louis Post-Dispatch* denounced the action as "high-handed." Though the paper did not oppose government ownership, it objected to an "arbitrary exercise of authority which is only technical at the best, and of which no shadow would remain except for the fact that the war still has a technical though not a de facto continuance." The influential *Springfield* (Massachusetts) *Republican* expressed a similar view, declaring, "It will be hard to convince people that any military necessity existed for commandeering the cables after the armistice had been signed." According to the *New York Times,* "Throughout the country, there is a feeling that considerations of public welfare furnish no warrant for Government control of cables, and speculation as to the real motive . . . is rife."[44]

The administration's conduct was also denounced on Capitol Hill, where Republicans no longer felt constrained by wartime patriotism to withhold their criticism of the president. Some voiced a sense of betrayal, for proponents of the Aswell Resolution had assured them that the measure would be invoked only in a war emergency. Senator Kellogg found it bad enough that the land lines had been seized; but then, "after the war is over we are met by the astounding proposition that as a war necessity . . . it is necessary to take over the cable lines." These measures, he said, were "part of a plan to fasten upon this country Government ownership of cables, telephones, and telegraphs," all "under the guise of a war necessity." Senator James Watson, an Indiana Republican, suggested that the takeover might be aimed at censoring the peace conference. In a speech at Columbia University on November 30 Charles Evans Hughes, a supporter of broad wartime authority, condemned the continuing use of emergency power: "With the ending of the war, we find ourselves with the familiar constitutional privileges and restrictions, and it behooves officers of the Government to realize that to make a pretence of military exigency for ulterior purposes when military necessity has ceased is simply an abuse of power which will not be permitted to escape censure."[45]

Faced with this escalating barrage the president decided to address the cable seizure in his State of the Union Message on December 2. The action, he said, was taken in preparation for the peace conference, so "news of the next few months may pass with utmost freedom and with the least possible delay from each side of the sea to the other." This explanation did not account for the seizure of the cables leading to Asia and South America; nor had the peace conference rationale even been hinted at by the postmaster general. The *New York Times* noted that Wilson's statement was "causing comment in Washington." To make matters worse, a *Washington Post* story several days later strengthened suspicions that the action was aimed at censoring the conference rather than assuring unimpeded news coverage. The *Post* reported that George Creel, the government's chief wartime propagandist, was going to Paris to ration dispatches sent to the United States and to provide "a centralized system of authentic outgivings." This article triggered a fresh round of attacks in Congress.[46]

The extent of the White House's failure to justify the cable seizure is indicated by the fact that it was denounced by Senator Gilbert Hitchcock, a Nebraska Democrat who supported the Aswell Resolution. Hitchcock charged that the takeover was "utterly unjustified" and "smacked of bad faith," for while the authority was given to "the administration for war purposes . . . it has been used to gratify the personal convictions, personal opinions, and personal wishes of the Postmaster General."[47]

The Drive for Permanent Control

Criticism of the cable seizure was directed principally at the government's choice of a war powers means rather than at the goal it sought to accomplish. Some of the strongest attacks came from papers such as the *St. Louis Post-Dispatch,* which tended to favor nationalization. Though many were upset by this disingenuous use of emergency power, such constitutional objections carried little weight in the heyday of Pragmatism. Moreover, their complaints were all but drowned out by a rising chorus of support for the concept of public ownership.

This rebirth of interest was an aspect of the postwar liberal dream of transforming society while it was still in a state of flux. Demands for nationalizing the rails and the wires, the merchant marine, docks, coal mines, oil wells, pipe lines, refineries, and the meat-packing industry came from an array of sources, including labor groups, liberal journals, the Hearst newspapers, and the Federal Trade Commission. The tremendous appeal of state socialism was evidenced by the Public Ownership League of America, whose membership jumped from 430 in 1917 to 3,400 by the end of 1919. The growth of the Committee of Forty-Eight was even more spectacular. Formed in early 1919 with the goal of building a new liberal party, the committee acquired 250,000 members within eight months. The first plank of its platform called for government ownership of natural resources, utilities, and railways. By early 1919 nationalization had become, as

Current Opinion described it, "the big issue of the near future," and one which it predicted would figure in the next presidential election. The *New York Times* was sufficiently alarmed by the prospect to launch an editorial campaign against such socialistic schemes.[48]

The enormous popularity of public ownership enabled the administration largely to ignore its critics. In late November Burleson named Theodore Vail his "personal adviser" on creating a "universal wire service and a unified cable system." This longtime advocate of consolidation recommended that the telegraph, telephone, and cable lines be placed under one management and that the cable companies be formally merged. In December the postmaster general asked Newcomb Carlton, whose earlier defiance had triggered federal control, to manage the cable lines. A Wire Operating Board was created to run the telephone and telegraph systems. It was chaired by a vice president of AT&T, the other members coming from Western Union, the Bell System, and an independent telephone company. In December Burleson issued a directive adjusting long-distance telephone rates; this order, which did not take effect until January 21, 1919, was said to be "part of the program of standardization" rather than a "war measure." He also ordered that beginning January 1 telegraphers would receive one or two weeks' paid annual vacation and a pay hike of 5 to 10 percent, though this was considerably less than what he had promised them earlier.[49]

After slumbering since its inception in July 1918, the wire experiment thus came to life with the signing of the armistice. Of the forty-six directives issued by the Post Office during the one year of federal control, only ten were handed down during the period of actual war. By contrast nine orders were promulgated in the first week following the armistice, while twelve more appeared before the end of 1918.[50]

As the government tightened its grip on the wires, it took steps to bring about permanent national ownership. The timing of this effort may have been influenced by the fact that in the November 1918 elections the Republicans won control of both the House and Senate. It appears that the president may have considered asking the outgoing Democratic Congress to nationalize the rail and wire systems prior to adjourning in March. On December 1, a day before the State of the Union address, Tumulty urged Wilson not to "advocate Government ownership or even hint at the permanent control either of the railroads, the telegraph, telephone, or cable lines in your Message. The result would be to divide the country on an economic issue when . . . you may be called upon soon to ask the backing of the country in favor of . . . the League of Nations." Instead, said Tumulty, "let the developments of the next two years determine the question of permanent ownership." Wilson partly heeded this advice. He made no mention of the land lines and promised eventually to return the cables. He did ask Congress, however, immediately to resolve the fate of the railroads and recommended that "complete government control, accompanied, if necessary, by actual government ownership," be given careful consideration. Though the president stopped short of endorsing this solution, he no sooner embarked for Paris than members of his cabinet began a drive to perpetuate federal control.[51]

In the case of the wires the crusade was led by the postmaster general, who prepared a bill to extend national control indefinitely and allow the Post Office to take steps toward acquisition of the telephone and telegraph companies. The measure, which was said to have President Wilson's approval, was introduced in the House on December 13. Meanwhile Burleson sought to generate public support for the "postalization" scheme through articles which he published in the *American Review of Reviews,* the *New York Journal of Commerce,* and *The Forum.*[52]

At the same time a similar campaign proceeded with respect to the railroads. On December 11 Railroad Director General McAdoo asked that the rail experiment be extended for five years. His concern was that Congress would be unable to solve the railroad problem before adjourning in March. If, as was likely, its Republican successor took no action, the venture would expire twenty-one months after peace was proclaimed, or in what McAdoo figured to be approximately two years. McAdoo considered this period inadequate for restoring the railroads to good condition; the "test" would "be an extremely unfair one for government control" and could "only result in failure." President Wilson endorsed the proposal, though he had said nothing about the need for an extension when addressing the matter nine days earlier. While some accused Wilson of duplicity, it is likely that since delivering the State of the Union Message, he realized that Congress could not possibly resolve the complex railroad question in the three months that remained.[53]

The McAdoo plan was universally regarded as a bid to improve the prospects for nationalization. This perception was reinforced when Assistant Director General Walker Hines said that the public needed a "test of Federal control under peace conditions . . . to contrast with a long experience of private control." The *New Republic* wrote, "If the government proves able to run the railways efficiently for five years, the demand for public ownership may become irresistible." By then, said the *Springfield Republican,* "half the people would have forgotten that the railroads ever had private management." The *New York Times,* however, denounced the scheme as "the straight road to Government ownership," while some Republicans saw the Burleson and McAdoo proposals as an effort to inaugurate socialism "under the guise of war necessity."[54]

The curtain fell on the Sixth-fifth Congress before it could vote on either of these measures. House committee hearings disclosed little support for extending telegraph and telephone control indefinitely or for allowing the Post Office to begin acquiring the companies. Burleson conceded that to his knowledge the takeover had not promoted the war effort in any way. Yet the committee was willing to continue the experiment through the end of 1919, beyond the anticipated date of peace, with perhaps another extension to follow. As for railroad control, McAdoo and Hines lobbied diligently for the five-year plan, but Congress terminated hearings in late February after it became clear that the matter could not be completed before adjournment.[55]

Mismanagement and Abuse

When time ran out on these extension efforts in early 1919, there was still strong public support for the concept of government ownership. The climate changed dramatically over the next few months. By summer the administration was forced to announce that it would abandon the experiments. This rapid disenchantment with federal control resulted primarily from the postmaster general's mismanagement of the wires. Within a short time he convinced the country that the advantages of nationalization were heavily outweighed by the dangers of governmental abuse.

For years Burleson had insisted that federal control would lower costs. Yet no sooner were the wires his than rates began to soar. In January 1919 long-distance charges were raised 18 to 20 percent, and by early June local rate hikes had been granted more than 250 telephone companies. On April 1 the price of sending a telegram went up 20 percent. These actions, which were prompted by a desire to strengthen the companies' financial position, were protested by consumers, merchants, and utility commissions, who objected in part to federal interference with state regulatory authority after the war had ended. The long-distance order was challenged in more than half the states, and in nearly a dozen cases the increase was blocked by the courts.[56]

It was widely believed the rate hikes were a fatal mistake. The *Portland* (Oregon) *Telegram* wrote that Burleson had "demonstrat[ed] the falsity of the theory that government control . . . makes either for economy or efficiency." According to the *Springfield* (Massachusetts) *Union,* "Many who have been favorable to government ownership, not only of wire-lines, but of railroads and shipping-lines, are getting ready to vote the Government out of the telephone and telegraph business at the earliest possible moment." The *New York World* predicted that these actions would doom "all measures of Government ownership or operation established in the name . . . of the Government's war powers when the exigency of war has passed." The most telling critique came from Congressman Aswell, sponsor of the wire bill and a friend of Burleson's. Aswell was "greatly disappointed and discouraged" by the telegraph rate hike, calling it the "death-knell" for any form of federal ownership. He apologized "to my people and to Congress . . . if government control means increase in rates."[57]

Support for federal control was further undermined by the fact that the postmaster general favored the giants of the industry, AT&T and Western Union, at the expense of the companies owned by Clarence Mackay. Western Union, which controlled 80 percent of the nation's telegraph lines, had been built by Jay Gould through acquisition of some five hundred smaller firms. The remaining lines and cables belonged to the Postal-Telegraph and Commercial Cable system, founded by Mackay's Irish immigrant father. In an age which honored small businessmen and reviled the trusts, Burleson's discrimination against the Mackay interests was most ill advised.[58]

Mackay had worked with the government in connection with the CTUA strike and had not opposed the Aswell Resolution. As soon as the armistice was signed, however, he asked that federal control be ended, stating that "the war no longer justifies . . . retaining these telegraph lines for war purposes." Not only did Burleson ignore this request, but a few days later he seized the cables as well. Given the Vail-Burleson goal of unification, Mackay had good reason to fear that his companies would be merged into the AT&T system. To prevent this he retained Charles Evans Hughes to file a lawsuit contesting the cable takeover. Though Mackay continued to cooperate fully with the government, the postmaster general thereafter treated him egregiously.[59]

Unlike his competitors, Mackay was not consulted in advance of the cable seizure, nor were his people named to any of the government's wire boards. Far more serious was Burleson's removal of Mackay from control of his companies, which were then turned over to his rivals. Newcomb Carlton was given charge of Commercial Cable in December 1918; the following March Postal-Telegraph was effectively put under the supervision of AT&T. The Mackay interests were also discriminated against financially. Western Union and AT&T secured lucrative compensation agreements from the postmaster general, netting them considerably more than they had earned during the period of federal control, but Postal-Telegraph was awarded less than half its actual earnings. Thus not only was the firm placed under the direction of its adversaries, but it was forced to subsidize them as well. Mackay declared at the time that "an organized effort was being made to use the power of the Postmaster General to eliminate our competition," a charge Burleson later all but admitted. Defending his conduct toward Postal-Telegraph, he described the company as "a parasite" that was "no essential part of a broad, comprehensive national system for the transmission of intelligence by wire."[60]

As Mackay recognized, his companies were ultimately saved by their "hold on public favor." Burleson even objected at one point that "Mackay has found the newspaper press of the country very serviceable in . . . his complaints against the Government operation of telegraphic service." The proadministration *New York World* led the attack on the postmaster general, writing, "Toward the Mackay lines from the start he has appeared to be inspired with a purpose at once hostile and discriminatory." Any chance of nationalizing the wires, it said, "has been killed by the feeling that the first result of Federal operation has been favoritism for one corporation at the expense of another." In Congress Senator Sherman voiced the outrage of many, warning that unless the wires were relinquished at once, when they "are returned to their owners it will be one owner, and by indirection there will have been accomplished what Mr. Vail was unable to accomplish by private enterprise."[61]

At Tumulty's suggestion Mackay prepared a lengthy account detailing the mistreatment of his companies under government control. In forwarding this letter to the president, Tumulty noted the unique injustice of the situation: "You will remember, when we had our controversy with the Western Union, that Mr. Mackay was the first to accede to your request and that Mr. Carlton who has been placed in charge of his lines under the Postmaster General's arrangements, was the individual who resented your interference in the settlement of the strike." The irony of federal power being used to crush a company that had cooperated with the government in order to reward one that had defied it perhaps explains why Burleson's abuse of the Mackay interests was so critical in the demise of wire control.[62]

The final element in the growing disillusionment was the postmaster general's unremitting hostility toward the telephone and telegraph workers. The *New York Times* had forecast an unhappy end to the affair, as had Felix Frankfurter, who feared that government control would leave the employees worse off than before. Burleson was stingy with regard to pay and refused to honor the War Labor Board policies allowing union membership and collective bargaining. In the unrest which ensued he alienated the public, labor, and even much of the business community.[63]

Burleson appointed a Wages Committee to study compensation; it had no funds and no authority, however, and accomplished nothing. The underpaid telephone employees never received a general wage increase from the government. When they sought pay hikes at the company level, management often met resistance from the Post Office. As a result telephone strikes occurred even when companies were willing to meet the workers' demands. The 5 to 10 percent increase awarded the telegraphers was less than what Western Union had promised to pay before the wires were seized. The CTUA reported that earnings actually fell, owing to reduced hours. Burleson added insult to injury by blaming the 20 percent telegraph rate increase on the paltry wage increase granted the workers.[64]

After meeting with the postmaster general in August 1918 Newcomb Carlton confidently predicted, "There will be no changes in the Western Union's labor policy as a result of the government taking over the lines." Western Union and many of the Bell companies in fact continued to fire anyone who joined a union. In the face of repeated CTUA protests Burleson asked Carlton to reemploy those discharged for union membership but refused to order the men reinstated with back pay and seniority. Moreover, in implementing this remedy Carlton discriminated against the CTUA by offering full reinstatement to those who agreed to join the company's employee association. Finally, Western Union later resumed firing those who joined an outside union despite an October 1918 Post Office bulletin stating that workers "must not be . . . discriminated against because they do or do not belong to any particular organization."[65]

Besides failing to protect the right to organize, the postmaster general prevented collective bargaining from functioning in companies which had already adopted it. The most notorious example of this involved New England Telephone & Telegraph, whose operators—all of whom were female—were represented by the International Brotherhood of Electrical Workers (IBEW). The women proposed a new wage scale in October 1918, two months before their contract was to expire. They were advised, however, that the company could no longer negotiate wages. The proposal was then submitted to the Post Office Wages Committee, which accepted the case but took no action on it. The matter was still pending in March 1919, when Burleson suddenly announced that the committee lacked jurisdiction. The issue, he explained, would instead have to be presented to the Wire Control Board.[66]

Thoroughly frustrated after five months of dealing with the Post Office, the operators wrote to the White House. In transmitting their message to Paris on March 27, 1919, Tumulty told the president that Burleson's treatment of labor "is so out of harmony with your attitude that I feel it a duty to bring it to your attention as unless steps are taken by you to modify the action the Postmaster General takes towards these people, there can be to my mind but one ending,—that is a general telegraphers strike throughout the country that may spread to other forms of labor." Burleson cabled Wilson the next day that the workers' claims were being "fully considered and fairly met" and that there was "no danger" of a walkout. The postmaster general then stalled for two more weeks. On April 10 he informed the operators that the Control Board could not resolve the case until the union resubmitted its wage proposal to company management, which would in turn make a recommendation to the Operating Board; after reviewing the matter, that body would submit a report to the Wire Control Board for final decision. This Kafkaesque ruling proved to be the last straw.[67]

The New England operators walked out on April 15. They were quickly joined by thousands of male employees belonging to the

IBEW. Telephone service in the Northeast was paralyzed, and the tie-up threatened to spread. When the strike was well under way, Burleson received a message from the president urging him to "mak[e] it evident to everybody that we are fair and open-minded and humane"; by then, however, the administration had already earned a quite different reputation. The White House was swamped with demands that it end the crisis. The *Springfield Republican* reported that "anti-Burleson feeling . . . was fully as catching as the influenza. Capitalist joined walking delegate in 'hoping the girls would win.' " The *Baltimore Sun* saw the strike as part of "a nation-wide revolt against the Burleson style of conducting public business," and noted that "the general public and the politicians are all united against him." One correspondent warned Tumulty "that from a party standpoint suicide is being committed." After six days Burleson was forced to capitulate. The New England operators won a generous wage increase, full reinstatement, and restoration of collective bargaining. As the *New Republic* observed, "At Boston, Mr. Burleson got his first sound absolute drubbing from his employees."[68]

Organized labor had been largely responsible for the chain of events that led to wire control. Within less than a year it came to regret the experience. Burleson was accused of "introducing into public office the traditional labor policy of the antebellum Southern plantation." Samuel Gompers was particularly bitter, declaring that the Postmaster General "needs only a wider field and a better opportunity to fit him for succession to some of the world's best known but unlamented ex-dictators. The only difficulty in Mr. Burleson's way is that the world has reached the decision that it wants no more dictators." At its June 1919 convention the AFL dropped its long-standing demand for nationalization of the telephone and telegraph and called for Burleson's resignation.[69]

"Abject and Exemplary Failure"

April 20, 1919, marked the turning point for the wire control venture. There were two "revelatory events" that day which, in the words of *Literary Digest,* "brought upon the Postmaster General a bombardment of criticism with editorial high explosives": one was Burleson's defeat by the New England operators; the other was an attempt by the *New York World* to syndicate an article highly critical of him. A telegram describing the piece was presented to Western

Union and Postal-Telegraph for transmission to newspapers throughout the United States and Canada. Neither company, however, would
accept the message. A telegraph official dismissed the incident as
simply "a case of an employee wanting to go easy on the boss," but
the country saw it in a more serious light. The *St. Louis Post-Dispatch*
observed, "If Government control means official suppression of news
and criticism of public officials, what will Government ownership
mean? If these things are done in the green tree, what will be done in
the dry?" For the *New York Evening Post* the occurrence was proof
that federal operation could lead to "surveillance over messages or
business personally objectionable to the ruling political powers."[70]

Equally significant was the fact that the episode involved a newspaper which many regarded as the chief organ of the administration.
The article's appearance thus revealed the extent to which Democratic leaders believed that wire control had become a political liability. While complaints that Burleson was harming the party had
been heard since the ouster of Clarence Mackay in March, they now
reached a crescendo. On April 20 the *Washington Star* reported that
the Democratic National Committee would ask President Wilson "to
decapitate Postmaster General Burleson as a member of the official
family." A cartoon in the *Chicago Tribune* depicted administration
leaders, huddled on the shore of a stormy sea of "unpopularity,"
banishing the postmaster general as a Jonah who threatened to ruin
the party.[71]

In a bid to pacify his critics and salvage the experiment, Burleson
decided to return the cables. This involved the jettison of worthless
cargo, since opposition from the British had kept him from ever
gaining effective control over these systems. On April 24 the postmaster general cabled President Wilson for permission to return the
cables, stating that it was "imperative in the public interest" and that
"full details of reasons will be given you upon your return." Burleson
may have hoped to present his critics with a *fait accompli,* for he
appears to have consulted no one but former Attorney General
Thomas Gregory. He could not, however, elude Joseph Tumulty, who
transmitted and received all cables between Wilson and the cabinet.
Burleson's wire of April 24 was in fact sent over Tumulty's name, and
began: "Following from the Postmaster General . . ."[72]

Tumulty immediately warned the president not to reply to Burleson
"until I can cable you further." He then sent a lengthy message
explaining that "there is no present source of irritation and popular

discontent affecting all classes of the people comparable with that growing out of the continuance of control over cables, telegraph and telephone lines by the Postmaster General." Instead of the token gesture proposed by Burleson, Tumulty urged that the wires be released in their entirety. Wilson agreed. On April 28 he approved a return of the cables and suggested that the postmaster general announce that the other systems would be restored as soon as protective legislation could be enacted.[73]

The president's cablegram put an end to plans for nationalizing the telephone and telegraph. To save face the postmaster general sought to create an impression that the decision to terminate wire control had been made "on his own motion." After receiving Wilson's communiqué, the Post Office reported that Burleson was recommending a return of the land lines; the next day it announced that permission had been received. The *New York Times* saw through the strategem, writing that "inherent probability supports the belief that the President, not Postmaster General Burleson, was the first to direct the return." Tumulty considered setting the record straight but ultimately decided to allow Burleson the benefit of the deception. The decision to end wire control did little to blunt the attacks on the postmaster general. The *New York World* saw the sudden change of course as "a confession that his administration has been disastrous," and many newspapers continued to demand his resignation. The *New Republic* facetiously cautioned that his departure would destroy the only tie holding the nation together: "We have one bond and one alone—getting rid of Burleson."[74]

The cables were returned to their owners on May 2, 1919, but the telephone and telegraph remained in government hands through the end of July. During that three-month interim Burleson continued at the helm, where in characteristic fashion he provoked further discontent. Even after it was decided to release the wires, the Post Office invited and approved applications for telephone rate hikes. At Tumulty's suggestion the president cabled Burleson that it would be "wise and prudent" to halt this practice. Though the postmaster general agreed to do so, he nevertheless approved more than sixty additional rate increases. Given this solicitude for the companies' interests, it is not surprising that the U.S. Independent Telephone Association later commended him for the excellent treatment accorded its members.[75]

Burleson was equally cooperative in helping the companies combat unionism. The triumph of the New England operators prompted other communications workers to strike. When the CTUA warned that the telegraphers might walk out to protest their treatment by the postmaster general, the *Springfield Republican* declared, "With Mr. Burleson so unpopular, even men in the employer class who hate the labor unions might be depended upon to wish the strikers success." The CTUA was also seeking to organize the telephone operators, and on June 2 it struck Southern Bell Telephone after fourteen of its members were fired. The union promised that the tie-up would spread unless the right to organize was protected. The postmaster general might have ignored this threat but for the fact that 265,000 telephone employees who belonged to the IBEW announced that they would soon join the walkout. Their participation would have produced a nationwide shutdown and virtually guaranteed a victory for the workers.[76]

In response Burleson on June 5 decided to return "control of operations" to the individual wire companies. This meant simply that while authority over rates, compensation, and working conditions remained with the Post Office, issues of union membership and union recognition would be determined by private management. Through this order, which one senator labeled "a piece of flimflam," the postmaster general sought to escape responsibility for a major strike, should one occur. The CTUA, outraged by this action, promptly extended its walkout to every telephone and telegraph company where its members were employed.[77]

The strike was easily crushed. Burleson not only refused to intercede on the workers' behalf but assured their defeat by keeping the IBEW from joining the walkout. After meeting with representatives of the AFL on June 14 he ruled that telephone employees would now be allowed to join unions and bargain collectively, and that anyone wrongfully discharged was to be fully reinstated. The telephone companies were warned to "comply strictly" with the order or face "disciplinary action." Unfortunately the AFL delegates failed to demand that the same rights be given the telegraphers. By the time they realized their mistake, it was too late; having neutralized the IBEW, Burleson refused to make any further concessions, and the CTUA was doomed. This use of war laws to check organized labor was not unique; the Justice Department would engage in similar action later that year.[78]

Because of the discredit Burleson had brought on the administration it was expected that when Wilson returned from Paris, he would ask him to step down. On July 8 the postmaster general denied that he had submitted his resignation, but the rumors persisted. On July 13, under the headline "Burleson May Quit Cabinet," the *Springfield Republican* reported that he had written to Wilson "on the subject of recent criticism and indicated a willingness to withdraw if he seemed to be in the way." Burleson's papers contain the penciled draft of a letter to the president in which he inquired "whether my continuance in the Cabinet is an embarrassment to you." The postmaster general added, "If by offering myself it will make your task the easier, I am not only ready but would be glad to do so." The two may have discussed the matter on July 16, when they met for an hour after the cabinet meeting. Though Burleson was never asked to resign, his political career was over. When the Wilson administration left office in March 1921, he returned to Texas, spending the rest of his life in seclusion.[79]

The wire experiment ended in what the *New York Times* aptly described as "abject and exemplary failure." Perhaps its most lasting effect was to discredit the principle of state socialism. In late April 1919 a banker noted that "while a year ago the great majority of the American people were moderately in favor of Government ownership, today the number has dwindled to the vanishing point." Of nearly six thousand newspapers surveyed, more than 75 percent opposed the idea. Railroad control became a victim of this reaction. In contrast to the wires, the government's record in running the railroads was a good one. Shippers, rail executives, and others who had long been critical of the venture, however, now found a receptive audience. The result was that in his May 20 message to Congress the president announced that the railroads would be returned at the end of 1919. Twelve months earlier in drafting the Indiana platform he had urged nationalizing these same properties. Largely because of the wire debacle Wilson, like many other Americans, had come full circle on this issue within the space of a year.[80]

Belated Blessings from the Court

The signing of the armistice had created doubts as to the continued validity of federal control. This was particularly true of the wire experiment, for the order raising long-distance telephone rates had been enjoined in many states. The administration no sooner decided to relinquish these ventures than their constitutionality was upheld by the Supreme Court. In a pair of decisions handed down on June 2, 1919, the justices reaffirmed their historic reluctance to review war powers legislation.

The suits, which were initiated in state court, contested the government's ability to use the war powers after the cessation of hostilities. One, brought by North Dakota, involved intrastate railway rates; the other, filed by South Dakota, dealt with in-state telephone charges. The rail schedule had been issued six months before the armistice but was not challenged by North Dakota until early 1919. The telephone order was promulgated in December 1918 and took effect the following month. In each case the result of federal regulation had been to raise rates above those previously approved by the states. The state courts sidestepped the constitutional issue but held that Congress had not authorized the executive to set local rates. The Supreme Court disagreed and therefore had to decide whether these war powers statutes could be invoked after the armistice to govern purely intrastate transactions. Though the question was carefully explored in the lower courts and in the briefs on appeal, the justices disposed of it as not warranting serious attention.[81]

The North Dakota Supreme Court noted the state's claim that "the [railroad] order is void on the ground that . . . if such powers are justified only as war powers, the justification ceased upon the signing of the armistice." It held, however, that the issue of whether "the military exigency" had "terminated" was nonjusticiable, for it involved "numerous intricate problems to be solved by the legislative and executive department." The dissent argued that courts may intercede if it is "demonstrated by proof . . . that the necessity for the exercise of such war powers does not exist." A concurring justice also thought the durational challenge was reviewable and concluded that "now that the war has ended, there is no longer any reason or excuse . . . to operate railways in disregard and defiance of the lawful police regulations of the several states. It is beyond the constitutional power of Congress and the national government." In an amicus brief filed with the U.S. Supreme Court the National Association of Railway and Utility Commissioners urged that the matter not be treated as a political question. Citing rulings concerning presidential exercise of the war powers, it declared that "the controversy is not removed from the sphere of judicial power simply because it relates to actions claimed to have been directed to a war end."[82]

In the South Dakota telephone case the state court majority over-turned the rate order on statutory grounds. The dissenters addressed the durational issue and concluded that where Congress has given war power to the president, he "is not subject to judicial control or interference." On appeal to the Supreme Court the state argued that the government could not set local rates under its peacetime powers and that mere incantation of the war powers did not guarantee the regulation's validity. Rather "it must appear affirmatively and not by inference that it was necessary as a war measure." The state empha-sized that while this requirement may have been met at the time when wire control was first adopted, there remained a question of whether the executive could enforce the measure after the armistice: "Even if Congress might authorize the President to change and increase South Dakota intrastate rates under the war powers . . . no attempt was made to exercise such power during the war or pursuant to any war purpose . . . The Postmaster General did not promulgate his order until after all necessity for the regulation of such rates as a war measure had passed." South Dakota thus employed a sophisticated durational attack, drawing a distinction between Congress's action during the war and the executive's subsequent enforcement efforts.[83]

The Supreme Court summarily rejected both of these challenges to continued federal control. In the North Dakota case it unanimously declared, "The complete and undivided character of the war power of the United States is not disputable." Since "the power which was exerted was supreme, to interpret it upon the basis that its exercise must be presumed to be limited was to deny the power itself." South Dakota's appeal fared no better. As to the initial adoption of the Aswell Resolution, the Court stated: "That under its war power Congress possessed the right to confer upon the President the author-ity which it gave him we think needs nothing here but statement, as we have disposed of that subject in the *North Dakota Railroad Rate Case.*" The Court recognized the state's separate contention that the executive had acted improperly because "there was nothing in the conditions at the time the power was exercised which justified the calling into play of the authority [conferred]." It rejected this claim as "concern[ing] not a want of power, but a mere excess or abuse of discretion," and concluded that it therefore "involves considerations which are beyond the reach of judicial power."[84]

There were several reasons why the *Dakota Cases* did not invite a reappraisal of the Court's traditional unwillingness to review war legislation. For one thing, the experiments were marked for extinction. A week before the appeals were argued, Burleson announced that wire control was to be terminated; and while the cases were under submission, Wilson disclosed similar plans for the railroads. Moreover, it appeared at the time that the government was in the midst of dismantling its other domestic war powers measures. Most of the restrictions imposed under the Food and Fuel Control Act had been lifted, and there were signs that the wartime prohibition of alcoholic beverages might be repealed. Under these circumstances the Court no doubt saw little need to interfere, for the political processes seemed to be working well to eliminate the last vestiges of the war laws. Also militating against intervention was the limited nature of the constitutional objection raised. In both suits the essence of the challenge was that the government had exceeded its enumerated powers and invaded the states' domain. Significantly, there was no contention that the Bill of Rights had been violated. Had such a claim been present, the case for judicial review would have been stronger, since individuals and even corporations have a greater need for judicial protection than do the sovereign states.[85]

The June 2 rulings upholding federal control did not slow the momentum for returning the rails and wires to private hands. They did, however, enable the postmaster general to implement the long-distance order in the eleven states where he had previously been blocked by the courts. Even before the decisions were announced, he granted nine rate hikes in these states; increases for seven more companies were approved the day the opinions were handed down. Later in the month he ordered all telephone companies that had been barred from adopting the new schedules to do so immediately after the injunctions were lifted.[86]

The hundreds of telephone rate advances awarded by the Post Office complicated the repeal of wire control. The companies were pleased with the higher schedules, and some faced financial ruin should they be nullifed when the experiment ended. Congress therefore provided that the rates approved by the postmaster general could remain in effect up to four months after the systems were returned, giving management an opportunity to seek comparable increases from the states. In June 1919, when the termination bill was being debated, Germany was about to sign the Versailles Treaty, and ratification was expected to follow swiftly. The provision continuing the federal rate schedules thus raised a question of whether the government could extend this war powers legislation into the period of formal peace.[87]

Perhaps because the measure initially provided for an extension of only ninety days, the Senate passed the repeal bill without addressing the constitutional issue. When the House committee proposed lengthening the period to six months, its chairman, John Esch of Wisconsin, noted that "in all likelihood this maximum period of six months will extend these rates beyond the declaration of peace." The committee defended this on the basis that other war laws contained similar provisions. Yet Esch admitted that "there may be doubt as to the validity of the war-made rates immediately upon the cessation of Federal control." While Kentucky's Alben Barkley thought a reasonable extension was proper, he added that this was "a judicial question and one upon which Congress as a matter of law can not pass."[88]

Owing to the Supreme Court's prior decisions, several House members believed it unlikely that the judiciary would overturn a war powers measure. Edward Denison of Illinois conceded that there was "a serious question as to the constitutional authority of Congress to extend Federal telephone tolls and charges for a period of several months after the wire systems have been completely returned to their owners and after the war has legally ended." Yet, he said, the legislature was on safe ground, partly because "the recent telephone cases . . . held that under its war power Congress possessed the right to confer upon the President the authority it gave him, and expressed the view that the purpose was so plain that it needed nothing more than a bare statement of it without further argument." John Moon of Tennessee, who had wanted to extend wire control indefinitely, was also influenced by the June 2 rulings. He appended to his remarks a memorandum prepared by the U.S. Independent Telephone Association entitled "Constitutional Authority of Congress, under Its War Power, to Temporarily Authorize Extension of Federal Telephone Rates beyond the Period of the War." The document cited several Supreme Court decisions but relied primarily on the *South Dakota Telephone Rate Case*.[89]

The rate extension debates demonstrate that in the period following the armistice Congress was not particularly concerned about the constitutionality of its actions. The Senate never addressed the issue, even after it was flagged by the House. The House committee report disposed of the problem on the basis that other statutes contained the same potential infirmity. When the bill reached the House floor, the matter was discussed by only a handful of representatives. The debates also reveal the Court's role in encouraging peacetime use of the war powers. As the remarks of Congressmen Denison and Moon indicate, some who had constitutional doubts were ultimately reassured by the judiciary's refusal to limit the scope or duration of the war powers. In this respect the experiments in federal control had a critical if unforeseen significance. Through the *Dakota Cases* they helped strengthen the government's confidence that it could continue exercising the war powers without fear of judicial interference. A prime example of this was the so-called War-Time Prohibition Act, which was adopted after the armistice to outlaw alcoholic beverages.

~ 3 ~

Wartime Prohibition:
"A Freakish Legislative Child"

Even more so than government ownership the prohibition of alcoholic beverages was an item on the reform agenda which benefited immensely from the war powers after the armistice. The Eighteeenth Amendment imposed Prohibition on January 16, 1920. Well before then, however, the United States had become bone-dry by virtue of the War-Time Prohibition Act. This war powers statute culminated a drive launched by the Anti-Saloon League of America in the 1890s. The dry crusade flourished under Progressivism, for the liquor industry symbolized big business at its worst. Not only had it corrupted state and local politics, but it was charged with having bred crime, poverty, and moral decay.[1]

By 1913, through a combination of local option and statewide prohibition laws, saloons had been banished from over 70 percent of the territory of the United States, with a majority of Americans living in dry areas. The key to the league's success lay in its adroit use of publicity as a lobbying device. Candidates for public office were queried on prohibition issues, and their views were disseminated to the voters through letters, circulars, and a host of league publications. The religious establishment also played an important role. Over the years the league had evolved into a federation composed almost entirely of local Protestant churches, and many of its officers were high-ranking ecclesiastics. As a result the organization had direct access to sixty thousand pulpits across the land. One Sunday in Illinois, for example, 2,500 ministers, acting at the league's request, addressed their congregations concerning a pending temperance measure. Politicians quickly got the message, including a state legislator who wrote the league: "While I am no more of a Christian than I was last year, while I drink as much as I did before, you have demonstrated to me . . . that there are more Anti-Saloon votes in my district than there are saloon votes; therefore I will stand with you both with my influence and my vote if you will give me your support."[2]

Though the league's goal was to outlaw the liquor traffic throughout the United States, its initial efforts were focused on state and local measures. By 1913 the group had achieved sufficient strength to begin exerting pressure at the federal level. In March of that year it scored a major triumph when Congress passed the Webb-Kenyon Act over President William Howard Taft's veto. This measure for the first time enabled states to bar the importation of all liquor, including that intended for a recipient's personal use. Absent such authority, some states had refused to adopt prohibition, not wishing to benefit out-of-state sellers at the expense of local business interests. During the next four years the number of dry states leaped from nine to twenty-six.[3]

On the heels of its Webb-Kenyon victory the league decided that it was time to press for nationwide prohibition. Most agreed that this could not be achieved simply by federal legislation. As one of the league's friends conceded, "Without a constitutional amendment the federal government is without power directly to prohibit the liquor traffic within the confines of any state in the Union." Inasmuch as forty states had either voted themselves dry or adopted local option laws, ratification by the necessary thirty-six states was not seen as a major obstacle. The more difficult task would be obtaining the two-thirds majority in the House and Senate needed to propose an amendment.[4]

The league resolved to employ the same strategy it had used at the state level. Reverend Purley Baker, the group's general superintendent, told delegates to the 1913 league convention: "From this time forth each and every candidate for Congress . . . should . . . be interrogated in a courteous, clear, dignified, written communication as to whether . . . he will support the submission of such an amendment, and the replies to such inquiries should be widely published . . . The great issue is now on and no unfriendly candidate for Congress . . . should receive the support of temperance people." More than fifty thousand speakers toured the country in support of dry candidates, while incumbents were bombarded with thousands of letters, telegrams, and petitions. The "drys," as prohibitionists were called, were aided by the war in Europe, for as other nations reduced their alcohol consumption in order to conserve foodstuffs, it was urged that America should do likewise. The cause received yet another boost when the National German-American Alliance, an organization heavily funded by the brewery industry, was charged with having secretly engaged in pro-German propaganda. Wayne Wheeler, the league's general counsel, later recalled that on election night in November 1916, "the lights burned late at our Washington office . . . Many hours before the country knew whether Hughes or Wilson had triumphed, the dry workers throughout the nation were celebrating our victory. We knew that the prohibition amendment would be submitted by the Congress just elected."[5]

The Sixty-fifth Congress proved a better friend than the league could have imagined. The United States' entry into the war gave a new sense of urgency to the arguments for prohibition. It also played on the Progressives' feelings of guilt. Many who were not called upon to risk their lives were only too eager to sacrifice the pleasure of drink. On April 4, 1917, two days after the new Congress has been called into special session, the league's proposed constitutional amendment was introduced in the Senate. The group might have secured immediate passage of the resolution but agreed to defer action until the president's war program was enacted. It was not until December 22 that the dry amendment was sent to the states. The measure contained a provision delaying its effective date until a year after ratification. One of the league's supporters, Congressman Edwin Webb of North Carolina, explained that this moratorium had been consented to because "the brewing business and the distilling business are legitimate at present in a number of States . . . [W]hile we prohibitionists desire to have the country go dry, we do not propose to let our zeal in that great cause destroy our sense of justice."[6]

Ratification proceeded at an astonishing speed. The Eighteenth Amendment was ratified on January 16, 1919, barely twelve months after it was sent to the states. H. L. Mencken, an avowed opponent of Prohibition, attributed the phenomenon to the war hysteria of the time. *Homo boobiens* was scientifically rowelled and run amok with the news that all the German brewers of the country were against the amendment . . . His nights made dreadful by dreams of German spies, he was willing to do anything to put them down, and one of the things he was willing to do was to swallow Prohibition. When he recovered from his terror, it was too late; the first article of the Methodist Book of Discipline had been read into the Constitution.

The league also deserved some credit. Its influence on Capitol Hill was a matter of common knowledge at the time. According to one Washington newspaper, "Every Congressman knows that if the ballot on the constitutional amendment were a secret ballot, making it impossible for the Anti-Saloon League bosses to punish disobedience, the amendment would not pass." The state legislatures where ratification occurred were even more tightly controlled than was Congress. While the war had accelerated the amendment process, it was the league that had assured its success.[7]

The Lever Act and Presidential Discretion

Despite the talk of fair play, the drys were unwilling to defer their utopia until January 1920, when the Eighteenth Amendment would take effect. The league's original strategy had been to obtain congressional approval of a constitutional amendment and then, while it was being ratified, impose prohibition on an interim basis under the war powers. This scheme was outlined by William Anderson, a member of the league's board of directors, in September 1917, before a grace period was added to the amendment: "It will be vastly easier from many angles to secure emergency war prohibition after Congress submits a prohibition amendment to the States . . .[T]he submission of this amendment by Congress will, in the judgment of the temperance forces, be followed by almost immediate collapse of the opposition to *war* prohibition." Anderson candidly acknowledged that circumstances had afforded a unique opportunity to obtain federal legislation in an area otherwise reserved to the states: "If an emergency, by opening a short cut which avoids the necessity for settling a lot of technical questions, enables the doing of certain desirable things with less delay and less friction than would be possible under normal conditions, that is one of the compensations of such a catastrophe as war." The league adhered to this plan even after the constitutional amendment was modified to include a built-in delay. Over the next two years it used its authority to obtain passage of three increasingly restrictive prohibition measures—the Lever Act, the War-Time Prohibition Act, and Title I of the Volstead Act. Each of these statutes was enacted under the war powers.[8]

In these efforts the league relied mainly on its influence with Congress, making little effort to win support from the administration. Besides believing that temperance was a personal matter, Woodrow Wilson feared that the question might split the Democratic party. Even among his closest advisers there was a sharp division on the issue. Secretaries Bryan, Daniels, and McAdoo were drys, while Postmaster General Burleson and Joseph Tumulty were opponents of Prohibition, or "wets." Unlike the experiments in federal control, where the initiative lay primarily with the executive branch, Prohibition was largely forced on an unwilling administration by a Congress dominated by the league. The same two-thirds majority that approved the Eighteenth Amendment was prepared, if necessary, to override a presidential veto.[9]

The first of the prohibition laws adopted under the war powers was the 1917 Lever Food and Fuel Control Act. As passed by the House, this conservation measure would have immediately halted all further production of beer, wine, and hard liquor. In a clear allusion to the pressure being applied by the league, Leonidas Dyer of Missouri charged that "some Members of the House are thinking more to-day of . . . their own personal welfare and their opportunity to return to Congress than about the great war"; he urged drys to content themselves with "the legal way to get prohibition"—by a constitutional amendment. When the bill reached the Senate, wets threatened a filibuster if the ban on manufacturing beer and wine was not deleted. In a remarkable tribute to the league's power, the administration asked it to consent to an amendment. The group insisted that Wilson put this request in writing, which he did. The league rejected the president's letter as inadequate; but upon receiving a second note, dated June 29, it agreed "as patriotic Americans" to permit modification of the bill's prohibition features.[10]

As signed into law on August 10, the Lever Act provided that the importation and manufacture of distilled spirits was to cease in thirty days; the supply on hand, however, was sufficient to last several years. As to beer and wine, the president was authorized to reduce their alcoholic content or curtail their production as he saw fit. Before the Prohibition amendment cleared Congress, the league had succeeded in freezing the nation's stock of hard liquor. Moreover, it had created a mechanism whereby popular pressure might force the president to cut off the supply of beer and wine. While some saw this compromise as a defeat for the drys, others, including the *Cincinnati Enquirer,* were appalled to discover that "the President of the United States [is] under orders to an officious and offensive lobby."[11]

For three months the administration showed no signs of exercising its discretionary authority under the Lever Act. In mid-November Wilson received a letter from the Federal Food Administrator, Herbert Hoover, warning that "The temperance advocates in the country, with whose ultimate ends I have the utmost sympathy, are raising a great deal of agitation for the further enforcement of . . . the Food Bill. This propaganda is having a reaction in some places in the refusal of the people to conserve other foodstuffs so long as food materials are being used by the brewers." Hoover recognized that the president's reluctance to act stemmed partly from a fear of "the discontent that might be created in the labouring classes." He recommended that the government steer a middle course by reducing the alcoholic content of beer to 3 percent and restricting the amount of grain a brewer could use to half that used before the war. Wilson accepted the suggestion in principle. He ordered that beginning January 1, 1918, brewers were to limit the alcoholic content of beer to 2.75 percent by weight and cut their grain usage by 30 percent.[12]

This action fell far short of satisfying the drys. When the league consented in June 1917 not to press its version of the Lever Bill, it expressly noted that the agreement "applies only to the pending Food Administration legislation. It will be our purpose to urge the passage of legislation prohibiting the waste of foodstuffs in the manufacture of beer and wines, at the earliest possible date." Nine months later the group complained to the president that the "waste of foodstuffs, fuel and man-power consequent upon the manufacture and sale of intoxicating liquors" was causing "deep and widespread unrest," and warned that it would seek to "absolutely prohibit the sale of all kinds of intoxicants for beverage purposes during the period of the war and demobilization thereafter." After receiving no reply to the letter, league delegates visited the White House but "came away with no more information as to the president's policy than when we went there."[13]

The Strange Case of the War-Time Prohibition Act

Within weeks of its unsuccessful meeting with Wilson the Anti-Saloon League began efforts to obtain stronger legislation from Congress. Among the bills proposed was one offered on August 29 by Senator Morris Sheppard of Texas as a rider to a pending agricultural appropriations bill. The measure was accompanied by a letter from the league requesting enactment of "immediate, emergency prohibition." On several prior occasions, the administration had been able to dissuade Sheppard from such action. In March 1918 Wilson told him that to deprive the working class of beer when this was not required for conservation purposes would "introduce a new element of disturbance in the labor situation which I should dread." In May the president, backed by Hoover, again asked Sheppard not to try to halt the manufacture of beer and wine. Wilson noted that since there were large stocks of liquor on hand but only a few months' supply of beer, "the consumption of whiskey would be stimulated and increased to a very considerable extent." Sheppard's most recent proposal sought to meet this concern by outlawing beer and wine production on May 1, 1919, followed two months later by a ban on the sale of all intoxicating beverages.[14]

Though the president opposed further prohibition legislation, he was willing to use his authority under the Lever Act as circumstances required. On September 6, hours before the Senate passed the Sheppard amendment, he ordered that, effective October 1, no foodstuffs could be used in brewing except malt already on hand, and that beer production would halt completely on December 1. This conservation measure, adopted at Hoover's suggestion, was no substitute for the pending Prohibition bill. It did not apply to wine, did not limit the sale of alcohol, and could be rescinded at any time. The league therefore pressed forward with the Sheppard amendment, which was signed into law on November 21, 1918, ten days after the armistice. Its overwhelming approval by a Democratic Congress, despite objections from the White House, lent credence to newspaperman Louis Siebold's claim that "the average member of Congress is more afraid of the Anti-Saloon League than he is even of the President of the United States." The so-called War-Time Prohibition Act placed the United States under nationwide prohibition on July 1, 1919, six and a half months before the Eighteenth Amendment would take effect.[15]

The war powers afforded the sole constitutional basis for this statute. Earlier, when the same Congress had passed the Prohibition amendment, it recognized that the government ordinarily could not restrict the production and sale of liquor within a state. The new law specified that it was adopted "for the purpose of conserving the man power of the Nation, and to increase efficiency in the production of arms, munitions, ships, food, and clothing for the Army and Navy"; it was to remain in effect only "until the conclusion of the present war, and thereafter until the termination of demobilization." As Representative Edward Voigt of Wisconsin declared, "It will be conceded by everyone that this proposed amendment would be unconstitutional if passed . . . in times of peace. The only authority that Congress has now for passing this amendment is the war power." Yet the validity of the War-Time Prohibition Act was far from clear. Not only did the terms of the law belie the notion that it was designed to deal with the war emergency; it may also have violated the Bill of Rights by taking property without just compensation.[16]

One bizarre feature of the act was that it did not take effect until the middle of the following year: the brewing of beer was to become illegal on May 1, 1919, and the sale of alcoholic beverages was not outlawed until July 1. While the delays were intended to benefit liquor dealers and banks whose loans were secured by whiskey, these goals could have been accomplished by the payment of compensation. That Congress instead postponed implementation for half a year seriously undermined any contention that the law was tied to the war. Senator Charles Thomas of Colorado was among those troubled by this point. Though he favored prohibition, Thomas did not believe that "the country should be deceived or deluded into the notion that any law is a war measure which becomes operative nine months after its enactment . . . [U]pon the assumption that this amendment is necessary to increase the efficiency of the soldier and of the workman . . . it is a contradiction in terms to enact that it shall not become effective until the 1st day of July, 1919."[17]

A second difficulty with the War-Time Prohibition Act was that insofar as it sought to curtail the production of alcoholic beverages for conservation reasons, it was seemingly unnecessary. The Lever Act already barred the manufacture of hard liquor, and in December 1917 the president had exercised his authority under that law to reduce the alcoholic content of beer and the quantity that could be produced. Moreover, as Wisconsin Congressman William Stafford noted, by the time the House took up the Sheppard amendment in late

September, Wilson had ordered that the breweries were to be closed on December 1, five months earlier than was called for by the pending legislation. Though the president had not acted against wine, the conservation argument for restricting its production was quite tenuous. As Representative Julius Kahn of California explained: "There is not a particle of food product that goes into the making of these light wines . . . You have to make wine out of those grapes or throw them into the waste barrel. You can not make anything else out of them. You can not make raisins out of them. You can not make preserves out of them. The only thing you can make out of the wine grape is wine."[18]

The act was also dubious as a mechanism for enhancing the efficiency of soldiers and defense workers. As the debates pointed out, the Selective Service Act of 1917 authorized the creation of dry zones around military camps and made it a crime to supply alcoholic beverages to uniformed members of the armed services. As for those employed in defense industries, a separate provision of the War-Time Prohibition Act allowed the president immediately to establish dry areas around "coal mines, munition factories, shipbuilding plants, and such other plants for war material as may seem to him to require such action." Even this provision was redundant, for Wilson had been given the identical authority by a law passed on September 12, 1918. Nor did Congress consider the problem urgent enough to mandate the creation of such zones.[19]

Another peculiarity of the act was its duration. Once the law took effect in mid-1919, it was to remain in force not merely "until the conclusion of the present war" but "thereafter until the termination of demobilization, the date of which shall be determined and proclaimed by the President." Of more than a hundred emergency measures enacted to deal with the war, this was the only one to contain such an unusual provision. When Senator Sheppard was asked why the law was to continue until the end of demobilization, a process which might take years, he candidly admitted, "It was put in with a view to the probability that the war might end much sooner than we thought." Senator George Norris of Nebraska made it equally clear that the goal was to preserve wartime prohibition until the Eighteenth Amendment took over: "With the ships at our disposal it will be a physical impossibility for [demobilization] to take place in less than two years . . . So that, so far as the prohibitory part of the law is concerned, there is not any doubt that it will hold its sway until the national prohibition amendment ... goes into effect." Wets denounced this feature of the act as "seeking by indirection to do that which Congress has no right to do," but their attempt to provide that prohibition would end with the armistice was easily defeated.[20]

As an emergency statute the War-Time Prohibition Act was thus a strange beast indeed. Rather than taking effect immediately, implementation was deferred more than half a year. Though the act ostensibly halted beer and wine production to conserve food, such action either had already been taken or was utterly senseless. As for ensuring the sobriety of servicemen and defense workers, the act addressed problems which were met by existing law. And while purporting to be a war measure, it was designed to remain in effect for as long as possible after the conflict had ended.

Unanswered Questions of Constitutionality

For some congressmen it defied credulity to maintain that this ill-fitting garment was designed for the war effort. To constitute a legitimate use of the war powers the statute would have to have been adopted for some emergency purpose. Opponents denied that the Sheppard amendment could in good conscience meet this test. They rejected the supposed war justification as "hypocritical," "political camouflage," and "pure humbuggery." Illinois Congressman Thomas Gallagher said, "Everybody who knows anything about the war and the provisions we have made for war-time prohibition knows that that is a fake argument pure and simple." Representative Voigt believed that the bill's "moving cause is the desire of the prohibitionists, under the guise of war necessity, to force their program on the people of this country, not only during the war but God only knows how long thereafter." The act's supporters all but conceded these charges. Moments before the final vote Senator John Shafroth of Colorado reminded his fellow drys that "those who believe in prohibition have been attempting for years and years to get such a measure through Congress"; the bill was a "compromise," he said, and "contains the very best terms [we] could get."[21]

In addition to claims that the act was not a proper exercise of the war powers, objections were made that the law violated the "just compensation" provision of the Fifth Amendment. Members of both houses noted that the July 1 ban on sales would totally destroy the value of existing liquor supplies. This aspect of the statute even concerned some of its supporters. Senator John Bankhead of Alabama confessed that "while I am in favor of prohibition, I am not in favor of confiscation." Senator Thomas, another dry, also felt that "a legal and a moral obligation rests upon the States of this Union and upon the Government, which have not only legalized but encouraged the traffic . . . to make due compensation under the Constitution." The Senate, however, defeated a proposal to pay for liquor held in bond. In the House, James Slayden of Texas observed that both France and Switzerland had paid compensation when they abolished the trade in absinthe. He denounced the Sheppard amendment as "a bit of high-waymanry that no other country, either as a reform or war measure, has resorted to. It proposes to take property from the citizen by the superior force of the State without compensation. That is downright robbery and disgraceful to the American Union."[22]

Most of the challenges to the War-Time Prohibition Act came from those who opposed it on the merits. Yet, as Donald Morgan has emphasized, "Constitutional settlements do not exist in a political vacuum, and the accommodation of special interests is a common ingredient." Whatever may have prompted it, the attack had sufficient force that one would expect someone to have risen in the act's defense. Nothing of the kind occurred. According to Representative Isaac Sherwood of Ohio the measure was "conceded by the leading lawyers on this floor to be unconstitutional," among them "the chairman of the committee in charge of this bill." William Gordon, also of Ohio, likewise stated that "the chairman . . . told me that this bill was unconstitutional, but he will vote for it just like all of these other fellows from these dry States." The chairman in question, Asbury Lever of South Carolina, was in the chamber when these statements were made. Despite the gravity of the charges, there is no evidence of his making any effort to refute them.[23]

This glaring indifference to constitutional issues typified the expediency and pragmatism of the times. It was further exacerbated by the fact that the Sheppard amendment came before Congress shortly before the 1918 elections. H. L. Mencken mocked the proceedings: "Congress is made up eternally of petty scoundrels, pusillanimous poltroons, highly vulnerable and cowardly men: they will never risk provoking the full fire of the Anti-Saloon League." The group's influence was openly acknowledged in the debates. Representative Jacob Meeker of St. Louis condemned the league as a "holy organization" whose members seek "to destroy every man . . . who dares to stand against them." "This bill," he claimed, "is here at their order and no other." Congressman Stafford predicted that "under the hysteria of the moment" the bill would "be passed through pressure of the Anti-Saloon Leaguers."[24]

In its pursuit of a dry utopia, the league for years urged reluctant members of Congress to ignore their constitutional doubts and refer them to the judiciary. In 1908, when the House was considering a prohibition measure many thought invalid, the league presented the Speaker, "Uncle Joe" Cannon, with a resolution stating: "Whereas certainty as to the constitutionality of such measure in this age of multiplying, varying, and conflicting precedents by divided courts, is impossible prior to its interpretation by the Supreme Court . . . all doubts as to the constitutionality of such measure should be resolved in behalf of the people and . . . the House should thereupon enact the same." In pushing another bill several years later the league argued that "until the Supreme Court has been allowed to have the last word upon such an important question . . . it may be doubted that Congress is justified in refusing to take action."[25]

The matter came to a head in 1913, when the Webb-Kenyon Act was before Congress. Even Wayne Wheeler, the league's principal lobbyist, was said to believe the measure invalid. This time, however, Congress was persuaded to leave such issues to the judiciary. In vetoing the bill on the ground that it was unconstitutional, President Taft deplored "the custom of legislators and executives . . . to remit to the courts the entire and ultimate responsibility as to the constitutionality of the measures which they take part in passing." Echoing the teachings of John Marshall, Thomas Cooley, and James Bradley Thayer, Taft declared: "The oath which . . . each Member of Congress takes, does not bind him any less sacredly to observe the Constitution than the oaths which the Justices of the Supreme Court take . . . The court will only declare a law invalid where its unconstitutionality is clear, where the lawmaker may very well hesitate to vote for a bill if of doubtful constitutionality because of the wisdom of keeping clearly within the fundamental law." Taft recognized that the danger inherent in a default by Congress was not that a measure might be invalidated but rather that it might be upheld. Indeed he correctly anticipated that the Webb-Kenyon Act would be sustained by the Court. In May 1916, eight months before the justices ruled, Taft wrote: "A President may veto a bill, Congress may pass it over his veto, the Supreme Court may sustain the law, and yet the Presi-

dent and the Court have the same serious doubt as to its validity . . .
In other words, the Court may . . . still not find the question so clear
as to overcome the presumption in favor of the validity of the law
because Congress has enacted it." It was thus critical, he said, "that
the constitutional validity of a measure should be fairly considered in
the legislature and by him who exercises the veto power."[26]

Congress ignored this principle when it approved the War-Time
Prohibition Act. That proponents made no effort to defend the law's
validity only strengthened the perception that the measure was a
constitutional fraud. When the legislation was first introduced, the
North American Review objected that "war measures are for war
times alone," and condemned the tendency to use " 'military necessity' as a stalking horse, behind which to secure the enactment of laws
for which there is no military necessity whatever, and which would
have no chance of acceptance without such a screen." The *Philadelphia Record* noted that "prohibitionists have made their fight upon
the grounds that abolition of alcohol was a war-time necessity. There
are many who have felt . . . they were insincere in this; that they
merely seized a war-time opportunity to make the enforcement of
their will upon others a peace-time permanency." Other journals
denounced the Sheppard amendment in even more scathing terms.
While many of these were located in cities where liquor traffic was
still permitted, there was apparent truth to their charge that the
measure sailed under false colors.[27]

Some placed their hopes in a presidential veto. Shaemas O'Sheel of
Brooklyn asked the White House to reject the statute out of consideration for the "plain people" of America: "You may never have been
a poor man, Mr. President, but you should realize that the only
harmless drink of which a poor man can purchase one glassful for five
cents, and all he needs for ten or fifteen cents, is beer. Men *will not*
drink water only; nor will men find solace in ice cream sodas."
Tumulty and Burleson also recommended a veto, citing constitutional
reasons and the risk of alienating urban voters. Had the Sheppard
amendment emerged from Congress in September, the president might
have followed their advice. Colonel House, who met with Wilson at
this time and urged him to sign the measure, noted that "he had in
mind to veto the bill" owing to its negative impact on federal tax
revenues. If Wilson harbored constitutional misgivings as well, he
kept them to himself.[28]

The bill did not reach the White House until late November, after the armistice had been signed. As the *New York World* observed, "For months discussion of 'war time' Prohibition has dragged along in the National Houses of Procrastination, until the war itself, in its active phase, has ended." The *New York Times* urged a veto, noting, "Prohibition as a war necessity would have been accepted by the country ungrudgingly. Prohibition as a war measure, enacted by Congress after the actual, if not formal, end of the war, stands or wabbles on a very different footing." The *St. Louis Post-Dispatch* declared, "The only shadow of legality attaching to the bill arises from far-fetched interpretations on the extent of the extra Constitutional war powers of Congress. But this bill did not gain the approval of Congress until the war from which a temporary extension of the congressional power is theoretically derived had already reached a de facto end." It was said that some members of Congress who had been pressured into voting for the bill were also hoping for a veto.[29]

The president signed the War-Time Prohibition Act into law on November 21, 1918. In his memoirs Joseph Tumulty opined that Wilson would have vetoed the legislation had it not been attached to an agricultural appropriations bill. This overlooks the fact that a few months earlier the president had told Colonel House that he was prepared to veto the measure in its entirety. His change of mind was probably a result of the recent election, in which the Republicans had won control of both the House and the Senate despite Wilson's appeal for the return of a Democratic Congress as proof that the country approved his leadership. Given the strength of the Anti-Saloon League, the odds were good that a veto of the prohibition bill would have been overridden. Such a defeat on the heels of the election would have further harmed his prestige at a time when support was needed for the peace plan and the League of Nations. Yet by dropping his objections to the War-Time Prohibition Act, the president made it a certainty that beginning July 1, 1919, the United States would become a dry nation.[30]

"No Beer, No Work"

Until then the Lever Act constituted the primary basis for federal regulation of the liquor trade. The administration proceeded to close the breweries on December 1 despite the signing of the armistice. As a result thousands of people were thrown out of work. A few weeks later Tumulty cabled the president that business and labor leaders were urging a resumption in the production of 2.75 percent beer. After replying that the prohibition would be retained until it was clear that there was no shortage of grain, Wilson advised Tumulty on January 17, 1919, that according to the Food, Fuel, and War Industries Administrations,

there is no longer any necessity . . . in continuing the ban on brewing. The problem therefore becomes purely one of temperance and I would be glad if the Cabinet would advise me whether . . . since the powers of the government in this matter were exerted as a war conservation measure, we are any longer warranted in suppressing brewing. If the Cabinet is of the opinion that we are no longer warranted in using the war powers for this purpose, I would . . . sign the necessary proclamation in the matter.

He thus appeared ready to lift all controls on beer, including the 1917 order limiting its alcoholic content to 2.75 percent.[31]

The cabinet proved less accommodating. On January 21 it counseled the president to allow only the production of "non-alcoholic drinks," explaining that it opposed broader action out of concern for the demobilization process. A similar recommendation came from the Food Administrator. Wilson followed this advice and on January 30 issued a proclamation allowing the manufacture of "beverages which are not intoxicating." The directive did not become effective until February 20, when it reached Washington and was sealed by the State Department. A second proclamation, dated March 4, terminated all restrictions on the use of foodstuffs in making beers that were not "intoxicating." These orders came none too soon, for without a resumption in brewing, the country would have run out of beer by the end of April.[32]

The brewers viewed the Lever Act proclamations as entitling them to renew production of 2.75 percent "war beer," a drink generally regarded as nonintoxicating. Their belief stemmed from the fact that the December 1 ban had applied to all "malt liquors, including near beer, . . . whether or not [they] contain alcohol." The president lifted this prohibition not simply for "non-alcoholic" beers but also for those that were "not intoxicating." The Food Administration, however, maintained that he had ended controls only on near beers containing little or no alcohol. This was also the interpretation of the Internal Revenue Commissioner, Daniel Roper, who enforced the Lever Act's beverage controls. Roper was a devout prohibitionist from the driest county in South Carolina. On March 13 he announced that brewers were permitted merely to resume the manufacture of beer containing less than 0.5 percent alcohol. This was the same standard he had said would be used to implement the War-Time Prohibition Act's impending ban on the production and sale of "intoxicating" liquor.[33]

Though these rulings appeared to sound the death knell for war beer, breweries across the country decided to defy the commissioner and resume production of 2.75 percent beer. In addition several brewers sued to enjoin the government from using the Lever Act or the War-Time Prohibition Act to interfere with war beer. They contended that 2.75 percent beer was not intoxicating and that Roper therefore lacked authority to ban it. The Bureau of Internal Revenue sought a Justice Department ruling on the matter, but Attorney General A. Mitchell Palmer chose to let the judiciary resolve the question. Until such a decision was obtained, he said, those brewing 2.75 percent beer would not be prosecuted.[34]

The administration's reluctance to halt the manufacture of beer no doubt reflected current labor conditions. From the outset 1919 was marked by a series of strikes which idled unprecedented numbers of workers from coast to coast. Cutting off the availability of beer might have been appropriate under the circumstances but for the fact that the sale of hard liquor—the supply of which was abundant—would remain legal until July 1. The U.S. Brewers' Association, echoing concerns raised earlier by Wilson and Hoover, urged that "in these days of unrest it is dangerous to have steady beer drinkers switch to whisky." The New Jersey Chamber of Commerce also recommended that beer production be permitted until the sale of distilled spirits had ceased.[35]

Even more serious was the possibility that eliminating war beer would lead to a nationwide general strike. The "No Beer, No Work" campaign was launched within forty-eight hours of Roper's announced intention to employ a 0.5 percent threshold under the War-Time Prohibition Act. By early March five hundred thousand workers were reportedly planning to walk out on July 1, with the number expected to reach several million. When Roper then decided to use the same standard in construing the Lever Act proclamations, it appeared that the protest might begin even sooner. The "No Beer, No Work" movement quickly collapsed after the AFL condemned the general strike as "an instrument of anarchy and revolution." The resentment which lay behind the campaign nonetheless manifested itself in other ways. On June 14 ten thousand workers gathered in Washington to insist that the War-Time Prohibition Act not be applied to war beer. The AFL endorsed the demand, and Samuel Gompers warned a Senate committee that "nothing could do more to bring about conditions here like those in Russia than taking away beer and wine from the workingman."[36]

The End of Wartime Prohibition?

Labor was not alone in seeking to modify the War-Time Prohibition Act before it went into effect. In late April the *New York World* called for the law's repeal, declaring it "a scandalous abuse of the technical war powers" which "is bound to create more public discontent and public disorder than any other act of Congress since the Fugitive-Slave law." Yet repeal was out of the question, for the Anti-Saloon League was, as Louis Siebold wrote, "the most potential political organization in the country." Wets therefore focused their efforts on the White House. No one worked more tirelessly to this end than Joseph Tumulty, who was once counsel to the New Jersey Liquor Dealers' League. Tumulty may have been particularly effective in these endeavors if, as Colonel House suggested, the president was not aware of his secretary's strong antiprohibition sentiments.[37]

Beginning in early May Tumulty sent cable after cable to the president at the Paris peace conference, urging that controls on beer be lifted in order to preserve industrial peace and protect the Democratic party. He reported, "The most violent reaction has taken place since the enactment of this law," and declared that "it would be disastrous to have a nationwide strike over an entirely extraneous issue." Moreover, he said, "our party is being blamed for all this restrictive legislation because you insist upon closing down all breweries and thus making prohibition effective on July first." By its terms the War-Time Prohibition Act was to remain in effect "until the conclusion of the present war and thereafter until the termination of demobilization." Tumulty suggested that if the first condition had not already been satisfied by the armistice, it would soon be fulfilled by the signing of the peace treaty. As to the act's second requirement, he proposed that if by July 1 "the number of men remaining in the service is no larger than the number desired for the regular army . . . cannot you declare by proclamation the demobilization complete for the purpose of this act?"[38]

Tumulty's efforts met with initial success. On May 12 Wilson expressed interest in lifting the two-week-old ban on the manufacture of beer and perhaps in canceling the imminent prohibition against sale. He requested the attorney general's opinion as to what action he could take. Palmer's response was entirely negative. As he interpreted the act, even if demobilization were deemed complete, Wilson could not proclaim that fact "at an earlier time than the conclusion of the war," which in his view had not yet occurred. "Therefore," said Palmer, "the only action you can take in the meantime would be to issue a public statement or send a message to Congress" noting that "the limitations imposed by the Act . . . maintain it in force until the termination of demobilization *after* the conclusion of the war." Rather than cabling the text of this letter, however, Tumulty sent a paraphrase which implied that Wilson could lift controls as soon as demobilization was "determined and proclaimed," even if the war had not yet ended within the meaning of the act.[39]

The president responded on May 20 by asking Congress to modify the War-Time Prohibition Act, stating that demobilization "has progressed to such a point that it seems to me entirely safe now to remove the ban upon the manufacture and sale of wines and beers, but I am advised that without further legislation I have not the legal authority to remove the present restrictions." While bills to this effect were being introduced, there was no chance that Congress would so defer prohibition until the Eighteenth Amendment took effect in January 1920. The *New York Times* reported that the power of the drys was such that "with probably not less than two-thirds of Congress in their control, and able to impose what policy they will, they have steadfastly refused to listen to any proposals for a postponement." Many thought that Wilson already had the power to lift these restrictions, and saw his request for additional legislation as an attempt to shift responsibility to the Republican Congress. An Anti-Saloon League spokesman noted that "the President signed this bill to be effective until demobilization is completed, and if it is complete," as his May 20 message had intimated, "he does not need any help from Congress to open the saloons."[40]

As July 1 approached, pressure mounted to relax the ban on wine and beer. Even drys seemed to agree that Germany's signing of the peace treaty on June 28 had ended the war for purposes of the act, but they insisted that the president's hands remained tied until demobilization was complete. On June 25 Tumulty cabled Wilson in Paris suggesting, "Will not the signing of peace be the opportunity for you to declare that demobilization is accomplished and that the object of the law having been satisfied, namely, the conservation of man-power, you would lift the ban by issuing a proclamation?" In a second message a few days later he warned, "There are only four days left until Nationwide prohibition becomes effective . . . Workingmen and common people all over the country cannot understand why light wines and beer cannot be permitted until the Constitutional amendment becomes effective." Tumulty urged that if Wilson were unwilling to lift the ban prior to July 1, he should at least promise that this would occur "as soon as the War Department notifies you demobilization is accomplished which, the best opinion says, will be August first." After receiving yet another wire from Tumulty, the president finally yielded. On June 28 the White House announced that beer and wine controls would be removed when demobilization was over, an event expected no later than September 1.[41]

Tumulty's victory was short-lived. The June 28 announcement came as a shock to the attorney general, for he had already informed the White House that its ability to annul the War-Time Prohibition Act did not hinge solely on demobilization. On July 1 Palmer cabled Wilson, "The impression seems to have gone out that the war time prohibition law will expire when the President proclaims demobilization has been accomplished." The statute's wording made it clear, however, that "the termination of demobilization could only come after the conclusion of the present war. The President therefore should not proclaim the termination of demobilization until after he has proclaimed the conclusion of the present war." In a separate statement Palmer explained that for purposes of the act the war could be deemed over only when the treaty was ratified. The attorney general's advice proved a disaster for the wets. On July 10, shortly after returning from Paris, Wilson told reporters that regardless of when demobilzation might end, beer and wine restrictions would not be lifted until the Senate approved the peace treaty.[42]

The Conversion of A. Mitchell Palmer

The president's yielding to Palmer was consistent with his past openness regarding prohibition. More surprising is the attorney general's rigid interpretation of the act's termination provision. The phrase "conclusion of the present war" might have been equated with the armistice or the signing of the treaty rather than with ratification by the Senate. Even the Anti-Saloon League initially so construed the law, and other statutes recognized that the term "end of the war" was a flexible one. Palmer also took a strict view of when demobilization could be deemed complete. When the Internal Revenue Bureau voiced doubt as to its ability to enforce the act, he promptly volunteered to assume the duty. This zeal contrasted sharply with his earlier record. As a congressman from Pennsylvania and a candidate for the Senate in 1914 Palmer had kept a low profile on the liquor question. Since then, however, he had developed a dislike for the German-American brewers, a distrust of labor, and an itch to be president. The result was that he became a champion for the prohibition cause.[43]

It was while serving as Alien Property Custodian, a post he assumed in October 1917, that Palmer began to sympathize with the dry cause. As overseer of enemy-owned property he became convinced that Germany was using its emigrants in a scheme to acheive economic supremacy over the United States. A month before the armistice Palmer told a Liberty Bond rally:

During the last 40 years, after Germany conceived her plan to colonize, subdue, and control the world, she began to plant on American soil a great industrial and commercial army . . . She planted that army in every city in the Union . . . As I have sat here in Washington, taking over this enemy property, I could piece together the picture of Germany's industrial and commercial organization upon this soil. I could see how we mistakenly welcomed these people into America for the purpose of exploiting our great resources.

After the armistice he warned that the "danger from German ambitions is not past and cannot be ignored" and called for a "decree of absolute divorce between German capital and American industry."[44]

According to Palmer the brewers were at the heart of this conspiracy. In September 1918 he charged that they, in collaboration with the U.S. Brewers' Association, had secretly tried to buy a major metropolitan newspaper in an attempt to spread German propaganda and influence domestic politics. Besides being "unpatriotic" and "pro-German," the industry had impeded the process of Americanization, for "it is around these great brewery organizations owned by rich men, almost all of them of German birth and sympathy, at least before we entered the war, that has grown up the societies . . . intended to keep young German immigrants from becoming real Americans." Palmer was able to take some action against the brewers in his capacity as Alien Property Custodian. Pursuant to the Trading with the Enemy Act, which defined *enemy* to include American citizens residing in enemy territory, he seized partial or full control of nine German-American breweries in the United States.[45]

One of these companies was the Anheuser-Busch Brewing Association of St. Louis. A quarter of the firm's stock belonged to Lilly Anheuser Busch, a U.S. citizen by birth. When her husband, Adolphus, died in 1913, Lilly went to Germany to visit her daughters and was trapped there when war broke out. In early 1918 the Alien Property Custodian seized all of her American property, including her shares in Anheuser-Busch. On returning to the United States a few months later Lilly sought release of her property, for under the act she was deemed an enemy only while residing in Germany. Palmer refused to grant her claim. Perhaps this was because her late husband epitomized the wealthy German-American whom he detested. Adolphus Busch came to this country at age eighteen and first worked as a steamboat clerk. He later fought in the Civil War, founded a brewery, and became one of the great philanthropists of his day. Though an American citizen, Adolphus was proud of his heritage and spent part of each year at a villa in Germany. His gifts included $300,000 to Harvard University for what is now the Busch-Reisinger Museum of Germanic Art and Culture and a grant to Washington University in St. Louis to endow a chair in German.[46]

After Palmer had taken no action for three months, Attorney General Thomas W. Gregory asked him about the case. In a lengthy reply the Custodian argued that Mrs. Busch was not entitled to return of her property unless she could prove that her residence in enemy territory was "merely of an accidental or temporary character." He also urged that her application be denied on grounds of loyalty. While there was no "evidence of personal disloyalty on the part of Mrs. Busch," he noted that her property "consists largely of an undivided interest in great brewery properties . . . and there are many facts and circumstances tending to cast doubt upon the loyal Americanism of some of those associated with her in business." He added that the Senate Judiciary Committee was then investigating the German-American brewers but did not explain how the alleged misconduct of others lawfully impaired her claim. Nor did Palmer mention that the Busch interests were actively supporting the war effort, or that the Busch-Sulzer Diesel Engine Company was producing submarine engines for the U.S. Navy.[47]

A few days later the president wrote Palmer that he was "distressed about the Busch case. The Attorney General told me . . . it was his unhesitating judgment that we had no legal right to retain the property. That being his judgment, it is embarrassing to resist Mrs. Busch's claim . . . Do you not think it is best to avoid any possibility of error in a matter of this sort?" The Custodian remained adamant, insisting that once an American citizen "voluntarily remains in enemy territory after he has had a reasonable opportunity to remove therefrom . . . his subsequent removal . . . will not give rise to any right to the return of his property." Such property, he said, should be sold at public auction. On November 20 Wilson advised Palmer that his position was legally "indefensible" and ordered the Busch claim granted "as soon as possible." Four other breweries Palmer had seized were released as well.[48]

Palmer's campaign against the brewers met with greater success after he became attorney general in March 1919. He was aided by a June 1919 Senate report which found that German-American brewing interests had attempted to influence public opinion against adopting prohibition legislation. Yet the Senate was unable to substantiate Palmer's charge that they had engaged in pro-German propaganda or other unpatriotic conduct. This failure was obscured by the report's title, *Brewing and Liquor Interests and German and Bolshevik Propaganda,* which conveyed the opposite impression. The Anti-Saloon League claimed that the document established a link between the brewers and "the political propaganda of the disloyal German-Americans." The report could not help but assist Palmer's efforts to close the breweries entirely.[49]

Political ambitions also shaped the attorney general's attitude toward the War-Time Prohibition Act. At one point during the 1912 Democratic convention there was talk of choosing Palmer as a compromise candidate. Though he declined the offer out of loyalty to Wilson, Palmer was thereafter obsessed with the presidency. As attorney general he was within striking distance of the White House; within months of the appointment it was rumored that he would lead the next Democratic ticket. During 1919 and 1920 Palmer used his position as the nation's top law enforcement officer to further this goal. Strict implementation of wartime prohibition was one of several strings in his bow.[50]

Like many aspiring politicians Palmer maintained cordial relations with the Anti-Saloon League. In May 1918 the organization wrote him that "a number of breweries," including the "Annhauser [sic] Busch Company and some of the Milwaukee Companies are largely controlled by alien Germans . . . Have you made any investigation? If not would you be willing to do so if we could give you any clue that would justify your taking such action?" Palmer was a step ahead of the group, for unknown to the public, he had already seized several breweries. The league was also grateful for his denunciations of the brewers, which had triggered the Senate investigation. It later thanked Palmer for his "splendid patriotic service" as Alien Property Custodian and helped secure his nomination as attorney general. There he continued to draw the organization's praise by opposing any relaxation of beer and wine controls and defending the 0.5 percent threshold for intoxicants. Not until late 1920, after having lost his bid for the presidency, did Palmer fall from the league's graces—this for suggesting that it was lawful to make hard cider for home use.[51]

The attorney general's support for prohibition also enhanced his standing with America's women, who in 1920 would figure significantly in a presidential election for the first time. In 1916 women enjoyed the presidential vote in only twelve states. By May 1919 this number had increased to twenty-nine, representing nearly two-thirds of the electoral college. The proposed Nineteenth Amendment was submitted to the states in June 1919. If it was ratified in time, 27 million women would be eligible to vote in 1920; even without it, the number would reach nearly 17 million. Experts generally agreed that women would favor the dry cause. The Anti-Saloon League was so sure of this that it broke its rule against endorsing other reforms and crusaded actively on behalf of women's suffrage. Using the same calculus, the liquor industry strenuously fought the movement. It thus appeared that a candidate with a strong reputation for enforcing prohibition would benefit greatly from the female vote in 1920.[52]

By popularizing himself with the drys the attorney general was certain to harm his reputation with organized labor. This prospect would once have given him pause. Palmer had backed the workers' cause during his six years in Congress, and he ran for the Senate in 1914 as a "radical friend" of labor endorsed by the AFL. The workers of Pennsylvania nevertheless voted heavily Republican, contributing to the failure of his Senate bid. Palmer's disenchantment with labor was intensified further by the strikes, riots, and bombings of 1919. Rumors of anarchistic plots had been circulating since early March. These suddenly acquired substance when, on May Day, postal officials discovered thirty-four bombs in the mails. Among those targeted for death were J. P. Morgan, John D. Rockefeller, Postmaster General Burleson, Justice Oliver Wendell Holmes, and Palmer himself. Violent May Day rallies occurred in many parts of the country. Then, on the night of June 2, bombs exploded within an hour of each other in eight cities, including one at the Palmer residence in Washington. In the debris police found the remains of a man presumed to have been one of the bombers, along with a leaflet declaring the beginning of "class war" in America.[53]

These events seemed to confirm the worst fears of Progressive reformers. The protectionist retreat that ensued was manifested by efforts to curtail strikes and silence radical elements in the working class. One of its most immediate effects was the attorney general's decision to ignore protests from labor and enforce the War-Time Prohibition Act against nonintoxicating beer.

The Troubled Campaign against War Beer

Once he had persuaded the president not to lift the restrictions on beer and wine, Palmer was in a position to control the pace of war prohibition. He had agreed for the time not to enforce Commissioner Roper's rulings, thereby permitting continued production of 2.75 percent war beer. Yet the Justice Department vigorously defended the 0.5 percent standard in the suits filed by brewers. On May 23 a U.S. district court held that 2.75 percent beer was not intoxicating and enjoined the government from employing the Lever Act or the War-Time Prohibition Act to interfere with the plaintiffs' manufacture of war beer. A month later the Court of Appeals set the order aside, ruling that while the acts applied only to intoxicating drink, an injunction against their enforcement was inappropriate. Instead the brewers' remedy was to defend any criminal action the government might bring by demonstrating to a jury that the beverage in question was not intoxicating.[54]

Though the Court of Appeals' decision was a setback for the government, since producers of nonintoxicating alcoholic drink could now avoid conviction, it was technically a victory, for the district court judgment granting an injunction had been reversed. The United States would therefore have had difficulty taking the case to the Supreme Court for a definitive ruling on whether war beer could be outlawed under the War-Time Prohibition Act. Another vehicle soon came along; nine days after the bombing of his home Palmer began enforcing the act against those violating the 0.5 percent standard. There was no longer a danger of prematurely eliminating the supply of beer, for the sale of whiskey and other intoxicating beverages would become illegal in a few weeks. The first of these suits, involving the Standard Brewery of Baltimore, was dismissed on July 1 after the trial court held the statute applicable only to intoxicating beer. The government promptly appealed the decision to the Supreme Court.[55]

The attorney general was unwilling to defer all further enforcement of the act until the appeal was resolved. The day the ban on sales took effect he announced, "Test cases on the sale of beverages containing more than one-half of one per cent. of alcohol will be brought immediately . . . in jurisdictions where such cases are not now pending . . . All persons violating the law might expect early and vigorous prosecution." He also issued a formal opinion sustaining the 0.5 percent standard. Palmer explained that "while there remains a question as to whether 2¾ per cent. beer is intoxicating . . . wholesale arrests" would not occur. There would, however, be no "amnesty" for those who "manufacture or sell beer pending an authoritative judicial construction of the law," and federal prosecutors were instructed to follow up on all violations reported by the public. As the *New York Times* observed, "Since there is no doubt that complaints will be filed by prohibition leaders, Anti-Saloon organizations, and others who are opposed to the sale of one-half of 1 per cent. beer, there can be no doubt that there will be prosecutions in such cases."[56]

The attorney general's policy in effect shifted responsibility for implementing the act from the Justice Department to the populace at large. The U.S. attorney in Brooklyn told local drys that "persons interested in enforcing the law should turn over any concrete information to the proper authorities," adding that he was "charged with prosecuting the violators of the law . . . not with searching out and detecting violations." The procedure saved department resources while deflecting criticism from those who might favor a more aggressive scheme. Prohibitionists were generally satisfied. One dry leader vowed that "the same efficiency which brought about the enactment of prohibition will be applied to its enforcement by the Anti-Saloon League."[57]

Though more than three-quarters of the country was already dry under state law, implementation of the War-Time Prohibition Act was felt in many of the nation's largest cities. Within a few weeks indictments were returned against brewers in Boston, Chicago, Los Angeles, Madison, New Haven, New Orleans, Philadelphia, Pittsburgh, Providence, San Francisco, Trenton, and Puerto Rico. In none of the suits was it alleged that war beer was intoxicating; rather the charge was merely that the beverage contained over 0.5 percent alcohol. Most of the cases were dismissed on the ground that the act applied solely to intoxicating drink. Only in Chicago, New Haven, and Pittsburgh did federal courts accept the Justice Department's argument that the statute could be enforced even against nonintoxicating malt liquors.[58]

Judges in some of these cases were asked to declare the act unconstitutional, but such claims were uniformly rejected. The War-Time Prohibition Act thus remained enforceable everywhere, though in some districts the government would have to prove defendant's beer was intoxicating. The Justice Department concluded, however, that it would be "virtually impossible" to obtain a conviction if such proof was required. Palmer therefore asked Congress to amend the act and announced that in the interim he would proceed against war beer only in "jurisdiction[s] where there has been no Federal court ruling interfering with prosecution."[59]

Palmer's assessment reflected the many experiments conducted to determine the properties of war beer, in which some subjects had consumed up to fifteen bottles at a time. The nearly unanimous verdict was that "no human being can accommodate inside himself at one and the same moment a sufficient amount of 2.75% beer to induce intoxication or even a slightly roseate state of mind." Even if the evidence had been less clear, the government would have faced serious obstacles, for juries in wet areas were unlikely to be very cooperative. This difficulty was observed in a case arising under New York's local option law, in which Sylvanus Ogden was charged with selling 5.39 percent cider in the dry town of Middleton. To Ogden's good fortune the county court sat in Goshen, which was wet. When the issue of whether the cider was intoxicating was put to a jury, defendant was acquitted. As the *New York Times* wrote, "Nearly twice the alcoholic content of contemporary beer is held by twelve good men and true as mild, harmless, and to be approved . . . The voice of juries is the protection of the State against new-fangled arbitrary restrictions . . . Probably our Dry friends will have to hear from a good many Goshens."[60]

As a result of the department's limited enforcement policy the manufacture and sale of war beer was halted only in the few districts where federal judges had accepted the 0.5 percent standard. In other wet areas the War-Time Prohibition Act was implemented solely as to hard liquor. A month after the sales ban went into effect, it was reported that "2.75% beer . . . is still being sold in New York and other large wet communities as well as in a majority of smaller wet centres." While this barely alcoholic brew had little appeal for the upper classes, it was popular in local taverns. The continued availability of war beer permitted the breweries to remain in business and kept thousands of saloons open in cities across the country. According to the St. Louis Brewing Association, while many bars had begun serving soft drinks and ice cream, it was 2.75 percent beer which enabled them to survive. The continued presence of this symbol of corruption was an affront to the Anti-Saloon League, which resolved to rid the country of the saloon before the Eighteenth Amendment took effect. The goal was achieved on October 28, 1919, with passage of Title I of the Volstead Act. This war powers measure amended the War-Time Prohibition Act so as to outlaw all beverages containing as little as 0.5 percent alcohol.[61]

The Dream Fulfilled

The War-Time Prohibition Act contained flaws which were detected before the law ever went into effect. Besides failing to define "intoxicating" beverages, the statute did not identify the federal agency responsible for its enforcement. And while it punished the sale of alcoholic beverages, the act made no provision for shutting down establishments where liquor was sold. When Congress convened in May 1919, drys wasted no time closing these loopholes. On June 27 the House Judiciary Committee offered a bill dealing with both the War-Time Prohibition Act and enforcement of the Eighteenth Amendment. The legislation was introduced by the committee's chairman, Andrew Volstead of Minnesota, but was drafted primarily by the Anti-Saloon League. Of its three parts only Title I pertained to wartime prohibition.[62]

Under Title I the Commissioner of Internal Revenue and the attorney general were jointly responsible for enforcing the War-Time Prohibition Act: the Bureau was to detect violators, and the Justice Department was to prosecute them. The measure resolved the uncertain status of war beer by specifying that "the words 'beer, wine, or other intoxicating malt or vinous liquors' in the War Prohibition Act shall . . . mean any such beverages which contain one-half of 1 per centum or more alcohol by volume." The bill made it a crime to operate any premises where intoxicants were produced, stored, or sold, and permitted such uses to be enjoined as a nuisance. The genius of this provision was that once an injunction had been issued, subsequent violations were punishable as contempt of court, with no right to jury trial. Landlords were made liable for penalties incurred by their tenants, and the property could be sold to collect any fines. Owners were thus discouraged from signing saloon leases, and those already having done so were given an out, for the act stated that "violation of this title upon leased premises . . . shall, at the option of the lessor, work a forfeiture of the lease."[63]

These amendments significantly broadened the War-Time Prohibition Act by outlawing conduct which until then had been legal. While the modifications made sense from a temperance standpoint, they raised serious constitutional questions. When the Senate debated the measure in September 1919, the armistice was ten months old and demobilization 92 percent complete. By the time the bill became law, the army was down to its peacetime strength. There was no doubt about Congress's ability to implement the Eighteenth Amendment, but its authority to adopt Title I was far less clear. Perhaps this is why the league combined the two measures, even though doing so would delay amendment of the wartime act. Representative John Tilson of Connecticut believed that they were "attached to each other like Siamese twins" because "so-called war prohibition is not able to stand upon its own merits."[64]

The most ambitious defense of Congress's right to amend the War-Time Prohibition Act had been made by Andrew Volstead in February 1919, during the closing days of the previous Congress. In a report supporting a bill identical to Title I he urged:

In the period of demobilization and readjustment to peace conditions there will necessarily be a vast number of idle men. Great dissatisfaction and no little suffering is inevitable . . . Riot and revolution due to a spirit of unrest engendered by the war are preached everywhere. Strikes and other industrial disturbances are imminent. Under the stress of such circumstances the usual precaution is to close the saloon, as it tends to greatly aggravate the evil.

Yet it was not apparent that the renewed strike activity was in any meaningful sense a product of the war. Nor did he explain how banning nonintoxicating beer would ease the situation. Perhaps sensing the weakness of this argument, Volstead advanced a more radical justification for amending the act: "If Congress finds that it . . . must maintain in the exercise of its war powers a situation which makes it necessary to enact this legislation, our courts can not review that finding . . . Congress and the Executive must determine what means are necessary for carrying on war. Courts can not be permitted to interfere." On this theory it was immaterial whether the measure was valid, for there was no danger of its being overturned. While Volstead cited no case authority, he was supported by more than a century of judicial practice. The Court's long-standing refusal to interfere with legislative exercises of the war powers was now being seized as an invitation to further abuse. As Pennsylvania's Henry Steele remarked with alarm, if Volstead was correct, "then Congress during war time has the absolute power to suspend any or all of the provisions of the Constitution designed to protect the liberty and property of the citizen."[65]

When the Volstead bill came before the new Congress, the House Judiciary Committee proved less willing to explore the constitutional issue than it had been in February. The earlier report recognized that the validity of the original War-Time Prohibition Act was distinct from the question of Congress's subsequent ability to expand its coverage. The June 1919 report glossed over this distinction, merely asserting that "as recently as June 26, four days ago, the Circuit Court of Appeals in New York sustained the validity of these acts." The committee's reticence may have stemmed from the fact that its prior defense rested on the demobilization process, which was expected to end in six or seven weeks. The Senate report on the bill was equally cryptic. Though it stated that "the question of the power of Congress to so define intoxicating liquors is fully discussed in the memorandum . . . which is herewith submitted," that memo dealt only with enforcement of the Eighteenth Amendment and did not address Congress's authority to make additional use of its war powers.[66]

Despite these efforts at evasion the matter quickly surfaced in the debates. It was universally conceded that Title I rested solely on the war powers, but its defenders never identified any war-related goal the measure could reasonably be said to further. Instead they relied almost entirely on the existence of a technical state of war. Congressman James Cantrill of Kentucky, a recent convert to the dry cause, said, "It is my duty as a legislator to give to the Anti-Saloon League ... a law which will enable them to enforce the ideas for which for years they have been contending." Maine's Ira Hersey was equally frank: "The people of this Nation, after a fair trial of the liquor traffic by a jury of the American people, have convicted it of the most infamous crimes and have said by that verdict that this great criminal of the ages must die ... [W]e, the representatives of the people, are now called upon simply to ... effectively execute and enforce the verdict of the people." Hersey added that though "certain legal questions are presented to save the prisoner," they posed no obstacle since peace had not yet been proclaimed. This position was enhanced by the June 2 rulings in the *Dakota Cases* upholding the government's continued right to enforce rail and wire control under the war powers. As Andrew Volstead noted, "Our courts have held within the last few days that that power still exists." The rulings thus reinforced Congress's willingness to make further use of its war authority.[67]

Only two members sought to rationalize Title I as a war measure. Representative Robert Luce of Massachusetts contended that since much of the world's capital had been destroyed, "there is still occasion to conserve the man power of the Nation. We must for many years command from all the people work and thrift and sacrifice; and how better can we [do this] than by abolishing industries and activities that produce nothing of value." By this ingenious reasoning the War-Time Prohibition Act might have been extended decades into the future. South Dakota Senator Thomas Sterling made a less ambitious attempt to justify Title I, urging that it was required to protect demobilization. Senator James Wadsworth of New York, a supporter of the measure, found this argument "curious," since the process was to end in a month. Tennessee's John Shields asked whether Sterling realized that "all the demobilization posts or camps, except the one in the State of New York, are located in States which have stricter laws concerning the ... disposition of liquors than even this proposed act; that this bill really is ... unnecessary and wholly gratuitous ... as to the other 47 States of the Union?" Shields added that existing federal law barred the sale of alcoholic beverages to members of the armed forces. It was therefore clear to him that Title I was not "a good-faith statute ... founded upon facts which would give Congress jurisdiction to enact it, but is really a prohibition law . . . under the guise of being for the protection of soldiers when it is not needed for that purpose."[68]

In the end Sterling abandoned his attempt to defend the act in terms of demobilization. Rather, he said, "the entire answer . . . is simply this: The law is on the statute books prohibiting the sale of malt and vinous liquors, and Title I of this bill provides for the enforcement of that law." Yet as the five dissenting members of the House Judiciary Committee recognized, the measure could not be supported on the simple theory "that the original act being valid and in force . . . any amendment thereof extending its provisions would likewise be valid." The proponents of Title I thus offered no plausible explanation of how it could be deemed a legitimate exercise of the war powers.[69]

Approximately a dozen members of Congress objected to the measure on constitutional grounds. They denounced it as "one-third fraud and two-thirds fake," "hypocritical," "indefensible and unjust." Congressman James Husted of New York decried the pragmatic tenor of the debate, noting that Title I "can be justified only upon the theory that the end justifies the means, and that is pretty shaky ground to stand on." Maryland's Charles Coady knew it to be irrelevant that "the ablest constitutional lawyers in this House have said that this bill is not constitutional," for, he asked, "what . . . is the Constitution among the followers and adherents of the Anti-Saloon League?" Congressman Clarence Lea of California envisioned the day "when the historian of the future reviews the record of this and the last Congress . . . What conclusion can he draw from such a situation that will reflect creditably upon the honor, wisdom, or patriotism of those responsible for such a freakish legislative child?"[70]

Andrew Volstead sought to discredit these attacks, claiming that "nearly every one that has objected to this bill because of its alleged unconstitutionality comes from a large wet city." While the challengers did include representatives from places such as Baltimore, Chicago, and St. Louis, they were matched by a nearly equivalent number from districts and states that had outlawed alcohol. One such congressman was Rufus Hardy, a former Texas judge who felt bound to oppose the measure because "while I would represent my people . . . I could not vote for an unconstitutional measure, such as Title I of this bill is, if every man, woman, and child in my district urged me to do it, because ... I would vote for it in violation of my oath of office and my obligation to support the Constitution." The bill nevertheless passed the House by a margin of almost 3 to 1 and cleared the Senate in two days without a roll call vote.[71]

An Unsuccessful Veto

When the Volstead Act reached the White House in late October 1919, President Wilson vetoed it, explaining:

I object to and can not approve that part of this legislation with reference to war-time prohibition. It has to do with the enforcement of an act which was passed by reason of the emergencies of the war and whose objects have been satisfied in the demobilization of the Army and Navy ... Where the purposes of particular legislation arising out of war emergency have been satisfied, sound public policy makes clear the reason and necessity for repeal.

Strongly suggesting that the legislature had exceeded its constitutional authority, Wilson cautioned that "in all matters having to do with the personal habits and customs of large numbers of our people we must be certain that the established processes of legal change are followed. In no other way can the salutary object sought to be accomplished by great reforms of this character be made satisfactory and permanent." As drafted by Tumulty the October 27 veto message was even more critical of Congress, but Wilson deleted a passage stating that in "legislation like this, so radical and fundamental in character, good faith and honesty shall be its foundation."[72]

In an editorial entitled "Mr. Wilson Vetoes a Lie" the *New York World* hailed the action as "one of the most scathing rebukes ever administered to a cowardly and faithless Congress." Though it was delighted by this rejection of "a calculated falsehood," the *World* was skeptical that such defiance of the Anti-Saloon League would long prevail. Indeed the Volstead Act became law within twenty-four hours. The House overrode the veto on the evening of October 27, virtually without debate. Congressman Volstead captured the sense of the body when, amidst cries of "Vote!" he exclaimed: "I do not believe that this House is anxious to discuss this question ... It has been voted upon in this House time and time again, and [it] seems to me that in view of the situation there is no occasion for prolonging the discussion."[73]

The Senate followed suit the next day, despite requests that the vote be delayed. Idaho's William Borah confessed, "I have never been satisfied in my own mind as to the constitutionality of the dry war-time prohibition act since the war ended," noting that "we passed during the war a great many acts which should have been considered as having served their purpose as soon as the war was over, whether technically the war has been ended or not." Charles Thomas of Colorado also had "very serious doubts" about the measure and urged the Senate not to "act so precipitately upon an important state paper emanating from the President of the United States." Alabama's Oscar Underwood believed that Title I was invalid but accurately predicted that rather than "defy the organized prohibition sentiment of the country," the Senate would "override the President's veto . . . and take chances on the Supreme Court holding the law unconstitutional."[74]

In light of the league's overwhelming influence there was little that could have prevented passage of the Volstead Act. Yet several factors tended to undermine support for Wilson's position. One was the growing fear of radicalism. When the act was initially debated in the House, Gilbert Currie of Michigan declared: "Reds and radicals stand for crime. Their favorite rendezvous is the saloon . . . When we have labor unrest and violent strikes, we close the saloons." There were 825,000 workers then out on strike, and an additional 435,000 coal miners threatened to join them November 1. According to the *New York Times* Congress was reluctant to ease "wartime prohibition at this time when the country is in the throes of strikes." Senator Henry Cabot Lodge of Massachusetts urged his colleagues that "to prevent this bill from becoming a law in the present disturbed conditions of the country would be a great misfortune."[75]

The president's objections to Title I also seemed inconsistent with his actions in the impending coal strike. On October 25 he told the miners that they remained bound by their contract with the government, "which was to run during the continuance of the war." Any attempt to abrogate the agreement was "unlawful," he said, for it came at a time "when the war itself is still a fact, when the world is still in suspense as to negotiations for peace, when our troops are still being transported, and when their means of transport is in urgent need of fuel." Yet in his Volstead Act veto two days later Wilson plainly indicated that the war emergency and demobilization were over. Even Senator Borah, who opposed prohibition, was "utterly bewildered to know when the war did end. We had a message from the President day before yesterday to the miners stating that the war was not closed and therefore their contract was not at an end. Now we have a message . . . to the effect that the war-time prohibition law is void because the war has closed." The *Nation* shared Borah's astonishment, asking, "Did the war end between Saturday and Monday?" The confusion no doubt resulted from the fact that because of his recent stroke, Wilson played only a token role in drafting the messages issued in his name.[76]

The force of the veto was further weakened by the president's unwillingness to lift wartime prohibition. If, as he implied, Congress could no longer constitutionally provide for the act's enforcement, didn't he have the right, if not the duty, to abrogate the measure himself? While the attorney general had said that Wilson's hands were tied until ratification, this reading of the statute was hardly obligatory. Senator Selden Spencer of Missouri was among those who suggested that "when the actual war has ended, and that army has been demobilized, the necessity for that war prohibition is ended. It did not mean . . . the technical paper ending of the war; it meant when the war as a fighting action has terminated, and when the process of demobilization had been substantially completed. Both those things are true now." If Wilson truly believed continued use of the act to be improper, there was no logical reason to cling to a rigid interpretation of its termination clause. Such inflexibility contrasted with the president's normal philosophy of expediency and may have been a consequence of his illness.[77]

Some believed that Wilson would resolve the contradiction by terminating the War-Time Prohibition Act, "ushering in a 'wet' period until January 16 when the prohibition amendment will go into effect." The White House announced, however, that the act would remain in force until the treaty was approved. Yet wets drew comfort from this news, for it was thought that ratification would be achieved before the end of November. The Anti-Saloon League reacted with alarm and urged pastors to oppose granting a "new lease of life to this foul, anarchistic, crime-breeding and riot-causing traffic." These fears were groundless, for it would be several years before any treaties were ratified. In the meantime the White House resisted all demands that it relax the War-Time Prohibition Act. As a result, through this war powers measure the league succeeded in keeping the United States bone-dry until the moment when the Eighteenth Amendment took effect.[78]

~ 4 ~

The High Cost of Living:
Recipe for Revolution

After the armistice the war powers played a major role in the government's campaign against rising prices. The cost of living had been of concern for years, but by mid-1919 it had become one of the most pressing issues facing the country. The administration responded by bringing criminal prosecutions against more than a thousand small businessmen and by indicting hundreds of striking workers. The government also used these powers to impose a comprehensive scheme of rent control in the nation's capital.

Prices before and during the War

Between 1898 and 1914 living costs in nonfarm areas of the United States rose nearly 40 percent. Though average wages kept even with inflation, a majority of working-class families did not enjoy a minimum standard of living. Inflation created different problems for those higher on the social ladder. As the sociologist Walter Weyl observed in 1912, "We are developing new types of destitutes—the automobileless, the yachtless, the Newport-cottage-less. The subtlest of luxuries become necessities, and their loss is bitterly resented." This "merely comparative poverty" of the middle classes, he said, had "the force of a revolutionary impulse." Walter Lippmann likewise noted that "the real power emerging today in democratic politics is just the mass of people who are crying out against the 'high cost of living.' "[1]

Inflation took its place as a key item on the reform agenda. It had been addressed by the three major parties in the 1912 elections. While the Republicans called for a "scientific inquiry," the Democrats and Progressives had proposed to combat high prices by attacking the trusts and lowering tariffs. Within two years of taking office Woodrow Wilson had signed the Underwood-Simmons Tariff Bill, the Federal Trade Commission Act, and the Clayton Antitrust Law. Yet none of these measures was likely to have a significant impact on the cost of living. Despite a 25 percent reduction in tariffs, duties remained high. While the Federal Trade Commission (FTC) was permitted to outlaw "unfair methods of competition," it was crippled by Wilson's appointment of strongly probusiness commissioners. And the Clayton bill was amended to such an extent in Congress that even the president pronounced it "so weak you cannot tell it from water."[2]

Many Progressives urged that stronger measures were needed to check profiteering by American business, including the nationalization of industry and direct regulation of prices. The difficulty was that the government lacked constitutional power to pursue these solutions except in extremely limited areas. As we have seen, its ability to take over private enterprise at best extended to entities engaged exclusively in interstate commerce. The authority to impose price controls was even more restricted, reaching only those interstate activities "affected with a public interest." Under this doctrine the Interstate Commerce Commission was able to set railroad rates, but beyond this there was little the government could do. The outbreak of war in Europe in 1914 had greatly increased the demand for American goods, and prices began to climb at a pace not witnessed since the Civil War. The situation only worsened once the United States entered the conflict. Between April and July 1917 the cost of food, clothing, and fuel rose 12, 19, and 28 percent, respectively.[3]

While the war had aggravated the problem, it also provided a means for its solution. Under the war powers the government not only experimented with public ownership but also set up an elaborate system of price controls administered by nearly a dozen agencies. The most important of these for consumer prices were the Food and Fuel Administrations, created under the 1917 Lever Food and Fuel Control Act. This statute barred setting any "unjust or unreasonable rate or charge" in the sale of food or fuel. Rather than fixing prices as such, the Food Administration determined the allowable markup for many staples; on other items dealers could earn no more than their average profit in the three years immediately preceding the war. A seller who exceeded these limits could lose its federal license, without which it was a crime to engage in the sale of food products. No restrictions were placed on farmers or ranchers, nor did the licensing provisions apply to retailers with annual sales below $100,000, thus exempting 95 percent of the nation's grocers. Yet the Food Administration was able to police small retailers through its control over their licensed suppliers. A grocer who ignored government price regulations was blacklisted, with the result that no wholesaler or manufacturer of foodstuffs could sell to him. The scheme was supplemented by a network of local Fair Price Committees, which issued "fair price" lists for retailers in most communities. Public pressure usually sufficed to secure compliance with these schedules, but where it did not, a merchant unable to justify his higher prices might be blacklisted.[4]

The Fuel Administration imposed ceiling prices on coal sold at the mine. Dealers in coal, coke, and charcoal were licensed under a system similar to that used by the Food Administration, and limits were set on their allowable markup. Producers and sellers of fuel oil were also licensed, mainly to regulate distribution, but in August 1918 the petroleum industry voluntarily agreed to a price freeze.[5]

The principal aim of wartime price control had been to stimulate production by assuring high profits while at the same time protecting the government as war purchaser. The ordinary consumer was of secondary concern. This explains why no restraints were imposed on food producers and why the retail price of many goods was not regulated. As a consequence living costs rose 40 percent in the year and a half of war. Clothing prices jumped 44 percent, while some regulated food items increased 50 to 100 percent. Wages barely kept pace with the cost of living, despite the fact that profits had grown considerably. In terms of real income industrial workers were no better off in 1919 than they had been three years earlier. Salaried workers, who constituted the backbone of the Progressive movement, fared much worse, for between 1916 and 1919 their real earnings fell by 20 percent.[6]

It was against this background that many reformers urged the preservation of price controls after the armistice. This scheme might be of far greater benefit to the consumer once the need to maximize production was no longer a factor. Early in 1918 the publisher William Allen White urged that "price fixing should be permanent, but not done by Wall Street." In October a symposium on postwar reconstruction proposed the "continuation of a scheme for fixing prices and controlling distribution." Most such advocates ignored the fact that the government's ability to regulate prices was strictly a function of its war powers. This dependency had been universally acknowledged in Congress when the Lever Act was adopted in 1917. During those debates Fiorello La Guardia recommended long-term federal supervision of food prices but recognized that this could not be achieved by statute. The New York congressman declared that price control should be "a permanent institution with us. After the war, if we are not careful, the speculators will soon be back to the old game . . . I have taken the first step toward that end. I have this day introduced a constitutional amendment giving power to the National Government at all times to regulate and control the production, conservation, and distribution of food supplies."[7]

Labor Draws the Line

Instead of being perpetuated, the system of price controls was dismantled following the armistice. Retail prices began to level off at the beginning of 1919, and restrictions were lifted as the danger of profiteering passed. By the end of March the Food and Fuel Administrations had ceased to function; they formally closed their doors on June 30. Controls were no sooner ended than consumer prices again began to climb. Between April and September the retail food index hit a new high, while clothing prices rose another 41 percent. As workers insisted on compensatory pay hikes, new strikes broke out among carpenters, machinists, longshoremen, and painters and in the building trades, the garment industry, and on street railways, to name but a few. In nearly two-thirds of the 1919 labor disturbances wages were a principal issue. The AFL noted that "no factor contributes more to industrial unrest and instability than excessive costs of necessaries of life . . . Labor has been compelled to struggle desperately to keep wages in some measure up to the cost of living."[8]

This strike activity provoked concern at several levels. First, it was certain to drive prices still higher. A *New York Herald* cartoon showed a stairway winding endlessly skyward, its steps labeled "High Cost of Living. Strike. Higher Wages. Higher Cost of Living. Strike

. . ." There were also fears that labor unrest might trigger broader social convulsions. Charles Forcey noted, "Most progressives were sure that the United States was in for a long period of heightened social tension . . . Much of the urgency with which [they] fought for social justice sprang from their feeling that if their 'constructive' solutions failed it would soon be too late." In April 1910, before becoming a candidate for governor of New Jersey, Woodrow Wilson had told a group of Princeton alumni that "unless America took accounting of herself . . . she would find herself in the throes of a revolution." He returned to this theme in the 1912 presidential campaign, warning that "some man with eloquent tongue, without conscience, who did not care for the nation, could put this whole country into a flame." For this reason, he said, society "stands ready to attempt nothing less than a radical reconstruction, which only . . . generous co-operation can hold back from becoming a revolution."[9]

Progressives viewed organized labor with particular foreboding. Union membership had increased tenfold since the turn of the century. A decade earlier Herbert Croly had cautioned that "militant unionists are beginning to talk and believe as if they were at war with the existing social and political order . . . The union laborer is tending to become suspicious, not merely of his employer, but of the constitution of American Society . . . [T]he literature popular among the unionists is a literature, not merely of discontent, but sometimes of revolt." The riots, bombings, and strikes of 1919 suggested to many that the United States stood on the brink of an upheaval similar to that which had transformed Russia two years earlier. Some believed the spark might be provided by the high cost of living. According to Lord D'Abernon, a British monetary expert, "80 percent of our present industrial troubles, and our Bolshevism, are due to this enormous displacement in the value of money. Changes in the value of currency in which wages, salaries, and other . . . remuneration are paid are the root cause of the prevailing unrest." Senator Henry Myers, a Montana Democrat, likewise noted that "The ever-rising cost of living is productive of Bolshevism and anarchy. It gives the Bolshevistic, anarchistic agitator a chance to go amongst the laboring men and embitter them . . . against their Government, and to tell them . . . they are not getting their share of the money and prosperity of the country."[10]

The matter came to a head in late July, when the Brotherhood of Locomotive Engineers asked President Wilson to "reduce the cost of the necessaries of life to a figure that the present wages and income of the people will meet." The railway trainmen endorsed the proposal, adding that if nothing were done by October 1, "steps looking to the enforcement of the demands would be taken." As if to emphasize the gravity of the situation, 250,000 railroad shop workers walked out on August 1, ignoring orders from their union to remain on the job. The action was triggered by the Railroad Administration's refusal to raise their pay seventeen cents an hour from the existing hourly level of sixty-eight cents. The spontaneous and defiant character of the walkout produced great alarm. Senator Albert Cummins of Iowa exclaimed, "Unless the relations between wages and and the cost of living are adjusted on some fair basis, the country is going to smash."[11]

The crisis escalated rapidly. On August 2 the rail unions replaced their insistence on a price reduction with a new demand. The *New York Times* announced the turn of events in an eight-column headline: "Brotherhoods Demand Government Ownership of Roads and a Share in the Profits, Following Strike Threat." This so-called Plumb Plan had been unveiled by the unions six months earlier but had long been given up as dead. Indeed the futility of seeking federal ownership from a Republican Congress had led the president to decide that the railroads should be returned at the end of the year. Labor, however, was now invoking more forceful means of persuasion. Some union spokesmen denied that they would use a nationwide general strike to force adoption of the Plumb Plan, but the secretary of the AFL told a House committee that such action was in fact being considered. This view was seconded by Glenn Plumb, who appeared before the same committee on August 7. Under a headline reading "Plumb Plan or Revolution, Says Its Author," the *New York Times* reported Plumb's belief that there would be "general strikes, within sixty or ninety days by the workingmen of the nation unless conditions were changed."[12]

The Brotherhoods' ultimatum spurred the administration to action. Tumulty advised the president that their demands were "the first appearance of the soviet in this country. If we trifle with it or appear indifferent to its spread, we will have Bolshevism and all of its attendant horrors . . . A few vigorous declarations today would be more powerful than machine guns later." A committee led by Attorney General Palmer recommended that the Lever Act be expanded and that its hoarding and profiteering provisions again be enforced. In a speech to Congress on August 8 Wilson urged, "There is no ground for some of the fearful forecasts I hear uttered about me, but the condition of the world is unquestionably very grave and we should face it comprehendingly." Imploring the nation to remain calm, he voiced hope "that the more extreme leaders of organized labor will presently yield to a sober second thought . . . and act like true Americans. They will see that strikes undertaken at this critical time are certain to make matters worse . . . for them and for everybody else." Wilson declared that high prices were due not to a "shortage of supply" but to "selfish and sinister" practices. He called on business to exercise self-restraint and warned that federal law would be invoked if necessary. He also asked Congress to provide better means of fighting inflation by amending the Lever Act, noting that while section 4 of the act "prohibits profiteering, the prohibition is accompanied by no penalty." In addition, he urged that the act be broadened to cover more commodities. Last, since the statute would expire with the proclamation of peace, he suggested adoption of "similar permanent provisions," limited for reasons of "constitutional power . . . to all goods destined for interstate commerce."[13]

The president's address quickly defused the threat of a general strike. Labor leaders reportedly displayed an "intense anxiety to refute the charge that they had threatened a strike in case the Plumb Plan was not adopted by Congress." By mid-August the shopmen had returned to work with a promise from the Railroad Administration to reconsider their demand for higher wages. In the end they accepted a raise of four cents per hour, much less than what they had sought. Yet the brief walkout was by no means a failure, for as one observer pointed out, it had the "effect of speeding up the belated efforts of the Administration and of Congress to find a remedy for the high cost of living—the broad issue on which the brotherhoods had based the necessity for their demands." These remedies consisted almost entirely of resorting to war powers legislation, much of which was adopted after the armistice.[14]

On August 12 the attorney general sent Congress a bill to amend the Food and Fuel Control Act as outlined by the president. It proposed expanding the definition of "necessaries" to include wearing apparel and food containers, and adding criminal penalties for profiteering and other conduct proscribed by section 4. The latter omission had proved harmless during the war, when the government could deal with violators through license revocation and blacklisting. With the termination of licensing, however, the defect became fatal. The amendments were swiftly approved by the House but were bogged down in the Senate by provisions dealing with rent control for the District of Columbia. As a result the bill was not adopted until October 22, 1919, two and a half months after Wilson had appeared before Congress.[15]

The Attorney General's Campaign: Bluff with a Bite

The administration was not idle in the interim. With the cost of living now front-page news, Attorney General Palmer seized control of a venture that was certain to place him in the limelight. He dissuaded the House from reviving the Food Administration, arguing that this might slow the bill's passage. Such a scheme would also have forced him to share the stage with another agency—a feature to which he could hardly have been indifferent. The connection between the cost of living campaign and Palmer's political ambitions was quite evident at the time. Indeed it was reported that the Senate's delay in amending the Lever Act was due partly to a Republican "fear that it would afford Mr. Palmer means for adding to his National strength and making him a contender for the Presidential nomination."[16]

On July 30, the day the Brotherhoods raised the issue, Palmer announced that the Justice Department would investigate the cost of living. He made it clear that the aim was to help the Progressive middle classes rather than organized labor. "The man who has suffered from high prices," he said, "has been the salaried man, the clerk. I wish we could do something to help him." By contrast, he explained later, "wage earners were in the class of the rich," for their income had kept up with the rising cost of living. The attorney general promised that though he could not yet attack profiteering directly, every available means would be used to discourage the practice. U.S. attorneys were ordered to employ the antitrust laws, as well as sections 6 and 7 of the Lever Act, which made hoarding a crime and allowed the seizure of hoarded goods. When asked how this war powers measure could be used to regulate living costs in time of peace, Palmer replied "these are not peace times. The Food Control act and other war acts are still in force; . . . the conditions throughout the country are part of the wartime conditions, and will be dealt with under both wartime and peacetime legislation."[17]

Shortly after Wilson addressed Congress, the attorney general moved to revive the network of Fair Price Committees. Committees were soon formed in three-quarters of the states to work with the Justice Department to "determine the fair margin of profits, and . . . to have published its list of fair prices." It was thought that these schedules would force most dealers into line, for shoppers would presumably refuse to pay more than the established price. Besides providing "education and moral suasion," the committees were to turn over any evidence of profiteering and hoarding to federal prosecutors. Such information not only might result in indictment but would also be used to subject a seller to public condemnation. Indeed the threat of censure was a key part of the campaign. U.S. attorneys were told to give the press "full details in all cases of profiteering and hoarding," including "the names of those involved, the amount of food involved, in fact everything connected with each and every case." Even the *New York Times,* which otherwise applauded Palmer's efforts, was concerned by this aspect of the program and suggested that "a Federal District Attorney should not call a man a profiteer unless sure that the charge is true."[18]

Sections 6 and 7 of the Lever Act afforded a firm basis for proceeding against hoarding, and on August 20 the attorney general reported that to date, federal agents had seized nearly twenty-five million eggs and two million pounds of pork. He repeatedly noted, however, that section 4 provided no means of prosecuting those who charged excessive prices. For this reason the administration had asked Congress to amend the act. In the meantime Palmer went to great lengths to frighten dealers into submission. As he explained to a Fair Price Committee in New York, "If we can make a few conspicuous examples of gougers and give the widest sort of publicity to the fact that such gougers have been and will be punished, in the future there will be little inclination to profiteer in this country." To this end the department took the incredible step of instituting criminal prosecutions under the sanctionless section 4.[19]

At least four such actions were brought during August 1919, all for profiteering in sugar. The suit against Joseph Mossew drew the most attention. The Binghamton, New York, retailer was fined $500 for selling sugar at fifteen cents a pound, four cents higher than the government thought appropriate. While the *New York Times* hailed it as "the first case to arise under the new law," there was no new law. In the days that followed, the press warned that Palmer "intended to prosecute every dealer guilty of selling at higher prices than those listed by the Fair Price Committees," a threat repeated by the attorney general himself. Mossew's conviction was overturned in May 1920. The U.S. Court of Appeals unanimously held that "the indictment is insufficient to charge a crime, and is therefore void," since "no penalty or punishment for a violation of the statute is prescribed." This result was virtually foreordained, but by the time the ruling was handed down, the case had served its purpose of deterring other would-be profiteers. Moreover, long before the conviction was set aside Congress had cured the problem by amending section 4.[20]

The attorney general sought to intimidate merchants in other ways as well. He stated that despite the difficulty of prosecuting individual profiteers, "a combination formed to raise prices can be punished." One of the criminal actions filed in August alleged a conspiracy to violate section 4 by charging excessive prices. Here, as in *Mossew,* the government's theory was fundamentally flawed. Section 9 of the Lever Act did outlaw conspiracies to engage in much of the conduct proscribed by section 4, but it did not cover combinations to charge high prices. The Justice Department also announced that once the Lever Act was amended, those who had engaged in profiteering during the preceding two years might be prosecuted. Palmer, apparently unconcerned by the constitutional prohibition against *ex post facto* laws, claimed that "the mere fact of adding the penalty after the law was passed doesn't mean that violators of the law from the time it became effective cannot be punished."[21]

It was no accident that all of the profiteering cases filed in August 1919 involved sugar. During the war the U.S. Sugar Equalization Board had purchased the Cuban sugar crop, which it then sold to American refiners. Under their contracts with the board these firms agreed to sell refined sugar at a set price through the end of 1919. By using the markups previously fixed by the Food Administration, the department arrived at a ceiling price for sugar without having to wait for the Fair Price Committees to complete their work. Sugar was also one of a handful of products still technically under license control. In August Palmer warned that dealers charging excessive prices would lose their licenses or face possible blacklisting, though there is no evidence that these sanctions were actually imposed.[22]

Between August and October the attorney general thus waged a vigorous fight against the cost of living without the aid of additional legislation from Congress. The most tangible aspect of the program involved hoarding. By the end of October there had been ninety-two confiscations under section 7 of the Lever Act and two indictments under section 6. Beyond this the department relied primarily on bluff, accompanied by an occasional prosecution for profiteering. In late September Palmer boasted, "We have not stamped out hoarding and profiteering, but already, by threats of prosecution, we have reduced prices of the necessaries of life more than 5 per cent . . . [A]fter we get the necessary law and initiate our prosecutions, I look for another drop of perhaps 5 or 10 per cent." This claim, while grossly exaggerated, clearly reveals the strategy employed during the early months of the campaign.[23]

Expanding the Lever Act

In the meantime the bill to amend the Lever Act was making its way through Congress. Wilson had asked that the law be extended, but according to the *New York Times,* "Republicans as well as Democrats in the Senate are opposed to continuing war powers, their chief contention being that war powers should be lifted as quickly as possible and the country allowed to return to normal conditions." The administration therefore sought only two changes in the law: first, to expand its definition of "necessaries," and second, to criminalize profiteering. There were nonetheless several attempts to continue the act beyond the formal end of the war. The failure of these extension efforts partly reflected a Republican unwillingness to enhance the authority of a Democratic president. It may also have stemmed from constitutional difficulties; if so, this was one of the few times in the postarmistice period when such concerns prevailed. By contrast, the constitutional objections to expanding the statute were almost totally ignored.[24]

All agreed that the war powers provided the only basis for amending the Lever Act. The original act specified that it was made necessary "by reason of the existence of a state of war," and its duration was limited to that emergency. North Carolina Senator Nathaniel Dial opposed any extension of the act, urging that it was too late to be making further use of these powers: "During war times it made no difference whether or not an act was constitutional or legal, whatever the Government wanted the people were willing to let it have. Now the war is practically over—not legally over, but to all intents and purposes it is ended—and . . . it is time to stop extending any war measures." As Senator Pat Harrison of Mississippi noted, the bill could not rest on the commerce power, for it "does not deal wholly with interstate commerce" but rather "with the individual in a State who is doing business intrastate." Iowa Senator William Kenyon, later a judge on the U.S. Court of Appeals, also believed that there was a question of "constitutional power" as to "whether we can fix a penalty for an unreasonable price for something that is in no way connected with interstate commerce." Senator Robert Owen of Oklahoma, who proposed continuing the law indefinitely, made no attempt to deny these assertions. Instead, when reminded that the Lever Act was adopted as a war measure, he replied, "Oh, I remember that very well, but these fundamental principles are so just and so sound that they ought not to be set aside, and since it is very easy to make them effective with the amendment I have proposed I think it ought to go in the bill."[25]

Similar objections were raised in the House. One member, however, made a serious effort to defend the bill's validity. George Huddleston of Alabama explained that according to Supreme Court decisions the war power "does not end immediately with the proclamation of peace. It continues for a reasonable time thereafter until the effects of war have passed, . . . until high prices which have arisen out of the peculiar conditions of the war have passed away." While Huddleston accurately stated the law, he made no attempt to show that the cost of living was a product of the war. The inflationary boom which began in the spring of 1919 was not easily traceable to the war. The conflict had been too brief for a backlog of unsatisfied consumer demand to have developed. After the armistice there was an adequate supply of necessaries despite the large number of strikes. As Wilson told Congress on August 8, 1919, the country was witnessing a "rise of prices in the face of abundance." He believed the crisis to be a moral one, produced by individual self-indulgence and greed on the part of business. While there was perhaps some merit in this explanation, it did not tie the problem to the war. Nor was the price spurt the result of continued deficit spending by government, for the level of federal expenditures had remained nearly constant.[26]

The rise in living costs was due largely to a credit expansion engineered by the Federal Reserve Board to assist the Treasury in floating the Victory Liberty Loan. By maintaining a low discount rate during the spring of 1919, the board allowed banks to increase reserves and make additional loans. The newly issued bonds, many of which were purchased on credit, could in turn be used as collateral to support additional borrowing. The postwar inflation was also fueled by a wave of speculative buying by merchants who sought to increase inventories in the self-fulfilling expectation that prices would continue to rise. This explains the phenomenon, noted by the president, of scarcity in the face of abundance. It also accounts for the sensational cases of hoarding uncovered in the late summer and early fall of 1919.[27]

Even if the high cost of living could be linked to the war, there remained the question of whether using the war powers to outlaw profiteering was consistent with the Bill of Rights. It was well established that as a matter of due process, when Congress "define[s] by statute a new offense . . . it should express its will in language that need not deceive the common mind. Every man should be able to know with certainty when he is committing a crime." The amendment to section 4 made it illegal to impose "any unjust or unreasonable rate or charge in handling or dealing in or with any necessaries; [or] to conspire . . . to exact excessive prices for any necessaries." Five years earlier the Supreme Court had invalidated a state law punishing conspiracies to charge a price higher than a good's "market value under fair competition, and under normal market conditions." This measure, said the Court, provided "no standard of conduct that it is possible to know," for the elements of the crime were "uncertain both in nature and degree of effect." The same flaw seemed inherent in the profiteering amendment to the Lever Act.[28]

Senator Hoke Smith raised the issue when Palmer appeared before a Senate committee in August. The Georgia Democrat thought the amendment "so indefinite" that the department might "have serious trouble in enforcing it," but he was more concerned at the prospect of "placing a doubt upon every man as to what would be an unreasonable and unjust profit and leaving him in a state of uncertainty about the conduct of his business." The attorney general replied that the problem would be redressed by Fair Price Committees, which would "publish a list of fair prices applicable to every community." The matter surfaced again when he testified in the House. Palmer now admitted that fair price networks were not yet established in a dozen states, though by the end of the year this figure would be reduced to six. At the city and county levels, however, there were only half as many committees as had existed during the war. It was thus clear that in many places a seller's only guidance would come from the vague words of the statute. Palmer nevertheless urged that this was acceptable, for while "many years ago" it had been held that "a man was

entitled to know the exact nature of the offense that he was committing," that principle "was exploded many times since." Nor, he added,
would such a rule apply here, for "it has been distinctly held the
due-process clause—although there are many, many lawyers who
dispute it—is not enforced against the law of Congress in war times."
In short, said Palmer, "the due-process clause of the Constitution is
abrogated by the war power."[29]

The House, apparently satisfied with the attorney general's explanation, approved the profiteering provision without change. In the
Senate, however, Hoke Smith persuaded the Agriculture and Forestry
Committee to offer an amendment providing that except in cases of
conspiracy, a dealer could be indicted for profiteering only if he
exceeded "a rate or charge fixed by a fair-price committee." Smith's
object was to "prevent prosecution where a merchant has no standard
from which he can tell what is a violation of the law. I simply do not
believe that we ought to turn loose upon the merchants of this country an act which will make it criminal to charge an unreasonable or an
unfair profit." Only a few senators voiced agreement with Smith, and
his proposal was defeated. The same fate befell a substitute amendment specifying that sellers who adhered to fair price guidelines could
not be prosecuted but which would have allowed the act to be implemented without restriction in areas where no committee existed.[30]

Some who shared Smith's concerns deliberately chose to overlook
the problem. Senator Reed Smoot of Utah, who seemed to concede
that the measure was invalid, went on to state: "If I thought this
legislation was going to be enforced in the United States very many
months . . . I never would support it . . . [B]ut, really, if we are going
to do a thing, let us do it. If it is bad, let it be bad and do not let us
try by putting in some words to make it a perfectly useless thing."
Senator Kenyon was equally pragmatic in deciding to support the bill:
"If it was to be permanent legislation, it would not secure my vote.
But the Attorney General has come to Congress, and the President has
done so, asking for this legislation. It is only going to be a period of
perhaps 30 days, and in the meantime the Attorney General may be
able to accomplish something by it. That is the only justification that
I can get into my mind for voting for it." Principle had yielded to
expediency. Contrary to the expectations of some, the profiteering
provision remained in effect for almost a year and a half and was
enforced vigorously until the eve of Wilson's departure from the
White House. Yet the constitutional infirmities which the attorney

general and Congress were so willing to ignore eventually proved fatal to the act.[31]

Rent Control for the District of Columbia

When Palmer testified before the Senate committee in mid-August, he stated that the profiteering amendment to section 4 was "so simple" that it could be enacted in three days. The process took much longer, mainly because the bill was expanded to regulate rents in the nation's capital. This measure was responsive to the president's August 8 request that Congress address the cost of living in Washington "as a useful example to the other communities of the country" and to "relieve local distress." The Ball Rent Law, as it was known, was the third rent statute to be adopted for the District of Columbia since the start of the war.[32]

The wartime expansion of the federal bureaucracy had led to a rapid growth in Washington's population. Landlords took advantage of the situation by raising rents, often by a third; those who refused to pay the increase were evicted. In January 1918 Wilson remarked that "the real estate proprietors of Washington are holding the Government up in a most outrageous and piratical manner." Four months later Congress responded with the Saulsbury Resolution, which barred the eviction of a tenant who continued to pay rent after the lease expired. This measure was to lapse at the end of the war. Before then it was expected that Congress would have created a District Rent Administration, to operate for a year after the proclamation of peace. Yet by the summer of 1919, when it appeared that peace might be at hand, Congress had still not approved such a bill. In anticipation of the end of rent control Washington landlords prepared for mass evictions. On July 11 Congress intervened by extending the Saulsbury Resolution until ninety days after the formal end of the war. This second of the District rent laws was not entirely altruistic, for as one House member observed, "We are all interested, many of us personally," and had it been possible, "we might have put it for six months or a year."[33]

When the administration's bill to expand the Lever Act was taken up a month later, Representative Huddleston suggested that "dwellings and dwelling rooms held for hire" be brought under its protection. "Profiteering in rents is just as oppressive as profiteering in food," he said. "We are suffering from it here in Washington and our constituents are suffering at home." Huddleston urged that nationwide rent control was proper as an "exercise of the war powers of Congress." After the House rejected his amendment, a Senate committee recommended simply outlawing "unreasonable and excessive" rents in the District of Columbia. The Senate then abandoned this proposal in favor of the more ambitious Ball bill, which was made part of the pending Lever Act amendments and adopted on October 22, 1919.[34]

The Ball Rent Law replaced the modest Saulsbury Resolution with an all-powerful Rent Commission. This body was authorized to determine "whether the rent, charges, service, and other terms or conditions of a lease or other contract for the use or occupancy of any . . . rental property, hotel, or apartment are fair and reasonable." If they were not, it could impose new terms of its own. The commission was also charged with issuing standard lease forms, and all rental agreements would be construed in conformity with the required provisions. Tenants could not be evicted after their lease expired as long as they paid rent, unless possession was required for the landlord's personal use. Regardless of when peace was proclaimed, this rent control scheme was to remain in effect for two years, until October 22, 1921.[35]

Congress chose to rest all of the District rent laws partly on the war powers, even though the Constitution gave it explicit authority to legislate for the nation's capital. To have relied only on the seat-of-government provision would have placed the statutes in jeopardy. One stumbling block lay in Article I, section 10, which bars states from "impairing the obligation of contracts." Some believed that this prohibition might apply to the United States if it interfered with leases solely under the District police power. Moreover, it was then accepted that the Fifth Amendment prevented Congress from impairing contractual obligations; as one writer put it, "Contracts have as substantial protection against federal action under the due process clause as they have under the contract clause against state action." The Ball law was particularly problematic, for it asserted direct control over rents. The Court had long held that price regulation was allowable only if a business was "affected with a public interest." Congress sought to meet this difficulty by expressly declaring that rental property in the District was so affected, but such a finding was not binding on the judiciary.[36]

The District rent laws took the government into uncharted waters.

While a few states had recently adopted rent measures, none was as sweeping as the Ball Act. The war powers seemed to afford a refuge from the doubts surrounding the measures. Like the attorney general, many held that legislation adopted under these auspices was exempt from constitutional limitation. Even those of more moderate persuasion believed that the Bill of Rights would apply in only a diluted form. The distinguished scholar Westel Willoughby thus asserted that "the power to wage war enables the government to override in many particulars private rights which in time of peace are inviolable."[37]

The war powers foundation of the Saulsbury Resolution was contained in a preamble which declared: "By reason of the existence of a state of war, it is essential to the national security and defense, and for the successful prosecution of the war, to establish governmental control and assure adequate regulation of real estate in the District of Columbia." Some, however, still believed the measure to be invalid. Senator James Reed charged that it "abrogates the terms of written contracts," and asked, "What are you going to do with the fifth amendment" or with the contracts clause, "a doctrine which in principle applies to the Federal Government?" The Missouri Democrat noted that there were other ways to prevent rent gouging, such as imposing an excess-profits tax on Washington landlords. At a minimum, he said, rent protection should be limited to federal employees. Reed cautioned that when Congress "shows its disregard for the Constitution and the laws of the land they sow the dragon's teeth, from which spring up . . . anarchists, and that class of socialists who disregard law and constitutions and property rights." Senator Frank Brandegee of Connecticut also thought the statute invalid, noting, "The only answer that is made to these criticisms . . . is that we are at war, and that Congress can do anything it wants when we are at war; that the due-process-of-law clause does not any longer exist." The measure's author, Willard Saulsbury of Delaware, apparently shared these concerns, for he sought Wilson's assurance that the Justice Department would defend the resolution's validity in court.[38]

The Ball Rent Law posed even more serious problems owing to its unprecedented interference with property rights and the fact that it extended far beyond the anticipated end of the war. The measure initially rested solely on the war powers, but several other bases were later added. In final form it stated that it was "made necessary by emergencies growing out of the war . . . resulting in rental conditions in the District of Columbia dangerous to the public health and burdensome to public officers and employees whose duties require them to reside within the District . . . and thereby embarrassing the Federal Government in the transaction of the public business." Representative James McLaughlin of Michigan, a member of the conference committee responsible for this language, stated that the law derived from three sources of power: Congress's authority over the nation's capital, the war power, and the government's "right to protect itself." As to the second of these, he declared that "a state of war exists; disturbed conditions following and due to the war will exist for a long time; and the war power of Congress continues while these conditions continue."[39]

As with the Saulsbury Resolution, the difficulty was not so much finding a source of power as avoiding conflict with the Bill of Rights. Several members objected that the Ball law violated the contracts clause and the Fifth Amendment. McLaughlin answered the first charge by noting that there was "no express limitation of that kind as to the power of Congress," but he ignored the fact that the due process clause was thought to do the same thing. Representative Ira Hersey of Maine believed the measure to be "clearly unconstitutional," and added, "The authors . . . know it; but they seek to escape by invoking the war powers . . . after the war is ended." Minnesota Senator Frank Kellogg was equally troubled. Describing himself as "just an ordinary country lawyer," the future secretary of state declared: "The war is over for all practical purposes . . . Hostilities ceased a year ago; thousands upon thousands have left the city, and more ought to leave it; and we now propose to initiate a system of price fixing in the District which will have an ultimate effect on the entire country." Absent a showing "that actual necessity exists for employment by the Government of more people than the housing facilities of the District will accommodate," he said, Congress lacked authority to adopt the statute as a war measure.[40]

In the face of these protests even the rent law's leading supporters agreed that it might not be a legitimate exercise of federal power. Representative Carl Mapes of Michigan conceded that he was not "absolutely certain . . . of its constitutionality" but found this no reason to vote against it. Displaying a remarkably casual air, the Michigan Law School graduate remarked that if the measure were "found to be unconstitutional," he would "see to it that a bill is passed that is constitutional." Illinois Senator Lawrence Sherman likewise noted, "There are a few provisions in the bill . . . that may not be sustained." Yet he preferred to leave the task of excising them to others, declaring that "there is enough to be enforced, enough that is valid, to furnish the remedy needed; enough that the courts, I think, will sustain." From these statements it is abundantly clear that Congress was again quite willing to invoke its war powers under conditions that were highly suspect. While the constitutional issues were discussed, they counted for little. In a familiar mood of pragmatic indifference, legislators preferred to take their chances with the judiciary rather than act responsibly themselves.[41]

In this particular case the temptation to ignore the Constitution was even greater than usual. While there was no recorded vote in the Senate, only eight votes were cast against the Ball law in the House. This minimal opposition was no doubt due to the fact that members were able to protect their own interests without fear of reprisal at the polls. As Ohio Representative James Begg observed, while most members of Congress leased property in Washington, their landlords had no voice on Capitol Hill.

I challenge you men who are in favor of this bill in this form to go back home and pass such a bill for your State. If you do, you will never get another vote from any man who owns property valued at as much as $500 . . . The reason . . . some of you are so ready to take it away from the people of the District of Columbia is because you think they can not get after you. They do not have a vote. You will not go back to your homes and talk that kind of stuff.

Indeed Begg reminded his colleagues that less than two months earlier they had rejected a proposal which would have outlawed profiteering by landlords throughout the country.[42]

The Ball bill provided that the Saulsbury Resolution was to remain in effect until sixty days after the new rent commissioners were appointed. Because of Wilson's stroke in early October the White House had not yet submitted its nominees to the Senate on December 1, when a federal court held the Saulsbury law unconstitutional. District landlords immediately commenced eviction proceedings against many tenants, while others were notified of huge rent increases. The *Washington Post* warned that unless the president acted at once, "hundreds of families will either be forced to leave the city or be evicted from their homes." The administration finally sent three names to the Senate on January 6, 1920, two and a half months after the Ball law had been adopted; eight days later they were confirmed. The life of the District Rent Commission, however, was not to be an easy one.[43]

The Campaign against Profiteering

The passage of the Lever Act amendments on October 22, 1919, breathed new life into the administration's efforts to check the rise in prices. Tumulty had complained to the attorney general in late September that the campaign was "lagging a bit," but the *New York Times* reported that the hiatus was only temporary: "As soon as the Department of Justice is given power under the amended law to prosecute profiteers there will be thousands of arrests in the country. An investigation has been completed, and the department is merely waiting the necessary law before undertaking its nation-wide crusade against food profiteers." Prices continued their upward climb, and by June 1920 the cost of living was 22 percent higher than it had been a year earlier. Meanwhile labor unrest kept the nation on edge. A Tennessee post of the American Legion urged Palmer to halt "the vicious profiteering" which, it said, "has done more than anything else to aid the radicals of the country in carrying out their propaganda." The attorney general assured the veterans that he would "bend every effort" to deal with the problem.[44]

Part of the campaign involved efforts to reduce consumption. The Justice Department created the Division of Women's Activities, which worked with local women's groups to promote thrift. In the December 1919 issue of the *Independent* Palmer declared that "the Government's fight against the high cost of living is the last campaign of the war" and urged consumers to exercise restraint. The Women's Division distributed complaint cards so that shoppers could turn in merchants who charged excessive prices. The attorney general explained that "the women of the country, in whose hands rests the power largely to control the cost of living through purchase, have been organized to . . . hunt out the profiteers and report violations of the Lever Act."[45]

The statute's criminal provisions were enforced by a unit in the department known as the Flying Squadron, which in April 1920 opened a branch office in New York City staffed by fifty investigators. A major problem was the uncertainty as to what constituted an "unjust or unreasonable" charge. According to Palmer, "This broad and general definition required more specific application and definition. The fair-price commissioners were therefore intrusted with the duty of conferring with the trade and arriving at rates, charges, and profits which would be mutually agreed upon as just and reasonable to the trade and to the consumer." Such agreements were apparently reached in many cities. In a few cases the department appointed national committees to set prices for an entire industry. On at least one occasion a federal grand jury issued a list of prices which it regarded as fair.[46]

Despite these efforts to clarify the act many sellers had no idea as to what the department would find acceptable. This resulted from the fact that fair price committees did not exist in a large number of communities, and even where they did function, price lists were not announced for all classes of necessaries. In New York City, for example, price and profit guidelines were released for food but not for wearing apparel. In an attempt to rectify the situation local clothiers met with the head of the Flying Squadron in May 1920. They came away empty-handed, complaining that he "was frankly determined to be vague on this point" and "loath to give his notion of a reasonable profit." In such circumstances merchants did business at their peril.[47]

The government secured its first conviction under the revised section 4 on November 14, 1919, when Charles and Julius Roth of New York City were found guilty of having profiteered in sugar two days after the amendment was adopted. By late December the department had filed nearly 180 criminal actions for profiteering and reported 100 seizures of hoarded goods. At least three hoarders were already in jail. The prosecutions in these first two months were more than twice the number brought under the Lever Act in the year and a half of war. Among those caught at this time was Jess Willard, the former heavyweight boxing champion. On December 12, five months after losing his title to Jack Dempsey, Willard was indicted for profiteering in firewood. He had been turned in by members of the Topeka fair price committee who had purchased wood at Willard's Kansas farm for $3.50 a cord, a price the U.S. attorney said was "double what it should have been."[48]

Sugar dealers were the most frequent target of the cost-of-living campaign, for during 1919 and 1920 the country faced a severe shortage of this commodity. In May 1919, before the "famine" began, sugar sold for 10.6 cents a pound; by June 1920 it had risen to 26.7 cents. The shortage was not a result of the war; at the time of the armistice, supplies appeared more than adequate for the coming year. The Food Administration had no sooner lifted controls, however, than consumption began to soar. By fall 1919 per capita use was nine pounds per year higher than before the war. This resulted partly from an increase in home canning and a heightened desire for sweets; but more important was the sudden demand for soft drinks once the sale of alcoholic beverages ceased on July 1. The situation was then aggravated by strikes and by the Equalization Board's eleventh-hour decision not to acquire the new Cuban sugar crop, triggering a panic among refiners, who suddenly had to fend for themselves. The sugar crisis, which had been caused largely by the use of the war powers to impose prohibition, was then dealt with through a further resort to those powers in the form of the Lever Act.[49]

The attorney general moved against the sugar famine on several fronts. There was no immediate danger of profiteering by refiners, who remained bound by their agreement with the board to sell at a fixed price until the end of 1919. To check gouging by domestic suppliers the Justice Department established ceiling prices for sugar beets and sugar cane; U.S. attorneys were told to prosecute growers who exceeded these limits. The greatest danger lay with wholesalers and retailers, against whom Palmer bore down with special fervor. Through late November the *New York Times* had reported nearly 50 suits against sugar dealers. A year later, the number of sugar profiteering cases had reached 455, with another 28 actions for hoarding. The department was given an additional weapon on November 21, 1919, when President Wilson authorized the attorney general to assume the duties once performed by the Food Administration. License controls were immediately tightened on sugar, and by the end of November the first in a series of license revocation proceedings had begun. Thereafter 19 dealers were prosecuted under section 5 of the Lever Act for violating sugar licensing regulations.[50]

The sugar famine broke in August 1920 as the 1921 Cuban crop began entering the market. The crisis passed without the Equalization Board's buying any of the 1920 crop, despite a last-minute attempt by Congress to make the purchase possible. In this ultimately futile endeavor Congress was again willing to invoke its war powers well after the armistice. The McNary Bill, which became law on December 31, 1919, authorized the board to acquire the 1920 Cuban crop. It also extended the Lever Act's license provisions to July 1, 1920, for domestic sugars and to the end of 1920 for Cuban sugars, even if the act had otherwise expired with the peace. Few questioned the propriety of this extension. The two senators from Louisiana, a sugar cane state, were among the exceptions. Yet several others who spoke out had less of an interest in the matter. Senator Ellison Smith of

South Carolina stated, "If it was during the war and conditions were abnormal by virtue of that fact, it would be a different question." In the House Carlos Bee of Texas observed that the Lever Act "was a war measure" and asked, "If peace is declared and the country returns to a peace basis, . . . what authority has Congress, then, to continue in time of peace a measure for the regulation of certain commodities?" The bill passed easily but came too late to allow purchase of the Cuban sugar. The extension of licensing also proved superfluous, for the Lever Act remained fully effective throughout 1920.[51]

The nation's clothing dealers were another principal focus of Palmer's attention. The price of attire, which had risen sharply during the war, increased another 47 percent in the last half of 1919. It was for this reason that Congress added wearing apparel to the definition of "necessaries" when it broadened the Lever Act in October 1919. The Women's Division sought to reduce clothing demand by promoting homemade and "made-over" garments. This had some amusing consequences. An Old Clothes Club was formed at Yale, where it was decreed that wearing a new suit on campus constituted "a serious breach of social etiquette." And at MIT students vowed to forgo such purchases for a period of three months. In Washington a member of Congress apppeared in the House wearing overalls, while in Manhattan a couple donned blue gingham for their wedding reception at the Waldorf-Astoria.[52]

The clothing campaign had a grim side to it as well. In his annual report for 1920 the attorney general noted that more than eighty prosecutions had been brought for profiteering in wearing apparel, a quarter of which had already resulted in convictions. The act was enforced even in cities like New York, where dealers had no guidance as to what constituted an allowable markup. On April 10 federal agents visited Joseph Nichthauser's men's shop in Brooklyn, where they found a raincoat priced at $45 for which he had allegedly paid $25 or $30. He was arrested, charged under the Lever Act, and released on $2,000 bail. The next morning's *New York World* announced, "Haberdasher Held as Price Gouger. Joseph Nichthauser of Brooklyn First Arrested by U.S. 'Flying Squadron.' " Later that day, the father of three took his life in what the *New York Times* described as "the first suicide resulting from the Government's war on profiteering."[53]

Fuel was the other major necessary protected by the Lever Act.

When the country's bituminous workers walked out on November 1, 1919, the president revived the Fuel Administration and placed coal prices under close supervision. These controls were lifted April 1, 1920, after the miners and operators accepted a pay award recommended by the Bituminous Coal Commission. Though the commission warned that mine owners might seek to pass the wage hike on to consumers, Wilson nevertheless decided to end the restrictions. He explained that he had considered making further use of the "war power of the Lever Act" but had rejected the option as improper. "There is at present no provision of law for fixing new coal prices for peace-time purposes, and unless and until some grave emergency shall arise, which in my judgment has a relation to the emergency purposes of the Lever Act, I would not feel justified in fixing coal prices."[54]

Attorney General Palmer did not share these scruples. On April 3, two days after Wilson had lifted coal controls, Palmer gave orders to prosecute any coal profiteering which resulted from the wage increases. By mid-May more than 140 Lever Act cases had been filed against fuel dealers, most presumably for sales of coal. In late June, while en route to the Democratic convention, the attorney general announced that coal profiteers were still being pursued. In July and August suits were brought against mine operators in Tennessee, Kentucky, and Virginia. The Flying Squadron continued to monitor wholesale and retail prices, and there were periodic reports of new coal indictments through the end of the year. Palmer stated that the number would have been even higher had federal courts in five key coal states not held the profiteering section of the Lever Act to be invalid.[55]

In October 1920 the Justice Department announced plans to discontinue the Fair Price Committees as well as the educational activities of the Women's Division. Criminal prosecutions continued to be brought, however, until February 1921, when the Supreme Court ended the affair by ruling that section 4 was unconstitutional. It is difficult to determine the full extent to which the Lever Act was invoked during the cost-of-living campaign. A December 1920 Justice Department report lists 1,049 suits for profiteering, 33 for hoarding, 13 under the coal regulations, and 1 for conspiracy. It is unclear whether these figures embrace the 180 profiteering cases filed in 1919; they obviously do not include those brought in 1921. It would thus appear that there were at least 1,100 prosecutions, and perhaps as many as 1,300, instituted under the Lever Act starting almost a year after the armistice. Though the war powers afforded the sole consti- tutional basis for this law, its criminal provisions saw more than 90 percent of their use long after hostilities had ceased.[56]

Politics and the Cost of Living

Large corporations were rarely indicted under the Lever Act. In- stead it was typically the small retailer who was selected for prose- cution. Herbert Hoover sensed this bias in the fall of 1919 when the venture was barely six weeks old. He urged the department to con- centrate "at the source of the stream and not at its mouth, as was now the belief of the public." With the arrest of Jess Willard the *St. Louis Post-Dispatch* asked, "Why angle for a minnow like Willard where there are oil whales to be harpooned?" By April 1920 even the *New York Times* was troubled; a week after Joseph Nichthauser's death it suggested that "a real improvement in the deplorable situation will have to come from something else than the catching here and there of a wretch who differs in luck rather than in depravity or ruthlessness from a multitude so vast that the jailing of them all would complete the ruin of the already despairing taxpayer." Shortly thereafter Sen- ator Irvine Lenroot of Wisconsin charged Palmer with "setting a few mouse traps around the country when he ought be setting bear traps. Not one thing is done to the big profiteers." Samuel Gompers agreed, declaring that the attorney general had gone after "corner grocers and small haberdashers for offenses which are of no moment at all in comparison."[57]

Despite his sensitivity to such criticism Palmer never succeeded in changing the direction of the campaign. Actions were brought against only a handful of big companies: in April 1920 Armour, Swift, and Wilson were charged with profiteering in meat; a month later the American Woolen Company was sued; in June prosecutions were instituted against the Gimbel Brothers department store and the Utah-Idaho Sugar Company, run by the Mormon church; the Amer- ican Sugar Refining Company was also indicted. None of these cases went to trial. The attorney general sought to explain the dearth of corporate prosecutions as a function of their added complexity. Yet by his own count these actions numbered fewer than a dozen and represented barely 1 percent of the criminal suits brought under the Lever Act.[58]

This almost exclusive concentration on local entrepreneurs seemed at odds with one of the main tenets of Wilson's Progressivism. During the 1912 campaign he had spoken with reverence of the man "who, if you will give him time enough and see to it that he is not swept off his feet, will build up a business more economical, more efficient, harder to compete with than the business which now, simply because it is big, can crush him while he is little." He had expressed the same view in *The New Freedom*, where he declared that the "man on the make" was "the man by whose judgment I, for one, wish to be guided." Yet in seeking to provide opportunities for these "pigmies" of capitalism, Wilson did not intend that they pursue merely a narrow self-interest. Rather, he hoped that individuals would place the public good ahead of private gain. "The American social spirit," he said in 1907, "insists upon a moral basis of human life, as distinguished from a selfish, inhuman greed." He later told a group of bankers that "those who control wealth [should] pay less attention to the business of making particular individuals rich and more attention to the business of making the country rich." By disregarding this principle, the small-time gouger forfeited any special claim to Wilson's sympathy.[59]

The peculiar focus of the profiteering campaign appears to have a political explanation. The venture began shortly after Congress submitted the suffrage amendment to the states. Palmer and others in the administration helped secure its ratification in August 1920, thereby assuring women the right to participate fully in the November elections. While inflation was a grievance shared by all, America's homemakers confronted it daily in shopping for their families. There was good reason to believe that a politician who won the battle against rising prices would reap a handsome reward at the polls. For this reason Republicans had been hesitant to give the attorney general any additional power under the Lever Act. When they finally did so in the fall of 1919, Palmer used his new authority to full advantage.[60]

The cost-of-living crusade was structured to maximize its appeal to women voters. The fact that the nominating convention was only eight months away called for a plan capable of gaining quick popular acceptance. A program aimed at distant producers and suppliers would have lower visibility, take longer to be felt in the marketplace, and generate less enthusiasm among consumers than one which targeted the neighborhood merchant. Sensing this, Palmer strenuously and successfully opposed a move in Congress to exempt small retailers from the ban on profiteering. Such a provision, he said, would "absolutely destroy this act," for

there is in almost every town and city a corner grocery store or a corner shoe-store retailer who is taking advantage of his limited circle of patrons . . .

We have more complaints of the retail gouger than of anybody else, possibly because he is the man that the people come directly in contact with . . . I would feel hopeless when it came to getting some relief for the people if I were restricted only to the great department stores and immense organizations.[61]

The importance of capturing the female vote was also reflected in the central role of the Women's Division. In each state its work was coordinated by a person who worked directly with the Justice Department. Directors existed at the county level, who in turn named chairpersons for cities and towns. Within these communities committees were formed, including a Complaint Committee to report suspected profiteers. Palmer noted that this elaborate organization was designed to "reach a considerable number of women," and it seems to have done just that. According to the department, the division distributed more than a million pamphlets, arranged for "innumerable newspaper and magazine articles," and answered thousands of requests for information.[62]

Because the war on profiteering was conducted simultaneously with the attorney general's campaign for the presidency, its political overtones were impossible to ignore. On November 26, 1919, the *New York Times* noted that "the attack on the high cost of living" was greatly responsible for the fact that "Mr. Palmer has come rapidly into national prominence." In mid-January it reported that he was the most conspicuous Democratic candidate, "a leader with a real appeal to a people aroused by the high cost of living, profiteeering and continuation of war taxes." Some believed political ambition to be the main force behind the antiprofiteering venture. The department sought to refute the idea when it met with members of the clothing trade, but the impression persisted. The *Chicago Post* later printed a cartoon which showed Palmer leaving Washington with a briefcase containing "Presidential Ambitions and Plans," telling Uncle Sam, "I'm going to reduce the high cost of living." In May the *Pittsburgh Dispatch* dismissed the crusade as "tinkling promises paraded around the country by Mr. Palmer's publicity representatives."[63]

In May 1920 Senator William Kenyon complained that only a few cases had been brought against corporate profiteers, and charged that "the Attorney General could have done vastly more by enforcing this law if he had not been so interested in running for the Presidency." It so happened that the Iowa Republican later headed a Senate subcommittee investigation into campaign expenditures by presidential candidates of both parties. Shortly after the Democratic convention was over, this committee turned up evidence indicating that Palmer may have been guilty of using the cost-of-living campaign to improve his political fortunes.[64]

The most damaging testimony came from Olivia Brueggeman, who testified at a hearing in St. Louis on July 9. She had been appointed by the Justice Department as executive secretary of women's activities in Missouri, a state which recently had given women the presidential vote. The ostensible function of the Missouri office was to encourage a reduction in consumption. This included arranging for speakers from Washington to address local women's groups. In at least one instance, said Brueggeman, the speaker devoted herself entirely to pushing Palmer's candidacy. Brueggeman testified that she and two other officers used Justice Department travel vouchers to attend the state Democratic convention, where one of the women was a voting delegate. Brueggeman was fired from her $150 a month post after it was learned she was a Republican. She then went to Washington and met with several Justice Department officials, including the head of the High Cost of Living Division, Howard Figg. "They asked if anything was being done for Mr. Palmer" and "whether we were for [him], and whether we were disseminating Palmer propaganda whenever we had a chance." Figg also questioned her about a weekly mailing the office was sending to hundreds of Missouri newspapers, wanting to know if these "could not be used to put in articles from time to time concerning Palmer . . . without looking like it was . . . [a] boosting article." In conclusion she agreed with Senator Kenyon that "in St. Louis the high cost of living was a campaign to boost Mr. Palmer for the presidential nomination."[65]

The Brueggeman testimony received prominent coverage in the press. Though Howard Figg denounced her story as "absolutely false," the *New York Times* noted that two hundred persons had attended the hearing and that Brueggeman "answered all of Senator Kenyon's questions sharply and clearly, and at no time appeared embarrassed or confused." Her charge that department travel vouchers were used to attend the state Democratic convention was corroborated by the chairperson and vice-chairperson of the Missouri campaign, and an office stenographer testified that she had once prepared a stencil dealing exclusively with the "Democratic program."[66]

The Missouri experience underlines the close connection between the cost of living campaign and Palmer's bid for the presidency. His failure to win the nomination at San Francisco, where he was at times second in the balloting, may have been due in part to the fact that prices did not begin to fall until after the convention. In April 1920 Howard Figg told a Senate subcommittee that the indictment of profiteers had not led to any appreciable decline in prices, and Palmer later acknowledged that "the criminal law is at best an imperfect instrument with which to deal with such a situation." That even the Justice Department doubted the efficacy of enforcing the act against the "man on the make" tends to reinforce the claim that these prosecutions were undertaken largely for their value as political propaganda.[67]

The Coal Strike Injunction

The attorney general's use of the Lever Act might have taken him farther down the road to the White House had he not employed it as a weapon against the nation's industrial workers. Whatever gains he may have made with consumers by hunting down profiteers were heavily offset by his alienation of organized labor. The decision to invoke this war law against the unions was consistent with early, traditional Progressive thinking. Though reformers sympathized with workers as individuals, they deeply distrusted lower-class efforts at cooperative action. Writing in 1909, Herbert Croly condemned the union laborer as "a bad citizen, and at times an inhuman animal, who is ready to maim or even to kill another man." Labor organizations were incompatible with democracy, he said, for they expected a man to place "allegiance to his union and to his class above his allegiance . . . to his country." According to Walter Weyl, "The middle classes are as much opposed to the trade-union as are the trusts." Progressives tolerated the unions but believed that their ultimate goals could be accomplished more safely through reform legislation.[68]

Woodrow Wilson shared these traditional views, seeing unions as the embodiment of selfish class interest. In 1907 he wrote that trade unionists "have neither the ideas nor the sentiments needed for the maintenance or for the enjoyment of liberty." Two years later he endorsed the open shop and accused unions of impeding production. But by 1912 Wilson was backing the right to organize, and as president he created the Department of Labor, signed several laws to protect workers, and through the War Labor Board helped to strengthen organized labor. Yet the administration's record after the armistice suggests that Wilson never entirely shed his early antipathy toward trade unions. His postmaster general bitterly opposed attempts by postal employees to organize and thwarted similar efforts by telephone and telegraph workers during the period of federal control. In August 1919, when a railroad strike seemed imminent, Joseph Tumulty denounced the Brotherhoods in characteristically Progressive terms as "a privileged group, struggling for further special privileges."[69]

This smoldering hostility burst into flame in the late summer of 1919 amid fears that the numerous strikes then occurring might be the harbingers of anarchy and revolution. The change in attitude was aided by a mistaken belief that labor had benefited unfairly from the war. The *Albany Journal*, for example, declared: "While the war was on, too much advantage of the opportunity was permitted and was taken both by profiteering capitalists and by profiteering labor organizations . . . [T]he effect has been to arouse a popular resentment against those who were trying to take advantage of conditions . . . , whether capitalists or labor leaders." The economist David Friday noted that after the armistice there was a sense that "high wages and 'extravagant living' indulged in by the laboring classes during the war could no longer continue." In actual fact real earnings were generally unchanged between 1916 and 1919. Yet the contrary perception made it easier for Progressives to vent their longstanding dislike of the unions.[70]

In his August 1919 address to Congress the president asked workers to refrain from strikes. In the weeks that followed, however, the labor picture grew worse. An unauthorized walkout by rail employees paralyzed the Southwest, and there were rumblings of a strike at the nation's steel mills. Against this backdrop the administration for the first time began considering more forceful action. The impetus came from Joseph Tumulty, who on August 22 urged that Wilson "fight to a finish the extortionate demands of the railroad brotherhoods," and that "preparations should be made to make good this position . . . It should be considered whether under existing law there is power to require and compel the railroad employees to continue at work. If there is not, a law should be drafted by the Attorney General conferring such powers upon the President . . . as an emergency measure." While the president issued a statement repeating his plea that there be no strikes, it soon became evident that Tumulty's suggestion had borne fruit. On August 28 the attorney general announced that anyone interfering with operation of the railroads or distribution of the mails would be prosecuted. He also asked the states to enforce local law against strikers. In the face of these warnings the Southwest rail walkout instantly collapsed.[71]

The administration had now reached a critical turning point, for it had gone on record as ready to crush future walkouts through resort to federal law. This constituted an ominous departure from the principle contained in section 20 of the 1914 Clayton Act, which stated that strikes and peaceful picketing would not "be considered or held to be violations of any law of the United States." In late September Palmer called for "an absolute industrial armistice in America for six months." Though the demand was not accompanied by a threat of sanctions, there was reason to fear that the government might take the same approach with other workers that it had against the trainmen. The uncertainty was dispelled when a nationwide coal strike erupted on November 1, 1919.[72]

The bituminous miners' real income in 1919 was no higher than it had been in 1902. Under the government-approved wage agreement of October 1917 their pay scale was frozen until the end of the war or March 31, 1920, whichever came first. A penalty clause provided that the increase granted in 1917 would be rescinded if a strike occurred during the life of the contract. Following the armistice the miners felt that they should be released from the 1917 agreement rather than having to suffer because a treaty had not yet been ratified. Wildcat strikes in Kansas and Illinois made it clear that the rank and file would take matters into their own hands if the United Mine Workers Union did not act. The UMW accordingly announced in September 1919 that it regarded the 1917 contract as terminated. The union demanded a 60 percent pay hike, a six-hour day, and a five-day week. When the operators refused to open negotiations, a strike was called for November 1.[73]

The administration sought to avert a walkout while at the same time preparing coercive action should these efforts fail. On October 24 Director General Walker Hines suggested to Tumulty that the walkout would violate section 9 of the Lever Act, which made it a crime "to conspire . . . to restrict the supply of any necessaries." The secretary agreed and drafted a message which was issued the next day over Wilson's signature. In language closely tracking that of the statute, the White House declared that the strike would constitute a "plan . . . to limit the facilities of production and distribution of a necessity of life and thus indirectly to restrict the production and distribution of all the necessaries of life." Moreover, said the president, it would come "at a time when the war itself is still a fact."[74]

The Lever Act was the government's primary weapon against the strike. Harry Garfield, the former fuel administrator, returned to Washington and promptly imposed price and distribution controls on coal stricter than those used during the war. On October 31, hours before the walkout began, a federal court in Indianapolis granted the Justice Department's request for an order barring the UMW from proceeding with the strike, distributing strike benefits, or otherwise conspiring to violate the Lever Act. The judge broadened the injunction on November 8 and gave the union seventy-two hours to cancel the walkout. The attorney general also asked Congress to extend the Lever Act until six months after peace was declared, "so that the Government will not be weakened in its fight against the striking coal miners." While the UMW withdrew the strike call, few of the 435,000 miners returned to work. At its peak the tie-up idled 75 percent of the soft-coal industry. Mines were shut down in twenty-one states, in twelve of which federal troops were called in to maintain order. The walkout ended in December, after the miners agreed to allow a presidential commission to settle the dispute. They were later awarded a wage increase of 41 percent.[75]

Palmer sought to minimize the adverse impact of the coal injunction on his standing with organized labor. Shortly before obtaining the order he explained that the government's method of dealing with the walkout was unlikely to be repeated: "The illegality of this strike can and will be established without in any way impairing the general right to strike . . . [T]he circumstances differentiate this case from the case of any other strike that has ever taken place in this country." Several months later he indicated that he had chosen the injunction route as being less oppressive than criminal prosecution: "Because they were laboring men . . . I forgave them the crime when they violated the Lever Act and went into a civil court to get my remedy . . . I could . . . probably have sent them to the penitentiary." Palmer also opposed the court's efforts to punish individual miners for contempt. In several Wyoming towns where martial law had been declared, federal troops arrested more than fifty strikers at bayonet point for allegedly violating the injunction; the men were released, however, when Palmer refused to prosecute them.[76]

The attorney general subsequently described his role in the coal strike as seeking to assure a fair fight. "Labor had become so strong," he said, "that she denied the right of capital to have the dispute adjusted by an impartial tribunal." In dealing with the walkout the department did threaten those mine operators, coal dealers, and fuel oil suppliers who tried to exploit the situation. Yet despite his efforts to present an image of neutrality, Palmer was bitterly denounced by labor and its friends. On November 9 the AFL declared, "The autocratic action of our government in these proceedings . . . staggers the human mind." *The Nation* condemned the attorney general as a "superficial and ambitious man" who, because "the Democratic nomination in 1920 [was] dangling before his nose," sought to ingratiate himself with the conservative southern wing of the party.[77]

A Broken Pledge

When the Lever Act was before Congress in 1917 labor leaders feared that its prohibition against disrupting the production and distribution of necessaries might be used to outlaw strikes, thereby curtailing the immunity contained in section 20 of the 1914 Clayton Act. When an amendment was offered to preclude such a reading, Congressman Asbury Lever of South Carolina persuaded his colleagues that the change was unnecessary. The proposed law, he said, did not "repeal or amend in the least particular either the Clayton Antitrust Act or any other act which deals with the right of men to strike for purposes of increasing their wages or bettering their living conditions. We do not believe that this affects that in the least." At the urging of New Hampshire's Henry Hollis the Senate adopted the labor proviso, but it was later deleted in conference. Senator George Chamberlain of Oregon, who had charge of the bill, said that there was no reason to "fear that in the administration of the food law anything would be attempted by the President . . . to prevent any labor or other organization from doing in a peaceful way all that they can now do under the Clayton law to protect themselves and their rights, without any saving clause in the bill under consideration. It is not necessary in this bill to protect those rights." To ensure AFL support, however, the secretary of labor informed Samuel Gompers, the federation's head, of President Wilson's assurance that "instructions could go forward and would from the Attorney General's office to the various district attorneys, instructing them not to bring cases against workmen in contravention to the provisions of the Clayton law." This promise was reiterated by Attorney General Thomas Gregory, although he later denied it. If there were any lingering doubts, they were put to rest by Paul Husting of Wisconsin, who announced on the Senate floor that he had been "authorized by the Secretary of Labor, Mr. Wilson, to say that the administration does not construe this bill as prohibiting strikes and peaceful picketing and . . . that the Department of Justice does not so construe the bill and will not so construe the bill."[78]

The president reportedly discussed the strike injunction with Attorney General Palmer. Yet it is difficult to believe that he would have approved the action had he been mindful of the pledge made in 1917. Dr. Edwin Weinstein has suggested that Wilson's fall 1919 stroke impaired his memory and judgment in areas which threatened his integrity. The promise not to enforce the Lever Act against organized labor almost surely fell into this category. A key tenet of the New Freedom was that government should operate neutrally, granting special privileges to none. The president had compromised this principle in 1913 and 1914 by approving legislation partially exempting trade unions from the antitrust laws. Having again to display such favoritism in order to win labor's support for the Lever Act may have been sufficiently troubling that Wilson was later unable to recall the matter.[79]

Because it violated explicit assurances which had accompanied the Lever Act, the coal injunction unleashed a storm of criticism, particularly from organized labor. It was reported that among Democratic leaders "this will weigh distinctly against Mr. Palmer," since the party could ill afford to nominate a person "for whom labor holds outright antagonism." Ironically, while the attorney general was blamed for this betrayal, he had not been part of the administration when the promises were made, and may not have learned of them until after the injunction had already been issued.[80]

The department's action was objectionable for other reasons as well. Even if labor was subject to the Lever Act, the sole remedy provided by the statute was criminal prosecution, in which an accused would enjoy the right to jury trial. The law did not authorize the government to proceed by injunction, the disobedience of which could be punished by the court without a jury. Nor was anything altered by Congress's concurrent resolution of October 31, 1919, giving the administration its "unqualified support" in handling the strike, for the measure did not amend the act or give the president any new authority. Moreover this was not a situation in which the executive could claim inherent power to obtain a restraining order, for coal mining was an activity whose regulation the Constitution left to the states. The Justice Department was no doubt aware of these difficulties, for when the strike was settled, the government dropped the contempt citations and insisted that the UMW not appeal the injunction.[81]

Finally, there was a question of whether this war powers legislation could be enforced nearly a year after the armistice. In his October 25 message to the miners Wilson had declared that "the war itself is still a fact," for "our troops are still being transported." This statement was no doubt intended to explain why the 1917 contract remained binding, as well as to justify use of the Lever Act. Forty-eight hours later, however, Wilson vetoed an expansion of the War-Time Prohibition Act on the ground that its aims "have been satisfied in the demobilization of the Army and Navy." *The Nation* charged that the government's case against the miners rested on "a flimsy pretext." According to Secretary of the Navy Josephus Daniels the cabinet regarded the inconsistency as a "big mistake & indefensible." The Justice Department sought to reconcile the president's statements by noting that the prohibition bill, unlike the Lever Act, involved new legislation. Yet it was unclear how this distinction could legitimize an exercise of authority deriving solely from the war powers once the administration had conceded that an emergency no longer existed. Felix Frankfurter expressed the feelings of many in writing that the government had displayed "shallow recklessness [by] invoking the injunction under plea of the war power."[82]

Quite apart from the illegality of the undertaking, there was simply no need to invoke the Lever Act against the coal miners. When it became clear that the injunction would not halt the walkout, the states began to deal with the situation themselves. Kansas led the way by placing its coal fields under receivership; fourteen mines were soon producing enough coal to avert a shortage there. North Dakota, Oklahoma, and Missouri took similar action, and Illinois, Arkansas, and Tennessee were about to do the same when the strike ended. On November 30 a governors' meeting in Chicago urged that "state governments take all possible steps to secure the production of coal." West Virginia arrested the local UMW leader under a wartime statute requiring able-bodied men to work at least thirty-six hours a week. Colorado modeled its efforts after the federal government's with similar results: in response to a state court injunction that they return to work, the Colorado miners announced that they were taking an "indefinite vacation." In Virginia the militia protected those desiring to return to work, and in Ohio Governor James Cox sought to negotiate a settlement after abandoning plans to seize the mines. The federal government's drastic and unauthorized action thus occurred in a setting where the states appeared willing and able to fend for themselves.[83]

From Injunction to Indictment

Despite the failure of the Indianapolis injunction the Justice Department continued to rely on the Lever Act as a strike weapon. In an article published in the *Independent* on December 13, 1919, the attorney general repeated his call for "an absolute industrial truce for six months." It was reported the same day that a federal court in Puerto Rico had used the Lever Act to enjoin a walkout by employees of the American Railroad. A month later Howard Figg told a group of clothiers that the department was planning to take similar action in the garment industry.[84]

The administration was no longer content, however, to proceed only by injunction. Palmer may have decided that he had nothing more to lose in seeking to appease public frustration with strikers. Shortly after the coal walkout ended in December, a grand jury convened in Indianapolis to investigate the conduct of the miners and operators. On March 11, 1920, 125 indictments were returned, a third of them against UMW officials. The men were charged under the Lever Act with conspiracy to restrict the supply and increase the price of coal. Though many of the counts were later quashed and the suit never went to trial, the case served as a warning to other unions. It was instrumental in causing Pennsylvania's anthracite miners to forgo a strike in May 1920 and instead to accept arbitration by a presidential commission.[85]

The colliers' decision proved a wise one, for as they deliberated at

Wilkes-Barre, Lever Act indictments were being returned in Pittsburgh against five participants in the "outlaw" railroad strike. This five-month walkout, which idled more than half a million men, occurred after Brotherhood leaders had twice capitulated to the government. In August 1919 the unions canceled a threatened nationwide strike at the president's request. After living costs continued to rise, another walkout was planned for February 1920, but it too was called off amid reports that the Justice Department would seek an injunction. Outlaw unions began to crop up. One of them, the Chicago Yardmen's Association, walked out on April 1. Before long the tie-up had spread to both coasts. When the Brotherhoods requested federal intervention against the insurgents, the administration was most sympathetic. As Director General Hines told the president, the strike constituted "a sinister and dangerous attack upon the established labor organizations and is an effort to . . . eliminate them, by reason of their patriotism and public spirit in supporting the policies you have established."[86]

From the attorney general's perspective the situation afforded an opportunity to please a strike-weary public while mending his fences with organized labor. On April 10, a day after the Brotherhoods asked for assistance, Palmer reported that U.S. attorneys were investigating the walkout. Meanwhile the Justice Department debated whether to proceed by injunction or by criminal indictment. After the experience at Indianapolis the choice could not have been difficult. It was made even easier by the strikers' lack of support within the labor movement and by Palmer's charge that the walkout had been engineered by the Industrial Workers of the World (IWW) and other radical groups. He warned on April 12 that if the men did not return to work immediately, they would be prosecuted for "conspiracy under the Lever law, on the charge of interfering with the dispatch of foodstuffs and necessaries of life."[87]

When this threat was ignored, a cabinet meeting was called for April 14, the first Wilson had attended since the previous August. The railroad question was brought up, but he had difficulty following the matter. Afterwards the Justice Department announced that it would invoke the Lever Act against the rail outlaws. Warrants were immediately issued in Chicago for the arrest of forty-one strike leaders around the country, all of whom were charged with conspiracy under the act. Separate criminal suits were filed against twenty-seven strikers in Los Angeles and seven men in Pittsburgh. In late June, as delegates streamed into San Francisco for the Democratic convention, additional indictments were issued against sixty-five members of the San Francisco Yardmen's Association. In Ohio, New Jersey, and New York the department used threats of prosecution to end the walkout. As with the previous winter's coal strike local authorities might have dealt with the problem had the United States not intervened. Kansas sued the outlaws even before Palmer did, and a week later strike leaders were indicted in Illinois. Other states would perhaps have done likewise had they been given a chance.[88]

During 1919 and 1920 the Lever Act thus saw significant use as a strike weapon. In addition to the 84 UMW officials cited for contempt in Indianapolis, more than 225 union members were prosecuted for walking off the job. Thousands of others were threatened with such action if they did not return to work. In April 1920, for example, the New York Merchants' Association asked for federal intervention in a dock strike which had shut down the Atlantic and Gulf Coast ports. When the Justice Department agreed, newspaper headlines warned: "Palmer May Act in Shipping Strike. Possibility That Lever Law Will Be Invoked to End Tieup by Longshoremen." The local U.S. attorney also promised to look into the other walkouts then plaguing the city. Though the government actually interceded in only a handful of strikes, these cases were sufficiently well publicized to make the prospect of indictment real. This may help explain why the number of walkouts fell sharply in the last half of 1920.[89]

After mid-1920 the administration bypassed several opportunities to employ the Lever Act. One involved a walkout by bituminous workers in Ohio, Indiana, and Illinois. In response to numerous pleas that he intercede, the president merely asked that the strike be ended. The same low-key approach was adopted when Pennsylvania's miners went on "vacation" in September. This reluctance to invoke the act cannot be accounted for by the fact that neither strike lasted more than a month, for their duration could not have been known when the walkouts began. Instead it was feared such action would have hurt the Democratic party in the November elections. Besides possibly further estranging labor, interference would have fueled Republican charges that the administration was "retaining, even after the war ended, broad powers that were either vested in or assumed by the President while the war was on as a matter of necessity." Unlike the occasional arrest of an obscure profiteer, strike intervention would have drawn immediate national attention. Tumulty, who had supported the coal injunction in late 1919, now urged Wilson to ignore a request for similar action from the governor of Indiana: "Governor Goodrich and his Republican friends . . . have for months been denouncing you for exercising autocratic control over private business and yet every day there come to us from Republican sources insistent demands that you again exercise that control." The president heeded this advice, and no further effort was made to enforce the Lever Act against striking workers.[90]

~ 5 ~

The War on Radicalism:
Prosecuting the American Heretic

The government's postwar employment of the Lever Act to curtail profiteering and discourage strikes was but an indirect attempt to deal with a perceived threat from the political left. The administration simultaneously launched a frontal attack on dissidents in the United States through resort to the Espionage and Sedition Acts. These war powers measures, adopted in 1917 and 1918, saw extensive use after the armistice in what the *New York Times* aptly referred to as the country's "war against radicalism."[1]

An Exercise in Appeasement

The Espionage Act was approved in the early summer of 1917, ten weeks after the United States had entered the war. While the statute did not expressly prohibit the dissemination of any particular views, its effect was to ban speech which might interfere with the war effort. Title I, section 3 of the act declared it a crime to make false statements with intent to impair the success of the U.S. military or promote that of the enemy. The section also prohibited the obstruction of recruitment and attempts to cause insubordination or disloyalty in the armed forces—offenses which could be committed either by word or by deed.[2]

These criminal provisions of the Espionage Act were augmented by Title XII, which granted the postmaster general broad censorship authority over the mails. It provided that "every letter, writing ... or thing, of any kind, in violation of any of the provisions of this Act is hereby declared to be nonmailable matter and shall not be conveyed in the mails or delivered from any post office or by any letter carrier." This section allowed Postmaster General Burleson to exclude from the mails any material he believed might interfere with enlistment or otherwise violate the act. Though Title XII denied him authority to open any "letter" not addressed to himself, he was free to examine and exclude newspapers, magazines, books, and circulars. In addition, the postmaster general claimed the right to revoke a publication's second-class mailing privilege if even a single issue were deemed nonmailable, thereby increasing circulation costs to what might be prohibitive levels. The magnitude of this censorship power cannot be overstated. Case law had firmly established that in determining whether a particular item was nonmailable the postmaster general did not have to afford the affected individual any opportunity to be heard. Though his decision could be challenged in court, it would not be overturned unless the postmaster general was found to have patently exceeded his authority. As a consequence the department's rulings were for all practical purposes conclusive.[3]

During World War I not a single bona fide spy or saboteur was convicted under the Espionage Act. Instead its criminal and postal provisions were directed at those who opposed the war on religious, philosophical, or political grounds and who had the temerity to express their views publicly. A contemporary report by the National Civil Liberties Bureau noted that "by far the largest proportion of all the cases ... involve members of the IWW, Socialist Party and Non-Partisan League."[4]

The IWW was hit particularly hard. Organized in 1905, the Industrial Workers of the World sought to replace capitalism with a system in which workers would exercise exclusive control over the management of industry. In contrast to the conservative craft unionism of the American Federation of Labor, the Wobblies espoused "One Big Union" for all workers including the unskilled, whom established labor had largely ignored. Employing the slogan "Every strike is a small revolution and a dress rehearsal for the big one," the IWW was feared and despised, particularly in the West, where it had organized workers in the timber, mining, and agricultural industries. Though it strongly disapproved of the country's entering the war, the organization "tried more to ignore [it] than to oppose it actively or officially." Yet because of their unpopular stance, as well as their radical philosophy and reputation for sometimes violent strikes, the Wobblies became targets for officially tolerated vigilante justice which sometimes resulted in death. In the fall of 1917 more than 165 IWW leaders were arrested and charged under the Espionage Act. Similar actions were later brought against the group's rank and file in federal district courts across the country. In his careful study Harry Scheiber found that "almost all the districts reporting high incidences of prosecutions were areas in which the IWW was active."[5]

If the Wobblies suffered most heavily from criminal enforcement of the Espionage Act, the Socialists bore the brunt of the statute's postal censorship provisions. In April 1917, within days of U.S. entry into the war, the Socialist party met at St. Louis and pledged its "continuous, active, and public opposition to the war through demonstrations, mass petitions, and all other means within our power." This resolution was promptly endorsed by nearly all of the more than one hundred Socialist newspapers and periodicals in the United States. The government was quick to retaliate. In the first three months that the Espionage Act was on the books, every major Socialist publication was suspended from the mails at least once, and some were excluded for weeks at a time. As of April 1918 the postmaster general had suspended the second-class mailing privileges of twenty-two Socialist journals, while many others were forcibly shut down by local vigilante groups. The result was that by mid-1918 most of the nation's Socialist periodicals had gone out of business.[6]

To the extent that American radicals threatened actual interference with the war effort, the Espionage Act afforded the government ample means for dealing with the situation. Conservative forces, however, fanned the flames of public antipathy to the point where the reaction became impassioned and irrational. Solomon Clark of the University of Chicago complained to George Creel, head of the Committee on Public Information, that "many public men and many of our prominent newspapers who have always bitterly fought socialism, the I.W.W.'s and even labor unions are taking advantage of the present crisis in an effort not purely patriotic to squelch all of these more or less radical organizations." The situation was exacerbated by the November 1917 Russian Revolution and by the ensuing Brest-Litovsk Treaty, through which Russia abandoned its allies and withdrew from the war. Wobblies and American Socialists were buoyed by these events, while the general public responded with anger and dismay. Not only was the Bolshevik takeover thought to have been German inspired, but it was increasingly feared that its success would spawn further proletarian uprisings in other parts of the world. The IWW, the most radical of the dissident groups in the United States, became even more deeply reviled. The National Civil Liberties Bureau reported that beginning in the fall of 1917 the press had released "a constant stream of false stories against the I.W.W. deliberately planned to create hatred and mob violence." The predictable effect of this propaganda campaign was to create what Robert Murray has described as a "hang-them-all-at-sunrise attitude," which only deepened as the war progressed.[7]

The Sedition Act of 1918 was a direct response to this widespread public hostility toward the IWW and other dissenting groups. Superpatriots were no longer content with punishing radicals if and when they disrupted the war. Instead they now demanded the total suppression of those holding heretical views, a task which could not be achieved under the Espionage Act itself. The shortcomings of existing law were exemplified by the acquittal of a Montana man who had criticized President Wilson and condemned America's role in the war. U.S. District Judge George M. Bourquin ruled that defendant's speech was nothing but "kitchen gossip and saloon debate" which, rather than interfering with the war, might at worst "create anger, disgust, and desire to punish the slanderer." To the extent that such remarks "cause or tend to cause breaches of the peace," he said, "they are offenses against the State of Montana, and can be prosecuted only in the courts of the State." Judge Bourquin noted that because of the "public impression that for any slanderous or disloyal remark the utterer can be prosecuted by the United States," the "United States attorneys throughout the country have been unjustly criticized because they do not prosecute where they cannot."[8]

Instead of seeking to correct this misapprehension or encouraging enforcement of the numerous state laws that punished sedition, Congress and the administration chose to accommodate the nation's mood. On May 16, 1918, Title I, section 3 of the Espionage Act was amended to prohibit broad new classes of speech whether or not they interfered with the war. The 1918 Sedition Act made it a crime to use any "disloyal, profane, scurrilous, or abusive language" concerning the Constitution, the armed forces, their uniforms, the flag, or the form of government of the United States. One could also be punished for using language intended to bring any of these things into "contempt, scorn, contumely, or disrepute." An antistrike clause made it a felony to urge curtailing the production of goods necessary to the war, if the words were uttered with intent to hinder its prosecution. By virtue of the existing Title XII all writings falling into one of these categories could be excluded from the mails. Moreover, under the 1917 Trading with the Enemy Act any book or newspaper deemed by the Post Office to be nonmailable under the amended espionage law could not be shipped or delivered by any other means. Finally, the Sedition Act authorized the postmaster general to terminate mail delivery to any person who "upon evidence satisfactory to him . . . is using the mails in violation of any of the provisions of this Act."[9]

The Sedition Act constituted a blatant attempt to appease "100 percent Americans." By drastically expanding the criminal and postal provisions of the Espionage Act, Congress sought to suppress those whose views were anathema to an aroused and intolerant public. Some of the Sedition Act's congressional supporters, most of whom came from states where the Wobblies had strength, acknowledged that the aim of the new law was to crush the IWW. Such a purpose was criticized by Georgia's Senator Thomas Hardwick, who charged that "the real—in fact, practically the only—object of this section is to get some men called I.W.W.'s, who are operating in a few of the Northwestern States." Hardwick urged that rather than have the federal government "jeopardize the fundamental rights and liberties of 100,000,000 American people," the states "ought to be able to handle those questions for themselves."[10]

Most of the measure's proponents took a more subtle tack, arguing that unless the government acted against the radicals, ardent patriots would take matters into their own hands. This was the position adopted by the Justice Department in pressing for the Espionage Act amendments. As an internal department memorandum explained, the bill would "extend the Federal penal laws over disloyal expressions . . . not in themselves effective propaganda, but which . . . present rather the evil of causing breaches of the peace." Another memorandum, which the department submitted to the Senate, argued that the Sedition Act was "made necessary because the disloyal remarks of the type indicated in the bill, instead of causing disloyalty, tend to cause a passionate loyalty which expresses itself in outrages and disorders."[11]

The same view was expressed repeatedly during the debates in Congress. Senator Henry Cabot Lodge of Massachusetts feared that "the cases which this law intends to cover will be dealt with by lynch law if we do not deal with it ourselves." A telegram was introduced from the mayor of Collinsville, Illinois, who blamed the murder of a German-American coal miner on the government's failure to punish those who made unpatriotic remarks. Senator Henry Myers of Montana, the architect of the Sedition Act, flatly stated that "one of its principal objects . . . is to prevent mob law." In a similar vein Minnesota's Knute Nelson warned, "If we allow men to go abroad and to utter sentiments which this proposed law prohibits, it will breed violence; the people will not submit to it. It is for the sake of keeping the peace of the country, to prevent a breach of the peace."

Yet, as Illinois Senator Lawrence Sherman noted, the proper remedy for vigilante justice was not the adoption of repressive federal legislation but rather the enforcement of state law. There was no indication that genuine efforts to preserve order at the local level had failed. To the contrary, said Sherman, "in every instance where a mob has acted it has been because the people themselves elect sheriffs and mayors, and maintain police departments who passively acquiesce in acts of lawlessness."[12]

The First Amendment, the Golden Rule, and Other Irrelevancies

Through the Sedition Act of 1918 the limits of public intolerance came to define the threshold for criminal indictment. Indicative of the degree to which the government hoped to purify the national discourse is a June 1918 Justice Department ruling forbidding false statements about the American Red Cross. There were grave constitutional difficulties to be overcome in adopting such a measure—difficulties not encountered by states such as Montana, whose sedition law Congress had chosen to copy. For one thing, the Constitution gave the federal government no general police power comparable to that possessed by the states. Moreover, in contrast to the states the central government was barred by the First Amendment from "abridging the freedom of speech, or of the press."[13]

These obstacles did not pass unnoticed in the debates. As for Congress's authority to enact measures for maintaining the peace in local communities, Senator John Shields of Tennessee said "We have no power to legislate for that purpose. That is a police matter of which the States have exclusive jurisdiction, except where it interferes with some Federal function." Senator Albert Cummins of Iowa likewise urged that "Congress in its efforts to forward the country in the prosecution of the war ought to confine itself to war . . . We ought not to attempt to usurp or take away the authority of the State to prosecute men for crimes that are not connected with the war."[14]

Objections based on the First Amendment were more numerous. Because of that proscription, said Senator Sherman, the Constitution "leaves any restriction upon the liberty of speech or of the press in the hands of the States." Senator James Reed of Missouri implored his colleagues not to "break down the liberty of speech in order to stop the ravings and rantings of an anarchist. It is not necessary to destroy the freedom of the press of a whole people because there may be some miserable wretch who prints an obscene or an indecent or disloyal thing. We need not grow alarmed and lose our heads." California's Hiram Johnson claimed to be "astonished" when he first read the proposed law: "This is a bill not for the punishment of disloyalty or of treason, but . . . to suppress the freedom of the press in the United States." Several members of the Senate noted the obvious parallel to the Sedition Act of 1798, a measure which had long since been repudiated as contrary to the principles of the First Amendment. In one respect the 1918 statute was less harsh than its predecessor, for it did not bar criticism of the president. Yet the 1798 law had permitted truth as an absolute defense; a similar proviso known as the France Amendment was deleted from the 1918 act at the insistence of the Justice Department.[15]

The constitutional problems posed by this attempt to outlaw the expression of radical views were generally thought to have been overcome by virtue of the war powers. Time and again the 1918 Sedition Act was declared to be a war measure, thus distinguishing it from the 1798 statute, which was passed when the country was officially at peace. As Senator Sherman observed, "It is not claimed . . . such legislation as this could be justified on other than war-power grounds." This was equally true of the provisions excluding material from the mails, for it was doubtful that they could have rested on the postal power alone. While a handful of senators argued that the First Amendment limited even the war powers, most congressmen took the familiar position that the Bill of Rights was wholly inapplicable in this setting.[16]

New Mexico Senator Albert Fall was particularly contemptuous in rejecting the First Amendment argument. When Senator Joseph France of Maryland renewed his efforts to allow truth as a defense to sedition, Fall replied, "If he offered the Ten Commandments, the Lord's Prayer, or the Golden Rule as an amendment to this bill, I would vote against it just upon the same principle that I voted against his first" attempt to protect "liberty of speech." The Justice Department, which had lobbied hard for the sedition law, helped reinforce this attitude. In a memorandum to Congress defending the constitutionality of the bill the department strongly implied that the First Amendment was irrelevant during wartime: "Our soldiers temporarily surrender their liberties of thought and speech and action in order that they may save them for the future. The whole Nation must subject itself to discipline until after the war. Otherwise in defending liberties in detail, we may lose liberty altogether." The memorandum took an extremely disparaging view of those who sought to defend the First Amendment: "There is no more dangerous element in this country than that which conscientiously battles for unlimited individual freedom of act and speech at this time. The persons assume the highest ethical and philosophical grounds, but their influences [sic] is as paralyzing as that of the fanatics whose motives are so earnest that they will commit arson, murder, or suicide to register their beliefs."[17]

The House of Representatives approved the Sedition Act in less than four hours. In their haste several members suggested that it was inappropriate even to discuss the question of constitutionality. William Green of Iowa agreed that the legislation denied rights "essential to the existence of a free government, whether in war or peace," but added that he would not "for that reason withhold my approval of the bill. When the administration comes in here and says that it must have certain things in order to carry on this war successfully, the responsibility must be upon it and not upon this House in this crisis of our affairs." The House Speaker, "Champ" Clark of Missouri, also acknowledged that the Sedition Act might be invalid but asserted: "The Chair has nothing to do with the constitutionality of the law. That is for the courts. The rule in this country . . . has been that the truth of an assertion can be offered in mitigation or defense. The Chair has nothing to do with that, and neither has the House. That also is for the courts."[18]

Those who were quick to dismiss the First Amendment may have been fortified by the belief that the Sedition Act would not be enforced against right-thinking Americans. Senator Henry Myers reminded his colleagues that they had little to fear, since the Constitution's speech or debate clause shielded utterances made in Congress. Senator Wesley Jones of Washington was troubled by the measure's breadth, remarking that "a man under entirely innocent circumstances . . . could be brought within the plain letter . . . of the act." Yet he was confident that "juries and courts will very well take care of persons who may be haled into court who have not intended to violate the spirit of the provisions." What this "spirit" was Jones did not say, though he was no doubt referring to the fact that the statute was intended to be used against Wobblies, Socialists, and other dissidents. As Henry Campbell Black wrote shortly after the measure was adopted, "No respectable citizen need go in fear of this law."[19]

Given the evolution of the Espionage and Sedition Acts, it is no wonder that they were enforced against American radicals well after the signing of the armistice. The underlying goal of the 1918 act had little if anything to do with the war. Instead, as in the case of federal ownership, prohibition, and price controls, the war powers were invoked to deal with a problem that was otherwise beyond the government's reach. The Espionage and Sedition Acts were, by their terms, limited to times "when the United States is at war." Yet the ideologies at which they were aimed did not vanish with the termination of hostilities. During the Red Scare of 1919 and 1920 the apparent threat from the American left escalated sharply, presenting a situation ripe for continued resort to these wartime laws.[20]

The Bolshevik takeover in Russia was accompanied by Lenin's assurance that it was the harbinger of revolution in Europe and the West. In December 1918 he issued "A Letter to American Workingmen," expressing confidence in "the inevitability of the international revolution" but recognizing that "it may take a long time" before such an uprising would occur in the United States. Early in 1919 the Third International was created to implement this program, and it called on Socialist parties everywhere to engage in immediate mass action. These events coincided with an abnormal degree of strike activity in the United States, accompanied by a wave of bomb scares, riots, and explosions. To the euphoric left wing of the American radical movement the country seemed on the brink of revolution—a specter deliberately encouraged by employers' organizations and a sensationalist press. It is now universally agreed that there was no objective basis for fearing an uprising in the United States. Yet from mid-1919 through early 1920 the nation's hysteria was quite real.[21]

The government's principal response to the Red Scare involved the arrest and detention of approximately three thousand suspected alien anarchists, of whom about six hundred were ultimately deported. This operation was not dependent on the war powers, for the Supreme Court had previously held that the United States possesses the "right to exclude or expel aliens, or any class of aliens, absolutely or upon conditions, in war or in peace, being an inherent and inalienable right of every sovereign and independent nation." The same could not be said for many of the other measures undertaken at the time, including the prohibition of war beer and the prosecution of strikers. These actions, like the protracted resort to the Espionage and Sedition Acts, would have been impossible without the ability to draw on the war powers.[22]

In seeking to protect itself against an apprehended threat to domestic order the country displayed a remarkable willingness to sacrifice basic political and civil rights. Perhaps this was natural, given the seriousness of the perceived danger. Yet the reaction was intensified by a new public mood which emerged after the armistice, one characterized by impatience, intolerance, and illiberalism. The habits of conformity instilled by the war left the majority unaccustomed and unwilling to tolerate those who criticized the established order. People were tired of sacrificing in the name of idealism and had grown disenchanted with high-mindedness itself. The lofty principles in whose name Americans had gone to war were hardly recognizable in the peace terms unveiled at Versailles. In short the Progressive garb of self-denying altruism had worn thin. If during the period of hostilities uniformity of expression had been imposed in the name of defeating Germany, it would now be demanded for the sake of national harmony and peace of mind. While basic liberties might suffer in the process, from a pragmatic standpoint such precepts were valuable only as means to an end. Once the goal was defined in terms of repressing dissent, freedom of speech became irrelevant.[23]

From Restraint to Enforcement

In resorting to the amended Espionage Act during 1919 and 1920 the Wilson administration was no more sensitive to the protection of constitutional rights than it had been during the war years. Indicative of its attitude toward even the mildest discord is the fact that all letters urging the president to veto the Sedition Act were forwarded by the White House to the Justice Department. As Harry Scheiber concluded, Wilson's last term in office witnessed "an unprecedented sacrifice of civil liberty in the United States," much of which might have been avoided had the president not "left the fate of civil liberties to subordinate officials, the judiciary, and the public at a time when few were inclined to be moderate and when regard for freedom of speech and press appeared to be the particular concern of unpopular dissident minorities." This indictment applies with especial force to the postwar years, when a virtual absence of presidential leadership enabled Attorney General Palmer and Postmaster General Burleson to abandon themselves to the hysteria of the times.[24]

The uses to which the Espionage and Sedition Acts were put after the armistice accorded perfectly with their principal underlying goal. The statutes' peacetime victims consisted almost entirely of Wobblies, Socialists, and others whose unorthodox views were repugnant to the patriotic masses. For a time the administration withstood the pressure. By the fall of 1919, however, after Mitchell Palmer had replaced Thomas Gregory as attorney general and the Red Scare was nearing its peak, the government finally succumbed.

Though it had pressed Congress to pass the Sedition Act, the Justice Department was keenly aware that the measure lent itself to abuse. A week after the law went into effect Attorney General Gregory warned his staff that "the wide scope of the act and powers conferred increase the importance of discretion in administering it. Protection of loyal persons from unjust suspicion and prosecution is quite as important as the suppression of actual disloyalty." The admonition proved ineffective. According to John Lord O'Brian, Gregory's special assistant for war work, "The general publicity given the statute . . . fanned animosities into flame, vastly increasing the amount of suspicion and complaints throughout the country. This, in turn, resulted in a large increase in the amount of prosecutions, backed up by strong local patriotic sentiment." In many parts of the country U.S. attorneys yielded to popular demands "for indiscriminate prosecution . . . in behalf of a policy of wholesale repression and restraint of public opinion." On several occasions O'Brian wrote department agents in San Francisco after having read press accounts of cases recently filed under the Sedition Act. "The newspaper description of the facts would in many of the cases," he said, "not seem to warrant an arrest." On October 28, 1918, the Justice Department instructed that no further indictments were to be sought under the Espionage and Sedition Acts without prior approval from the attorney general.[25]

This order came only two weeks before the armistice. Its effect was to curtail greatly the number of new Espionage and Sedition Act cases. From time to time the department granted permission to institute criminal proceedings, but in the vast majority of instances consent was refused. The department was also liberal in authorizing the dismissal of pending suits that had not yet gone to trial. A month after the end of hostilities Gregory ordered U.S. attorneys to submit information concerning persons who had been convicted under the Espionage or Sedition Acts "in preparation of the sifting out of unjustified . . . convictions." These efforts were undertaken despite his warning, issued shortly after the armistice, that "violations of the war statutes, all of which are still in force, must be prosecuted." Gregory apparently regarded the Espionage and Sedition Acts as falling into a special category which called for the exercise of extraordinary restraint.[26]

On March 5, 1919, A. Mitchell Palmer replaced Gregory as attorney general. For the next several months Palmer continued his predecessor's policy of making guarded use of the Espionage and Sedition Acts. Typical of his early attitude was the department's handling of a March 14 letter from the U.S. attorney in Omaha, who wrote, "Now that the war is over, I am inclined to believe that all of the foregoing [espionage] cases should be dismissed, and I am submitting the evidence for your consideration." Permission was immediately granted. Hundreds of other suits were dropped as well, including one filed against John Reed, the young Harvard-educated Socialist whose *Ten Days That Shook the World* provided an eyewitness account of the Bolshevik Revolution.[27]

Palmer's initial reluctance to enforce these statutes was also to be seen in the Justice Department's March 31, 1919, announcement that it no longer desired the cooperation of "various private organizations formed during and since the war to detect offenders against the laws of the country and to aid in securing the prosecution of seditionists, agitators and others." The *New York Times* asserted, "The Attorney General has perhaps been a little hasty" in his action, warning that "bad as was the German spy, he was not worse nor more dangerous than is the would-be destroyer of all civilized government." Palmer also proceeded to review those cases in which convictions had already been obtained. By June 1919 the president had commuted the sentences of approximately one hundred persons who had been found guilty of violating the Espionage and Sedition Acts.[28]

Had the attorney general continued down this path, the criminal provisions of the Espionage and Sedition Acts might have fallen into disuse. As the year progressed, however, the clamor for federal action against the extremists grew to a point where Palmer could no longer resist. He subsequently described the situation to a Senate subcommittee:

There were more strikes than there had been for many, many years . . . At that time the country was stirred up; there is no question about that. Those demonstrations of force, followed by insidious propaganda in all these industrial disturbances, seemed to awaken our people. I remember . . . the morning after my house was blown up. I stood in the middle of the wreckage of my library with Congressmen and Senators, and without a dissenting voice they called upon me in strong terms to exercise all the power that was possible to the Department of Justice to run to earth the criminals who were behind that kind of outrage.

The pressure was unrelenting: "I was shouted at from every editorial sanctum in America from sea to sea; I was preached upon from every pulpit; I was urged—I could feel it dinned into my ears—throughout the country to do something and do it now . . . and do it in a way that would bring results to stop this sort of thing in the United States." Palmer might have added that he was then a leading contender for the presidency, a fact which made it even more difficult for him to ignore the demands for repression or the charges that he had failed to protect the nation against the threat of subversion.[29]

The consequence was that the attorney general abandoned the cautious and forgiving course he had previously followed. Just as the Sedition Act had been adopted to mollify an angry public, the department's decision to resume its enforcement was likewise a gesture of appeasement. Even the Socialist party, a major target of the federal antisedition campaign, was surprisingly understanding of the position in which the government found itself in 1919. Seymour Stedman, a party leader, later acknowledged that "when I say the country went wild, I do not mean either the courts or the Department of Justice . . . [T]he courts of the country . . . in a sense stood between a raging, unreasoning mob in this country and the people who were the defendants."[30]

The turnabout came a few weeks after the bombing of Palmer's home. In mid-June the department devised a scheme for the mass arrest and deportation of alien radicals, which it implemented at the end of the year. Later that month the president expressed his desire to jettison the case-by-case review of those convicted under the acts in favor of a general amnesty. The day the treaty was signed Wilson cabled Tumulty:

It is my desire to grant complete anmesty and pardon to all American citizens in prison or under arrest on account of anything they have said in speech or in print concerning their personal opinions with regard to the activities of the Government of the United States during the period of the war. It seems to me that this would be not only a generous act but a just act to accompany the signing of the peace. I do not wish to include any who have been guilty of overt crimes, of course, but I think it would be a very serious mistake to detain anyone merely for the expression of opinion.

Besides freeing many who were then incarcerated, such a policy would have halted further enforcement of the Espionage and Sedition Acts, at least as to American citizens. Palmer strongly opposed the idea. Tumulty advised the president on June 28, "The Attorney General thinks you ought to wait until you return before granting complete amnesty. . . He says there have been no convictions of people for mere expression of opinion. Every case has been a conviction for obstructing the war under statute." Whether or not Wilson accepted this sophistry, he yielded to Palmer's objections and temporarily shelved the amnesty plan.[31]

Interestingly, while he was resisting the president's efforts to terminate these war statutes, the attorney general was urging Congress to enact new sedition legislation on the ground that the 1917 and 1918 measures were no longer enforceable. According to Palmer, while existing law "might possibly be invoked against seditious utterances and acts, . . . I have felt that it was limited to acts and utterances which tended to weaken the waging of actual hostilities. This view seems to be generally accepted." This disingenuous claim was undoubtedly intended to excuse the fact that until then the Justice Department had not responded to the radical threat. In the same vein the attorney general later complained that Congress had failed to provide him with adequate tools, and boasted that "we have been compelled to clean up the country almost unaided by any virile legislation." Yet amidst these protestations Palmer admitted that he had "nevertheless . . . caused to be brought several test prosecutions in order to obtain the final ruling of our courts as to the espionage law and its application to acts committed since the cessation of the activities of our armed forces."[32]

Three Case Studies in a Statistical Void

Certainly the Espionage and Sedition Acts were invoked to punish activity occurring after the armistice. The difficulty is forming an accurate notion of the extent to which this happened. The figures contained in the attorney general's annual reports are of little assistance, for they do not indicate when the offense in question was committed. The report for the year ending June 30, 1919, states merely that since the signing of the armistice, "sporadic instances of apparent violations have come to the attention of the department, but comparatively speaking, the number of actual cases arising since that time has been small." We do not know how many of the 968 cases commenced during this fiscal year were based on postarmistice conduct. The same is true of the report for the 1919–20 fiscal year, which fails to reveal which of the approximately forty new cases involved "test prosecutions" for utterances made subsequent to the armistice. During fiscal 1920–21, only six new suits were filed; the attorney general's statement that "violations of the so-called disloyalty sections of the espionage act have greatly decreased" at least suggests that these actions were based on recent conduct. When he testified in front of the Senate Judiciary Committee in January 1921, six weeks before leaving office, Palmer confirmed that the Espionage and Sedition Acts had been invoked to the very end. "If you don't want the laws enforced," he said, "the best way to settle the matter is to repeal the laws."[33]

The inadequacy of the statistical data is exacerbated by a factor noted years ago by Zechariah Chafee, namely that "a great many of the Espionage Act cases have never been reported in detail in print." As to suits arising after the armistice, the lack of publicity may have been attributable partly to the fact that during 1919 and 1920 Attorney General Palmer was lobbying for a permanent sedition law. Central to that effort was his claim that the existing statutes were no longer enforceable. This may also account for certain inconsistencies in his public statements concerning the acts. In the spring of 1919, several months before asking Congress for new legislation, Palmer stated that these laws would only "become inoperative with the formal declaration of peace." Yet in the fall of 1920 he told a group of Socialists and labor leaders, who had complained about his continued use of the Sedition Act, "I have seen to it that no prosecutions under it have been instituted since the Armistice." This statement was belied by his own November 1919 report to Congress, which conceded that a number of test prosecutions had been brought based on conduct occurring after the armistice.[34]

The picture thus remains clouded. From the case reports and press accounts, however, one can obtain a fairly clear idea of the type of person who fell victim to the Espionage and Sedition Acts in the years following the armistice. One of the few documented suits brought while Thomas Gregory was attorney general involved Morris Zucker, a prominent Brooklyn dentist. Zucker was arrested on November 29, 1918, after making a Thanksgiving Day speech in which he criticized the conduct of U.S. troops in the war and suggested that American capitalists had circulated false stories of German atrocities. For these remarks the Socialist dentist was found guilty of violating the Sedition Act and sentenced to fifteen years in prison.[35]

Another individual who was targeted under the Sedition Act after hostilities had ended was Jacob Isaacson, the New York City publisher of *Freedom* magazine. The April-May 1919 issue of this anarchistic journal contained an article attacking the recently launched Victory Loan drive. Though he had not written the offending piece, Isaacson, a Russian alien, was arrested in mid-May and held on $2,500 bail. The local U.S. attorney, Francis Caffey, requested permission to seek Isaacson's deportation, and if that failed, to prosecute him under the amended Espionage Act. The Justice Department replied on June 5, three days after Palmer's house had been bombed, advising Caffey to reverse the procedure and seek deportation only as a last resort. The U.S. attorney was instructed to proceed under the Sedition Act, "and if an indictment is returned . . . the same should be prosecuted vigorously." Isaacson was indicted two months later. His attorney, Harry Weinberger, sought a dismissal in exchange for Isaacson's consent to be deported, but the attorney general twice refused these requests. On the eve of trial, after Weinberger had made a personal visit to the Justice Department, the government agreed to drop the case once the defendant had been shipped out of the country. The matter ended on June 20, 1922, when Jacob Isaacson was deported to Russia aboard the S.S. *Berengaria*.[36]

In the Isaacson case, as in every other known instance where the

Sedition Act was invoked after the armistice, the defendant's speech had no measurable impact on the war effort. To be sure, the Victory Loan floated in April 1919 bore a connection to the war, but the article Isaacson published was hardly addressed to an audience of potential investors. In a letter to Palmer, Harry Weinberger explained that the piece had appeared "in an anarchist magazine, with only anarchist readers, and the Liberty Loan was in no way hurt." The attorney general had no answer for Weinberger, but four months earlier, in response to another critic of the Isaacson prosecution, the Justice Department candidly admitted that its postarmistice enforcement of the Sedition Act had nothing to do with the war. "The Act is enforced not as a matter of war strategy or war policy, but because it is a war penal law, the enforcement of which is the duty of this Department as is the case of any other penal law."[37]

Perhaps the most remarkable suit brought under these acts was that filed against Charles Steene, Frank Preston, and William Hotze in upstate New York. Their offense was distributing a handbill in November 1919, a year after the armistice, urging President Wilson to release those still imprisoned for having violated the Espionage and Sedition Acts. The leaflet, which referred to the statutes' victims as "political prisoners," showed pictures of federal inmates being abused. It declared that

American citizens, charged with no crime against persons or property and guilty only of expressing their political, industrial and religious beliefs, are subjected to these tortures in your prisons. These people were convicted in violation of the spirit of the Declaration of Independence and the Constitution of the United States. Their conviction was made possible only by the war hysteria prevailing at that time. Whatever justification those conditions gave no longer exists. The war is over. No justification exists, or ever did exist, for these brutal and inhuman tortures inflicted on defenseless victims by your agents and representatives. In the name of Liberty and Justice we demand the release of all prisoners whose alleged crimes consisted in the peaceable expression and maintenance of their political opinion, industrial activities or religious beliefs.

The men were tried and convicted under the very statute they had dared to criticize. The district judge rejected their claim that the Sedition Act was no longer enforceable and found that the circular impermissibly suggested "that the form of government of the United States and the Constitution upon which it rests have proved inadequate to secure justice for American citizens." As such, he said, the handbill "was well calculated to have the effect of arousing the contempt, scorn, contumely, and disrepute which Congress sought to prevent." The defendants were sentenced to eighteen months' imprisonment. Their convictions were set aside by the Supreme Court in 1921, after the government belatedly confessed error and admitted that there had been insufficient evidence of intent to violate the act.[38]

The Prosecution of the Seattle Union Record

At almost the same time Charles Steene was distributing leaflets in Syracuse, the government was employing the Espionage and Sedition Acts at the opposite end of the country against the *Seattle Union Record*, a newspaper which had erred by sympathizing too closely with the IWW. The prosecution arose out of the so-called Centralia Riot, in which one Wobbly and four members of the American Legion were killed during an Armistice Day parade in Centralia, Washington. The violence occurred after the Legion had decided to march on the local IWW hall. To this day it is unclear which side was responsible for triggering the incident. The nation's press immediately placed the blame on the Wobblies and called for an end to the radical menace. At first the Justice Department seemed to agree that state law was adequate to deal with the tragedy. Two days after the event the *New York Times* reported, "Although no comment was made by Attorney General Palmer or his assistants, it is understood that the view of the department is that in this particular crime the perpetrators should be held for first degree murder under the laws of the State of Washington." Local officials quickly arrested the Wobblies thought to be responsible, eleven of whom were tried for murder. A state court later convicted seven of the men of second-degree murder, and they received sentences ranging from twenty-five to forty years in prison.[39]

The *Times* was mistaken in its belief that the Centralia affair would be treated as a state matter. The killings came in the midst of nationwide coal and steel strikes and at a time when the country was already in a condition of alarm over the radical threat. A few weeks earlier the Senate had approved a resolution demanding that the attorney general report "whether or not the Department of Justice has taken legal proceedings, and if not, why not . . . for the arrest and punishment of the various persons within the United States who during recent days and weeks . . . have preached anarchy and sedition." Palmer responded to this request three days after the Centralia killings. He explained that a number of jurisdictions, including Washington, had adopted sedition legislation, and that "the several States through their law-enforcing machinery have at their command infinitely greater forces than the United States Government for detecting and punishing these seditious acts." Yet the attorney general intimated that additional prosecutions would be brought and mysteriously stated that he had "caused a number of other lines of activities to be pursued by my department which from the confidential nature thereof I can not disclose at this time." It soon became evident that the Centralia Riot had afforded Palmer a perfect opportunity to answer his critics.[40]

The entree came in the form of a telegram to the attorney general from Clarance Blethen, editor of the proestablishment *Seattle Times*. Blethen was hardly a dispassionate observer of the Centralia affair; a former lieutenant colonel in the U.S. Army and an officer in the Washington National Guard, he was undoubtedly in sympathy with the American Legion. His wire of November 12 objected to a front-page editorial in that day's *Seattle Union Record*, "the paper that led the general strike in Seattle last February." According to Blethen the editorial declared that "violence begets violence. Anarchy calls for anarchy. That is the answer to the Centralia outrage." The Justice Department also received messages from the local Chamber of Commerce and from American Legion posts around the country urging Palmer to take swift action. The Legion's Hollywood, California, post recommended that "all guilty of seditious statements or acts be immediately incarcerated or deported."[41]

On November 13, the day before he responded to the Senate, Palmer ordered Robert Saunders, the U.S. attorney in Seattle, to interview Blethen concerning the *Union Record* and, "if publication violates any provision of amended espionage act institute criminal prosecution." The paper, which was owned by the Seattle Central Labor Council, meanwhile published additional articles suggesting that the Wobblies were not necessarily at fault and claiming that the incident was the latest in a series of illegal acts committed by former servicemen. An editorial entitled "Don't Shoot in the Dark" urged fair-minded persons to let the facts unfold rather than succumb to the mounting anti-Wobbly hysteria.[42]

The administration may have been inclined to go after the *Union Record* even before Blethen entered the picture. *The Nation* had recently reported that the Seattle paper had not been very cordial to President Wilson during his visit to the city in late September. In three-inch letters covering four columns of the front page, the *Union Record* had printed the word WHY? followed by a series of questions which included: "Why do you not ask the immediate repeal of the espionage law?"; "Why is it that under the espionage law working men and women mainly were convicted and not one German spy was prosecuted?" Like Charles Steene and his friends, this journal would fall prey to the very statute it had ventured to criticize.[43]

Federal prosecutors lost no time in moving against the *Union Record*. Upon receiving Palmer's wire, U.S. Attorney Saunders obtained a search warrant under the Sedition Act and federal marshals raided the *Union Record* offices, where they seized files and subscription lists. Though printing activity was halted temporarily, the paper resumed publication after the raid. Clarance Blethen, who had closely monitored the proceedings, was incensed that the *Union Record* had not been completely shut down. In an impassioned telegram to the attorney general sent within hours of the raid, the *Seattle Times*'s editor warned that permitting the paper to continue "means most extraordinary encouragement of red radicals and anarchy. If Union Record resumes publication riots are almost certain to follow. In addition influence of loyal press will be completely smashed. For God's sake do not permit this triumph of Bolshevism over Americanism." The following day, after Saunders received a wire from Palmer inquiring why the entire *Union Record* plant had not been seized, U.S. marshals took possession of the premises and announced that they were under instructions to hold it indefinitely. Despite this interference the *Union Record* continued to publish by using a rented press at another location. The editors even put out an "extra"edition while their offices were being ransacked, reporting details of the federal raid. Approximately a week after the takeover a U.S. commissioner ruled that the warrant authorizing seizure of the *Union Record* had been improperly issued and ordered the government to surrender possession of the plant.[44]

In addition to its attempt to halt publication of the *Union Record,* the Justice Department instituted criminal proceedings against the paper's staff. On November 13, when federal agents raided the *Union Record* offices, they arrested E. B. (Harry) Ault, the editor, along with two members of the Board of Directors—Frank Rust and George P. Listman. The defendants were charged with having violated the Sedition Act and were released on $5,000 bail. Fortunately for the government, the case would not go to the grand jury for several weeks. In the interim Saunders obtained permission to enlist the services of six private attorneys from Associated Industries, an anti-labor group, who had volunteered to help comb the newspaper's files for evidence supporting the government's case. On December 2 indictments were returned against Ault, Rust, and Listman and against Anna Louise Strong, a member of the *Union Record* staff, charging each of them under the Espionage and Sedition Acts.[45]

The indictments represented a significant victory for Attorney General Palmer. News of the federal raid on the *Union Record* and the arrest and indictment of its staff received front-page coverage in newspapers across the country. Palmer personally acknowledged many of the letters and telegrams that poured into the Justice Department from American Legion posts and other advocates of suppression. In some instances he urged his correspondents to press Congress for adoption of a permanent sedition law.[46]

The suit against the *Union Record* was based on articles appearing on fourteen different dates, all after the armistice. Mention of a few of them will suggest the flavor of the government's case. One was an editorial by Anna Louise Strong, published in February 1919, assuring the residents of Seattle that during the impending general strike the workers would maintain order, provide for feeding infants and the sick, and guarantee the availability of food at reasonable prices. The piece was said to violate the Sedition Act because it was "disloyal, scurrilous, and abusive, about the form of the government of the United States"; was intended to bring the government and the Constitution "into contempt, scorn, contumely, and disrepute"; and was designed "to incite, provoke, and encourage resistance to the United States when the United States was at war."[47]

Another allegedly seditious piece was a poem by Strong entitled "Signed!" published on June 30, 1919, two days after the signing of the treaty. The verse suggested that both sides in the war had brought suffering upon the innocent. Its last few lines expressed the widely shared sense of disappointment at the peace terms which had emerged from Versailles:

> And I thought: "Let us face
> At last the naked fact.
> THEY were like beasts
> And WE were like beasts.
> We won, thank God, not they!
> And we take

> What we CHOOSE,
> Even as they would have done
> By law of club and fang.
> But there is NO HONOR LEFT
> And no high sounding aims
> For ANY of us!"

According to the indictment this poem constituted an "attempt to obstruct the recruiting and enlistment service of the United States"; contained "disloyal, scurrilous, and abusive language" which tended to bring the government, the Constitution, and the military "into contempt, scorn, contumely, and disrepute"; and sought to provoke resistance to the United States and favor the cause of its enemies.[48]

Other articles said to violate the Sedition Act referred to the American Legion as "Plutes' Pets" (bringing the uniform of the United States military into contempt and disrepute); suggested that "when the Workers' government comes into power, President Wilson will probably get three years for murdering Gene Debs of Atlanta" (bringing the government into disrepute and encouraging resistance to the United States); predicted the inevitability of revolution (bringing the government and Constitution into disrepute and encouraging resistance to the United States in time of war); urged public employees and other workers to strike for better conditions (encouraging resistance to the United States, promoting the cause of its enemies, and urging curtailment of production essential to the war); and solicited funds to secure bonds for "members of the I.W.W. now confined in jails and penitentiaries throughout this country." As to the last offense, the department charged that it was part of an effort to encourage resistance to the United States by "depicting as heroes and martyrs, Kate O'Hare, Eugene V. Debs, Hulet M. Wells, William D. Haywood, . . . referred to . . . as 'political prisoners,' which said crimes included the offenses of seditious conspiracy, and . . . violation of . . . the Espionage Act."[49]

This was all the government could come up with after an exhaustive search. Saunders later told the attorney general: "As a precaution I had all of the files of the Union Record from May 18, 1918 to the date of the indictment carefully examined in order to discover any articles [other] than those set out in the indictment plainly violative of the Espionage Act. I found none." Absurd though the case may seem today, the Justice Department was determined to press forward with it. In an autobiography written in 1935 Anna Louise Strong stated that the *Union Record* arrests "were hasty and ill-considered," and that after the state Democratic party complained to Washington, "our case was quietly dropped behind the scenes." In actuality the government refused to dismiss the indictments despite numerous requests that it do so. One such plea came from Anna Louise Strong's father, the Reverend Sydney Strong, pastor at Queen Anne's Congregational Church in Seattle. Another came from Anna Louise Strong herself, who asked Paul Kellogg, editor of *The Survey*, to intercede with the attorney general, unaware that Palmer was personally supervising the *Union Record* case. Her letter, written the day after she was arrested, was passed on to the attorney general, who must have read the following passage with amusement: "I notice in your last number an article by Attorney General Palmer. He seems to talk like a sensible man, not like the representatives of his Department which are running the office here. I wonder whether any of you people are in touch with him and could let him know what is really happening here."[50]

While these appeals to the Justice Department fell on deaf ears, U.S. District Judge Jeremiah Neterer proved considerably more receptive. The judge did not address the defendants' argument that the Espionage and Sedition Acts had ceased to be operative with the signing of the armistice. He did find, however, that none of the articles cited by the government fell within the prohibitions of the acts. The poem "Signed!" he said was no more than an expression of "opinion with relation to the peace treaty," while Strong's February 1919 article related solely to "the industrial strike that was imminent in Seattle, and not to any war activities." Judge Neterer found that the other allegedly seditious pieces dealt with "strikes, securing bail for prisoners, . . . expressing opinion with relation to . . . industrial conditions, . . . and venturing opinion that revolution is inevitable if conditions continue; but nowhere is there apparent any statement advocating any change other than by constitutional methods." All of the *Union Record* indictments were dismissed.[51]

The government decided not to appeal this ruling. It did so not because of outside pressure, as Strong later suggested, but because the local U.S. attorney became convinced that the matter should not be pursued. On March 6, 1920, shortly before the time to appeal would expire, Saunders wired Attorney General Palmer advising against seeking review. Two days later in a lengthy and rather remarkable letter Saunders outlined the basis for his recommendation:

I personally conducted and argued this group of cases and pressed vigorously for a favorable decision . . . I have come to the deliberate conclusion that the Court's decision is correct, since I am inclined to believe that, generally speaking, the attack on the constitutional form of government, et cetera, must be direct in order to violate the Espionage Act. Perhaps this would not be the rule during an active state of war and hostilities, but, in my judgment, the rule of law is in some degree, at least, measured by all of the circumstances, times and conditions surrounding the commission of the alleged offense.

This letter was written nearly four months after the United States had first moved against the *Union Record.* Its dispassionate and almost apologetic tone contrasts sharply with Saunders's earlier zeal toward the case. The dramatic change in attitude no doubt reflected the fact that by March 1920 the Red Scare had nearly run its course.[52]

Judge Neterer's order in the *Union Record* case served to protect freedom of the press. Yet the decision was based not on the First Amendment but on a finding that because the articles had nothing to do with the war, they did not fall within the scope of the Espionage and Sedition Acts. In so ruling he appears to have read more into the statutes than Congress intended. There was nothing in the relevant clauses of the Sedition Act which required a connection between defendants' speech and the war effort. Instead it was seemingly enough for the government simply to prove that the unpatriotic remarks were made during a technical state of war. The latter interpretation was advanced by the Justice Department in the *Isaacson* case and is amply supported by the legislative history. Congress's principal aim in adopting the Sedition Act was to silence those whose beliefs were upsetting to the majority, regardless of their relation to the war. Viewed from this perspective the *Union Record* prosecution was entirely justified, for it could not have accorded more perfectly with the statute's underlying goal.

The *Union Record* indictment and the U.S. attorney's correspondence in the case clearly indicate that the newspaper was targeted for prosecution because the majority in Seattle was offended by its strongly prolabor stance. One extraneous paragraph in the indictment thus charged the journal with "pretending . . . to advance the interests of laborers as a class . . . not by political action . . . but by the continual . . . employment of unlawful, tortious, and physical means and methods . . . to be accomplished in part by local strikes, industrial strikes, and general strikes of such laborers." The defendants' crime lay in having angered the local business community: it will be recalled that the case was initiated at the insistence of the *Seattle Times*, with encouragement from the American Legion and the Chamber of Commerce.[53]

In a letter to Attorney General Palmer sent shortly after the *Union Record* was seized, Robert Saunders acknowledged that the action had been taken to mollify the local populace.

Public feeling was such that nothing except legal action could have prevented the raiding and destruction of the Union Record plant by the inflamed public, and also raids upon its news-stands and agencies all throughout the Western District of Washington . . . [T]aking action under the Espionage Act, and thus in effect preventing the further circulation of the paper at this time, was the only possible step that could have been taken by legal authority to prevent destruction of property and loss of life and further complications of the situation in this territory.

The U.S. attorney had greatly exaggerated the danger, for as he knew, the newspaper continued to publish during the takeover of its plant, yet no incidents of violence occurred. That the *Union Record* was prosecuted because its philosophy was objectionable to many in Seattle finds further confirmation in Saunders's letter to Palmer advising that the suit be dropped without an appeal: "I may say this much, that since the indictment the general tone of the Union Record has been very much less offensive to the great majority of the community who entirely disagree with all of the ideas finding advocacy in the Union Record. To sum up, I think the purposes of the indictment have been accomplished." In its skirmish with the *Union Record* the Justice Department may have lost the battle, but it won the war. While the criminal actions were dismissed, the government achieved its goal of forcing the paper to express itself in more conventional terms.[54]

Wobblies, Commies, and the Committee of Forty-Eight

The federal response to the Centralia Riot did not end with the prosecution of a newspaper which had supported the Wobblies. The government also used the occasion to go after the IWW itself. By doing so the administration fulfilled the hopes of the many congressmen who had supported the Sedition Act with precisely this end in mind. The U.S. attorney in Seattle immediately saw the potential for launching a full-scale attack on the radicals. When Attorney General Palmer first directed him to consider possible action against the *Union*

Record, Robert Saunders urged a much grander scheme in which he would seek indictments against the IWW's officers, members, and organizers under both the Penal Code and the Espionage Act. As Saunders explained: "The Centralia murders were . . . intended to obstruct all federal military activity by subjecting ex-service men to fear of assassination after discharge as well as by persuading them not to enter service and to resist draft. Procedure I outline is seizure all I.W.W. records[,] literature[,] and paraphernalia[,] arrest all I.W.W.[,] thorough investigation[,] and final prosecution where evidence supports above outline of federal crime." An ambitious theory perhaps, but one designed to ensnare the entire IWW within the net of the Espionage Act.[55]

The U.S. attorney also began to explore using the Espionage and Sedition Acts to prosecute the local AFL unions which operated the *Union Record*, and whose ranks had to some extent been infiltrated by Wobblies. Saunders floated the idea in a letter to Palmer on November 17: "I know that there is no intention on the part of the government to either unnecessarily draw the A.F.L. into a fight or to complicate the coal miners' strike with I.W.W. prosecutions. The trouble arises out of the fact that most of the mining organizations out here are I.W.W.s as well as A.F.L." A week later Saunders took a more definite approach. Declaring that the IWW had taken over the AFL in western Washington, he recommended to the attorney general "that the leaders, organizers, officers and distributors should be unrelentlessly [sic] prosecuted . . . for conspiracy to violate the terms of Section 3 of the amended [Espionage] act on the ground that they have combined not only to hinder the war, but against the government, the uniform, the flag, etc."[56]

Given the wrath provoked among organized labor by the recent coal strike injunction, it is not surprising that nothing came of the scheme to indict the Washington AFL. The Justice Department did, however, follow through with Saunders's plan to prosecute the Wobblies. Ironically by this time the IWW had been all but destroyed as a radical presence. The wartime suits under state and federal law, together with numerous instances of mob violence, had decimated its membership rolls. The IWW abandoned its militant tone to the point where it more closely resembled a debating club than a revolutionary sect. Yet the legend established in the prewar years continued to haunt the public imagination. If nothing else, the ghost might still be put to rest.[57]

In the wake of the Armistice Day killings ninety Wobblies were arrested in Centralia and Tacoma, though it was unclear what was to be done with them. On November 14 the mayor of Centralia declared, "The State has taken charge of certain I.W.W. prisoners for prosecution, and the Federal Government is taking charge of otl :rs." The next day, however, all ninety men were charged under the Espionage Act, and the U.S. attorney promised that "as soon as we can get to it all I.W.W. held in Seattle will also be charged with violation of ... the espionage law." Such action was quite acceptable to the Washington attorney general, who, on November 18, urged Palmer that while the state could handle the murder cases, federal law should be employed against the IWW on a broader basis. Palmer assured him that "this Department intends to take action in any cases wherein the laws of the United States warrant." On November 20 the state began murder proceedings against eleven of the Wobblies. Several weeks later a federal grand jury was convened at Tacoma; according to U.S. Attorney Saunders those IWWs "against whom definite murder charges cannot be brought will face Federal charges."[58]

The grand jury was not as cooperative as the Justice Department might have hoped, though the government did not come away empty-handed. On December 3, 1919, indictments were returned against Pete Anderson, Gus Kangas, John Korpi, Alfred Lampinen, and Eva Rumpinen. The five were charged under the Sedition Act in what Robert Saunders described as a "general movement ... against Russian Bolshevikis." The fate of these individuals is unknown. On Christmas Eve three more Wobblies were arrested on the basis of a secret indictment returned a few days earlier. They were accused of having violated the Espionage and Sedition Acts by distributing radical literature. Taken into custody were William Randall, secretary of the Tacoma IWW; A. Gross, a local organizer; and R. E. Eddy, operator of a Tacoma bookstore; a fourth man named in the indictment, A. G. Grant, was never found. The case against Eddy was dismissed, but Randall and Gross were both convicted.[59]

The government's campaign against the Wobblies appears to have taken it beyond the state of Washington. Though Congress expressly limited use of the Espionage and Sedition Act to times "when the United States is at war," the Justice Department made no pretense that its postarmistice prosecutions were in any way war related. The point is illustrated by a March 1919 letter to Palmer from the U.S. attorney in Phoenix asking permission to prosecute two Wobblies for circulating a book entitled *The War, What For*. In explaining why the two should be indicted under the Sedition Act the U.S. attorney placed no importance on the book's title. Instead, the key was that they "were very active organizers for the I.W.W. . . . These two men . . . have both been very active since in the spreading of I.W.W. propaganda and inciting labor troubles, strikes, etc. We regarded them both then and do now as very dangerous and undesireable [sic] citizens, and feel that the defendants in both cases should be prosecuted, and so recommend." Like Morris Zucker, Jacob Isaacson, Charles Steene, Frank Preston, William Hotze, Anna Louise Strong, and her colleagues at the *Union Record*, the IWWs of Washington, and doubtless many others whose names are unknown, the Arizona Wobblies were targeted because they were heretics whose political and economic beliefs ran counter to those of a frightened and intolerant majority.[60]

Nearly a year after the Centralia episode the United States invoked the Espionage and Sedition Acts against two alleged members of the Communist party, John Jassinka and J. Juodis. They were indicted at Chicago in October 1920, charged with distributing literature in Illinois, Michigan, Wisconsin and California which was said to be "disloyal and abusive" to the government. The men were found guilty on November 17, 1920.[61]

One did not have to be a Wobbly or a Communist to be threatened with prosecution under the Espionage and Sedition Acts. Groups far less radical faced similar treatment if their views were sufficiently unconventional. The Committee of Forty-Eight was unpopular with superpatriots owing to its interest in government ownership, and perhaps because a November 1919 poll showed that 93 percent of its roughly 250,000 members favored repeal of the Espionage and Sedition Acts. This liberal organization was made up largely of business and professional people who sought to chart a political course which would avoid the extremes of both left and right. These distinctions were too subtle for the American Legion. When the committee attempted to hold a convention in St. Louis in December 1919, the Legion prevented it from meeting at the Statler Hotel and forced the management to cancel the group's reservations. The Legion warned that unless the Justice Department made sure the committee did not meet in St. Louis, the veterans would see to it themselves.[62]

With the aid of a judicial restraining order the convention began. Yet the attorney general's special assistant in charge of disloyalty cases told the Legion that he would "send stenographers to every session, and that reports of all discussions would be made." The promise was kept. On December 11 the *New York Times* reported, "Attentive representatives of the Department of Justice were at the conference when the second day's session opened . . . Verbatim reports of all speeches and discussions have been ordered made." One of the items on the group's agenda was a plank demanding "repeal of the Espionage law and release of 'political prisoners.' " No indictments resulted from the meeting, but the government's brazen attempt at intimidation may have succeeded in part. The platform the committee ultimately adopted called for "the immediate and absolute restoration of free speech, free press, peaceable assembly and all civil rights guaranteed by the Constitution." All references to the Espionage Act and to political prisoners, however, had been deleted.[63]

The documented instances in which the Espionage and Sedition Acts were applied to postarmistice conduct are not great in number. Yet they reveal a pattern of enforcement against those who, in the eyes of the majority, had strayed too far from the path of orthodoxy. Regardless of how many such cases were brought, the country had every reason to believe that the acts were being vigorously enforced. This perception stemmed from the fact that after the armistice the government initiated and tried a considerable number of Espionage and Sedition Act cases, many of them based on prearmistice activity. In the first half of 1919 there were probably three hundred suits filed or heard under these laws. During the 1919–20 fiscal year forty-one cases were instituted and fifty-nine went to trial, of which forty-seven resulted in conviction. In 1920–21, six more actions were commenced while twice that many were tried. In covering these cases the press often failed to note that defendant's speech had occurred during the war. On occasion the facts were simply misstated. A March 1919 *New York Times* story thus reported that H. E. Kirchner was "convicted under the espionage act because of statements made in a recent speech at Elizabeth, West Virginia . . . He was sentenced to two years' imprisonment." Kirchner was actually indicted in January 1918 for a speech given long before the armistice. Such misinformation only strengthened a public belief that was already grounded in fact and contributed to the atmosphere of chill and repression which prevailed throughout 1919 and 1920. That climate was made even more oppressive by the system of postal censorship which continued to operate during these same years.[64]

~ 6 ~

Censorship and the "Cowed Mind": Perpetuating the Aura of Repression

The Espionage and Sedition Acts, in combination with the Trading with the Enemy Act, enabled the postmaster general to function as a national censor. Any newspaper, book, or magazine which he deemed to be in violation of the acts could be barred from the mails, in which case its distribution in interstate commerce by any other means was also prohibited. All further mail delivery could be terminated indefinitely to those who published the offending material. If the violator was a newspaper or a magazine, the postmaster general might revoke its second-class mailing privilege, thereby at least quadrupling the cost of sending future issues through the mails.[1]

In contrast to the criminal provisions of the Espionage and Sedition Acts, the system of postal censorship did not depend on convincing a judge or jury that the statutes had been violated. The Post Office could unilaterally declare a violation to have occurred, thereby triggering any or all of the legal sanctions at its disposal. While an aggrieved individual might ask the courts to reverse the postmaster general's decision, judicial review was virtually certain to be fruitless. As a result, the postmaster general was able to take action having ruinous effects even though the alleged violation might not be provable in a court of law.[2]

This discrepancy between the postal and criminal enforcement provisions would have been reduced or eliminated if the administration had followed a Justice Department suggestion made shortly after the Sedition Act was adopted. A memorandum prepared for John Lord O'Brian in May 1918 urged that the postmaster general submit any material to the attorney general before determining it to be in violation of the act. The memo explained:

In the work of suppressing unlawful propaganda there seems to be nothing more important than that the interpretation of the Espionage Law should be concentrated in the Department of Justice . . . It seems the matter is quite important enough to warrant the Attorney General in insisting that matters shall not be declared as violating the Espionage Act unless it is so declared by this Department. If the Post Office Department will simply send over here such matter as it thinks violates the act, we will promise a speedy agreement or disagreement of that opinion. The Postmaster General can then decide upon his action.

For whatever reason, the proposal was never adopted. Instead, the departments enforced the law independently of each other.[3]

During the war years the Post Office had carried the laboring oar on the Censorship Board, an agency created under the Trading with the Enemy Act to monitor communications between the United States and foreign countries. With the armistice, the president and the postmaster general were both eager to terminate these controls, but other cabinet members persuaded Wilson to continue the board at least until the treaty was signed. In the spring of 1919 Burleson and Tumulty again sought to end censorship of the foreign mails, but without avail. The postmaster general, however, showed no inclination to surrender censorship authority over the internal mails. Indeed, in late February 1919, when Burleson was urging dissolution of the Censorship Board, Wilson suggested to him that it was time to halt the system of domestic surveillance: "I cannot believe that it would be wise to do any more suppressing. We must meet these poisons in some other way." Burleson scrawled across the president's note, "Continued to suppress and Courts sustained me every time."[4]

That the president and the postmaster general were prepared to lift all restrictions on foreign mail strongly indicates that the continuation of official censorship was no longer justified by war conditions. Burleson's determination to continue monitoring the domestic mails undoubtedly reflected his antipathy toward the radical left, a feeling which was in no way alleviated by his limited belief in government ownership. Writing in the February 1919 issue of *Forum,* the post-master general defended his scheme for taking over, or "postalizing," the telephone and telegraph partly on the basis of "national defense." Like the mails, he said, the wires "constitute a means for covering intelligence." This notion of government using its control over the means of communication to ferret out threats to the state was hardly new. One of the main reasons why England and other nations had claimed a monopoly over the post "was the desire to use the mail facilities for an official espionage on private correspondence with a view to discovering who were the enemies of the sovereign or his ministers." While the Espionage and Sedition Acts did not allow the Post Office to open private letters, its ability to censor the radical press was virtually complete. The postmaster general of course enjoyed the same authority over establishment journals, but they only rarely felt the sting of these laws. As with the criminal provisions of the acts, postal sanctions were reserved almost exclusively for IWW, Socialist, and other leftist publications.[5]

The Pursuit and Destruction of The Masses

A classic instance of the use of the Espionage and Sedition Acts to suppress a radical journal involved *The Masses,* a monthly periodical published in New York City by Max Eastman. The Post Office resorted to a combination of censorship devices to destroy a magazine which the Justice Department was twice unable to convict in the courts. Although the attack on *The Masses* occurred prior to the armistice, it vividly illustrates a process which was employed against other leftist publications between 1919 and 1921, including most notably *The Liberator,* a magazine Eastman founded as a successor to the ill-fated *Masses.*

The Masses described itself as "a Revolutionary and not a Reform Magazine; a Magazine with a Sense of Humor and no Respect for the Respectable; Frank; Arrogant; Impertinent; Searching for the True Causes; a Magazine Directed against Rigidity and Dogma wherever it is found; Printing what is too Naked or True for a Money-Making Press; a Magazine whose final Policy is to do as it Pleases and Conciliate Nobody, not even its Readers—A Free Magazine." As the U.S. Court of Appeals noted, while the journal was "revolutionary, not only in matters political, but in art and literature and religion as well," it was "not revolutionary . . . in that it desires to overturn existing forms of government by force of arms." *The Masses* had been published in Greenwich Village since 1911. Until the government intervened, it had a monthly circulation of 20,000 to 25,000 copies and "passed freely through the mails to subscribers throughout the United States."[6]

The August 1917 number was ready for mailing in early July. Like many previous issues of the magazine, it contained articles and drawings opposing the war. It was the first, however, to appear since the Espionage Act was approved. On July 5, two days after copies were presented for mailing, the New York City postmaster informed Eastman that on instructions from Washington the August issue was "unmailable under the Act of June 15, 1917." The Post Office was at first unable to specify which parts of the magazine were objectionable, which suggests that the decision to bar the August issue had been made before it ever appeared. After more than two weeks' delay the government identified four cartoons and four text passages which, it said, tended to obstruct recruitment and encourage insubordination in the armed forces.[7]

In an effort to reverse the Postmaster General's order the editors first appealed directly to the president. Eastman knew Wilson personally and, though a Socialist, had supported the president's reelection. On July 12 Eastman, John Reed, and Amos Pinchot asked Wilson to look into the situation. He replied the following day, stating that their letter "has been read with a great deal of interest and sympathy. I am going to take the matter . . . up with the Postmaster General to see just how the case may best and most justly be handled." According to Burleson the president told him that he knew the editors: "These are well-intentioned people. Let them blow off steam!" Burleson replied that he was "willing to let them blow off steam, providing they don't violate the Espionage Act." He told Wilson, "If you don't want the Espionage Act enforced, I can resign. Congress has passed the law and has said that I am to enforce it." Having provoked a stronger reaction than he perhaps expected, the president retreated. He advised Burleson to "go ahead and do your duty." The postmaster general then prepared a formal letter explaining his rejection of the August issue, which Wilson sent to Pinchot on July 17.[8]

The attempt at presidential mediation having failed, the magazine filed suit in federal court seeking an order compelling the New York postmaster to release the August issue. During oral argument on July 21 Judge Learned Hand agreed with petitioners that under the act "a publication could not be condemned as unmailable which did not in fact violate the law and so bring upon the publishers a criminal charge." A few days later Hand issued a now famous opinion finding that the August number did not violate the Espionage Act. According to Eastman, "Judge Hand also remarked—and years after he called my attention to this with a grin—that if the magazine *had* violated the law, the proper procedure was to indict the editors. That passed unnoticed by us, however, and for a day we felt triumphant." The victory was short-lived. Government attorneys traveled to Hanover, New Hampshire, where U.S. Court of Appeals Judge Charles M. Hough was vacationing. On July 26, the same day Hand issued an injunction against the Post Office, Hough stayed the ruling.[9]

While the August issue languished in the New York City post office, the staff went ahead with production of the September edition. This number was considerably more restrained. When it was presented for mailing, the government raised no objection to its contents but refused to accept it as second-class mail. As Eastman later recalled, the publishers "were invited to Washington to show cause why our mailing privilege should not be revoked on the ground that we were irregular in publication, and therefore not 'a newspaper or periodical within the meaning of the law.' " By statute, to be eligible for a second-class mailing permit it was necessary that a publication "regularly be issued" at stated intervals, at least four times a year, and that it disseminate information "of a public character." The editors explained that the only reason *The Masses* had not been issued "regularly" was interference by the government. Yet, said Eastman, "this did not seem sufficient 'cause,' and our mailing privilege was revoked because we had not mailed the August issue!" The magazine immediately asked Judge Hough to revoke his stay order on the basis that the Post Office was putting it to unfair use. Hough denied the request but "permitted himself to remark that the act of the Postmaster General in revoking our mailing privilege on the ground of an omission for which the postmaster himself was responsible seemed to him 'a rather poor joke.' "[10]

Eastman once more tried the personal touch, this time meeting with Burleson himself, "hoping to dissuade him from destroying so valuable a property." The effort came to naught, though the postmaster general later told the newspaperman Edward W. Scripps, who had arranged the meeting, "Why, we *love* Max Eastman!" Just how much affection was felt is revealed by a report Burleson sent to the Senate at this time in which he denounced *The Masses* as "a leader in organized propaganda to discourage enlistments, prevent subscriptions to the Liberty Loan and obstruct the Draft act." Yet the postmaster general refused to give Congress any specific reasons for his action against the magazine, declaring that "such information was incompatible with the public interest."[11]

At this point *The Masses* filed a second lawsuit, this to force the Post Office to accept the September issue as second-class mail. The petition was rejected on September 12 by Judge Augustus N. Hand, who agreed that "in September the editor adopted a somewhat milder and less pronounced tone than in August," but held that since the August issue was deemed to violate the Espionage Act, *The Masses* was not entitled to a second-class permit. "That which must be regularly issued," said Hand,

is a lawful magazine. If the publication contains matter in violation of law, it ceases to be a mailable publication at all, and hence can lay no claim to regularity of issue. It was for this reason that the Masses was held by the Department not to be regularly issued and not for the absurd reason suggested at the argument that transmission had been interrupted by the stay of Judge Hough. A more important ground of revocation than regularity of publication was the illegality of matter contained in recent issues.[12]

In desperation Eastman again wrote to the president, urging that the government's treatment of *The Masses* and other left-wing journals posed a "grave danger to our civil liberties." Wilson answered on September 18, explaining that in wartime normally innocent speech may become dangerous; he confessed that "the line is manifestly exceedingly hard to draw and I cannot say that I have any confidence that I know how to draw it. I can only say that a line must be drawn and that we are trying, it may be clumsily but genuinely, to draw it without fear or favor or prejudice." Thus ended *The Masses'* fight to recover its second-class permit. Without it the journal could no longer afford to use the mails, for third-class mail cost at least four times as much as second class.[13]

Eastman and his staff were determined to keep the magazine alive. They completed a combined November-December number which was to be sold on newsstands rather than distributed through the mails. Its back cover carried a notice urging readers to have their local news dealer carry *The Masses,* explaining that "loss of our second class mailing privilege is, of course, playing havoc with our distribution. Undoubtedly, we shall sustain very material damage because of the Post Office's actions." Nonetheless, said the editors, "we are throwing all our energies into the newsstand sales until we can get back into the mails."[14]

By the time the issue appeared, the Trading with the Enemy Act had become law, making it a crime to ship or distribute any material found nonmailable under the Espionage Act. Since only the August number of *The Masses* had been so designated, the new law should not have affected dissemination of subsequent issues. Eastman had taken pains to avoid further difficulties with the Post Office, even sending advance copies to the postmaster general with an offer to incorporate any changes he might suggest. The November-December issue was in fact never declared nonmailable and thus did not fall under the ban of the Trading with the Enemy Act. Yet confusion as to how the statute would be interpreted had the same effect as an outright ban on shipment.[15]

This unfortunate turn of events was precipitated by a November 2, 1917, Court of Appeals ruling reversing Learned Hand's decision in the *Masses* case and finding that the postmaster general had properly excluded the August issue from the mail. In an opinion by Judge Henry Rogers the tribunal rejected Hand's narrow interpretation of the Espionage Act, which required that a publication "in so many words directly advise or counsel a violation of the act." Instead, it was enough that "the natural and reasonable effect of what is said is to encourage resistance to a law," if the words were used in an "endeavor to persuade to resistance." A concurring opinion read the majority as holding that a writing would violate the Espionage Act if it had even the "indirect effect" of discouraging recruitment or enlistment. The judges also emphasized that Burleson's determination that a publication had violated the Espionage Act "must be regarded as conclusive by the courts, unless it appears that it is clearly wrong"—a showing which had not been made in the case at bar.[16]

This decision was a severe blow to *The Masses.* The damage was compounded by the next day's *New York Times,* which incorrectly reported that the effect of the ruling was to outlaw all further distribution of the journal. The *Times*'s headline read:

COURT FINDS MASSES
UNFIT TO BE MAILED
Reversal of Injunction Against
Postmaster Opens the Way
for Criminal Action.
MEANS END OF MAGAZINE
New Law Forbids Distribution by
Any Agency of Publications
Barred from the Mails.

The article went on to state that "arrangements had been made by the Masses Company to distribute its publication in other ways than through the mails, but the new methods are made ineffective" by the Trading with the Enemy Act. New York City newsdealers immediately announced that they would not handle the November-December issue of *The Masses* for fear of being criminally prosecuted. The editors explained that the dealers were under an "erroneous impression that if the Government once determines an issue of a publication to be non-mailable all its future issues are non-mailable." The Justice Department backed *The Masses* on this point, announcing that federal law barred distribution of "the particular number of a magazine which had been declared in violation of the Espionage act, but did not make it unlawful to handle copies of the magazine as such."[17]

Newsdealers nevertheless continued their boycott, concerned that under the Court of Appeals' broad reading of the Espionage Act they could otherwise face indictment. That ruling, said the *Times,* had created "great alarm" in publishing circles, for it "was the first intimation that there was danger of jail for writers and publishers of articles as long as they took pains with their language and used circumlocutions, instead of expressly advocating resistance to the draft, or other treasonable acts." The ease with which a journal might be found to have violated the act was said to pose in turn new and substantial risks for those handling such publications. Indulging in a highly dubious interpretation of the law, the *Times* warned:

According to the Trading with the Enemy act, . . . a newsdealer may today sell a magazine on the supposition that it is inoffensive, but that newsdealer is liable to prosecution if the postal authorities the next day come to the decision that the magazine violates the Espionage act. The result of this is that the newsdealer handles all newspapers and publications at his own risk and is not excused for handling non-mailable or seditious matter because he handled it before it was declared non-mailable or seditious.

Not surprisingly, the November-December *Masses* never appeared on the newsstands. With the magazine effectively barred from the mails and unable to reach its readers by any alternate route, *The Masses'* seven-year existence came to an abrupt end. What Max Eastman aptly described as the "unnatural death of the *Masses*" occurred entirely as a result of the postmaster general's unilateral determination that the August 1917 issue violated the Espionage Act.[18]

If Burleson was correct in his assessment, the government need not have settled for merely putting *The Masses* out of business but might also have put the editors behind bars. While Learned Hand had hinted at this option, the Court of Appeals literally invited it. In his opinion for the majority Judge Rogers declared, "If the magazine is nonmailable . . . it may be that the editor has committed a crime in publishing it, for which, upon conviction, he may be fined not more than $10,000, or imprisoned for not more than 20 years, or both." The Justice Department took the cue. Less than three weeks after the Court of Appeals decision the Masses Publishing Company and seven of its staff were indicted under the Espionage Act. The case against four of the defendants—Max Eastman, John Reed, Floyd Dell, and Josephine Bell—rested exclusively on articles or poems that had appeared in the August 1917 issue. The alleged violation was identical to that which the Post Office had relied on with such devastating effect. The difference was that the claim now had to be proved in court to the satisfaction of a judge and twelve impartial jurors.[19]

The feat proved too much for the government. In April 1918 a nine-day trial before Judge Augustus Hand ended in a mistrial, the jury deadlocking at 9 to 3 for conviction. After federal prosecutors announced that the defendants would be retried, the president received letters from several influential supporters and advisers, urging that the case be dropped. For a moment it appeared that Wilson might be persuaded. He told one correspondent that "the matter has been giving me a great deal of thought, and troubled thought at that, but I have not yet been able to come to a conclusion that satisfies me." Eastman meanwhile met with Colonel House and Solicitor General John W. Davis after failing to secure an interview with the president himself. On June 6 Attorney General Thomas Gregory and the president met and decided that the editors should be tried again. The case was heard in October 1918 and resulted in another hung jury, this time with only four jurors voting to convict. In January 1919 the Justice Department announced that it would abandon the case. The postmaster general had succeeded in destroying *The Masses* on a charge the government was twice unable to prove in court.[20]

The Siege of The Liberator *and Other Radical Publications*

Several months after the death of *The Masses* Max Eastman launched *The Liberator*. Many former staff members, including John Reed and Art Young, appeared on the masthead, and the format of the two journals was quite similar. Eastman explained, however, that *The Liberator* would differ from its predecessor in one key respect: "Of necessity it would be less rambunctious. Some things we felt deeply must be left unspoken; on others we would have to temper our speech to the taste of the Postmaster General." Indeed the magazine's editorial policy was so cautious that John Reed resigned in protest. Yet despite these adaptations the new venture encountered stiff opposition from the government.[21]

A variety of devices was employed against *The Liberator*. The Post Office blocked delivery of each issue until the department's solicitor determined whether or not it violated the Espionage and Sedition Acts. No issue was ever found to be nonmailable, but the delays in granting approval were at times substantial. The magazine's first number, dated March 1918, was presented for mailing sometime in February; as of mid-April it was still being held by the New York City Post Office. Thinking that Eastman might try to circumvent this restriction by mailing copies from Connecticut, Solicitor William Lamar on April 11 warned the postmaster at Bridgeport that "the March and April issues of this publication are now being examined in this office to determine whether or not they carry matter violative of the Espionage Act. Should any copies of these issues reach your office for either dispatch or distribution, you are directed to hold them for further instructions from this office." The Post Office finally released the March issue in late April, after having detained it for nearly two months.[22]

The solicitor encouraged local postmasters to withhold delivery of subsequent numbers of *The Liberator* if they were "in doubt as to their mailability . . . and submit samples to this office for a ruling." Even though approval was invariably granted, the department made it clear that the magazine's future was an open question. Thus, in advising the New York City postmaster that the November 1918 issue was acceptable for mailing, Lamar noted that this was "notwithstanding the fact that it contains much matter the mailability of which is very doubtful under the Espionage Act." By the end of 1918 the process of granting clearances had been reduced to a week or two—still a significant delay for a journal whose content was topical in nature.[23]

In addition, the department refused to grant *The Liberator* a second-class permit. In late January 1918, acting on a tip from the director of Naval Intelligence, Lamar alerted postal officials that *The Masses* would soon be revived as *The Liberator* and recommended that any request for second-class privileges be given "careful examination." His advice was followed with a vengeance. *The Liberator*'s application was filed on February 11, 1918. The March issue optimistically noted that its application for second-class status was "pending." Month after month the department accepted copies of the magazine for mailing, yet the permit was not forthcoming. In October 1918, after the matter had been under submission for more than eight months, Lamar advised that "no action . . . be taken at this time," explaining that "the whole question of this publication has been under investigation, and several issues found to contain matter the mailability of which is very doubtful under the Espionage Act." In the interim *The Liberator* was distributed through the much more costly third-class mails. The application was still pending in July 1919, when Max Eastman's sister, Crystal, made a futile visit to the solicitor's office. In September 1920 *The Liberator*'s attorneys were given a hearing by the postmaster general and were assured that a ruling would be made within days. Months passed, however, without a decision.[24]

It is difficult to understand the department's perverse treatment of *The Liberator*. Because no copy of the journal was ever excluded from the mails, the regularity-of-issue argument used against *The Masses* was inapplicable. The various justifications which the Post Office offered for refusing the second-class permit were far from convincing. One explanation was that the magazine had somehow violated the amended Espionage Act, though the department never found any issues unmailable on this ground. Another contention was that *The Liberator* did not meet the requirement that second-class mail contain information of a "public character," a condition the postmaster general distorted to mean that it be of "public benefit." Finally, the Post Office said that the journal, while having made an "insidious attempt to keep within the letter of the law," contained "revolutionary matter" which might incite arson, murder, or assassination. Since Criminal Code section 211 made such material nonmailable, it was claimed that second-class status could also be denied on this ground. Yet every issue of *The Liberator* had been examined carefully by the department, and none was found to violate the Criminal Code or any other federal statute.[25]

The Liberator's request for second-class status was still pending when the Wilson administration left office. On May 25, 1921, more than three years after the application was filed, President Warren G. Harding's postmaster general, Will H. Hays, determined that Burleson's conduct had been unjustified. If the magazine had violated the Criminal Code or the Espionage Act, said Hays, it should have been excluded from the mails and its editors prosecuted. Inasmuch as neither of these actions had been taken, there was no basis for denying it the same privileges enjoyed by other lawful publications. Hays accordingly granted the permit and refunded more than $11,000 in excess postage *The Liberator* had been forced to pay as third-class mail.[26]

Despite Postmaster General Burleson's best efforts *The Liberator* survived until 1924. Its success in weathering the storm was based on several factors, including the fact that newsstands and express companies continued to handle the magazine. Since none of its issues was found to have violated the law, distributors had less reason to fear prosecution than in the case of *The Masses*. Demand for the journal was also phenomenal, largely because its first number began serializing John Reed's account of the Russian Revolution; circulation quickly became double that of its predecessor. *The Liberator* was also better financed than *The Masses,* which had been cooperatively owned by the editors and had difficulty generating capital. *The Liberator* was publicly held, with Max and Crystal Eastman owning 51 percent of the stock. Additional funds were raised by selling shares at $10 apiece. Finally, after operating for nearly a year without a second-class permit, the journal was able to increase its price by a third, thereby offsetting the increased cost of third-class mail.[27]

The Liberator was only one of many radical journals which the Post Office attempted to suppress in the period following the war. In his annual report for 1919 Burleson explained that

enforcement of the espionage and trading-with-the-enemy acts has been carried on throughout the year. The character of the disloyal and seditious matter found in the mails since the signing of the armistice has differed materially from that which the department dealt with during . . . the war. It is now of a radical, revolutionary type, having for its object the solidification of the revolutionary elements in this country and the overturning of our present form of government by force.

He noted that, in addition to excluding such material from the mails, he had "found [it] necessary to revoke the second-class mail privilege of some publications because their contents consisted more or less of matter which was nonmailable under the espionage and other laws."[28]

In a report filed in November 1919 Attorney General Palmer claimed that there were 471 "radical publications" circulating in the United States, more than 100 of them in English. "All of these," he said, "are read and translated by the Department of Justice in cooperation with the Post Office Department. A force of 40 translators, readers, and assistants is employed for this purpose, and daily reports are received on the radical articles that appear." The Post Office report for 1920, under the heading "Enforcement of the Espionage and Trading-with-the-Enemy Acts," declared, "During the year the department continued to find in the mails much matter of a radical, revolutionary type, both in the English and in foreign languages . . . This matter has been dealt with in the manner which the law provides."[29]

Concern was occasionally voiced as to the use of war legislation to impose censorship long after the armistice. Congressman James Byrnes of South Carolina, speaking on the House floor in December 1919, observed that the Post Office was still enforcing these statutes against the IWW and other radical groups: "The only law they have is the espionage law . . . [U]nder that law they have been stopping some publications. But I doubt if we have the right to do it . . . The espionage law is so worded that it clearly applies to the act of an individual the object of which is to obstruct hostilities or give aid to the enemy." In September 1920 the Post Office solicitor also expressed doubt as to the legality of continuing to enforce these war measures. Yet Lamar advised against altering the practice "unless and until the courts determine" otherwise. Postmaster General Burleson subsequently raised the question with President Wilson, who suggested that it be taken up by the cabinet. Nothing evidently came of this, for the department enforced these laws against the leftist press until Burleson's final day in office.[30]

The Post Office and Justice Departments together reviewed every issue of nearly five hundred radical newspapers, a process which obviously took time. As a consequence, even where no objectionable material was found, out-of-town circulation of these papers was often delayed three to five weeks, destroying any news value they might have had. For example, on January 9, 1919, the solicitor finally notified the Chicago postmaster that the November 30, 1918, issue of *Il Nuovo Proletario,* an Italian-language Wobbly newspaper, was acceptable for mailing. The department took almost a month to advise officials in Youngstown, Ohio, that the December 18, 1918, issue of *Revolutionary Age* was mailable. The *Chicago Socialist* was closely watched throughout 1919 and 1920, with delays sometimes exceeding three months. During this period five issues of the *Socialist* were declared nonmailable under the Sedition Act, including one dated December 4, 1920.[31]

An internal Post Office memorandum indicates that in the first three months after the armistice more than seventy-five periodicals and pamphlets were barred from the mails. Of these at least a fifth were IWW publications. A rare instance in which such censorship may have had a plausible link with the war involved Arthur Griffith's "How Ireland Has Prospered under English Rule and the Slave Mind," published by the Irish Protective League. In January 1919 this pamphlet was ruled nonmailable under the amended Espionage Act owing to the danger it presented for "friction between the United States and her Allies at the Peace Conference." The ban was lifted in October 1919, three months after the conference ended.[32]

One newspaper receiving particularly close scrutiny was the *Seattle Union Record,* which the Post Office began monitoring shortly after the February 1919 general strike. Seattle postmaster Edgar Battle was instructed to send two copies of each issue to Solicitor Lamar for review, though the department consistently found the paper mailable under the Espionage and Sedition Acts. On November 15, 1919, however, in the wake of the Centralia Riot, Battle denied the *Union Record* all further access to the mails. U.S. Attorney Saunders and Attorney General Palmer applauded the move, and on November 18 Palmer suggested that the Post Office might also revoke its second-class mailing privilege. The exclusion had a major impact on the *Union Record,* which depended on the mails to reach fifteen thousand out-of-town subscribers, who accounted for more than 20 percent of its circulation. The newspaper sued to enjoin the postmaster's order, but on November 25 a federal court denied relief on the basis that the matter should first be presented to the postmaster general. A few days later Solicitor Lamar advised Battle: "There is no law under which a publication as such can be denied the privilege of the mails. Only individual issues which contain matter which the law prohibits can be excluded. You will therefore consider each issue of the Seattle Union Record and hold up only such as appear to be in violation of law." The blanket exclusion was lifted two weeks after it had been imposed.[33]

Several periodicals earned the distinction of having their second-class permits withheld for even longer periods than Max Eastman's *Liberator.* The *New York Call* and the *Milwaukee Leader,* two of the largest Socialist dailies in the country, lost their second-class privileges in late 1917 for allegedly violating the Espionage Act. Following the armistice they unsuccessfully petitioned Burleson for reinstatement. Their efforts to have the federal judiciary overturn the postmaster general's action were equally unavailing. The papers did not obtain redress until the Harding administration came into office. When Will Hays granted second-class privileges to *The Liberator,* he noted that similar action was being considered for the *Call* and the *Leader.* Their permits were finally restored on May 31, 1921, after having been suspended more than three and a half years.[34]

The *Milwaukee Leader* may have suffered more than any other newspaper in the postarmistice period. Not only did the Post Office bar the *Leader* from the second-class mails, but it also refused to deliver mail to the *Leader* through at least the end of 1920. During the spring of 1919 such an embargo was also employed against Socialist party headquarters in Chicago. This sanction, which the postmaster general could invoke against anyone believed to have violated the Sedition Act, appears to have been used sparingly. Attorney General Gregory had been deeply troubled by the provision, noting that it allowed the Post Office to "inflict . . . a penalty worse than a money fine and one which in some cases might conceivably destroy a whole enterprise." The cutoff had the intended effect of making it extremely difficult for the *Leader* to maintain contact with readers around the country. In an attempt to evade the blockade, the paper had its mail sent to the addresses of supporters in Milwaukee. The device did not always work. In August 1920 the postmaster at Cheyenne intercepted a letter from the *Leader* to one of its Wyoming subscribers explaining that it had been necessary to increase rates and asking that payment be sent to another address. The letter recounted the journal's difficulties in some detail.

The restrictions that war legislation placed on commerce have very nearly all disappeared. One barrier after another is being removed that captains of industry may again resume trading with our former enemy. But ... the Espionage Act, designed to crush the freedom of speech and press of the common people, is still in full force ... This condition hits The Leader harder than any other Socialist publication. For not only is The Leader's second class mail right revoked, in addition no mail of any kind is delivered to The Leader, but is returned to the sender with the notation stamped on the face of the envelope, "Mail to this address undeliverable under the Espionage Act." This alone is an immense financial loss to us.

The Leader noted that the necessity of using the third-class mails meant that postage costs on an annual subscription were "about eight times as great as under the second class rate."[35]

It is not clear why Burleson treated *The Leader* with particular harshness. The answer may lie in the fact that its editor, German-born Victor Berger, was a prominent Socialist who, because of his opposition to the war, was sentenced under the Espionage Act to twenty years in federal prison. Though the conviction was later set aside by the Supreme Court, feeling against Berger was so strong that the House of Representatives refused to seat him in the Sixty-sixth Congress, to which he had been elected. The tide of hostility which swept over Capitol Hill may have invaded the Post Office Department as well. Yet the critical point is that with the virtually unlimited discretion he possessed under the Espionage and Sedition Acts, the postmaster general did not need a reason to bar a publication from the mails or to deny it second-class privileges or to terminate its mail delivery. This capricious authority, which Burleson wielded frequently in the early postwar years, had a powerful inhibiting effect on freedom of expression.[36]

A Repressive Status Quo

The administration's continued enforcement of the Espionage and Sedition Acts created a chilling climate for the nation's press. Though instances of self-censorship are difficult to document, we have already encountered several examples. Max Eastman adopted such a restrained policy at *The Liberator* that John Reed quit the staff. And according to the local U.S. attorney, prosecution of the *Seattle Union Record* caused that newspaper to become "very much less offensive."[37]

The aura of oppression that prevailed throughout 1919 and 1920 was noted by a number of contemporary observers. One of the first was Senator William Borah of Idaho, who was shielded from possible reprisal by the speech or debate clause of the Constitution. Speaking three months after the armistice, Borah charged that the Espionage and Sedition Acts had created "a complete system of licensing the press" which enabled the postmaster general to "encompass the whole field of public opinion." Though the war had ended, "there is a belief that this censorship still obtains . . . that it is still in existence, and that the law may still be invoked. That belief results in the same hesitancy to discuss public questions in a frank, open, sincere, and candid way . . . as during the war." An article by William Hard in the May 10, 1919, *New Republic,* entitled "Mr. Burleson, Espionagent," lamented that "free speech seems to be an antique Jeffersonian Victorian liberal sentimental dogma, with few believers left."[38]

In December 1919, thirteen months after the armistice, Frank Cobb of the *New York World* delivered a stirring and widely reprinted address to the Women's City Club of New York. He quoted a passage from Thomas Jefferson praising the "spirit of resistance to government" and added, "If the author of the Declaration of Independence were to utter such a sentiment to-day, the Post Office Department could exclude him from the mail, [and] grand juries could indict him for sedition." Cobb urged that "what the United States needs more than anything else to-day is the restoration of the free play of public opinion. That requires first, the reestablishment of the freedom of discussion," along with an end to the government's "power of damnation over all dissenting political and economic beliefs. If the guaranties of the Bill of Rights are to be overridden in the name of superpatriotism, the newspapers themselves will be the ultimate victims . . . and we shall have no public opinion at all except that which cringes under the lash of officeholders."[39]

In early 1920 the *Baltimore Sun* suggested that prolonged use of the Espionage and Sedition Acts might have caused irreparable harm. Many had

assumed as a matter of course that as soon as the war ended the free expression of opinions would be resumed . . . But there have been two unexpected and alarming developments in this connection. The first is that a considerable proportion of the people seem, as a result of the suspension of their habit of thinking, to have lost the habit. The mental facilities seem to have atrophied from disuse. The second is that an even larger proportion of the people have grown so accustomed to censorship and suppression that they want them continued. They don't want free speech and free assemblage and a free press anymore.

A few weeks later Ernest Hopkins, president of Dartmouth College, declared that "censorship and propaganda have been actively at work to such an extent that freedom of thought and speech, such as the Constitution of the United States expressly guarantees, are impossible." The situation had improved little in August 1920, when Walter Nelles of the National Civil Liberties Bureau commented on the "prevalence of the cowed mind." He recognized that prosecutions for sedition seemed to have abated for the moment and that "as a direct agency of repression, the Espionage Act is dormant. An observer finds almost daily evidence, however, that we are living in its wake. I think it has done more harm to people out of jail than to those it imprisoned . . . [I]t is upon the minds of the people out of jail that fear of punishment for heresy has wrought devastation."[40]

Not everyone was reduced to a cringing condition. On February 21, 1919, a Michigan state court judge urged President Wilson to seek repeal of the amended Espionage Act and pardon those convicted under it. "If there was any necessity for its existence on the statute books during the war," he wrote, "now that the war is over there is no further reason for this repressive legislation." While the act had resulted in an "almost complete silencing of the expression of radical thought," the judge made it clear that the chill was not confined to leftists: "I do not know, because there has been no opportunity under the terms of the Espionage act to talk about it, in the way I would like to talk about it, whether this tyrannical piece of legislation strikes any other Democrat in the same way it strikes me." His apprehensions may have been justified, for the White House promptly forwarded the letter to the Justice Department. The same procedure was followed with the many other petitions and letters received from citizens' groups demanding an end to the acts' enforcement and release of those held under them.[41]

During 1919 calls for repeal of the Espionage and Sedition Acts were issued by the League for Amnesty of Political Prisoners, by former governor Charles Whitman of New York, and by the National Civil Liberties Bureau. In September Albert DeSilver, the bureau's director, urged Attorney General Palmer to drop criminal proceedings against Jacob Isaacson, the anarchist who had criticized the Victory Loan drive. DeSilver wrote:

It is very unfortunate that prosecutions should continue to be brought under the Espionage Act nine months after the termination of hostilities. The only possible supposed justification for interference with the right of the citizen freely to discuss public affairs . . . lies in the existence of a forcible threat against the safety of the country. While I realize that technically a state of war still exists, nevertheless it is manifest that the United States [is] under no present threat of danger and accordingly there can no longer be any possible supposed justification for the curtailment of the right of free discussion.

It was in reply to this letter that the Justice Department conceded that it was enforcing the Espionage and Sedition Acts "not as a matter of war strategy or war policy" but simply because these penal laws were still on the books.[42]

In June 1920 Charles Evans Hughes told the graduating class at Wellesley College that "the policy of denying free expression of political opinions is death to the Republic"; in a thinly disguised reference to the Sedition Act he condemned "the attempt to repress political opinion with which we do not agree." The *New York Times* immediately blasted Hughes for "arguing, by implication and innuendo, for an unpermissible 'right' of persons and parties within the United States to seek to destroy, not to change, the Government," adding that "his generous liberality, his intellectual hospitality, cannot be admired too much."[43]

Though the *Times* was not among them, some establishment publications—including the *Nation,* the *New York World,* and the *Baltimore Sun*—did criticize the administration's protracted use of the Espionage and Sedition Acts. The same was true of the Pennsylvania State Federation of Labor, which in late 1919 passed a resolution insisting that the attorney general take steps "to restore to the people of Pennsylvania the constitutional rights of free speech, free press, and free public assemblage," including repeal of the Espionage Act and release of political prisoners. While the Justice Department ignored this protest, those less closely allied with the establishment did not always find such forgiveness. When Charles Steene and his friends distributed leaflets calling for amnesty and repeal, they were indicted. The *Seattle Union Record* also found that public criticism of the acts could be dangerous. Its front-page condemnation of these measures during President Wilson's stay in the city may have contributed to the decision to prosecute the paper two months later. The Committee of Forty-Eight, which opposed the Espionage and Sedition Acts throughout 1919, avoided a similar fate, perhaps because in response to Justice Department intimidation it significantly muted its demands.[44]

Within Congress there were efforts to terminate the wartime sedition laws. Some, including Representative Meyer London of New York and Illinois Senator Lawrence Sherman, had opposed these measures from the outset. Others, such as Miles Poindexter of Washington, had once strongly defended them. As Senator Poindexter explained in November 1919, though the legislation "was necessary during the war, . . . even then along with the good that it did in punishing disloyalty it had a most unfortunate effect by virtue of a widespread and perhaps cultivated misunderstanding of suppressing loyal and wholesome and necessary criticism and denunciation of . . . public employes and officials." Between December 1918 and September 1919 this dissatisfaction manifested itself in a host of bills seeking partial or complete repeal of the Espionage and Sedition Acts. None of the measures was reported favorably by committee. As a result the Sedition Act remained in effect until March 1921, when it was finally repealed as part of an omnibus bill which removed from the books most legislation adopted during the war.[45]

Opposition to these laws was not strong enough to effect their repeal during 1919 or 1920. Yet it did help prevent adoption of a permanent sedition act, for which there was considerable support at the time. Attorney General Palmer, after requesting such legislation in June 1919, submitted a draft bill in November. Wilson urged Congress to adopt the measure, stating that "towards passion and malevolence tending to incite crime and insurrection under guise of political evolution there should be no leniency." More than eighty proposals were introduced in the Sixty-sixth Congress, including the Sterling Bill, which the Senate approved in January 1920; it died in the House, however, after the much more drastic Graham Bill was substituted in its place. The latter measure was so extreme that it was opposed even by many proponents of a peacetime sedition law.[46]

Congress was for several reasons reluctant to rescind the Espionage and Sedition Acts before 1921. One of them, however, was surely not the excuse feebly offered by the Senate Judiciary Committee—that "it was impracticable to repeal the law, because it included search warrant and other provisions necessary for the enforcement of prohibition." Had this been a genuine concern, the committee might easily have recommended a limited repeal.[47]

Republicans contended that the Democrats wished to retain the legislation in order to stifle criticism of the Versailles Treaty. While these charges may have been in part politically motivated, there was some foundation to them. The cabinet had opposed canceling domestic censorship restrictions until peace terms were agreed on. Moreover, the administration had defended its postarmistice seizure of the cables on the basis that the action was necessary to protect the treaty process. And in early 1919 the Post Office blocked "How Ireland Has Prospered under English Rule and the Slave Mind" on the ground that it could adversely affect the peace conference. Fear that the Espionage and Sedition Acts might be used to secure ratification of the treaty led some to demand their immediate termination. In January 1919 Senator Joseph France, a Maryland Republican, urged return of the wires and repeal of the sedition laws, declaring: "Now, as never before in our history, as we . . . are approaching the time when we must consider treaties which may fix the obligations of our country to other nations for generations to come, are the absolute freedom of the press and fearlessness and freedom of speech and discussion indispensable." Two months later, in what the press described as "a sensational address," Republican Senator Lawrence Sherman challenged President Wilson to "remove the limitations upon a censored press and censored free speech that we may combat with him in an open forum and on equal terms."[48]

In late July, after the treaty had been presented to the Senate, Senator France charged that the administration was using the Sedition Act to prevent free discussion of the League of Nations proposal. This accusation was triggered by an editorial in the *Baltimore Sun,* a Democratic newspaper, denouncing the Justice Department for attempting to suppress Thomas F. Millard's *Democracy and the Eastern Question,* a book critical of Japan and its treatment of China. The *Baltimore News* believed that such "censorship . . . to help the league of nations propaganda" was "more concerned to keep the Senate in the dark than the public." The incident, said Senator France, revealed "the apparent purpose of the administration to foist this scheme upon the people by a well thought-out campaign, cleverly combining propaganda with repression."[49]

Whatever the merits of the treaty theory, it would account for only some of the opposition to rescinding the Espionage and Sedition Acts. Had this been the sole factor at work, it is likely that one of the repeal bills would have been approved by the Republican-controlled Congress. Most Republicans and many Democrats, however, wished to retain these statutes as a weapon in the government's fight against radicalism. Meyer London, the lone Socialist in Congress, correctly observed that "what has taken place under the so-called espionage law is that men are being prosecuted and persecuted, very often by well-meaning officers, because to these officers the doctrines which the accused advocate seem to be subversive of well-ordered society." While none took issue with this statement, there was no apparent sympathy when London urged his colleagues "to repeal the obnoxious espionage law" and "stop this unjust, unfair attack upon the Socialist philosophy." In proceeding against such heretics, the administration was operating exactly as Congress had envisioned when it broadened the Espionage Act in 1918. Indeed, some members cited the presence of Socialists and other dissidents as a reason to preserve and perpetuate these wartime laws. Senator Knute Nelson of Minnesota urged that "instead of repealing the espionage law, in my opinion we ought to have it extended . . . in order to stem this most iniquitous propaganda that is now being carried on in this country . . . It is our duty as legislators to do what we can to protect the American people against this poisonous spirit of anarchy and sedition. The Constitution never was intended for the protection of people of that kind." Lee Overman of South Carolina charged that the effort to repeal the laws was itself part of "a propaganda on the part of the Bolsheviki" and said that his Senate committee was investigating the situation.[50]

Retention of the Espionage and Sedition Acts also appears to have been favored as a means of discouraging strikes, which many regarded as radically inspired. At a time when walkouts were occurring on an unprecedented scale, the Sedition Act held some promise, for it made it a crime to "urge, incite or advocate any curtailment of production . . . of any . . . products, necessary or essential to the prosecution of the war . . . with intent . . . to cripple or hinder the United States in the prosecution of the war." According to Senator France this section "was considered by many—not merely by the labor unions themselves, but by some commentators on the law—as being an antistrike provision." The clause had been one of the bases for prosecuting the IWW, and labor was concerned as to its possible application to traditional union activity. In lobbying against an extension of the amended Espionage Act, the Amalgamated Clothing Workers charged, somewhat extravagantly, that "though it was aimed against German spies, [the Act] was only used to curtail and restrict, directly and indirectly, the legitimate activities of labor

unions." The Pennsylvania Federation of Labor warned that legislation, "which ostensibly aims to punish . . . any advocacy of a change
of Government by violence . . . may readily be construed, as was the
espionage act, to apply to any vehement protest against existing
conditions." For the same reasons that organized labor fought a
continuation of these laws, others supported them. The *Baltimore
Sun* reported that it was the antistrike potential of the Sedition Act
which explained the Senate Judiciary Committee's refusal to vote out
a repeal bill.[51]

Opposition to the Espionage and Sedition Acts because of their
chilling effect on speech and their impact on the treaty process was
thus counterbalanced by their value in the fight against radicalism.
The result was a stalement in which neither side could alter the status
quo. While no new sedition legislation was approved during 1919 or
1920, the wartime laws were not repealed.

Not with a Bang but a Whimper

Even though the Espionage and Sedition Acts remained in place
until 1921, public hostility was strong enough to hamper their enforcement in many parts of the country. One of the places most
affected was New York City, whose large immigrant community
tended to look favorably on radicals and dissenters. In 1918 juries in
the Southern District of New York twice refused to convict the editors
of *The Masses*. In February 1919, a month after the government
dropped the *Masses* prosecution, another New York jury deadlocked
in the case of Scott Nearing, a prominent Socialist who was indicted
under the Espionage Act for his antiwar pamphlet "The Great
Madness." The two jurors who voted to acquit Nearing had both
been born in Russia, a fact that caused the prosecutor to complain of
"the cosmopolitan character of the population in the District." The
New York Times was upset, noting that "the sedition law has worked
out unequally. Offenders against it in the West have been dealt with
according to the law. In the East men who have committed precisely
the same offenses have gone free. It has become almost impossible to
convict a seditionary in New York. Precisely the same degree of
evidence that serves to convict one in the West is enough at most to
hang a jury in New York." Charles Whitman cited the lack of geo-
graphic uniformity as reason to repeal the Espionage and Sedition
Acts, remarking that "nowadays it depended largely upon what sec-

tion of the country one was in as to what sentiments could be expressed."[52]

The situation grew worse with time. In May 1919 a front-page article in the *New York Times* about the amended Espionage Act observed that "some lawyers hold now that it is ineffective because of the difficulty of getting a jury to convict under a law intended solely for war-time conditions." Six months later the paper reported, "As armistice day receded . . . both the Department of Justice and the Post Office Department found it increasingly difficult . . . to enforce the wartime meaning of these statutes." In January 1920 Attorney General Palmer made an oblique reference to the problem, urging, "There can be no real effectiveness . . . in our legal prosecutions of sedition unless [they] are backed by the sympathetic and hearty efforts of all elements of good citizenship."[53]

The reluctance of juries to support federal enforcement of the Espionage and Sedition Acts was reminiscent of Colonial resistance to British law and of the abortive prosecutions under the 1850 Fugitive Slave Act. However discomfiting it may have been, the reality was one the Justice Department could not ignore. It may partly account for the government's spring 1919 decision to review all cases that were still pending under the Espionage and Sedition Acts. One of those suits involved John Reed, who had been indicted for a September 1918 speech in the Bronx, where he declared that "the sending of allied troops to Russia was an adventure of brigands." In April 1919 the department announced that it was dropping the case because "the termination of hostilities had created a situation in which the ends of justice could not be especially served by placing the defendant on trial." This explanation would have applied to most if not all of the pending prosecutions. A more likely reason for the action was the fact that Reed's suit would have been heard in New York City, where federal juries had proven most uncooperative. Only six months earlier a jury in Manhattan had refused to convict Reed in the second *Masses* trial, and this was followed by the acquittal of Scott Nearing.[54]

If one must speculate as to the *Reed* case, it appears that a number of sedition prosecutions were specifically abandoned because of anticipated jury resistance. In the Jacob Isaacson matter, for example, the article he had published criticizing the Victory Loan was written by Arthur Turner, an American citizen. Turner was indicted along with Isaacson but eluded arrest until after the government had agreed to dismiss the suit against Isaacson. The government then decided to drop the Turner case as well, reasoning that because Turner—like Scott Nearing and the *Masses* defendants—was a citizen, a New York jury would be unlikely to convict him.[55]

A similar phenomenon occurred in the *Seattle Union Record* case. One factor causing the U.S. attorney to advise against an appeal in March 1920 was "the condition of the public mind after the cessation of active hostilities. This only goes to show the probability of securing a verdict of guilty . . . though it is clearly material to a consideration of the whole case." That jury resistance was an obstacle even in western Washington suggests that the government's problem had become a serious one. At about the same time *The Independent* reported that "from the prosecutors' point of view, great difficulty long has been apparent in getting convictions for treason or sedition." This popular opposition may help account for the fact that only six cases were filed under the Espionage and Sedition Acts after June 30, 1920. Yet, though their actual enforcement had been reduced to a trickle, the statutes' presence on the books continued to chill freedom of expression.[56]

It was recognized in some circles that the public's negative reaction to these laws might not be confined to the jury box. In mid-1919 segments of the press warned that unless enforcement was ended, the consequences could be "politically disastrous" for the Democratic party. One journal suggested that the attorney general's "campaign on radicalism" might "in some measure recoil on him," recalling that "it was just such a drive, apprehended to endanger freedom of press and speech, that resulted in the extinction of the old Whig party and the birth of the Republican party." Lest history repeat itself, several of the president's advisers urged that the administration make no further use of the Espionage and Sedition Acts and that pardons be granted those who had been convicted under them.[57]

Wilson had considered taking such action in June 1919 but yielded to the objections of Attorney General Palmer. At the end of March 1920 Joseph Tumulty resurrected the idea, noting that "most of our associates in the war have already granted amnesty and America ought not to be the last to act." The concept appealed to Wilson, who instructed Tumulty to solicit the views of Palmer, Burleson, and Secretary of War Newton Baker. Within a week, however, the "outlaw" railroad strike irrupted, rekindling fears of anarchy and dampening the spirit of forgiveness. On April 15 Tumulty sent the president an urgent note advising that he delay the amnesty. "The time when you ought to do it is most important," he said, "and I am afraid this is not the psychological moment." The tenor of his letter suggests that Wilson may have been on the verge of acting. If so, the interruption proved costly, for no general amnesty was ever granted.[58]

Wilson may have been influenced to abandon the plan by a letter he received from the attorney general on April 19. Palmer objected to an amnesty and to the secretary of war's proposal to "declar[e] that from a specified date further arrests and prosecutions for the mere expression of opinion were not to be made." The latter, said Palmer, "would imply that such arrests and prosecutions had been made in the past and that others are contemplated. As a matter of fact, there have been no arrests or prosecutions for mere expression of opinion." As for a general amnesty, the attorney general observed that "the majority of those who were charged with a violation of the Espionage law have already been released after service of their terms of imprisonment." The 214 people still in prison and those whose cases were on appeal were undeserving of mercy, for they represented "a kind of men whose presence at large among society in either peace or war times is a menace to its existence . . . Their offenses approached the borderland of treason." Since this group included men such as Dr. Morris Zucker, Victor Berger, and Eugene V. Debs, it is difficult to believe that even Palmer accepted this explanation. Later in the same letter the attorney general offered another objection to the amnesty proposal which may come closer to revealing the true basis of his opposition: "A proclamation of general amnesty of the character which is being considered would be a confession on the part of the Government that we have made many prisoners for political reasons, or have convicted them for a mere expression of political opinion, and would constitute a serious reflection upon the administration of the laws by the courts of the country." These words were written at the height of Palmer's campaign for the presidency, when more was at stake than simply the reputation of the judiciary. If the courts had erred in their application of the Espionage and Sedition Acts, it was the attorney general who had made the initial determination to prosecute political dissidents under these laws.[59]

William Gibbs McAdoo, the president's son-in-law, was one of Palmer's chief rivals for the Democratic nomination. He too was concerned about the possible impact of the sedition prosecutions on the impending election. Yet McAdoo, who had not been responsible for the acts' enforcement, suggested a different solution from the attorney general's. In a letter to Wilson in May 1920 the former treasury secretary declared that

continued imprisonment . . . for seditious utterances during the war is offending the great mass of men and women in the country of liberal thought and tendencies. These are your friends, and it is to these to whom we must look for support in the coming campaign . . . [I]t would be a wise thing from the standpoint of justice and for every other consideration, to release all of these so-called political prisoners,—to extend a general amnesty, as it were.[60]

In the end the president stood by his attorney general, although the matter continued to bother him. A month before the 1920 election Wilson told Palmer, "I feel the embarrassment of pressing the suits now which began under the authority of the Espionage Act, because I think the country feels that the time for that is past." He urged the Justice Department to drop these cases as "the fair and wise thing to do." The attorney general continued to feel otherwise, and in characteristic fashion the president did not press the point. When Wilson left office in March 1921 nearly a hundred Espionage and Sedition Act prosecutions were still in the course of litigation.[61]

There are a number of interesting parallels between the 1918 Sedition Act and that of 1798. Both were enacted out of fear that a foreign revolution might otherwise spread to the United States. When the smoke had cleared, however, the danger of a Jacobin uprising proved to have been as illusory as that of a Bolshevik coup. And in each instance the sedition law spawned by the crisis was used as a weapon of political oppression, only to lapse on the administration's last day in office. Yet there are also some key differences between these historical episodes, one of the most significant of which is the type of reaction they engendered.[62]

The country's repudiation of the Sedition Act of 1798 was swift and decisive. Largely because of the Federalists' enforcement of the statute, they were swept from power in 1800. Thomas Jefferson's election to the presidency constituted a victory for freedom of expression and was celebrated as such in both word and deed. In his inaugural address Jefferson made indirect reference to the recently expired Sedition Act, declaring that "every difference of opinion, is not a difference of principle. We have called, by different names, brethren of the same principle. We are all republicans: we are all federalists. If there be any among us who wish to dissolve this union, or to change its republican form, let them stand undisturbed, as monuments of the safety with which error of opinion may be tolerated where reason is left free to combat it." Within days of assuming office Jefferson granted full and unconditional pardons to those still imprisoned under the Sedition Act. As he later explained to Abigail Adams, his action flowed from a conviction, shared by the electorate, that the statute was "a nullity, as absolute and as palpable as if Congress had ordered us to fall down and worship a golden image; and that it was as much my duty to arrest its execution in every stage, as it would have been to have rescued from the fiery furnace those who should have been cast into it for refusing to worship the image."[63]

In contrast to this supreme triumph of principle, the Sedition Act of 1918 departed the scene almost unnoticed, one of a host of statutes terminated by the Act of March 3, 1921. A victory, perhaps, but not so much for freedom of speech as for a nation grown weary of living under the cloud of wartime laws. Nor was its repeal followed by any immediate relief for the act's victims. Between 1918 and 1921 Woodrow Wilson commuted the sentences of several hundred political prisoners. His successor was urged to complete the process by granting an amnesty to the 150 to 200 persons still jailed for having expressed their views. Yet whatever else Harding's election may have stood for, it did not represent a protest against the Espionage and Sedition Acts. Despite pleas from civil liberties groups, the new president refused to issue a general pardon and instead adopted Wilson's case-by-case approach. On Christmas Eve 1921, nearly eleven months after taking office, Harding released Eugene Debs and 23 others in hopes of defusing the amnesty movement. Over the next year and a half he commuted the sentences of an additional 41 persons. Not until December 1923 was the last prisoner freed—this under a pardon from President Calvin Coolidge. The end came—not with a bang but a whimper—nearly three years after the Sedition Act had been repealed. In contrast to 1801, the response was halting and equivocal.[64]

This difference is partly explained by the nature of the groups targeted by the two sedition laws. The act of 1798 was employed by the Federalists to silence their main political opponents. All who were indicted under the statute appear to have been Jeffersonian Republicans, most of them newspaper editors but one an outspoken member of Congress. Such a bold and foolhardy undertaking was destined to produce a far more sweeping reaction than the Wilson administration's campaign against the Wobblies and other political outcasts, for whom little public support existed."[65]

In addition, freedom of expression enjoyed a loftier status at the close of the eighteenth century than it did after World War I. The Republicans framed their opposition to the Sedition Act partly in terms of federalism, arguing that the general government was exercising powers the Constitution had reserved to the states. Yet their objections were also based on principles of natural law which bound the government even in the absence of specific constitutional limitations. For those who subscribed to such tenets the wrong embodied by the Sedition Act was egregious and intolerable and was certain to have more profound consequences than would ensue in the rudderless days of Pragmatism.[66]

This is not to say that the reaction to the 1918 law was utterly devoid of principle. The juries that refused to convict in 1919 and 1920 may well have been protesting on behalf of liberty. Idaho Senator William Borah, once a supporter of the 1918 Sedition Act, was surely moved by conviction when in late 1923 he charged that "intolerance, bigotry, [and] prejudice" had led to the imprisonment of many who "expressed their political views upon matters of government." He believed that by freeing the last of the prisoners, President Coolidge "has gone as far as lies within his power to destroy the precedent which might obtain by reason of these prosecutions for political opinions." Yet to pragmatists of the late Progressive era such principles had a much less sacred quality than in the days of Thomas Jefferson. It is difficult to imagine the Founding Fathers agreeing, as Justice Holmes wrote in the summer of 1918, that "free speech stands no differently than freedom from vaccination." Though under the right circumstances one might become excited about freedom of expression, it would be unlikely to take on the fervor of a holy cause or arouse many of one's countrymen. It is disappointing but not surprising that the response to the 1918 Sedition Act was so much weaker than the reaction which had shaken the country 120 years earlier.[67]

~ 7 ~

Judicial Review:
Its Hour Come Round at Last

In decisions handed down in late 1919 and early 1920 the Supreme Court abandoned its longstanding unwillingness to review federal war powers legislation. One of the cases, *Hamilton v. Kentucky Distilleries,* involved several suits brought by liquor dealers in Kentucky and New York to enjoin the War-Time Prohibition Act's July 1, 1919, ban on the sale of whiskey. In October 1919 a U.S. District Court in Kentucky ruled the statute unconstitutional, while a few weeks later in New York Learned Hand found the law to be valid. In a companion case filed by the Jacob Ruppert brewery Hand upheld the recent Volstead Amendment, which expanded the act to cover nonintoxicating beer. The three rulings were appealed directly to the Supreme Court, where they were argued together in late November. If war prohibition were to be invalidated, time was of the essence, for Prohibition would take effect under the Eighteenth Amendment on January 16, 1920. The Court handed down its decision in *Hamilton* in mid-December, unanimously upholding the ban against whiskey. Three weeks later in *Ruppert v. Caffey* the proscription against war beer was sustained by a vote of 5 to 4.[1]

Though neither statute was overturned, the decisions broke sharply with tradition. Rejecting a position of more than a century, the Supreme Court announced that congressional exercises of the war powers were now subject to judicial scrutiny. This dramatic turnabout was the work of a conservative Court which, since the signing of the armistice, had seen the government repeatedly invoke its war powers in contexts many people regarded as a sham. The widespread public perception that these powers were being abused, combined with the prospect that the pattern might continue indefinitely, made the Court's policy of blind acquiescence no longer tenable. Had Congress terminated the remaining wartime laws in the first half of 1920, the implications of these rulings might have remained unexplored. When the repeal efforts failed, however, lower federal courts began to implement these new decisions by blocking further enforcement of war powers legislation. The full import of *Hamilton* and *Ruppert* became clear on February 28, 1921, when the justices held the antiprofiteering provisions of the Lever Act to be unconstitutional.[2]

The Federal Control and Espionage Act Cases

Earlier in 1919 the Supreme Court had upheld a number of war powers measures without any hint of what was to come. In the *Dakota Cases,* decided in June, it affirmed the government's right to continue regulating intrastate railroad and telephone rates, refusing to address a contention that the laws were no longer enforceable because "all necessity for the regulation of such rates as a war measure had passed." Chief Justice Edward Douglass White declared that Congress's authority under the war powers is plenary and supreme, leaving no room for judicial interference. Any challenge to the postarmistice implementation of these laws, he said, "concerns not a want of power, but a mere excess or abuse of discretion in exerting a power given," and thus failed to raise a constitutional question. The cases gave the Court little reason to reconsider its noninterventionist stance. Congress had not exercised its war powers after the armistice, and any risk of abuse on the part of the executive branch was minimized by the fact that the rail and wire control experiments were in the midst of being dismantled. Nor was there any suggestion that through prolonged enforcement of these war measures the United States was interfering with liberty or property interests secured by the Bill of Rights. Rather, the sole objection was that by acting beyond the scope of its peacetime powers, the government had invaded the domain of the states.[3]

Between March 1919 and March 1920 the Court issued eight

decisions sustaining convictions under the Espionage and Sedition Acts and again suggested that the Constitution may not be invoked to overturn legislation adopted under the war powers. The constitutional issues differed markedly from those presented in the *Dakota Cases.* It was not claimed that the acts were beyond the scope of the war powers or that their duration was improper, for all of the indictments were based on conduct occurring before the armistice. What was in dispute was whether enforcement of the statutes violated the First Amendment freedom of expression.[4]

The briefs for the United States in the Espionage and Sedition Act cases assumed that the Bill of Rights applied to war powers legislation but urged that appellants' speech was unprotected for several reasons. First, the government argued that the "constitutional freedom of the press applies to restraints previous to publication, and not to responsibility after publication." In support of this position it cited Blackstone and a 1907 Supreme Court decision written by Justice Holmes. Moreover, said the government, even if the First Amendment did apply to subsequent punishment of speech, it did not protect utterances aimed at inducing others to break the law. Finally, it urged that freedom of speech does not include "the unlimited right to publish a seditious libel"; rather, "the power to punish the publication of language dangerous to the existence of the Government . . . impliedly granted by the Constitution, is not taken away by Article I of the Amendments."[5]

In sustaining the convictions under the Espionage and Sedition Acts the Supreme Court scrupulously avoided any suggestion that the Bill of Rights might operate as a check on Congress's war powers. Instead of explicitly adopting the government's assumption that the First Amendment applied even to war legislation, the Court strongly intimated that this constitutional restraint was wholly inoperative in the face of such measures. In *Schenck v. United States,* the first of the cases to be decided, Justice Holmes wrote for a unanimous Court that even if the First Amendment were not "confined to previous restraints," nevertheless "the character of every act depends upon the circumstances in which it is done . . . The question in every case is whether the words used are used in such circumstances and are of such a nature as to create a clear and present danger that they will bring about the substantive evils that Congress has a right to prevent. It is a question of proximity and degree." In formulating this test for when speech can be punished, Holmes might not have been addressing the First Amendment at all. Instead, as Fred Ragan has argued, the justice may simply have been deciding when, purely as a matter of criminal law, words may constitute an "attempt" to commit a forbidden act.[6]

Yet even if he were writing of the First Amendment, Holmes clearly implied that it offers no security where Congress has chosen to abridge freedom of expression in wartime: "We admit that in many places and in ordinary times the defendants in saying all that was said in the circular would have been within their constitutional rights . . . When a nation is at war many things that might be said in time of peace are such a hindrance to its effort that their utterance will not be endured so long as men fight, and that no Court could regard them as protected by any constitutional right." Though the protected character of speech was said to depend on the "words used" and the "circumstances in which" they were uttered, the Court upheld Charles Schenck's conviction without any such analysis of the leaflets he sent to men eligible for the draft. It was enough that the "tendency and the intent" of the circulars was to obstruct the draft, whether or not they posed a "clear and present danger" of producing such a harm. By conspicuously failing to examine the specific facts of the case, the Court suggested that "so long as men fight," the only relevant "circumstance" in determining the constitutionality of restrictions on speech is the fact of war itself. Whatever safeguards the First Amendment may afford "in ordinary times," it provides none when the nation is at war. In *Frohwerk* and *Debs*, decided a week after *Schenck*, the Court again dismissed appellants' First Amendment claims without considering whether their statements created a risk of obstructing the war. Holmes wrote for the Court in both cases, stating in *Frohwerk*, "We do not lose our right to condemn either measures or men *because* the Country is at war." Yet as the decisions strongly suggest, though war itself may not impose such a ban, Congress is free to do so under its war powers.[7]

The decisions in *Schenck*, *Frohwerk*, and *Debs* can thus be read as exempting war legislation from the constraints of the Bill of Rights. It is also possible—though by no means clear from the cases—that the Court applied the First Amendment and upheld appellants' convictions because the protection which it affords was seen as minimal. To this extent the clear and present danger test was, as Robert Cover wrote, "born . . . as an apology for repression." Less than a year before the decisions were handed down, Holmes told Learned Hand

that the only difference between free speech and freedom from vaccination was "that the occasions would be rarer when you cared
enough to stop it but if for any reason you did care enough you
wouldn't care a damn for the suggestion that you . . . might be
wrong." For Holmes and the rest of the Court at this time the First
Amendment imposed no restraint on the majority's "natural right" to
silence "the other fellow when he disagrees."[8]

The other Espionage and Sedition Act cases decided in 1919 and
early 1920 likewise suggest that the Court was unwilling to apply the
First Amendment to war powers measures. Adhering to the position
staked out by Holmes in *Schenck*, the majority summarily rejected
appellants' free speech claims without evaluating the nature or circumstances of the offending speech. Holmes and Louis Brandeis dissented in *Abrams, Stilson, Schaefer,* and *Pierce,* but it was Holmes
whose view of the First Amendment had changed, not the Court's.
The majority in *Schaefer* was quite explicit as to the basis of its
Espionage Act decisions, for it dismissed as a "curious spectacle" the
idea that the Constitution could be "adduced against itself" so that
the "right of free speech" might restrict the power to wage war. This
"strange perversion of . . . precepts," said Justice Joseph McKenna,
was an attempt "to justify the activities of anarchy or of the enemies
of the United States." Where war legislation was being enforced
during wartime, as it was in these cases, the government's authority
was seemingly without limit.[9]

December 1919: A Contemporary Perspective

The challenges presented in *Hamilton* and *Ruppert* were distinguishable in a number of important respects from the suits involving
federal control and seditious speech. The War-Time Prohibition Act
was adopted after hostilities had ended and did not take effect until
almost six months after the armistice. The act was then expanded
nearly a year after the cease-fire to outlaw the production and sale of
war beer. These facts contrasted sharply with the *Dakota Cases,* in
which the laws in question were passed during the war, and with the
sedition appeals, in which wartime statutes were applied to prearmistice conduct. In addition, the private interests threatened by the
War-Time Prohibition Act involved traditional property rights rather
than novel and unprecedented free speech claims which, in the eyes of
Justice McKenna, were advanced on behalf of anarchists and traitors.

Finally, the Espionage and Sedition Acts sought to regulate activities in the national government's sphere, whereas control over the manufacture and sale of liquor historically fell within the exclusive domain of the states.

Despite these differences, had the prohibition statutes constituted the only instance of Congress's exercising its war powers after the armistice, the Court might not have felt compelled to make new law. The cases, however, presented themselves at a time when the need to establish a limiting principle had become overwhelming. In October 1919, a month before the prohibition cases were heard by the justices, Henry Campbell Black suggested that the most dangerous legacy of the war was "the facile habit of legislators and executives ... to forget that their powers are circumscribed by constitutional limitations, or pervert constitutional grants of authority to entirely unintended uses." After canvassing the uses made of the war powers since the armistice, Black concluded that "there was no pretense that any of these measures was connected with the mobilization of the country for the purpose of the war ... [T]here seemed to be a vague idea that laws and agencies brought into being for the war might be indefinitely extended over into times of peace so long as any conditions persisted which could in any way be attributed to the effects of the war."[10]

These words would have struck a responsive chord in anyone reading the newspapers in the fall of 1919. *Hamilton* was argued in the Supreme Court on November 20 and decided on December 15. During this four-week period the daily press brimmed with tales of the government's ongoing enforcement of war powers legislation in a range of settings. The various streams of activity we have examined in earlier chapters came together at this point to produce a torrent the Court could no longer safely ignore. The government was seeking to break the nationwide coal strike. The Indianapolis injunction had failed to end the walkout, and federal authorities were threatening to seize the mines if operators did not agree to a proposed government settlement. In early December UMW officials were arrested and charged with having violated the injunction, and the Justice Department warned that mine owners were to be investigated on possible Lever Act charges. Meanwhile, the Fuel Administration had imposed severe restrictions on coal. These were eased somewhat when the walkout ended on December 11, but Attorney General Palmer announced that Lever Act indictments would be sought against any dealers who flouted the regulations or charged excessive prices.[11]

The government was also employing the Lever Act to check profiteering. Two days after *Hamilton* was argued the attorney general took on the wartime functions of the Food Administration. Authorities were moving to control the price of coffee, milk, and Thanksgiving turkeys, and prosecutions had been initiated against dealers in shoes, fuel oil, and other necessaries. The sugar famine was then at its height, and the Lever Act was being invoked against those who sought to profit from the shortage. In mid-December the Senate approved a bill to extend the life of the Sugar Equalization Board. The president and the attorney general were urging Congress to continue the Lever Act to prevent it from expiring should the treaty be ratified. On December 12 Senator Arthur Capper of Kansas proposed that the government be given emergency power to regulate profiteering in all industries.[12]

The Espionage and Sedition Acts also figured prominently in the news at this time. On November 23 the *New York Times* ran a full-page story describing the ongoing war against radicalism. A week and a half later headlines declared that the *Seattle Union Record* staff had been charged under the acts. On December 4 it was reported that the postmaster general had been sued for refusing to restore the *New York Call*'s second-class privileges. Soon thereafter the Justice Department announced that ninety Wobblies would be prosecuted under the Sedition Act in connection with the Centralia Riot. And on December 12 New York Congressman Isaac Siegel introduced a bill expanding the Espionage and Sedition Acts to punish those who preached anarchy.[13]

While the *Hamilton* case was under submission, the Court was thus frequently reminded that the government was continuing to enforce war legislation on a number of fronts. The situation was exacerbated by the fact that prospects for peace collapsed suddenly in mid-December. The day before *Hamilton* was argued, the Senate failed to ratify the Versailles Treaty on three separate votes, though Republicans were confident of passing a resolution offered by Senator Henry Cabot Lodge of Massachusetts to formally terminate the war with Germany. It was also expected that President Wilson might now be willing to compromise on the treaty and that ratification would follow swiftly. On December 2 the *New York Times* noted, "The Republican plan is to have the status of peace declared before . . . the Christmas holidays." The outlook changed quickly, however, for it became evident that Wilson would make no concessions, while support for the Lodge resolution "virtually died out." The Senate killed an attempt to bring the peace resolution to a vote and refused to reconsider the treaty. All hope that the state of war might end soon had been extinguished.[14]

The War-Time Prohibition Act epitomized the danger of permitting unfettered peacetime use of the war powers. A great many people regarded the statute as a constitutional fraud. The *Washington Post* declared that while it was approved "as a war measure under the war powers," the "deed was done under false pretense, closely bordering upon chicanery." According to the *San Francisco Chronicle,* "War-time prohibition was not enacted as a war measure, but only as a pretended war measure." The *St. Louis Post-Dispatch* described the act as "a sham, based wholly upon false premises, specifically passed to meet conditions that do not exist." The *Chicago Tribune* was troubled by the long-range implications, recognizing that the treaty stalemate could "continue for months or years. That being the case, the United States might remain indefinitely under war-time legislation. When a law does not serve its purpose, when it alleges a cause and works to a different effect, it produces a disrespect for law." Though these denunciations generally came from wets, the criticism was nonetheless a serious one. For the Court to continue its practice of declining to review such legislation could lead to further abuse of the war powers, while at the same time undermining the judiciary by portraying it as "blind" to that which "all others can see and understand."[15]

The Court Charts a New Course

It was against this background that the Supreme Court decided to abandon its traditional attitude toward war powers legislation. Indeed the justices in *Hamilton v. Kentucky Distilleries* initially voted 5 to 4 to hold the War-Time Prohibition Act unconstitutional. Justice Brandeis convinced Holmes, however, that the loss inflicted on the liquor industry did not constitute a taking of property under the Fifth Amendment. Once Holmes switched sides, the law's validity was assured. As Brandeis later explained, "Gradually they all came with me." He once said that Holmes "is very powerful when he changes his mind," and *Hamilton* was undoubtedly a case in point. Yet to achieve this unanimity, modifications had to be made in the Court's opinion which were of extraordinary significance. While the War-Time Prohibition Act was sustained 9 to 0, the decision took the momentous step of establishing that war powers legislation would no longer be immune from judicial review.[16]

Plaintiffs challenged the act on several bases. They urged that the law had expired by its own terms and that it had been impliedly repealed by the one-year grace period contained in the Eighteenth Amendment. The Court rejected both of these arguments. In addition, plaintiffs contended that by destroying the value of whiskey held in bond, the government had taken their property without just compensation. Finally, they claimed that even if the measure was valid when adopted in November 1918, it was no longer constitutionally enforceable owing to the passing of the war emergency. While the Court disagreed with these contentions as well, it broke entirely new ground in doing so.[17]

Hamilton was faithful to tradition in one respect. The justices refused to consider whether the War-Time Prohibition Act was a bona fide war measure, stating, "No principle of our constitutional law is more firmly established than that this court may not, in passing upon the validity of a statute, enquire into the motives of Congress." Beyond this, however, the Court entered new waters. Addressing the Bill of Rights contention first, Justice Brandeis declared in unequivocal terms that "the war power of the United States, like its other powers and like the police power of the States, is subject to applicable constitutional limitations." The novelty of this proposition, dropped by the Court almost in passing, was betrayed by the meager authority cited in its support. Besides the 1866 dictum in *Ex parte Milligan,* Brandeis noted four other cases, none of which involved or even mentioned the war powers. Conspicuously absent were the six Espionage and Sedition Acts decisions issued earlier in the year, for the majority there had rejected appellants' First Amendment claims without clearly indicating that the war powers are limited by the Bill of Rights. Having held that the War-Time Prohibition Act was subject to the Fifth Amendment, the Court ruled that there had been no taking since the law's seven-month delay gave dealers a reasonable opportunity to dispose of liquor held in storage.[18]

Brandeis needed no prodding to declare that Congress's use of the war powers is controlled by the Bill of Rights. Only five weeks earlier he had joined Holmes's dissent in *Abrams v. United States,* urging that defendant's Sedition Act conviction violated the First Amendment. In the initial draft of his opinion in *Hamilton* Brandeis thus explained that the War-Time Prohibition Act was "subject, of course, to every applicable constitutional limitation," including "the Fifth Amendment."[19]

His first draft, however, took a very different approach to the claim that the act "became void . . . by reason of the passing of the war emergency." This contention was similar to the durational challenges summarily rejected in the *Dakota Cases,* and Brandeis proposed the same treatment here: "To state this question is to answer it. The whole responsibility for the conduct of war and the making of peace is imposed, within their respective spheres, upon Congress and the President. Whether they agree or disagree as to what is necessary or desirable, this Court is powerless to control the exercise of the judgment vested in them, or either of them." He acknowledged the resemblance to a pair of decisions announced five years earlier involving Congress's power to regulate Indian affairs. In those suits the Court recognized that the validity of legislation banning the sale of liquor in certain territory was dependent on the continued presence of Indians there. "In both cases," said Brandeis, "the court suggested that after the practical disappearance of the Indian wards of the Government the prohibition might not be within the constitutional power of the United States . . . because the power expired with the expiration of the guardianship, just as the present power will expire with the ending of the war emergency." Yet the parallel was misleading, for "the existence of Indians upon the lands . . . is not a legislative matter, but purely a question of fact which must be established before the court. The existence of the war emergency, on the other hand, is not a judicial question but is solely one for the legislative and executive branches of the Government. In other words, it is a political and not a judicial question." The draft thus concluded that "the necessity for the continuance of war-time prohibition is not a question for judicial cognizance." According to this theory, as long as the government did not violate the Bill of Rights, it was free to enact and enforce legislation under the war powers any time it wished.[20]

In later versions of the opinion Brandeis deleted all references to the political question doctrine and replaced them with language suggesting that the allowable duration of the war powers is a legitimate matter for judicial review. Though plaintiffs did not dispute that the War-Time Prohibition Act had been proper when adopted shortly after the armistice, the Court was willing to assume "that the implied power to enact such a prohibition must depend not upon the existence of a technical state of war, terminable only with the ratification of a treaty of peace or a proclamation of peace, but upon some actual emergency or necessity arising out of the war or incident to it." With respect to the subsequent enforceability of such a measure, Brandeis now relied on the Indian cases as establishing that "a statute valid when enacted may cease to have validity owing to a change of circumstances." The Court conceded "for the purposes of the present case, that . . . the continued validity of the war prohibition act under the changed circumstances depends upon whether it appears that there is no longer any necessity for the prohibition of the sale of distilled spirits." While *Hamilton* stopped short of a square holding to this effect, it strongly implied that the enactment and enforcement of war powers legislation are both dependent on actual war necessity, the presence of which may be ascertained by the judiciary.[21]

On the question of how strict it would be in determining the existence of such an emergency, the Court emphasized that where Congress is exercising "the war power . . . a wide latitude of discretion must be accorded." Brandeis stated that "it would require a clear case to justify a court in declaring that such an act, passed for such a purpose, had ceased to have force because the power of Congress no longer continued." Under this test the War-Time Prohibition Act remained enforceable, for it appeared from "facts of public knowledge" that demobilization was still under way and that other war-related activities, including federal operation of the railways, were not yet terminated. Unlike *Ruppert,* the case did not present the additional question of whether the statute was reasonably related to the war emergency. On this point the plaintiffs in *Hamilton* had agreed that "prohibition of the liquor traffic is . . . an appropriate means of increasing our war efficiency," and that the act was within the scope of the war powers while the emergency endured.[22]

The dramatic changes which occurred between the initial and final versions of Brandeis's *Hamilton* opinion were prompted by the Court's more conservative members. These justices, four of whom had originally joined Holmes in voting to find the act invalid, insisted that the draft be modified before they would join it. Mahlon Pitney served as a broker in the process. In exchange for the majority's abandoning its political question approach, Justices Pitney, James McReynolds, and two others—most likely Willis Van Devanter and William Day—changed their votes, producing a unanimous decision to uphold the act. These four justices were no doubt troubled by the prospect of the war powers being used indefinitely for purely domestic purposes. Pitney, who was the least conservative of the group, had voted frequently to strike down federal and state laws which, like the War-Time Prohibition Act, interfered with private property interests. McReynolds, Day, and Van Devanter shared these concerns and also opposed federal attempts to control matters traditionally regulated by the states. The concessions they obtained in *Hamilton* would help check future exercises of the war powers and were apparently worth the price of voting to uphold a law whose effects would be felt for only another month.[23]

One may ask why Brandeis was willing to modify his opinion, for once he had persuaded Holmes that the act did not violate the Fifth Amendment, there were enough votes to sustain the measure. Brandeis may have felt pressure from Chief Justice White and others in the majority who wished to avoid a 5-to-4 ruling on a matter as controversial as war prohibition. After the decision was announced, the *New York Times* found it "fortunate and salutary that there was no dissenting opinion. Bitter as is the disappointment of the Wets, they cannot murmur against this unanimous decision of the highest court."[24]

Brandeis's flexibility may also have stemmed from a realization that the government's unbridled use of the war powers posed a threat to civil liberties. Ten days before *Hamilton* was argued, he and Holmes had dissented in *Abrams v. United States* on the ground that defendant's speech was protected by the First Amendment. Brandeis would also dissent in two other Espionage Act appeals then under submission. These cases vividly demonstrated the inadequacy of the Bill of Rights as a shield against abuse of the war powers. Brandeis was therefore perhaps in a receptive mood when his brethren suggested creating the additional safeguard of permitting the judiciary to review the continued enforceability of such measures.[25]

The government's indiscriminate use of the war powers may have troubled Brandeis for another reason as well. Though he had backed many reforms involving state intervention in the social and economic spheres, Brandeis sought to maximize the scope of individual freedom. He believed centralization of power and the "curse of bigness" to be as unacceptable in government as they were in private business and thus rejected Herbert Croly's New Nationalism as a cure for the nation's ills. That these concerns were much on Brandeis's mind as he drafted the opinion in *Hamilton* is revealed by the memoirs of Dean

Acheson, his law clerk at the time. Reacting to reports that the states might deal with the pending coal strike by seizing the mines, Acheson said, "I am a States rights man," to which the justice replied, "Of course, so am I. What I have had impressed on me in my public life and private practice is that man's activities have outrun his abilities. He must go back to the smaller unit." When Day, McReynolds, and Van Devanter insisted that the war powers not serve as an automatic justification for federal incursions into the states' domain, they undoubtedly struck a responsive chord.[26]

Holmes shared these concerns as to the states' role in the federal system and may have encouraged Brandeis to accept the changes sought by Pitney and company. Holmes had dissented in the 1904 *Northern Securities* decision, writing that if the Sherman Antitrust Act could be applied to appellant's business, "I can see no part of the conduct of life with which on similar principles Congress might not interfere." During the war years he corresponded with Harold Laski about the alarming growth of central government in England and the United States. Laski attributed this phenomenon to reformers' claims that "State government . . . must . . . be overridden if progress is to be made," citing prohibition as a case in point. It was also significant that the war powers measure at issue in *Hamilton* was adopted after hostilities had ended. In May 1919 Holmes defended his decision in *Debs* on the basis that the Espionage Act provisions involved there "were proper enough while the war was on. When people are putting out all their energies in battle I don't think it unreasonable to say we won't have obstacles intentionally put in the way of raising troops." As his initial vote in *Hamilton* suggests, Holmes viewed peacetime exercise of the war powers more skeptically, a concern that may have caused him to favor language cautioning against their further use.[27]

The Split over War Beer

Though Brandeis had greatly strengthened the *Hamilton* opinion, he was dubious as to the judiciary's ability to check abuse of the war powers. He told Felix Frankfurter in 1923, "You might as well recognize that during a war . . . all bets are off." Brandeis was willing to deliver a warning to Congress, but he may not have expected the Court ever to enforce it. To this extent the unanimity of decision in *Hamilton* was deceptive, for it masked a fundamental disagreement over the Court's actual readiness to overturn war powers legislation.

This cleavage became apparent a few weeks later in *Ruppert v. Caffey,* when the 1919 amendment to the War-Time Prohibition Act was upheld by a vote of 5 to 4. Brandeis again wrote for the majority, but McReynolds, Day, Van Devanter, and Clarke now dissented.[28]

As posed by appellants, the main issue in *Ruppert* was: "Is there *now* such actual war emergency or necessity in this country as would in any reasonable aspect warrant the enforcement of the new and extensive prohibitions contained in the Act of October 28, 1919?" This involved two separate questions: first, whether a war emergency existed when the amendment was adopted; and second, assuming such an emergency, whether the prohibition of concededly non-intoxicating drink was a permissible means of dealing with it. The first issue was disposed of by *Hamilton,* where the Court held that there was a sufficient war emergency in October 1919 to allow continued enforcement of the War-Time Prohibition Act. "For the same reasons," said Brandeis, "the Act of October 28, 1919, was not invalid, merely because it was new legislation."[29]

The question of whether a ban on war beer was a permissible means of coping with the emergency had not been addressed in *Hamilton.* As appellants noted, "It does not follow that because Congress may exercise the power of prohibiting intoxicants in war time, it can go further and ban non-intoxicants as an incident to this implied incidental power." They urged that to sanction such an expansive view of federal authority "would strip the States of all their powers" and might eventually result in "one consolidated government in place of our present federal system." The majority was unpersuaded. Brandeis began from the premise that "the war power of Congress to effectively prohibit the manufacture and sale of intoxicating liquors in order to promote the Nation's efficiency . . . is as full and complete as the police power of the States to effectively enforce such prohibition in order to promote the health, safety and morals of the community." Since many states had found it desirable to regulate nonintoxicants under their prohibition laws, the federal government could surely do likewise. It was enough that "Congress might reasonably have considered some legislative definition of intoxicating liquor to be essential to effective enforcement of prohibition" and that the chosen definition "was not an arbitrary one." Having found that the statute fell within the scope of the war powers, the majority rejected appellant's claim that the measure had taken its property without just compensation.[30]

From the dissenters' standpoint, the majority was far more lenient in reviewing this act of Congress than seemed called for under the principles set forth in *Hamilton*. Justice McReynolds's dissenting opinion conveyed a sense of betrayal.

By considering the circumstances existing when the War-Time Prohibition Act was challenged, in order to reach the conclusion announced in *Hamilton* . . . this court asserted its right to determine the relationship between such an enactment and the conduct of the war; the decision there really turned upon an appreciation of the facts . . . [T]he power of Congress recognized in the *Hamilton Case,* and here relied upon . . . should be restricted . . . to actual necessities consequent upon war. It can only support a measure directly relating to such necessities and only so long as the relationship continues.

The dissenters had read more into *Hamilton* than was there. That case did not deal at all with the "relationship between such an enactment and the conduct of the war," for the adequacy of this connection had been conceded by the parties. In *Hamilton* the Court simply had no occasion to consider whether an exercise of the war powers must relate directly to an existing war emergency. Moreover, while the Court had closely examined the facts, it did so only to determine whether a war emergency still existed. The belief that *Hamilton* promised more exacting scrutiny of war powers legislation may have stemmed from the opinion's statement that the "power to enact such a prohibition must depend not upon the existence of a technical state of war . . . but upon some actual emergency or *necessity* arising out of the war or incident to it." Yet the word *necessity* here did not refer to the need for a particular statutory enactment but rather to the emergency Congress had chosen to address.[31]

Whatever the source of this confusion, there was sharp disagreement as to how close a connection was required between an existing war emergency and a measure ostensibly designed to deal with it. The *Ruppert* majority was willing to give Congress every benefit of the doubt, hypothesizing as to the reasons for outlawing nonintoxicating drink. The dissent was less accommodating. The question for Justice McReynolds was whether it "truthfully" might be said that imposing such a ban late in 1919 "could afford any direct and appreciable aid in respect of the war declared against Germany and Austria." He concluded that there was "no reasonable relationship between the war declared in 1917, or the demobilization following . . . and destruction of the value of complainant's beverage"; nor was there any basis to find that the law would "aid in an appreciable way" the proscription against intoxicating liquors. "It is not enough," said McReynolds, "merely to assert such a probability; it must arise from the facts." In the eyes of the dissenters, "well settled rights of the individual . . . and powers carefully reserved to the States, ought not to be abridged or destroyed by mere argumentation."[32]

Despite these differences as to the appropriate degree of scrutiny, the Court had agreed that legislation enacted under the war powers was subject to judicial review. In this respect, *Hamilton* and *Ruppert* marked the end of an era. From now on the constitutionality of war powers measures could be challenged on any of three possible bases: (1) that no war emergency existed either when the law was adopted or when its enforcement was later sought; (2) that the statute bore no reasonable relation to an existing war emergency; or (3) that the act, while otherwise a proper exercise of the war powers, violated restrictions found in the Bill of Rights. The first avenue was the most problematic, for the Court in *Hamilton* merely conceded its availability "for the purposes of the present case." The propriety of the second line of assault was clearly established by *Ruppert*, but under the majority's deferential approach it would be difficult to invalidate a war statute on this ground. A challenge based on the Bill of Rights stood the best chance of success, for though the Court had rejected such contentions in *Hamilton* and *Ruppert*, it did so on the basis of established precedent, suggesting that the same standards governed here that applied to other federal legislation.[33]

The implications of *Hamilton* and *Ruppert* passed almost unnoticed at the time. Most of the reaction came from wet cities and focused on the fact that the Court had upheld the prohibition laws, rather than on the principles of review it had articulated. The *New York Times* was "glad that a wild Bacchic explosion, a New Year's Eve of wastrels, is not to be," but was troubled by the fact that "the power of Congress to decide what a citizen shall drink has been established by the highest court in the land, and will be a precedent for future efforts of Congress to control his other habits." The *Chicago Tribune* greeted *Hamilton* with dismay, reporting that it would close four thousand saloons in the city and put twelve thousand people out of work shortly before Christmas. "It is wrong," said the *Tribune*, "to govern a nation in peace by laws which were passed for definite purposes when it was not at peace." The *San Francisco Chronicle* declared:

The position of the Court is sustained by technical reasoning, which is not persuasive. Even those who are in perfect sympathy with the conclusion reached ought to recognize that there is grave danger in any precedent leading to a custom of the courts to use legal technicalities based on forced assumptions to transfer to the Federal Government powers intended to be reserved to the states, especially when as an incident property lawfully acquired is thereby rendered valueless.

The *St. Louis Post-Dispatch* also saw *Hamilton* as enhancing rather than limiting federal power, writing that the Court had put "all the responsibility for the continuation of war-time legislation, when the emergency of war has passed and every reason for war restrictions has vanished, on the Congress of the United States."[34]

Few of the nation's legal journals even commented on the decisions. Of those that did, most failed to mention the fact that the Court for the first time had asserted its right to review the constitutionality of war legislation. One notable exception was Thomas Reed Powell of the Columbia Law School. Writing of *Hamilton* in the *Political Science Quarterly,* he observed that "though the war emergency was found not to have passed when the suits involving the statute had been brought, there was an implied concession that there might come a time when the validity of war legislation originally constitutional would be destroyed by change of circumstances." The only other exception was the *Harvard Law Review,* which declared that the principles announced in *Hamilton* and *Ruppert* came as a "staggering blow to what was thought a basic conception of our governmental system." The issue of "whether or not the war emergency has passed," it said, should have been treated as "an exclusively political question" whose resolution "is peculiarly appropriate for Congress, and peculiarly inappropriate for the court." The *Review* was pleased by the result in *Ruppert* but found it "startling" that "by the narrow margin of a single vote the court has repudiated a doctrine which, applied, might make an error of the justices in prophesying the outcome of an armistice result in irreparable disaster."[35]

Intermezzo: An Elusive Peace

The Supreme Court was not alone in its concern over the prolonged enforcement of wartime laws. In commenting on the *Hamilton* decision the *San Francisco Chronicle* observed that the country was "gradually becoming accustomed—and it is very dangerous—to the usurpations of Congress." It also denounced the ongoing use of the Lever Act, charging that "price fixing is no proper part of a peace policy." Charles Evans Hughes, who told the American Bar Association in 1917 that Congress's war powers were virtually unlimited, had begun to have second thoughts. Hughes was now defending many of those targeted under the Lever Act after the armistice. In a well publicized speech at Wellesley College in June 1920 he described the continued use of the Espionage and Sedition Acts as "nothing short of a reign of terror." A week later he told an audience at Harvard that "through a fiction, permissible only because the courts cannot know what everyone else knows, we have seen the war powers, which are essential to the preservation of the nation in time of war, exercised broadly after the military exigency had passed and in conditions for which they were never intended." While lawyers such as Hughes attempted to block the administration's enforcement campaign through resort to the courts, renewed efforts were made in Congress to repeal the wartime laws. Had these endeavors succeeded in the first half of 1920, further intervention by the judiciary might have been unnecessary.[36]

After the Senate again rejected the Versailles Treaty in March 1920, serious thought was given to finding an alternative means of ending the war. At an international level this meant terminating the state of war with Germany, adjusting claims, and effecting a resumption of trade. Domestically the goal was to abrogate the Espionage and Sedition Acts, the Lever Act, and the other statutes whose existence was tied to the technical state of war. Unfortunately for those seeking a return to normalcy, the issue was heavily entwined with politics. The president, who refused to abandon hope for the treaty, would not support any peace measure that might lessen the chances of ratification. Even a purely domestic resolution was objectionable, for it would reduce pressure on the Republican Senate to achieve the same end by approving the treaty. The Republicans, who were not especially eager to repeal the war laws, hoped to benefit from the president's intransigence by blaming the Democrats for the fact that peace had not been restored. As a result it was not until March 3, 1921, Woodrow Wilson's last day in office, that a peace resolution was finally approved.[37]

The GOP made its opening move on April 1, 1920, introducing a resolution declaring an end to the war with Germany and proclaiming the war over for purposes of those laws tied to its continuance. The Porter Resolution had been drafted by the Republican members of the House Foreign Affairs Committee and was expected to win approval on a partisan vote. Most Democrats opposed the international aspects of the measure, which they said unconstitutionally interfered with the president's power to negotiate peace. According to the *New York Times,* however, "that part of the resolution which would abolish the war regulations . . . has strong support, and, if not bound up in the resolution which proposes to end war with Germany . . . would be accepted by both houses without a partisan division."[38]

No one seriously expected the Porter Resolution to become law. Though Wilson had made no public statement on the matter, it was universally conceded that he would veto the measure owing to its international implications. Indeed, the president privately had told his physician, Admiral Cary Grayson, "If they pass a resolution declaring peace with Germany, I will then express my views in a message—which I know will be extremely distasteful to the Senate. I do not doubt but that they may try to impeach me for it." It was equally certain that Congress could not muster the necessary two-thirds majority to override a presidential veto. Yet doomed though the measure was, the Republicans figured to gain from it. The majority report accompanying the Porter Resolution declared that "the laws conferring extraordinary powers upon the President for the duration of the war are still in full force and effect and constitutional rights are still suspended. Many of these laws are extremely drastic and could be justified only as war necessities; but since the war has, in fact, long since ceased the justification for these laws no longer exists." A minority report replied that if the Republicans were sincere in their desire to terminate the war laws, they should repeal them "instead of . . . attempting to pass unconstitutional legislation for the purpose of embarrassing the executive."[39]

The House took up the peace measure on April 8, approving it the next day by a margin of 242 to 150—well short of that necessary to override a veto. During the debates Claude Kitchin accused the Republicans of "false pretense and hypocrisy" in claiming to support the measure when in fact "if they knew it could become law, they would not favor it." The South Carolina Democrat charged that the GOP was particularly opposed to repealing the Lever Act.

The big corporate interests . . . have demanded of the Republican leaders . . . that the Lever food-control act should be the last act that is repealed, because in these times of . . . great contests between capital and labor, it is the only act by which they can hold a club over organized labor and shout "injunction, contempt proceedings, jail sentences, the Lever Act". . . . The Republicans in Congress dare not at this session repeal the Lever Act, because they fear to disobey the orders of the big corporate interests.

Three days later the government began to enforce this statute against the striking railway workers.[40]

The Senate did not consider the Porter Resolution until more than a month later. In the interim the Democrats introduced a number of bills to terminate the domestic war laws without affecting the state of war with Germany. On May 9, shortly before the Senate was scheduled to debate the resolution, Wilson put an end to speculation that he might compromise on the issue. Denouncing the peace resolution, the president demanded that in the upcoming national elections Democrats campaign for ratification of the Versailles Treaty without reservations. It was now absolutely clear that if peace were to be restored during Wilson's administration, it would have to come through legislative action. Many Democrats were upset, for the president's role in prolonging the state of war could prove harmful at the polls in November.[41]

Rumors that this dissatisfaction might cause Democrats to break ranks proved ill founded. After a minor amendment offered by Philander Knox of Pennsylvania, the peace measure was approved 43 to 38, with only three Democrats voting in its favor. One of the renegades was Senator David Walsh of Massachusetts, who had supported the resolution in order to "remove the chaotic state of neither peace nor war" produced by the deadlock; "the Chief Executive," he said, "will not accept any changes in the treaty," and "the Senate will not accept the treaty . . . as submitted by the President."[42]

The Knox Resolution, as it was now called, won easy approval in the House, though still shy of what was needed to override a veto. George Huddleston, an Alabama Democrat, supported the proposal, saying, "Harsh war laws are yet being harshly enforced. Their time of usefulness has passed." Stephen Porter of Pennsylvania, the measure's Republican author, believed that the legislation would force the president "to state whether or not he intends to relinquish the extraordinary war powers vested in him by Congress . . . or if he intends to remain a dictator." One Republican even suggested that when the president "finds that Congress, by a great majority in both its branches, has insisted by this resolution upon having peace, the veto will not be forthcoming."[43]

Wilson vetoed the measure on May 27, stating that it would "place an ineffaceable stain upon the gallantry and honor of the United States" to make peace "without exacting from the German Government any action by way of setting right the infinite wrongs which it did." The *New York World* applauded the move, charging that the Knox Resolution "was a mean, miserable, cowardly subterfuge, conceived in political malice. Not a man who voted for it ever expected that it would take effect. The only purpose behind it was a partisan purpose, born of a campaign effort to make the President take the responsibility for continuing the state of war." An attempt by the House to override the veto met with failure.[44]

Having done their best to embarrass the president, the Republicans decided to back an exclusively domestic peace resolution that would enjoy sufficient bipartisan support to survive a veto. Action would have to occur quickly, however, since Congress was due to recess in early June and would not meet again until after the elections. Maryland Senator Joseph France urged that Congress should if necessary "remain in session and mercilessly strip from the Executive every one of those enormous powers which were conferred for the period of the war." The Republicans chose as their vehicle a measure introduced in the House by Andrew Volstead on June 1. Perhaps because its prospects were excellent, several key war statutes were exempted from the resolution, including the Trading with the Enemy Act, the Espionage and Sedition Acts, the Lever Act, and the District of Columbia rent law. The Republicans sought the best of both worlds; while they hoped to take credit for restoring peace at home, they were unwilling to surrender the government's ability to continue prosecuting radicals, strikers, and profiteers.[45]

Claude Kitchin's prophecy had come true. In defending the exclusion of the Lever Act, the House committee report made no mention of the law's utility as an antistrike weapon but noted that the "provisions against profiteering . . . are very much more drastic and effective than any law Congress can pass under its peace power." This reluctance to terminate the Lever Act reflected the fact that the cost of living remained a source of great concern. Congress had just appropriated $500,000 for the Justice Department's campaign against profiteering, and federal grand juries were then in the midst of returning indictments against the railroad "outlaws," who were still out on strike.[46]

Even though it would not terminate all of the war laws, the Volstead Resolution constituted a major step toward restoring peace at home. Democratic Congressman William Igoe of Missouri unsuccessfully sought to have the Lever Act repealed as well. The resolution nevertheless had almost universal support. Tom Connally, a Texas Democrat, declared that he would "vote for the bill as the best measure possible under the circumstances." A similar view was expressed by Wells Goodykoontz, a West Virginia Republican, who had wished the resolution broadened but decided that "if I cannot get a whole loaf I will take a half." The House passed the Volstead Resolution on June 3 by a margin of 326 to 3. The next day the Senate made a minor amendment and then adopted the measure without a roll-call vote. The House accepted the change in the early morning hours of June 5, the last day of the session.[47]

It was understood at the time that a president could sign bills into law only while Congress was in session. The Volstead Resolution reached the White House on June 5, prior to the 4 P.M. adjournment hour. Wilson, however, pocket-vetoed it and ten other measures because they had not arrived "in time for their proper consideration." Since this announcement was not made until after Congress had adjourned, the fact that there were enough votes to override the veto became irrelevant. Whatever merit the president's explanation may have had as to the other bills involved, it was questionable with respect to the peace resolution. Except for the exemption of a handful of laws, the Volstead measure was virtually identical to the domestic portion of the Knox Resolution, which Wilson had kept for six days and vetoed a short time earlier. It seems unlikely that this one-paragraph enactment would have required further study on his part.[48]

As it turned out, Wilson had ample time to review the peace resolution. One of the eleven measures pocket-vetoed on June 5 was a bill creating a federal power commission. It had been overwhelmingly approved by both houses of Congress and presented to the president five days before the end of the session. Senator Wesley Jones of Washington, chairman of the Senate Commerce Committee, described Wilson's failure to sign the bill as "little short of a calamity to the country."   These events transpired barely three weeks before the start of the Democratic convention, a fact which may help account for the miracle which was performed at the White House on June 10.

While meeting with Wilson that day, Attorney General Palmer announced that contrary to accepted wisdom, the chief executive could sign legislation up to ten days after it was presented to him (excluding Sundays), even if Congress had adjourned. Through this feat of constitutional interpretation the attorney general single-handedly resurrected the eleven bills which were thought to have died on June 5. The *New York Times* noted that the attorney general's opinion, which caught everyone by surprise, "may result in the rescue of some very important measures."[49]

Wilson lost no time taking advantage of the reprieve. He signed the Federal Water Power Act immediately upon receipt of Palmer's advice, one day before the extended period would have expired as to it. Seven other bills were also salvaged by the ruling. They included a law permitting non–English-speaking persons to enlist in the army and a measure appropriating $35 so that Michael MacGarvey, a laborer at Governors Island, could purchase a new set of false teeth. Under Palmer's formula the president might have signed the peace resolution as late as June 17. That day came and went without any action being taken.[50]

The White House never offered a formal explanation for its refusal to approve the Volstead Resolution. In an interview with Louis Siebold of the *New York World,* printed on June 18, Wilson recognized that continuation of the war statutes was "irksome to a great many of our citizens" but placed the blame on the Republican party, which "has never reflected a sincere desire to ameliorate the effect of measures adopted for protecting the country in time of war. The Republican policy has been rather to exaggerate the effect of these measures." In a statement difficult to square with the historical record, Wilson denied that his administration had misused the war statutes and challenged his critics "to prove that the power given the government during the war has ever been unjustly used . . . [or] that any man has been punished for expressing his opinion." He praised the Lever Act, which would not have been affected by the resolution, and said that the "time for repealing it is not yet." Wilson also stated that "as long as these laws are on the statute books they must be enforced." For those unhappy with the situation he offered a simple remedy: "With the ratification of the Peace Treaty the operation of laws that were enacted to safeguard the interests of the country in the war would automatically cease."[51]

Congressman Porter was thus correct in his prediction, made after the first peace resolution was vetoed, that Wilson would "retain and continue to use these drastic war laws as a means of compelling the Senate . . . to surrender its prerogatives and ratify the treaty." The president's intransigence also reflected a rigidity of thought which had resulted from his illness. Dr. Edwin Weinstein has noted that "after his brain lesion, his metaphors often controlled his thinking. He maintained his principles of morality, honor, and duty: these categories, however, contained what others interpreted as unrelated and contradictory elements. In his classification, Wilson reduced complex issues to all-or-none questions of right or wrong, and of morality or immorality." In the president's mind the idea of peace was inextricably bound up with the treaty. He may have been incapable of grasping the notion of a domestic peace distinct from an international one, or of a peace resolution which did not constitute an inherent repudiation of his labors at Versailles.[52]

Even had Wilson signed the Volstead Resolution, the Lever Act, the Espionage and Sedition Acts, and several other key war laws would have remained in effect. He was therefore only partly responsible for the fact that war legislation continued to operate well into 1921. The Republicans nevertheless made the most of his opposition to the peace efforts. Their 1920 platform declared: "The President clings tenaciously to his autocratic war time powers. His veto of the resolution declaring peace and his refusal to sign the bill repealing war time legislation . . . evidenced his determination not to restore to the Nation . . . the form of government provided for by the Constitution. This usurpation is intolerable and deserves the severest condemnation." The Democrats by contrast supported Wilson's actions and campaigned for "immediate ratification of the treaty without reservations which would impair its essential integrity." The voters expressed their desire for a return to normalcy with unmistakable clarity, repudiating the Democrat James M. Cox and giving the Republican candidate Warren Harding the most lopsided presidential victory the country had ever seen.[53]

When the outgoing Sixty-sixth Congress reconvened on December 6, 1920, Andrew Volstead introduced a new peace resolution nearly identical to that which Wilson had pocket-vetoed in June. The measure provided for terminating the Espionage and Sedition Acts but exempted the Lever Act, the District rent control law, and several other war powers measures. Retention of the Lever Act was again defended on the ground that its antiprofiteering provisions were "broader . . . than anything we can pass under peacetime powers," for "under the war powers we can deal with local business . . . instead of only interstate and foreign commerce." Volstead, however, was now challenged by members of his own party. Indiana's Oscar Bland reminded the House that the Lever Act had been employed as an antistrike weapon, most notably against the coal miners of his own state. "To say that you want it to remain the law on account of profiteering is a mere subterfuge. It is cowardly to refuse to face the strike question on its merits . . . Why should this government longer hide behind a law passed for war-time purposes only? . . . If the security of the government of the fathers depends upon a state of war perpetually existing, we should find it out now."[54]

The recent elections had no doubt weakened Republican determination to preserve the Lever Act. In addition, the measure was by now all but superfluous, for since mid-1920 the cost of living and the number of strikes had both declined considerably. On December 13 the House dropped the exemption for the Lever Act and approved the peace resolution by a vote of 324 to 0. House leaders proclaimed the action as "one of the first steps taken by the Republican majority to fulfill the campaign pledge to put the country on a peace-time basis." In the Senate the measure was expanded further so as to repeal rather than merely suspend the 1918 Sedition Act; the House accepted the amendment on March 1.[55]

Two days before he left the White House, Woodrow Wilson was again presented with a resolution seeking to restore within the United States the peace that had descended on Europe more than two years earlier. While the president might have pocket-vetoed this measure as well, the gesture would have been futile, for in the November elections the Republicans had won control of the House and the Senate. This extinguished any lingering hopes for the treaty and assured passage of a fourth peace resolution, should that be necessary. Having held out to the end, Wilson signed the Volstead Resolution on March 3, 1921, bringing down the curtain on the most potent and despised of the wartime laws.[56]

The Demise of the Lever Act

Wilson's rejection of the first two peace resolutions enabled the government to continue implementing the war laws until his last day in office. Of the measures involved the Lever Act was the most widely employed. The validity of these efforts came under heavy attack in the courts as federal judges were asked to apply the principles set forth in *Hamilton* and *Ruppert*. By October 1920 challenges to enforcement of the Lever Act had severely crippled the government's campaign against profiteering. This would have been proof enough that the judiciary had accepted the responsibility to review war powers legislation. A few days before Congress officially terminated the Lever Act, however, the Supreme Court declared the statute unconstitutional.

The prohibition decisions suggested three bases on which an exercise of the war powers might be questioned. In applying these standards in 1920 and 1921, judges were unwilling to rely on either of the first two grounds—that the war emergency had lapsed or that the statute was not related to it. All of the decisions overturning war laws rested on a finding that the measure violated the Bill of Rights.

Durational arguments that the war emergency had passed were usually rejected out of hand. Some judges ignored *Hamilton*'s requirement that use of the war powers "must depend . . . upon some actual emergency or necessity arising out of the war," saying it was enough that the country "was still officially at war." Others cited *Hamilton* as establishing that a war emergency existed without inquiring whether conditions might have changed in the interim. One court, in finding that the War-Time Prohibition Act was enforceable in December 1920, acknowledged that the passage of time was relevant but took judicial notice "that nothing has since occurred to change the status existing when the Hamilton Case was decided." A Georgia district court ruled that the question was a political one, stating that "Congress and the President are the constitutional judges of states of war and peace and their decisions should be abided in patience by . . . courts."[57]

The sole exception to this failure to apply the prescribed durational analysis occurred in the case of a Polish citizen charged with having entered the United States illegally in August 1920. Though the district court rejected the petitioner's constitutional claim, it first determined that the entry ban was related to an existing war emergency. The judge noted that under *Hamilton* a war law might be struck down "on the theory that, the reason for the statute having ceased," then "the validity possessed by the statute during wartime has failed." The court held that with respect to this specific war measure "the reason has not yet ceased. We have as yet no peace with Germany. Our troops are yet upon her soil. The court may not say, with the completeness and satisfaction that seems to be required, that there is no longer necessity for a watchfulness of the entry of immigrants across our border . . . We do not have here the 'clear case' which must exist before the court may thus hold a law of the United States inoperative."[58]

Many courts were equally inhospitable to challenges based on the Bill of Rights. In ten cases decided between March and October 1920, however, the federal judiciary overturned sections of the Lever Act on the ground that they violated the Fifth and Sixth Amendments. The first of these rulings was issued in Arizona three and a half months after *Hamilton* was decided. The suit involved an indictment under section 4 of the Lever Act for exacting an "unjust or unreasonable" charge in the sale of firewood; the wood in question was sold for six dollars—two dollars above what the Justice Department considered a fair price. The court voiced "sympathy" with the government's efforts to control profiteering, but agreed with defendant that "the statute nowhere defines . . . what shall constitute an unjust or unreasonable rate or charge"; as a consequence "no individual can know in advance . . . whether he has violated the statute or not." The judge held the provision unconstitutional and quashed the indictment.[59]

A week and a half later a federal court in St. Louis dismissed sugar profiteering charges against the L. Cohen Grocery Company, finding that section 4 possessed "an indefiniteness, vagueness, and uncertainty which is dangerous, beyond excusing, to the property and liberty of innocent men." Echoing concerns raised when the act was before Congress, the judge warned that "no self-respecting man would remain in business, if his fortune, good name, or liberty is to be determined solely by the heated and prejudiced views of what is unjust and unreasonable . . . entertained by a jury personally embarrassed and harassed, it may be, by the inordinate rise in prices of all commodities." A few days after these words were written, Joseph Nichthauser committed suicide in Brooklyn following his arrest for selling a raincoat at what federal agents deemed an unreasonable price.[60]

In late April the profiteering provisions were held unconstitutional by a federal court in Detroit. Even though the local Fair Price Committee had set a maximum charge for milk, the judge enjoined enforcement against the plaintiff dairies, finding the Lever Act "too vague, indefinite, and uncertain to satisfy constitutional requirements or to constitute due process of law." The decision led to the dismissal of all subsequent profiteering suits in the eastern district of Michigan. At about this time a similar ruling was handed down in Colorado, causing the Justice Department to abandon its profiteering campaign there. By mid-June 1920 the provisions had also been invalidated on vagueness grounds in Texas, Kentucky, Nebraska, and Pennsylvania. In the Nebraska case the court declared that, like other statutes, "war measures must equally stand the test of constitutional limitations, and must fall, if rights guaranteed by the fundamental law are infringed."[61]

The Lever Act contained a severability provision which limited any judgment of unconstitutionality to the specific "clause, sentence, paragraph, or part thereof directly involved in the controversy." As a result, the decisions striking down the unreasonable-price clause did not affect the section 4 prohibitions against hoarding necessaries or conspiracies to restrict their supply. It was under the latter provision that the Justice Department had indicted the striking coal miners and rail employees. Two courts nonetheless invalidated section 4 in its entirety, thereby curtailing the act's utility as an antistrike weapon. One of these rulings, issued in Indiana on May 26, 1920, resulted in dismissal of all but five counts filed against the UMW for its role in the 1919 strike. Charles Evans Hughes argued on behalf of the union that section 4 was unconstitutional because of its exemption of farmers, ranchers, and dairymen. The district judge agreed, holding that the statutory exclusion was so arbitrary as to violate the due process clause of the Fifth Amendment. This decision put an the end to all further enforcement of the Lever Act in the state of Indiana.[62]

The Justice Department's efforts to prosecute the railroad outlaws met a similar fate in Pennsylvania. Several of the men named in the Chicago indictment were arrested in Pittsburgh on charges of conspiring to limit facilities for transporting necessaries. The case came before District Judge W. H. Seward Thomson on a government request to transfer defendants to Illinois for trial. Thomson had previously held that section 4 was not unduly vague, but in a decision issued on October 21 he agreed with the Indiana court that the exemption of farmers was "unjust and arbitrary in the extreme, violating both the letter and the spirit of the Fifth Amendment." This ruling not only freed the three railroad workers but also rendered section 4 completely unenforceable in the western half of Pennsylvania. According to the *Pittsburgh Daily Dispatch* the case was "considered by Federal authorities here a momentous one by reason of the number of Lever Act prosecutions which are pending and which are to come." Since the court in Philadelphia had earlier struck down the "unjust or unreasonable" price clause, the antiprofiteering provision was now a dead letter throughout the state.[63]

These cases present only part of the picture, for decisions upholding the Lever Act outnumbered those invalidating it nearly two to one. Some federal judges were simply unwilling to overturn a law enacted under the war powers. District Judge Frank H. Rudkin of Spokane, when faced with a claim that section 4 was impermissibly vague, agreed that "there is great force in this argument, and that it finds support in many adjudications and declarations of the Supreme Court." He even quoted *Hamilton* for the proposition that war measures are subject to the Bill of Rights. Yet he rejected defendants' challenge, stating that "a decision of such far-reaching consequences, involving . . . the very life and foundation of the government, should come from the court of last resort, and not from this or any other inferior court." This was one of the first cases to raise such an argument, but the same hesitancy undoubtedly affected other judges as well.[64]

Though fewer than a dozen courts held the Lever Act unconstitutional, this was enough to create serious enforcement problems during the last half of 1920. In mid-May, when only three or four such rulings had been issued, the Justice Department conceded that they had sown "much confusion and uncertainty in the conduct of cases under this law, to the embarrassment of the government and the public." By late fall the section 4 antiprofiteering clause was unenforceable in Arizona, Colorado, Indiana, Nebraska, and Pennsylvania and in significant areas of Kentucky, Michigan, Missouri, and Texas. The department noted that "great difficulty has been experienced by the investigative force because of judicial doubt as to the constitutionality of the act."[65]

The impact was particularly severe as to coal. At the end of 1920 the attorney general stated that "anthracite is practically all produced in the State of Pennsylvania, where the Lever Act prohibiting the making of unreasonable charges is unconstitutional in the opinion of United States district judges." The soft coal situation was reported to be only slightly better: "In five of the ten principal bituminous coal-producing States—Indiana, Colorado, western Kentucky, Pennsylvania, and Missouri—prosecutions under the Lever Act were prevented by decisions of the United States district courts holding the act unconstitutional." To circumvent these rulings the department began seeking indictments against coal suppliers in states other than those in which the mines were located. Early in 1921, for example, it filed suit against some Pennsylvania coal operators and distributors in New York federal court, where the statute was still generally enforceable, on the theory that defendants' acts of profiteering in Pennsylvania had increased retail coal prices in New York.[66]

At the government's request the Supreme Court agreed to review the Lever Act cases on an expedited basis. Ten appeals were argued together in mid-October 1920. Those contesting section 4, many of whom were represented by Charles Evans Hughes, alleged that the measure was invalid on durational grounds and also because it violated the Bill of Rights. As to the first claim, one brief explained that under the test articulated in the prohibition cases the question was "whether any actual war emergency exists at present, nearly two years after the Armistice." It went on to urge that the "slight evidence of emergency which the Court was able to adduce in disposing of [*Hamilton* and *Ruppert*] has disappeared, and now there is no war or wartime condition anywhere in the land, and all that remains is the fiction of a *de jure* state of war." The challengers also asserted that section 4 was so vague and indefinite as to violate the Fifth and Sixth Amendments; that by regulating prices it deprived sellers of liberty and property protected by the Fifth Amendment; and that by exempting farmers and food producers, it created an arbitrary classification contrary to the due process clause. In addition to these constitutional arguments, it was maintained that section 4 should not be construed to apply to the sale of goods.[67]

While the United States contended that section 4 was constitutional, its lead argument was that the issue of validity was a political question. The solicitor general "readily conceded that ordinarily legislation of this kind is not within the power of Congress to enact." Yet, he said, because it was adopted under the war powers, the government had an absolute right to enforce the measure without judicial interference: "During the period of an armistice Congress possesses all the powers which it possessed as a result of the declaration of war and is, as it has been during the entire period of the war, *the sole judge* of the extent to which it is necessary to exert these powers in order to properly protect the country and to meet any emergency that it thinks may probably arise before peace is fully accomplished." This suggested that the Court was precluded both from reaching the durational issue and from striking the measure on Bill of Rights grounds. The claim was remarkable in light of the *Hamilton* and *Ruppert* decisions handed down less than a year before. Even more astonishing is that the government cited these cases as supporting its political question stance, stating that "it was for these reasons that this Court held constitutional a prohibition act passed six days later than the Act now in question. These cases are conclusive of the question now made."[68]

The government's utter misreading of *Hamilton* and *Ruppert* passed unnoticed in the rather confused brief filed by the L. Cohen Grocery Company. Its lawyers admitted that the document had been prepared in advance, and that after a "perusal" of the brief of the United States they decided not to make any changes. "In fact," they said, "the proposition involved here is so nearly self-evident, that counsel are almost impelled to apologize for their own argument." Fortunately the point was ably addressed in an amicus brief filed by the Lake and Export Coal Company, which had been indicted two months earlier for profiteering in West Virginia. "The question here presented," said amicus, "is plainly a judicial question. Otherwise Congress would be the sole judge of the extent of its war powers and could exercise them at will and as despotically as it pleased, and in time of peace as well as in war . . . The justiciability of this question was, indeed, recognized and assumed in the recent wartime prohibition cases."[69]

The appeals remained under submission more than four months. When the decision in *United States v. L. Cohen Grocery Co.* was announced on February 28, 1921, it came as something of an anticlimax, for the Lever Act was then within days of being repealed. The ruling was nevertheless a momentous one. Speaking through Chief Justice White, the Court held that section 4 was so vague and uncertain as to be "void for repugnancy to the Constitution." Having concluded that the measure violated the Bill of Rights, the Court did not need to resolve the durational issue. As the chief justice explained, "The question of the existence or nonexistence of a state of war becomes negligible," since under the decision in *Hamilton*, "the mere existence of a state of war could not suspend or change the operation upon the power of Congress of the guaranties and limitations of the Fifth and Sixth Amendments," which had been violated here. Justices Pitney and Brandeis concurred separately; without reaching the constitutional issues, they argued that the section 4 proscription of an "unreasonable rate or charge" was meant to apply only to "compensation for services, rather than the price at which goods are to be sold."[70]

Cohen Grocery shortened the life of the Lever Act by only seventy-two hours. Yet the ruling was fatal to scores of profiteering actions then pending in federal courts around the country. One of Attorney General Palmer's last official acts was to dismiss the special staff he had hired to enforce the Lever Act. On March 12, 1921, his successor advised U.S. attorneys to dismiss any remaining profiteering and hoarding cases. Some of the suits abandoned involved large corporate profiteers against whom indictments had been sought only late in the game. These included actions against the "big five" meat packers, several coal companies, the giant American Sugar Refining Company, and Gimbel Brothers department store. After having been thwarted by lower federal courts in many states, the government's campaign against the high cost of living had at last been brought to a halt.[71]

The *Cohen Grocery* decision stands as a landmark in American constitutional history. In the War-Time Prohibition Act cases handed down fourteen months earlier the principles of review that Brandeis articulated had appeared so innocuous as virtually to escape notice. In the context of the Lever Act, the consequences proved devastating. This was only the second time in the Court's 130-year history that a piece of war powers legislation had been held unconstitutional. It was the first such decision to have any precedential value, for the prior case had been overruled a year after it was rendered. The *Cohen Grocery* ruling was undoubtedly made easier by the fact that Congress was on the verge of repealing the Lever Act. Yet that action may in turn have been hastened by the adverse rulings which had halted the measure's enforcement in many parts of the nation. The demise of the Lever Act was thus a genuine triumph for the canons of judicial review which the Court had announced in *Hamilton*.[72]

~ 8 ~

The Tug-of-War over Rent Control:
A Futile Exercise in Defiance

The war powers saw their most protracted use in the area of rent control for the District of Columbia. From 1919 to 1925 Congress was engaged in a running battle with the federal judiciary over the constitutionality of the rent scheme. In the course of this struggle the Ball Rent Law was extended on three successive occasions. While only the first of these renewals was based explicitly on the war powers, all three relied on the alleged presence of a war emergency to enhance the scope of federal authority. In reviewing these actions the Court had to move beyond its prior decisions, for here the purported emergency was invoked not to gain access to the war powers but as a ground for relaxing the prohibitions of the Fifth Amendment. Appeals involving the rent law reached the Supreme Court in 1921 and again in 1924. In the second of these cases the justices expressed doubt that a war-related emergency still existed in Washington. When Congress ignored this warning and continued the regulations for still another year, the courts put an end to the matter by declaring the statute unconstitutional.

The Rent Commission's Shaky Debut

The Ball Rent Law was approved in October 1919, but because the White House was slow in submitting its nominees to the Senate, the rent commissioners were not confirmed until early 1920. To give the new commission time to organize itself, Congress had provided that the more modest protections of the Saulsbury Resolution would remain in effect until sixty days after the commissioners assumed office. This transitional scheme was disrupted when, in December 1919, the Saulsbury Resolution was struck down by the U.S. Court of Appeals. Although the court did not cite *Hamilton,* which had been decided nine days earlier, it followed the principle that "the Constitution is not superseded by a declaration of war." The Saulsbury Resolution was found to violate the Fifth Amendment by depriving landlords of the use of their property and by arbitrarily freezing rents only on dwellings occupied at the time of its passage. The court suggested that its ruling would produce only "temporary embarrassment" since the Ball Rent Law had already been adopted as a replacement for the stricken resolution. The decision nevertheless caused panic as landlords took advantage of the regulatory vacuum to raise rents. The appointment of the District Rent Commission, however, appears to have come in time to prevent any serious harm to the city's tenants.[1]

Washington landlords promptly challenged the new law. A test suit was brought by Louis Hirsh, who had leased a piece of commercial property to Julius Block for a term expiring December 31, 1919. When Block refused to vacate the premises after that date, Hirsh sued for possession. The municipal court and the supreme court of the District denied the claim, ruling that Block was entitled to occupancy as long as he continued to pay rent. Hirsh took the case to the U.S. Court of Appeals, where it was heard by the same judges who had recently invalidated the Saulsbury Resolution. On June 2, 1920, the court overturned the Ball Law on the grounds that it deprived landlords of property and denied the right to a jury trial. The majority noted that while the rent law had been adopted under the war powers, this "adds nothing to the constitutional power of Congress." Quoting from Brandeis's opinion in *Hamilton,* the court declared that "the war power of the United States, like its other powers and like the police power of the states, is subject to applicable constitutional limitations." In a companion case the Court of Appeals explained that its ruling in *Block* rendered the Ball law "totally void" and left the Rent Commission "without jurisdiction" to proceed in any other cases. The local courts announced that landlord-tenant disputes would be dealt with "as if the Ball act or the Saulsbury resolution had never been passed."[2]

The Rent Commission continued to hear cases and issue rent adjustment orders, but its actions were utterly without effect. Landlords could have such rulings set aside by appealing to the District Supreme Court, though most simply disregarded the commission. If a tenant refused to pay the demanded rent, an eviction action was commenced. Three weeks after the Court of Appeals decision the *Washington Post* reported: "Proceedings of landlords against tenants are flooding the municipal court, where from 75 to 100 landlord-tenant cases have been heard every day for the last week. Washington landlords apparently have succeeded for the present in eliminating the rent commission in the settlement of disputes with their tenants." In these cases courts applied the old landlord-tenant law "as if the rent commission were not in existence."[3]

The ruling in *Block* was appealed to the U.S. Supreme Court. The case was argued in March 1921, three days after the Court issued the *Cohen Grocery* decision, which involved a different title of the same 1919 statute. The Ball law differed from the other World War I measures reviewed by the Supreme Court, for it rested on both the war powers and Congress's authority to govern the District of Columbia. Congress deliberately did not rely solely on its power over the District for fear the act might be found to violate the Fifth Amendment. *Hamilton* had not yet been decided when the Ball law was approved, and it was thought that complete immunity could be obtained by invoking the war powers. This notion had since been put to rest. It no longer mattered whether Congress had acted under the war powers, the District of Columbia power, or a combination of the two: the legislation was in any event subject to the constraints of the Bill of Rights.

In the Supreme Court the rent law was defended partly as an attempt to deal with a continuing war emergency: "The shortage of houses in the District of Columbia is one of the evils which have arisen from the rise and progress of the war." It was also urged that the measure was a valid exercise of Congress's "plenary police power in the District of Columbia." Louis Hirsh suggested, however, that the source of power was irrelevant. Citing *Hamilton* he explained, "War carries many and grievous afflictions, but among them is not the abrogation, temporary or permanent, of the constitutional limitations upon the power of Congress." The only pertinent question was whether the rent law was consistent with those restrictions.[4]

The Court implicitly agreed. In a 5-to-4 decision upholding the Ball measure on April 18, 1921, neither the majority nor the dissent asked if Congress had properly used the war powers as a basis for the law. Rather, wrote Justice Holmes for the Court, "the question is whether the statute is . . . an attempt to authorize the taking of property not for public use and without due process of law, and for this and other reasons void." The relevant inquiry was whether "circumstances have clothed the letting of buildings in the District of Columbia with a public interest so great as to justify regulation by law." If the war was immaterial as a possible source of congressional power, the existence of a war-related emergency was critical in determining whether housing had become sufficiently "affected with a public interest" to satisfy the Fifth Amendment. As Holmes noted, "Circumstances may so change in time or so differ in space as to clothe with such an interest what at other times or in other places would be a matter of purely private concern."[5]

Congress had addressed this issue in section 122 of the Ball Rent Law, which declared that the measure was "made necessary by emergencies growing out of the war . . . resulting in rental conditions in the District of Columbia dangerous to the public health and . . . embarrassing the Federal Government in the transaction of the public business." Moreover, section 106 specifically provided that in the District, "all (a) rental property and (b) apartments and hotels are affected with a public interest." According to the government these congressional findings that the war emergency necessitated rent control were decisive, "unless that conclusion be essentially absurd and such as no rational mind could draw." The justices unanimously disagreed, declaring that not only must the judiciary ascertain whether there is a sufficient emergency to permit exercise of the war powers, but it must also determine if an alleged exigency satisfies the due process clause. Thus, said Holmes, "a legislative declaration of facts that are material only as the ground for enacting a rule of law, for instance, that a certain use is a public one, may not be held conclusive by the courts." Yet such a determination was entitled "to great respect," and "in this instance Congress stated a publicly notorious and almost worldwide fact. That the emergency declared by the statute did exist," he concluded, "must be assumed."[6]

There being a "public exigency" sufficient to "justify the legislature in restricting property rights in land," the remaining question was "whether the statute goes too far. For just as there comes a point at which the police power ceases and leaves only that of eminent domain, ... regulations of the present sort, pressed to a certain height, might amount to a taking without due process of law." The rent law was found acceptable on this score, largely because it was a temporary measure due to expire in another six months. "A limit in time, to tide over a passing trouble," said Holmes, "well may justify a law that could not be upheld as a permanent change." The Court intimated that though the war-induced housing shortage was then sufficient to allow rent control in the District, an extension of the scheme might be unconstitutional. The four dissenting justices strenuously argued that even existing conditions were inadequate to support the severe restrictions imposed on Washington landlords. In a companion case, *Marcus Brown Holding Co. v. Feldman,* the Court on the same basis upheld New York's emergency rent control, also by a vote of 5 to 4.[7]

The impact of *Block* was immediately felt in the capital. Since the Court of Appeals ruling ten months earlier the Rent Commission had proceeded to decide cases involving thousands of tenants. Most landlords had ignored its rulings and collected whatever rent they chose. As a result of the Supreme Court's action tenants could now sue for rebates, estimated at several hundred thousand dollars. Under the law landlords were liable for double the amount of any overcharge, the excess going to the federal government. The Rent Commission's workload skyrocketed. Within seventy-two hours of the Court's decision it received 133 new complaints, and it soon had to hire additional staff.[8]

Block v. Hirsh was quite significant in constitutional terms. The decisions in *Hamilton, Ruppert,* and *Cohen Grocery* had established the Court's authority to review congressional exercises of the war powers, both to see whether a challenged law fell within their scope and to assess its compatibility with specific constitutional limitations. Yet besides triggering access to the war powers, an emergency may effectively enhance Congress's ordinary legislative powers by easing the restrictions of the Bill of Rights. The latter situation was presented by the District rent control case. While the Court in *Block* recognized that war-related exigencies may at times justify measures that otherwise would be unconstitutional, it left no doubt that here too the judiciary would independently determine whether an emergency was truly present. The decision added significantly to the evolving framework of judicial review over expansions of federal power premised on a war emergency.

A Seven-Month Extension

In narrowly upholding the District rent law the Supreme Court emphasized that the statute was "put and justified only as a temporary measure" which might "justify a law that could not be upheld as a permanent change." By reserving the right to verify that a claimed war emergency existed, the Court made it clear that attempts to extend such a scheme beyond "emergencies growing out of the war" might render it invalid. This admonition was lost on Congress. Two months after *Block* was decided, Delaware Senator Heisler Ball introduced a bill to continue the District rent law for an additional seven months. The measure was approved in August 1921, so that instead of expiring that fall, rent control would now "remain in full force and effect until May 22, 1922."[9]

Congress did its best to link the new extension to the war. A House report found that "the effect of the war on the housing problem still exists in the city of Washington, and that there is a necessity for the continuation of the Rent Commission and its supervisory functions." The report also said that the action was required by the international disarmament conference which was to be held in the capital in November. In the debates it was observed that on July 2, 1921, Congress by joint resolution had declared an end to the war with Germany and Austria-Hungary. Some urged that this precluded any further exercise of the war powers, but others noted that the declaration had not ended the technical state of war, for no treaties had yet been ratified. Like the original Ball law, the measure was also based on the government's authority over the District of Columbia.[10]

On the issue of constitutionality, congressmen exhibited a range of responses to the recent decision in *Block*. Some, apparently ignorant of *Cohen Grocery*, doubted that the judiciary would ever strike down a war powers enactment. Others misread *Block* as authorizing Congress to regulate rents in Washington for as long as it wished. Most participants in the debate realized that a more subtle analysis was called for. Senator Ball opened the committee hearings on the extension bill by explaining that when the Court upheld the rent control law in April 1921 it did so "on the ground of an emergency existing at that time. The question for the committee to consider is whether that emergency still exists. If there is no emergency existing now, the decision of the Supreme Court probably would not cover the validity of the act." Yet after framing the issue as it did, the committee failed to find that any such conditions were present in the District.[11]

Testimony at the hearings revealed that there was no longer a scarcity of rental housing in Washington and that the specific emergency conditions relied on in *Block* no longer existed. One rent commissioner stated that since the peak of the war the District's population had fallen by nearly a third. While there were still one hundred thousand more people in the city than at the start of the war, there were over six hundred vacant apartments and houses available for rent. According to Senator Frank Gooding of Idaho, "On every street, every few houses, you see a sign in the window 'for rent' or 'for sale.'" Florida Senator Duncan Fletcher agreed: "There is not now, according to the testimony which is before us, a shortage of housing facilities in the District of Columbia." He reminded his colleagues that *Block v. Hirsh* "distinctly said that the fact that we may now say that the emergency continues to exist is not conclusive on the court at all."[12]

No serious effort was made to refute these assertions. Senator Ball admitted that rather than a general scarcity the problem was "a shortage of proper housing facilities for employees drawing reasonable salaries." A House committee report candidly stated that the aim of the extension was to attain "more equitable rental charges." This was not the same emergency that had confronted the government when the Ball law was first adopted. As Senator Miles Poindexter of Washington emphasized,

It is said . . . that a public emergency continues to exist, and that the same reasons for the enactment of this legislation exist to-day which existed when it was originally enacted in 1919 . . . That condition was the absence of living quarters for the employees of the Government who were brought here to do war work. To-day a very different reason is urged in behalf of this act . . . It is stated, even by the proponents of the bill, that the reason why this bill should pass is that the rents which are being charged to people in certain instances are too high. That is not a public emergency.

The same point was made by Florida's Duncan Fletcher, who urged that if federal workers could not afford the going rent, "the remedy . . . is, in some way, to increase the salaries."[13]

In voting to extend the Ball Rent Law in August 1921 Congress thus addressed a problem distinct from that which was held sufficient to survive constitutional challenge in *Block*. From the standpoint of one seeking shelter, there is little to distinguish unaffordable rental costs from an inadequate supply of housing. Yet a Court imbued with laissez-faire might sharply differentiate the two situations. It was one thing to tolerate price control where supply and demand were temporarily distorted by war; it was quite another to sanction government regulation which interfered with the normal operation of the market.

Housing costs in the District of Columbia were not a result of gouging on the part of landlords. Between December 1914 and May 1921 rents rose 29 percent, or less than 5 percent a year. This was less than half the increase in the overall cost of living in the capital, which climbed more than 67 percent during the same period. Average rent inflation in other major urban areas was double that of Washington; of thirty-two cities studied, only three had lower increases than the District. This experience was no doubt due largely to the Saulsbury Resolution and the Ball law. Yet the fact is that given the cost of living in Washington, and in comparison with conditions elsewhere, rent increases in the capital were quite modest. Rather than having been guilty of profiteering, District landlords had not come close to holding their own against inflation.[14]

The reason why federal workers could not afford housing was that their pay scale had not kept pace with the cost of living. The real income of government employees had been declining for years. By 1920 the purchasing power of their annual pay was 25 percent lower than in 1914 and only half of what it had been in 1895. In a study of real wages Paul Douglas found that for the period 1890 to 1926 "no other class of labor seems to have suffered the economic losses which the government employees have suffered." By extending District rent control, Congress was forcing Washington's landlords to bear the brunt of a problem caused largely by the government's own stinginess as an employer.[15]

The unfairness shown federal workers and landlords in the capital is hardly surprising, for they had no voice in selecting those who ruled them. The city's residents chose no members of Congress, nor did they even vote for the three commissioners who governed the District, all of whom were named by the president. Senator Poindexter noted the helpless condition of the District's citizens in condemning the rent law extension:

There are but few communities in the United States where it would have been possible for a legislative body, controlled by the people upon whom the burdens of the legislation were to fall, to go to the extent that Congress has gone in this legislation in dealing with a people who are politically submerged, a people who have so long been denied any participation in the Government which deals with their property and their lives that . . . Congress works its will upon them practically without consulting their wishes.[16]

Yet while the city's landlords would suffer from a continuation of rent control, tenants would benefit greatly. During the August 1921 debates it was noted that landlords were already sending out rent increase notices in anticipation of the October 21 expiration of the Ball law. Among those who would be adversely affected were many of the nation's lawmakers. Representative Roy Woodruff of Michigan stated that he had been seeking an apartment for six weeks, and he feared that it would become "even harder than it is at present if the law is not extended." Congressman James Begg claimed that he would be evicted if rent control expired. While the Ohio Republican doubted that anyone was "more conservative along every line than I am," he was in favor of this extension. Representative Marion Rhodes of Missouri, complaining that he was already paying "at least twice as much rent as is fair and right," urged that "passage of this bill is the only remedy there is in store for us."[17]

This element of self-interest helped overcome any constitutional scruples Congress might have had. It also defused charges that peacetime imposition of rent control involved "communistic legislation" that "leads you right down the toboggan slide to Socialism." The bill to continue the Ball law until May 1922 won overwhelming approval in both houses.[18]

A Wolf by the Ears: Two More Years

Senator Ball had assured his colleagues on several occasions that the August 1921 rent law extension would be the last. The Committee on the District of Columbia, he said, "only asks to have the law extended for seven months, to tide over the winter months. Then, from April until October, when there is no great demand, because there are not as many people living in Washington, we feel that the rentals and the prices will adjust themselves and no further legislative action will be needed." In January 1922, however, another member of the committee, Atlee Pomerene of Ohio, proposed continuing the Rent Commission for an additional two years, through May 1924. The measure was approved by Congress after brief debate and was signed into law by President Warren Harding on May 22, 1922, a few hours before rent control would otherwise have expired.[19]

Unlike its predecessor, the latest extension did not rest on the war powers, for treaties with Germany and Austria-Hungary had been ratified in November 1921. Instead the May 1922 continuation was based solely on the power to regulate the District. Yet in an attempt to justify the protracted interference with rights of private property the act's opening paragraph stated that "the emergency described in Title II of the Food Control and the District of Columbia Rents Act still exists and continues in the District of Columbia, and . . . present housing and rental conditions therein require the further extension of the provisions of such title." The emergency referred to was a lack of accommodations for government workers drawn to Washington by the war. It was far from clear that such a shortage still plagued the city.[20]

In defending this extension the House report relied heavily on a March 1922 Supreme Court decision which again sustained New York's emergency rent control laws. In *Edgar A. Levy Leasing Co. v. Siegel* the Court concluded that as of September 1920 rental housing in New York City was still clothed with a sufficient public interest to permit continued rent regulation. Justice John H. Clarke noted for the six-member majority that "the warrant for this legislative resort to the police power was the conviction on the part of the state legislators that there existed in the larger cities of the State a social emergency, caused by an insufficient supply of dwelling houses and apartments." New York had carefully documented the existence of this shortage. Moreover, said Clarke, the Court could not "ignore the notorious fact that a grave social problem has arisen from the insufficient supply of dwellings in all large cities . . . resulting from the cessation of building activities incident to the war." He emphasized that it was a similar emergency—"a very great shortage in dwelling house accommodations"—which a year earlier had been the basis for upholding the identical New York statute in *Feldman* and the District of Columbia rent law in *Block*.[21]

Given the Court's emphasis on the importance of a shortage in the supply of housing, it is no wonder that in extending the Ball law for another two years Congress recited that the action was necessitated by the same emergency that had prompted the 1919 rent control law. Yet the debates showed that there was no longer a housing shortage in the capital but that the problem was rather one of price. Housing costs were already high relative to income; if controls were lifted, the situation might become worse. Congress, having imposed rent control, feared that it now had a wolf by the ears. In describing "The Emergency" a House report stated that "failure to extend the act will result in the most vexatious attempts at extortion, excessive and exorbitant increases in rent, and will greatly inconvenience and harass many of the poorer and humbler citizens of the District." It was said that landlords, expecting rent control to end on May 22, were already advising tenants to vacate unless they paid higher rent. While these concerns were certainly legitimate, they involved a very different emergency from those which the Court had found adequate to support rent control in *Block, Feldman,* and *Siegel.*[22]

Personal interest again played a role in extending the rent law, despite renewed cries that the scheme was Bolshevistic. Early in the debates Senator Poindexter charged that "if every Senator and every Representative who is a beneficiary of some action of the commission in cutting down the rent which he is paying . . . would refuse to vote, the number of votes in behalf of the bill would be very greatly reduced. " He noted that in addition to members of Congress, "judges of the courts which construe and pass upon the law are tenants who have likewise been liberally dealt with by the commission in fixing the rents which are to be charged to them." Among those so benefited, he said, were a judge of the District of Columbia Court of Appeals and a member of the U.S. Supreme Court.[23]

The facts of the case to which Poindexter referred had already appeared in the local press and were aired again before a House committee. The property in question was the Meridian Mansion, one of Washington's largest and most modern apartment houses. Its tenants included eight U.S. senators; four members of the House; Constantine Smyth, chief justice of the District of Columbia Court of Appeals; and Associate Justice Clarke of the U.S. Supreme Court. On April 21, 1921, three days after the Ball Rent Law was revived by the Court's ruling in *Block,* two of the occupants—Senators Thomas Walsh of Montana and Andrieus Jones of New Mexico—filed complaints with the Rent Commission seeking reductions in their rent. The building's owners in turn sought permission to raise all rents, a step opposed by five U.S. senators, a former senator, and Chief Justice Smyth.[24]

Though the commission was seven months behind in processing complaints, the Meridian Mansion case was taken up at once. On December 30, 1921, the commission issued a revised schedule of rents. Some tenants were awarded sizable reductions, while others were given increases greater than the owners had asked. Rents were lowered for all of the complaining public officials and for some prominent individuals who had not objected to the requested increase, among them Justice Clarke and several congressmen. Senator Walsh's rent was cut by a third, while Justice Clarke's was lowered from $290 to $230 a month. Counsel for the building's owners suggested that this "glaring discrimination in favor of influence, wealth, power, and luxury, and against the poor" was tied to the fact that the commissioners' appointments were due to expire on May 22, 1922. "View it as you will . . . it is 'fawning and favoritism,' the 'bending of the pregnant hinges of the knee' to greatness, the desire to court influence in order to secure the perpetuity of their job, that controlled the Rent Commission in the fixing of the schedules."[25]

If this case was at all typical, such courtesies stood the commission in good stead. Only one of the eight senators from Meridian Mansion voted against the two-year extension bill, and one other did not vote; the remaining senatorial tenants supported the measure, providing one-sixth of the affirmative votes cast. In the House three of the four Meridian Mansion tenants voted to extend the commission, while the fourth did not vote. Congress also provided that the incumbent commissioners, whose terms were about to end, could continue to serve until other appointments might be made by the president.[26]

The favors extended the judicial tenants of Meridian Mansion may have been repaid as well. In March 1922, shortly after his rent was reduced by 20 percent, Justice Clarke wrote the Court's opinion in *Siegel,* sustaining New York's rent control law on the basis of a "notorious" housing shortage said to exist "in all large cities of this and other countries." This at least implied that rent regulation remained valid in Washington, and the decision was so interpreted by proponents of the two-year extension bill. When the new District rent statute was later challenged, it was upheld by a unanimous three-judge panel of the Court of Appeals, one of whose members was Chief Justice Smyth. In neither of these instances can it be shown that the justice's vote was swayed by his prior experience with the commission. As with the congressional occupants of Meridian Mansion, the most that can be said is that the facts suggest a possibility that such influence was at work. Yet, inasmuch as maintaining the appearance of fairness is as important as preserving fairness itself, it would have been better had these officials not participated in the legislative and judicial proceedings which determined the Rent Commission's future.[27]

The Taft Court's Dilemma

A challenge to the May 1922 rent law extension arose out of a commission decision involving the Chastleton, another luxury apartment house. An August 1922 order lowered rents for all of the building's residential and commercial tenants retroactive to March 1. The owners contested the ruling in the District of Columbia Supreme Court, alleging that no housing shortage or other emergency existed at the time of the extension or when the order was issued. When the suit was dismissed, review was sought in the U.S. Court of Appeals, which upheld the rent law extension in a ruling joined by Chief Justice Smyth. The case was then taken to the U.S. Supreme Court, where it was argued in March 1924.[28]

There was reason to believe that the District rent law might now receive a less cordial reception than it had three years earlier in *Block*. While the high court had rebuffed several attacks on the constitutionality of rent control, critical to each of those cases was the existence of a housing emergency. While *Chastleton* hinged on the same issue, it was now quite possible that the justices would conclude that conditions in Washington no longer permitted the imposition of rent control.[29]

The makeup of the Supreme Court had also changed considerably since *Block* was decided in April 1921. Chief Justice White had died in May 1921, allowing William Howard Taft to assume the office he coveted more than the presidency. Before the end of 1922 additional vacancies occurred owing to resignations by Justices Clarke, Day, and Pitney. President Harding appointed George Sutherland, Pierce Butler, and Edward T. Sanford in their stead. Of the five-member majority in *Block* only Holmes and Brandeis were still on the Court. Except for Sanford the new appointees were conservatives who were generally hostile to government interference with private property and freedom of contract. Taft, Sutherland, and Butler could be expected to oppose the highly restrictive District rent scheme and to join forces with Justices McKenna, McReynolds, and Van Devanter, the dissenters in *Block*.[30]

The Taft Court was particularly suspicious of wage and price regulation. The ability to determine the rate at which goods and services are exchanged is, in Robert McCloskey's words, "the very keystone of the free enterprise system. Any state interference . . . infringes vitally on freedom of contract, which is the holy of holies for the knights-errant of laissez faire." That keystone had been weakened by the Court under Chief Justice White, which, in the face of war emergencies, had upheld the fixing of railway wages and the use of rent control in Washington and New York. These decisions were consistent with the established rule that rate regulation was permissible if a business was "affected with a public interest." Taft, however, thought this principle a threat to private property, and he equated many interventionist Progressive doctrines with those of the "Bolshevicki." He believed that the Supreme Court should act as a "bulwark to enforce the guaranty that no man shall be deprived of his property without due process of law." Nor was he alone in these views. The dissenters in *Block*, three of whom remained on the Court, had condemned rent control as symptomatic of a belief that conditions "are not amenable to passing palliatives, and that socialism . . . is the only permanent corrective."[31]

This hostility to wage and price regulation had manifested itself by the time *Chastleton* was heard. In *Adkins v. Children's Hospital*, decided in April 1923, the Court struck down a minimum wage law for women and children in the District of Columbia. The majority noted that this federal statute was not limited to businesses "affected with a public interest," and that unlike the rent measures upheld earlier, it was not confined to a temporary emergency. In a rare dissent Taft urged that an exception to laissez-faire was appropriate here since the law sought to aid those "peculiarly subject to the overreaching of the harsh and greedy employer." He carefully avoided deciding whether a measure applicable to all workers would be constitutional, suggesting that he might look differently on a rent statute that protected all classes of tenants, the weak as well as the strong.[32]

A few months later in *Charles Wolff Packing Co. v. Court of Industrial Relations* the Taft Court overturned a Kansas law fixing wages in certain businesses declared by the legislature to be "affected with the public interest." Writing for a unanimous Court, Taft emphasized that there were strict limits on when a business might be subject to rate regulation. The appellant's meat packing operation did not qualify as a public utility, nor did it fall into a category of enterprises traditionally regarded as "exceptional," such as operators of inns, taxicabs, and gristmills. It was urged that meat packing fell into a third class of "businesses which though not public at their inception . . . have risen to be such and have become subject in consequence to some government regulation." Taft warned that where it was sought to defend wage or price controls on this last theory, the measure would be closely scrutinized: "The mere declaration by a legislature that a business is affected with a public interest is not conclusive of the question whether its attempted regulation on that ground is justified. The circumstances of its alleged change from the status of a private business and its freedom from regulation into one in which the public have come to have an interest are always a subject of judicial inquiry." In concluding that meat packing did not meet this test, the Court noted that in *Block* the conditions which clothed housing with a public interest had involved "great temporary public exigencies recognized by all." While Kansas argued that wage fixing was necessary to avoid strikes and restrain food prices, the chief justice, in language boding ill for the District rent law, rejected the notion that the prevention of economic harm is a sufficient emergency to justify rate regulation: "The public may suffer from high prices . . . in many trades, but the expression 'clothed with a public interest,' as applied to a business, means more than that the public welfare is affected by . . . the price at which a commodity is sold or a service rendered."[33]

Without a "great temporary public exigenc[y]" of war the validity of rent regulation in the District of Columbia appeared to be in serious jeopardy. The Taft Court had even hinted that the decisions upholding rent control in *Block, Feldman,* and *Siegel* were unlikely to be duplicated. In December 1922 Justice Holmes declared for eight members of the Court that

a strong public desire to improve the public condition is not enough to warrant achieving the desire by a shorter cut than the constitutional way of paying for the change . . . The late decisions upon laws dealing with the congestion of Washington and New York, caused by the war, dealt with laws intended to meet a temporary emergency and providing for compensation determined to be reasonable by an impartial board. They went to the verge of the law.

Later, in *Children's Hospital,* the Court held that the District minimum wage law had not been "passed to meet a sudden and great emergency" and emphasized that this had been the critical factor in "the *Rent Cases.*"[34]

While there were thus grounds to believe that the Court might invalidate District rent control, other factors militated against such a ruling. The rent law was set to expire in May 1924, less than three months after *Chastleton* was argued. Under these circumstances a decision overturning the law might be dangerously provocative. The Court's power to void federal legislation was under heavy attack at the time. Senator Robert La Follette's proposal that Congress be allowed to override a judicial veto was part of his 1924 Progressive party platform, as was his plan for popular election of all federal judges. Judicial review was a major issue in the 1924 campaign, with the Republican and Democratic candidates urging voters to reject the La Follette reforms.[35]

The chief justice was keenly sensitive to the position in which the Court then found itself. As early as September 1922 he observed, "We are facing now another of the half-a-dozen attacks in its history which have been made upon the Supreme Court and its powers under the Constitution." Taft was troubled enough by these proposals to mention them in a 1923 Memorial Day address, though he was hopeful that they would be killed by the House and Senate Judiciary Committees. His optimism ultimately proved well founded, but in the interim prudence counseled restraint in the review of federal legislation.[36]

The Court had another reason to proceed cautiously at this time. Besides looking to Congress for protection, the chief justice was then lobbying for a bill designed to reduce the Supreme Court's caseload. The so-called Judges' Bill would shift a large number of cases from the Court's mandatory appellate jurisdiction into the discretionary certiorari category. The measure, drafted by Taft with help from McReynolds, Van Devanter, Day, and Sutherland, was first introduced in 1922. When nothing came of that effort, Taft enlisted the American Bar Association, with whose help the bill was reintroduced early in 1924. In February of that year McReynolds, Van Devanter, and Sutherland testified on its behalf, and in April the Senate Judiciary Committee reported the bill favorably. Passage was far from assured, and Taft campaigned vigorously, particularly in the Senate, where opposition was the strongest. While the measure was under consideration, the justices had every incentive to avoid a confrontation with Congress. Between January 1924 and February 1925 when the Judges' Bill was pending, the Court struck down only one federal statute, the invalidity of which was compelled by a decision handed down four years earlier.[37]

Conservatives like Taft faced a dilemma in *Chastleton*, for their antipathy toward price controls was checked by important institutional concerns. Given that the rent law would soon expire, the balance might have been expected to tip in its favor. Yet the calculus was complicated by developments which came to a head after the Court took *Chastleton* under submission. At the opening of the Sixty-eighth Congress in December 1923 the first of several bills was introduced to further extend District rent control. On March 15, two days after the Court heard arguments in *Chastleton*, a House subcommittee proposed that the rent law be continued twenty-six months, so that instead of expiring in May 1924, it would remain in effect until August 1926.[38]

A House report accompanying this bill noted that many tenants had urged continuation of the rent law, and stated that "conditions in the District of Columbia which prompted the enactment of the original legislation on rentals approved October 22, 1919, and the extensions thereof . . . not only continue to exist . . . but in the lower priced rental properties appear to be growing worse." It explained that while the situation was originally "believed to be temporary," it was now thought "to have become chronic and more or less permanent." The committee had given "careful consideration" to continuing the rent law indefinitely but decided "for the present" to seek a less ambitious remedy. As with the extension adopted two years earlier, the problem was the cost of rental housing, not the overall supply. The report noted that while hundreds of apartments were vacant, many were at "such high rentals and the surplus is so small" as to make it "clear that the emergency has not passed." The committee also expressed fear that if the rent law were allowed to expire, "a period of greatly increased rentals and wholesale evictions" might ensue.[39]

A survey conducted for the Senate likewise found that the physical housing stock was "more than sufficient . . . to meet the requirements of the District and there are many vacant apartments and houses," but added that "the rents asked for these are high and beyond the reach of the average income." To rectify the situation, the survey urged that Congress not "attempt to force prices down to the level of the existing salary scale" of federal workers, for this could "result in material harm to the best interests of the National Capital and the government itself." Instead it recommended that the government "eliminat[e] the difference between the pay of its employees and the prices asked for housing accommodations." Congress ignored this advice, for it was cheaper to regulate rents than to raise the salaries of the city's federal workers.[40]

In proposing what would be the fifth extension of District rent control since its inception in 1918, the House committee was confident that the measure would be sustained. It stated that "the Supreme Court of the United States has held constitutional and valid similar prior regulatory rent legislation," and noted that while *Block* and *Feldman* were 5-to-4 decisions, Taft's arrival had made the vote 6 to 3 in *Siegel*. A minority report suggested that *Block* might soon be overruled: "The new judges who have mounted the bench since that opinion was handed down . . . are not likely to align themselves with the pronouncement of Mr. Justice Holmes . . . We confidently assert that the present Court will repudiate the opinion of Mr. Justice Holmes at the very first opportunity and relieve the community of the baneful effects which ensued and still exist as a result of that judicial pronouncement." These predictions were repeated when debate opened in the House on April 14. If the Court wished to renounce its decision in *Block,* the vehicle for doing so was at hand.[41]

The End Proclaimed

The ruling in *Chastleton* was handed down on April 21, 1924. In a brief opinion by Holmes, joined by all of his brethren save Brandeis, the Court applied the reasoning of *Block.* The question was whether in the three years since that case was decided circumstances "had so far changed as to affect the constitutional applicability of the law." When Congress extended the act in May 1922, it had stated that a wartime housing emergency continued in effect; but, said Holmes, the finding was not conclusive, for "a Court is not at liberty to shut its eyes to an obvious mistake, when the validity of the law depends upon the truth of what is declared." Moreover, even if such conditions obtained in May 1922, the relevant time was three months later, when the commission had issued its order against the Chastleton. Insofar as Congress's "declaration looks to the future," wrote

Holmes, "it can be no more than prophecy and is liable to be controlled by events." The case was remanded for a determination of whether a housing emergency existed in Washington in August 1922.[42]

Had the opinion stopped here, it might have had little impact, for the lower courts could have found that a scarcity of affordable housing warranted an extension of controls. The Court, however, foreclosed this possibility. Holmes noted that "the exigency ... upon which the continued operation of the law depended" was a housing shortage caused by "the sudden afflux of people to Washington" during the war. That crisis might have passed by August 1922, owing to reduced "Government ... demand for employees" and "extensive activity in building." As to the fact that rents might be high, Holmes declared, "If about all that remains of war conditions is the increased cost of living, that is not in itself a justification for the act." The Court thus rejected as constitutionally inadequate the very emergency Congress had relied upon for the 1922 statute, and which it was then in the process of invoking as the basis for a further extension.[43]

While the Court refrained from invalidating District rent control, it strongly implied that given the conditions existing in 1922, the measure should be struck down on remand. The decision cast an even darker shadow over the rent law, for in the final paragraph of the opinion Holmes wrote, "If the question were only whether the statute is in force today, upon the facts that we judicially know we should be compelled to say that the law has ceased to operate." In this remarkable dictum the Court declared that regardless of what the situation might have been in 1922, present circumstances were such that continued enforcement of rent control would be unconstitutional.[44]

Shortly after the ruling was announced, Brandeis wrote Felix Frankfurter that "to fully appreciate the rent decision, recent Congressional record & files of Washington papers on proposed extension of law to 1926 must be consulted." The extension bill had not yet cleared Congress, but there was little doubt that it would pass. Had the measure not been pending, *Chastleton* might have been resolved without addressing the constitutional issues. The justices would also certainly have avoided making a wholly gratuitous pronouncement as to the current validity of rent control.[45]

Justice Brandeis demonstrated that the case could have been decided entirely on nonconstitutional grounds. When Holmes circulated a draft of his opinion, Brandeis replied that it was "admirable, if the constitutionality should be considered at all. My present impression is that it should not; and that I shall want to concur only in the reversal. But I want to look into the record further." The landlords had argued that even if the rent law were valid, the commission's order was improper for failure to comply with the act's notice requirements. After studying the facts, Brandeis prepared an opinion concluding that the order was void as to two appellants who had received no notice of the proceedings. With respect to the third appellant, Brandeis believed that his suit for injunctive relief had correctly been dismissed, for he had already appealed the rent order to the District Supreme Court. Since the case could be disposed of on these grounds, Brandeis believed that "to express an opinion upon the constitutionality of the acts, or to sanction the inquiry directed, would therefore be contrary to a long-prevailing practice of the court."[46]

The majority was by this time determined to reach the constitutional issues and summarily rejected the bases of decision suggested by Brandeis. On the statutory notice point Holmes found the argument not "sufficiently clear." As to the contention that the third appellant had an adequate remedy through his pending appeal, Holmes said it was "open to . . . doubt whether in a proceeding under the law [he] could assail its validity." Had the Court been so inclined, it might have asked the parties to clarify these questions rather than using them as an excuse to discuss the statute's validity. A few years earlier Brandeis had suggested to Frankfurter that "the remedy for the prevailing discontent with the U.S. S[upreme] C[ourt] must be sought . . . [i]n refusing to pass on constitutional questions if the case can be disposed of on any other." This principle of judicial self-restraint was flagrantly ignored in *Chastleton*.[47]

The Court violated another of Brandeis's precepts as well: "refraining from all constitutional dicta." In the first draft of his opinion Holmes rightly made no reference to existing conditions in Washington, for they were completely irrelevant to the case at hand. He addressed the issue only at the insistence of members of the Court who wished to invalidate the rent law then and there. After reading Holmes's initial draft, Justice Sutherland replied, "I voted to go further and declare the emergency to have passed on what we know." Van Devanter reacted similarly: "I . . . am still inclined to the view that we should end it now, but I have not had an opportunity to take it up with others who also had that view. There are strong reasons, as it seems to me, why we should determine the matter now. Many landlords and many more tenants are concerned. They should not be left in a state of uncertainty for the year or so that would be required for further proceedings in the lower courts." Justice McReynolds's response to Holmes referred specifically to the pending rent control extension bill: "I should much prefer to have you say that facts within the knowledge of the court make it entirely clear that no emergency exists & the act is no longer in force. This will put an end to miscievous [*sic*] agitation now going on in Congress & clear the air."[48]

Three years earlier in *Block* Justice McKenna had dissented, urging that the District rent law be declared unconstitutional. He was now content to remand the case for further findings. In contrast to Sutherland, Van Devanter, and McReynolds, the latter two of whom had also dissented in *Block,* McKenna found Holmes's first draft "Very Excellent" and was generally "in full accord." His only caveat concerned one phrase, beside which he wrote in the margin: "Is not this judgment and a criticism in some degree of Congress? The latter is to [be] avoided at this time." Holmes deleted the offending clause. This incident dramatically confirms that at this particular juncture the Court was anxious to avoid crossing swords with Congress.[49]

In his second draft Holmes made a grudging effort to satisfy those who wished to put an end to rent control, stating, "If the question were only whether the statute is in force today we might not hesitate to say that the emergency has ceased." He circulated the revision "in hopes of compromise" but without success. The chief justice "corrected" the draft "in accord with [the] majority view." The quoted sentence was modified to read, "If the question were only whether the statute is in force today, upon the facts that we judicially know we should be compelled to say that the emergency has ceased." The final version was even stronger; the words "the emergency has ceased" were replaced by the unequivocal declaration that "the law has ceased to operate." The Court had thus adopted a middle ground between those who, like Holmes and McKenna, hoped to avoid any pronouncement on the rent law's validity and others, like Sutherland, Van Devanter, and McReynolds, who wished to declare it unconstitutional.[50]

Chastleton was a masterpiece of judicial statesmanship. The Court had effectively assured the end of rent control in the capital but without invalidating the statute. That task, with its potential for alienating a Congress on whose good will the Court depended, was left to the local judiciary of the District. Should Congress extend the rent law again, the decision provided clear directions that the measure was to be held unconstitutional. All of this was achieved in conformity with the principles of stability and continuity that Chief Justice Taft held so dear. Though the Court had reached a different result from that in *Block,* it did so by following rather than repudiating the analysis of that decision. To underscore the point, Holmes wrote for the majority in both cases. Finally, by insisting that the *Chastleton* opinion be reworked, the Chief Justice was able to "mass" eight justices behind the decision, thereby providing the "weight and solidarity" he believed vital to the Court's institutional credibility. Even Brandeis contributed to the sense of accord, describing his separate opinion as "concurring in part," without adding that it was also a dissent. Moreover, Brandeis volunteered that if the case had "required us to pass upon the constitutionality of the District Rent Acts, I should agree . . . to the procedure directing the lower court to ascertain the facts."[51]

Congress Defies the Court

The ruling in *Chastleton* came in the midst of the debates on the latest rent extension bill. The decision quickly became a focus of concern, with reactions to it running the spectrum from dutiful submission to outright defiance. In the end Congress paid no heed to the Court's dictum and continued the life of the Rent Commission for another year.

Representative Ira Hersey of Maine had supported the previous extension law but believed that a repetition of that action was now precluded. While the opening clause of the bill claimed that "the emergency described in . . . the District Rents Act still exists and continues," Hersey observed:

The war laws have all been repealed except this one. We attempt to hold it in force by stating something that we know is not true. There is no war emergency existing in the District of Columbia . . . Rents have increased 45 per cent in all of the cities; and because they have increased is that a war emergency? . . . The Supreme Court says in their opinion that the war emergency no longer exists and that this rent law we seek to extend . . . has become void. Let us respect the highest court in the land, and, above all, let us respect our conscience and our oath of office under the Constitution.

Senator William King of Utah later commented on the same language of the bill, describing it as "a legislative inexactitude. Some persons who speak directly might say it was a legislative lie." King, who had opposed the 1922 extension, predicted that in light of *Chastleton* the pending measure was certain to be overturned.[52]

Massachusetts Representative Charles Underhill, who once favored extension, declared that to continue the law again would be to adopt the premise of Senator La Follette's proposed constitutional amendment. Underhill submitted that "those in the House who are opposed to the general proposition that Congress shall have the power to override the decisions of the Supreme Court—those men who believe that is contrary to the traditions of our Government and to the best interests of the Nation as a whole, should, as a matter of principle, vote against this report." Kansas Representative Jasper Tincher pointed out to his colleagues that by renewing the District rent control act, "you invite hundreds and hundreds of lawsuits, every one of which will be decided against the Government by the court upholding itself, and the United States Government pays 40 per cent of the expenses of those cases." Moreover, he said, "it is unfair to the people of the District, and it is unfair to Congress to ask us to stultify ourselves and pass a law in direct conflict with the Constitution of the United States after the court has said that it would be unconstitutional."[53]

Others argued that *Chastleton* did not necessarily preclude a further extension of the rent law, for the Court's statement as to the lack of a housing emergency had been made in the absence of a contrary determination by Congress. The most recent legislative finding had been issued in 1922, when the previous extension was adopted. Representative James Begg of Ohio declared: "If this Congress should . . . incorporate in this bill the statement . . . that a national emergency in housing in the District does exist as a result of the war, I will prophesy that the Supreme Court will never inquire into the finding of fact." Walton Moore of Virginia thought that the Court should "ascribe very great weight, if not final authority, to the declaration of Congress," adding: "We are not moved by any disrespect for the court in taking the step now proposed. We invite a further careful consideration of the question by the court as to whether it should defer to the declaration made by the legislative body."[54]

The notion that a congressional finding of emergency should be dispositive was in direct conflict with *Block* and *Chastleton;* for Holmes had stated that a "legislative declaration of facts . . . may not be held conclusive by the courts," and that "the court may ascertain as it sees fit any fact that is merely a ground for laying down a rule of law." If presented with a new legislative finding, the Court might change its mind as to whether an emergency existed, but *Chastleton* made it clear that housing costs alone could not justify a rent control scheme. Yet it was just such an exigency upon which the latest extension was based. By resting the measure on the very conditions the Court had said were constitutionally inadequate, Congress was adopting an extremely confrontational stance.[55]

A number of legislators asserted frankly that the principles set forth in *Chastleton* were wrong and that the case should be ignored. William Hammer of North Carolina told the House, "The courts have no power to annul a declaration of Congress as to the necessity of a law passed by it." In support he cited Justice McKenna's opinion for the Court in *Commercial Trust Co. v. Miller,* decided a year earlier. There, in ruling that the Alien Property Custodian's authority to seize enemy property had not lapsed in the fall of 1921, McKenna stated that "the power which declared the necessity is the power to declare its cessation, and what the cessation requires. The power is legislative. A court cannot estimate the effects of a great war and pronounce their termination at a particular moment of time, and that its consequences are so far swallowed up that legislation addressed to its emergency had ceased to have purpose or operation with the cessation of the conflicts in the field." *Miller,* however, was readily distinguishable from *Chastleton,* for it presented no question of whether the act was unconstitutional owing to a cessation of the war emergency. The sole issue was whether, in light of changed conditions, the statute should be construed to have expired. On this point the Court understandably deferred to Congress, which had specifically provided that the law was to remain in effect until Germany agreed to pay U.S. claims. That the decisions were compatible is suggested by the fact that not a single justice in *Chastleton* mentioned *Miller,* though it was surely still fresh in their minds. Even if the cases were unreconcilable, *Chastleton,* as the more recent of the two decisions, would control. Robert Luce of Massachusetts reminded his fellow representatives that "what men may have thought the law [was] is now of no consequence . . . The court spoke last Monday and said what is now the law."[56]

New York Congressman Fiorello La Guardia nevertheless contended that "the principle laid down in the Commercial Trust case . . . is sound and is the law on the question." A day after *Chastleton* was announced, he stated that "the House cannot agree with the viewpoint expressed in the court's decision. It is another instance of legislative progress being retarded by judicial decisions." The following week he declared that "as legislators it is our duty to meet the defiance suggested in the opinion handed down. It is for the legislature to . . . decide as to the existence of an emergency and not for the court to decide." Echoing Senator La Follette's philosophy of congressional supremacy, La Guardia declared that the issue "is whether or not the judicial branch of this Government will dictate to the legislative branch what shall and what shall not be law." Yet even La Follette acknowledged that until the Constitution was amended, Congress was bound by the rulings of the Supreme Court.[57]

The local press likewise urged that *Chastleton* be given no heed. Two days after the case was decided, the *Washington Post* advocated adoption of the extension bill, noting that "large elements of the local public demand and need this relief." On May 17, 1924, less than a month after the Court expressed its view that the District rent law "has ceased to operate," President Coolidge signed a bill continuing the measure for another year. In doing so he set the stage for what was to be the final round in the struggle over rent control in the nation's capital.[58]

The Judiciary Stands Firm

Within a week of the *Chastleton* decision landlords sued in the District of Columbia Supreme Court to enjoin further action by the Rent Commission. On May 10, after reviewing evidence showing that there was no longer a shortage of rental housing in Washington, Justice Wendell Stafford announced that he would rule in the landlords' favor. He agreed that "high prices for homes do not prove that an emergency exists . . . Everything we buy is higher now than it ever has been before." It was thus apparent even before Congress approved the extension bill that the local courts would treat rent control as a nullity. A Washington attorney wrote Calvin Coolidge suggesting that, in light of Stafford's ruling, it was pointless to sign the pending continuation bill. The president obviously thought otherwise.[59]

On May 19 Justice Stafford issued a temporary injunction against the Rent Commission, explaining that he felt bound by the Supreme Court's dictum in *Chastleton*: "It would be nothing less than effrontery, in view of that decision, to declare that the emergency was not at an end." Though his order technically protected only the two landlords who had sued, the *Washington Post* saw it as "a mortal blow" which would "render the rent commission powerless." The Department of Justice agreed that it "will virtually put the rent commission out of business."[60]

The commission later conceded that this ruling had "sounded the death knell of the rent law in Washington," but at the time it was unwilling to admit defeat. Cases were heard "as usual," even though, as the press observed, "all any other property owner has to do to keep the hands of the rent commission off his property is to invoke the equity court to issue another restraining order based on . . . the contention that the housing emergency no longer exists." The District of Columbia Supreme Court refused to issue a blanket injunction against the commission, reasoning that there might be "things to be done . . . in respect to its old proceedings which may be found to have been taken before the emergency had ceased." Yet on a case-by-case basis injunctions were liberally granted, with the result that the commission was prevented from fixing rents on fifty of the larger apartment houses in Washington.[61]

As the *Washington Post* described the situation in May 1924, the "status of the rent commission today is that of a body created by Congress . . . hanging in the air, with no place to go." It could no longer order rent reductions, and tenants were not protected against eviction if they refused a demand for increased rent. Most Washington municipal courts allowed landlords to recover possession in such cases, even if a tenant had continued to pay rent at the former rate. While tenants were free to file complaints with the commission, few bothered to do so, knowing that a landlord could easily obtain an injunction against the proceedings from the District Supreme Court.[62]

The Rent Commission's one hope lay with the District of Columbia Court of Appeals. This was extinguished in early November 1924, when that court, in the case of *Peck v. Fink*, held the most recent rent law extension to be unconstitutional. In finding that the commission lacked authority to lower Jacob Fink's rent, the court explained that under *Chastleton*

the emergency giving rise to the . . . legislation had ceased to exist on the date of the opinion, or April 21, 1924 . . . The order here involved was entered subsequent to this authoritative declaration by the Supreme Court, namely on May 2, 1924. While it is true that after such declaration, or on May 17, 1924, Congress purported to continue the legislation in force for still another year, there was no constitutional basis for the legislation . . . The opinion of the court is so clear and direct as to leave no room for doubt as to its meaning, and our plain duty is to apply it in the case before us.[63]

A day after the Court of Appeals ruled in *Peck* the Rent Commission announced that it would hear no more contested cases until the matter was finally resolved by the U.S. Supreme Court, so as not to "merely clutter up court calendars with endless suits." The commission's defeat became final on January 5, 1925, when the justices decided not to review the case. The attempt to continue the rent scheme for another year had proved utterly futile. The only persons to benefit from the extension were the rent commissioners, their attorney, and a secretary, each of whom was able to draw another twelve months' salary from the federal treasury.[64]

The wolf that Congress had grabbed in 1918 was at last set free. For the first time in over six years rents in the District of Columbia could rise to market-determined levels. Soon after the Court of Appeals ruled in *Peck* it was reported that "tenants, particularly those in modest quarters, the scarcest sort of dwelling in Washington, are facing evictions. They have asked permission of the President to pitch tents in public parks, and this permission has been denied . . . These are the people who are facing the Winter with nowhere to go." Yet the consequences were not as severe as expected. In spring 1925 the Rent Commission conducted a survey to determine what had happened to rents following the end of control. The study was undertaken a year after Justice Stafford's injunction and six months after the decision in *Peck*, affording landlords ample time to seek increases. During this period rent hikes were demanded from 45 percent of those in small houses and 30 percent of apartment dwellers; the average increase was 15 percent for house renters and 8 percent for apartment dwellers. The investigation focused solely on those lower-income dwellings whose rents had once been fixed by the commission. Since in most of these cases rents were presumably set below what the owner desired, the survey no doubt overstated the extent of increases following deregulation. The wolf had turned out to be rather tame.[65]

The Last Hurrah

One would expect Congress and the president to have been sufficiently chastened by the 1924 extension debacle to banish thoughts of a further continuation. Yet this was not the case. Calvin Coolidge mystified conservative supporters by his sympathy for the tenants of Washington, who urged him to press for additional rent legislation. In October 1924 he pursued a request by the Tenants League for permission "to use the Ellipse as well as Army tents and camping outfits, should the necessity develop, for as many persons as shall be made homeless by eviction." Permission was denied after the secretary of war said that tents could be lent only to "recognized veterans organizations," and that use of the Ellipse would be "objectionable as . . . entirely foreign to the purpose for which the parks of Washington were created and are maintained, namely: for the pleasure of all the people." The lack of alternative remedies may have persuaded Coolidge to seek permanent rent control for the District. The president's bill, drafted for him by the Rent Commission, was introduced in both houses of the lame duck Congress on December 29, 1924.[66]

It was one thing for Coolidge to have signed the earlier 1924 extension bill, which had passed Congress with enough votes to override a veto. It was quite another for this Republican president to step forward as a champion of rent control. In a letter to Coolidge's secretary the head of the Franklin National Bank voiced alarm that while Coolidge had recently been "elected by the millions of conservative Republican and Democratic voters—yet, almost his first act (if the papers are right) is to fall for the socialistic propoganda [sic] of this commission in its efforts to perpetuate itself indefinitely." Thomas Blanton of Texas, who had led the House fight against the previous extension, was incredulous that "such a bill would come from Calvin Coolidge," for it "carries socialistic ideas further than many socialists . . . would be willing to hang as a millstone around the neck of this Republic." Remarking that he "had more confidence in the sane, conservative character and disposition of the President of the United States," Blanton added, "I am forced to the conclusion that he is getting this pink rash."[67]

There was a more plausible explanation for Coolidge's seemingly uncharacteristic behavior. His close identification with the tenants of Washington probably reflected his embarrassment a few years earlier when, as vice president–elect, he and his family arrived in the capital, found themselves unable to rent a house they could afford, and were forced to take rooms at the New Willard Hotel, where they lived until moving to the White House in August 1923. Coolidge described the incident in his autobiography and recommended "that an official residence with suitable maintenance should be provided for the Vice-

President . . . The great office should have a settled and permanent habitation and a place, irrespective of the financial ability of its temporary occupant." The experience may account for what, to his followers, was an inexplicable chink in the president's laissez-faire armor.[68]

Joint hearings on a new rent control extension were held in January 1925. The following month committees in both houses recommended that the Rent Commission be continued for two years. No action was taken on Coolidge's bill for a permanent law. The Senate report noted that owing to the rulings in *Chastleton* and *Peck,* "The rents act is not functioning at the present time." Nevertheless, under the heading "Continuation of War Emergency," the report stated that "present rental conditions constitute an emergency . . . attributable in part to the war," and that "rental property . . . in the District is clothed with public interest." The exigency was identified as "excessive rents," identical to that relied upon in the ill-fated 1924 extension. Though the Supreme Court and Court of Appeals had made it clear that this was not an adequate justification, the Senate committee, in a belligerent mood, declared that "the facts it has ascertained . . . force it to disagree with the judicial knowledge that was asserted in the Chastleton case to the effect that the emergency conditions growing out of the war have terminated." That Congress should seriously consider another extension of rent control was perhaps not unexpected, for this was the same body that had spurned the Court nine months earlier by extending the rent law until May 1925.[69]

The bill failed not because of any second thoughts about defying the judiciary but as a result of massive lobbying by real estate and financial interests. As early as October 1924 property owners in the District had promised vigorously to oppose another continuation of the rent law. According to the Rent Commission, once President Coolidge submitted his extension bill to Congress in December,

Washington realty brokers and operators undertook a campaign of national propaganda and sent to real estate brokers throughout the United States, and even in Canada, circular letters urging them to write to the President, their Senators, and Congressmen, opposing further rent legislation . . . They pointed out that if the legislation were continued here as it had been in New York State it might spread throughout all the large cities of the country.

The realtors met with Coolidge but so angered him by remarks published afterward as to prompt a White House announcement that "real estate men interested in defeating the bill will have no more audiences." The giant New York Life Insurance Company dramatized its opposition by refusing loans to property owners in the nation's capital, advising disappointed borrowers that "in view of the pending legislation now before Congress . . . known as 'The District of Columbia Rent Act'—this Company feels that it cannot safely make any further commitments for loans secured by mortgages on real estate for residential purposes within the District of Columbia." The company added, "We can only hope that this legislation may be defeated, so that Washington may continue to be as it has been in the past, an outlet of our funds for investment."[70]

The real estate industry had also fought the May 1924 extension bill, but that effort paled in comparison with the 1925 campaign. Members of Congress could no longer vote to continue rent control without fearing reprisal at the polls. The specter that the states might begin duplicating the District rent law had made the issue one of national concern. Indeed, New York's rent control law, first adopted in 1920, had already been extended several times and was not due to expire until 1926. Representative Thomas Blanton of Texas asked his colleagues,

Are you surprised that New York has such a law? Why, with all of its foreign citizenship . . . you should not wonder at its laws. I told you once before how I stood at the intersection of Fifth Avenue and Broadway and saw that procession of foreigners march down the street from 9 o'clock A.M. until 6 in the afternoon without a break in it, 25 to 30 abreast, and every one of them of foreign citizenship. They were still passing there when I left late that afternoon. They could get almost any kind of socialistic law passed there . . . Is the Congress of the United States going to take the New York law as a model for the rest of the country? God forbid.

Had the bill come to a vote before Congress adjourned, the odds would have been heavily against its passage. As it was, opponents prevented the measure from being considered. The Ball Rent Law expired on May 22, 1925, bringing to a close the final chapter in the government's use of its war powers after the 1918 armistice.[71]

The episode is a fitting one with which to conclude, for it highlights the great distance the federal judiciary had come in the six and a half years since hostilities ended. Having begun with a rule which virtually immunized congressional exercises of the war powers from scrutiny, the courts ultimately succeeded in halting a rent control law whose roots lay in the war powers and which had been extended repeatedly on the ground that a war emergency continued to exist. In contrast to *Cohen Grocery*, in which the Lever Act was invalidated on the verge of its repeal, the District rent decisions were issued in the face of a defiant and unrepenting Congress. In this tug-of-war over rent control the principles announced in *Hamilton* were severely tested but proved equal to the task.

~ 9 ~

Preserving the Legacy:
The Timing of Judicial Intervention

In the wake of World War I the Supreme Court decreed that laws passed in the name of war are subject to judicial scrutiny. Emergency action—whether taken by the executive alone or with the authorization of Congress—may be reviewed by the courts to assure its constitutionality. This fundamental principle is of great significance today, for since *Hamilton* was decided in 1919, the government's opportunities to exercise extraordinary power have increased considerably. World War II was not formally terminated until 1951, six years after the surrender of Japan; the Korean War emergency remained in effect until 1978, twenty-five years after the truce. In addition, there are currently some 470 statutes which augment the president's authority in wartime or whenever he believes that a national emergency exists. One of these measures, the International Emergency Economic Powers Act, was invoked by President Ronald Reagan to declare national emergencies and impose embargoes against Libya, South Africa, and Nicaragua. Indeed, because of a series of domestic and international crises the United States has been in a state of emergency almost continuously since 1933.[1]

The Continuing Potential for Abuse

One of the principal dangers posed by the war powers in the World War I era was that the government might use them to invade the regulatory domain of the states. Since 1937 this states' rights objection has been rendered obsolete by the Court's expansive reading of the commerce clause. Today there is practically no facet of American life which Congress may not regulate if it wishes, on the theory that the activity affects interstate commerce.[2]

War and emergency measures may still be challenged under the Bill of Rights or as violating the separation of powers between the executive and Congress. While the latter doctrine concerns the structure of government, the Court has emphasized that "the declared purpose of separating and dividing the powers of government ... was to 'diffus[e] power the better to secure liberty.' " Separation of powers was not an issue in the immediate post–World War I years, for President Wilson secured statutory authorization for virtually all of his administration's war powers actions, including seizure of the telephone and telegraph; control of the railroads; prohibition; the prosecution of strikers, profiteers, and radicals; and censorship of the press. The landscape changed dramatically with the rise of the "Imperial Presidency," an institution which has endured despite attempts by Congress after Vietnam and Watergate to reclaim its lost authority. This increased centralization of power in the executive has seriously impaired the constitutional system of checks and balances. The Iran-Contra affair of the Reagan presidency is but one reminder of the fact that administrations often feel no obligation to obtain legislative approval before taking major action in the foreign and domestic fields.[3]

There is a recurring danger that the executive will exceed its constitutional authority and invade the legislative sphere. This may occur if a president goes to war without the sanction of Congress. The 1973 War Powers Resolution did little to alleviate this risk, as witnessed by the invasion of Grenada, the bombing of Libya, and the granting of military aid to the Nicaraguan Contras. On the domestic front, separation of powers may be violated if the executive seeks to enforce policies of his own making or implements the law contrary to the intent of Congress. Even where he follows existing legislation, there is no assurance that his conduct has the approval of Congress. Most of the nearly five hundred war and emergency statutes upon which a president can draw are relics of a bygone day and may have been adopted with quite different conditions in mind. The 1976 National Emergencies Act addressed this problem by providing that an emergency declared by the president can be terminated by concurrent resolution of Congress. In 1983, however, the Supreme Court held the legislative veto to be unconstitutional; as a result it now takes a joint resolution to end an emergency. If a president vetoes this resolution, a two-thirds vote of Congress is needed to halt the use of emergency authority. He may thus be able to proceed even though his conduct is opposed by a majority of Congress.[4]

Judicial Review in Time of Crisis

While the potential for abuse of war and emergency power has grown considerably over the past fifty years, the federal courts have been extremely cautious about interfering with such actions. There are a number of institutional limitations that restrain the exercise of judicial review in time of war. One major difficulty is that judges may not be able to obtain or evaluate the information necessary for resolving the constitutional questions presented. Much of the relevant data is likely to be protected against compulsory disclosure by executive privilege. In *United States v. Nixon* the Supreme Court seemed to imply that a presidential claim of national security might trump any attempt to obtain such material; in dictum it stated that courts "should not jeopardize the security which the privilege is meant to protect by insisting upon an examination of the evidence, even by the judge alone, in chambers." If the Court adheres to these standards, it would be difficult for the judiciary to assess independently the nature of a claimed emergency or the validity of the measure at issue.[5]

Moreover, courts are likely to think twice before challenging the commander in chief at a time when he enjoys the enthusiastic, if not hysterical, support of the country. To confront the president in the midst of a national crisis could result in long-term damage to judicial prestige. Federal judges have no real ability to enforce their judgments and must depend on either voluntary compliance or the resources of the executive branch. As Tocqueville observed, "Their power is enormous, but it is the power of public opinion." For this reason, he said, judges "must be statesmen, wise to discern the signs of the times, not afraid to brave the obstacles that can be subdued, nor slow to turn away from the current when it threatens to sweep them off." Instances of judicial defiance by the federal executive are notoriously rare, no doubt in part because courts have made an art of discretion. Norman Redlich has remarked: "The Supreme Court has emphasized that it does not back away from its responsibilities because of a fear of noncompliance, a position which, of course, the Court must assert to preserve its moral authority. But, surely, the fear that this country . . . would suffer grievous harm if a president defied a court order, or refused to enforce one, must influence both the president and the Supreme Court in certain areas."[6]

Also militating against judicial intervention in a period of crisis is the fact, noted by Clinton Rossiter, that "the Court, too, likes to win wars." Learned Hand saw this phenomenon at work in the World War I sedition cases, commenting that "their Ineffabilities, the Nine Elder Statesmen, have not shown themselves wholly immune from the 'herd instinct.' " Justice Robert Jackson likewise recognized that the Constitution in wartime "is interpreted by judges under the influence of the same passions and pressures" that affect their countrymen. At such times courts may hesitate to become involved. The concern here is not that an order might be ignored but rather that it would be obeyed, to the possible detriment of the war effort.[7]

Hamilton v. Kentucky Distilleries and its progeny established the proposition that federal exercises of the war powers are subordinate to the Constitution and subject to judicial review. In actual application that precept has been tempered by prudence and expediency, by a recognition that in periods of crisis there is a need for flexibility and discretion which defy the simplicity of doctrinal absolutes. Justice Jackson put it squarely: "It would be impracticable and dangerous idealism to expect or insist that each specific military command in an area of probable operations will conform to conventional tests of constitutionality." Instead, implementing the Constitution requires bridging the gulf that separates the ideal world from the real. Alexander Bickel wrote: "There are no absolutes that a complex society can live with in its law. There is only the computing principle that [Edmund] Burke spoke of—adding, subtracting, multiplying, dividing . . . Even absolute rights that the legal order seems, absentmindedly, to create, if very rarely, do not endure. Circumstances erode them. Better to recognize from the first that the computing principle is all there is, ought to be, or can be." However discomforting the thought, principle subsists in an atmosphere of adaptation and compromise.[8]

The judiciary's willingness to oppose the political branches only after an emergency has passed is amply documented by the historical record. Prior to World War I the Court struck down federal exercises of the war powers on eight occasions, all coming well after hostilities had ended. In one instance—*Ex parte Milligan,* decided in 1866—the justices acknowledged the importance of the fact that the war was over: "During the late wicked Rebellion, the temper of the times did not allow that calmness in deliberation and discussion so necessary to a correct conclusion of a purely judicial question . . . *Now* that the public safety is assured, this question . . . can be discussed and decided without passion or the admixture of any element not required to form a legal judgment." The World War I cases adhered to the same pattern. Despite the portentous language of cases such as *Hamilton,* every challenge to war legislation was rejected until 1921, when *Cohen Grocery* invalidated the antiprofiteering provisions of the Lever Act. The *Chastleton* decision dooming the District of Columbia Rent Law was issued in 1924, more than five years after the armistice.[9]

Following *Chastleton* the justices were not again called on to apply the principles of *Hamilton* until World War II. Between 1943 and 1950 the Court upheld the constitutionality of every war statute that came before it, including those providing for the relocation and internment of 120,000 Japanese-Americans living on the West Coast. In two cases executive action was overturned on the basis that it exceeded the scope of the authorizing legislation. *Ex parte Endo,* decided late in the war, ruled that the War Relocation Authority could not detain citizens whose loyalty was conceded. *Duncan v. Kahanamoku,* issued in 1946, held that military trial of civilians in Hawaii violated the Organic Act of 1900. In light of this evidence a historian at midcentury might have concluded that *Hamilton* had fallen on barren ground. Clinton Rossiter wrote in 1950 that "whatever limits the Court has set upon the employment of the war powers have been largely theoretical, rarely practical."[10]

Within a few years there were signs that this era of judicial hospitality might be nearing an end. In *Dennis v. United States,* handed down in 1951, the Court upheld the Smith Act convictions of the leaders of the American Communist party after giving the statute a narrowing construction to render it compatible with the First Amendment. A year later in *The Steel Seizure Case* the justices ruled that President Truman's takeover of the steel mills to avert a nationwide strike during the Korean War exceeded his authority, including his "power as Commander in Chief of the Armed Forces." This was one of the rare instances in which the Court intervened during a period of active hostilities. The explanation lies partly in the fact that Truman's conduct was not only unauthorized by Congress but was also contrary to an existing statutory scheme for handling emergency labor disputes. The justices also emphasized that the government's hands were not tied, for "the power of Congress to adopt such public policies as those proclaimed by the order is beyond question." The ruling was nevertheless an auspicious one in terms of fulfilling the promise of *Hamilton*.[11]

Between 1955 and 1967 the Court under Chief Justice Earl Warren struck down a series of war powers statutes that infringed on political and civil rights. One group of cases curtailed the scope of court-martial jurisdiction. The Uniform Code of Military Justice was invalidated insofar as it allowed military trial of those no longer connected with the armed services, of civilian dependents of military personnel, and of civilians employed on bases overseas. Another set of decisions dealt with attempts to suppress the Communist party. In 1964 the justices held unconstitutional a section of the Subversive Activities Control Act denying passports to party members. Three years later they overturned another provision of the act that made it a crime for communists to work in defense plants. In the latter case the chief justice declared that "the phrase 'war power' cannot be invoked as a talismanic incantation to support any exercise of congressional power which can be brought within its ambit. '[E]ven the war power does not remove constitutional limitations safeguarding essential liberties.'"[12]

The final area in which *Hamilton* bore fruit under the Warren Court involved government attempts to strip persons of their citizenship for military-related conduct. *Trop v. Dulles* struck down a law providing that anyone dishonorably discharged from the army after being found guilty of wartime desertion would lose his nationality. Though the case arose from action taken at the height of World War II, it was decided in 1958, long after the war was over. *Kennedy v. Mendoza-Martinez* invalidated a statute allowing citizenship to be stripped from those leaving or remaining outside the United States during wartime to evade military service. This 1963 ruling, which dealt with conduct occurring in World War II and the Korean War, came a year before the United States escalated its military presence in Vietnam. The Court noted that its holding would not "frustrate the effective handling of the problem of draft evaders who leave the United States."[13]

The judiciary beat a quiet retreat when suits were brought testing the constitutionality of the Vietnam War. All of the early challenges were dismissed by the lower courts as nonjusticiable. By 1970, as opposition to U.S. engagement became widespread, federal judges showed a greater readiness to address the merits. In most of the latter cases, however, courts found that there was sufficient congressional participation to validate the president's actions, despite the absence of a formal declaration of war. There were a few notable exceptions. In *Mottola v. Nixon* Judge William T. Sweigert refused to dismiss a suit filed by four law students and intimated that the Vietnam War was unlawful. Before Sweigert ruled on the merits, however, an appellate court ordered the case dismissed. The judiciary's boldest moment came in July 1973, when Judge Orrin Judd ruled in *Holtzman v. Schlesinger* that the U.S. air war in Cambodia was unconstitutional. An injunction barring further bombing was immediately stayed, and the Court of Appeals subsequently ruled that the suit was nonjusticiable. The Supreme Court refused to hear any of the Vietnam cases, apparently satisfied with the lower courts' rejection of challenges to the war. The federal judiciary likewise declined to interfere with the Reagan administration's military activities in Central America.[14]

The notion that courts may oversee executive branch conduct in time of crisis is one which cuts sharply against the grain. History demonstrates that, almost without exception, federal judges have been unwilling to intercede during periods of national emergency. While the principle articulated in *Hamilton* has technically endured, it is in constant danger of succumbing to judicial abdication. In seeking to avert a war powers confrontation with the president, courts tend to be drawn to either of two extremes. On the one hand they may be tempted to engage in a purely ceremonial exercise, the foreordained outcome of which is to approve the executive conduct in question. On the other they may conclude, as did many judges faced with challenges to the Vietnam War, that the matter involves a so-called political question to be resolved exclusively by Congress and the president. Both approaches are equally fatal to the concept of judicial review.

Scylla: Ritualistic Approval

If during a period of crisis a court proceeds to the merits of a case that significantly challenges the exercise of emergency power, it is almost inevitable that the decision will be in favor of the government. As *Mottola* and *Holtzman* demonstrate, should an occasional district court have the temerity to do otherwise, the ruling is likely to be stayed and reversed on appeal. The net effect is to create a body of case law, some perhaps from the Supreme Court itself, sanctioning practices that would be intolerable in ordinary times. As Alexander Bickel has argued, "It is no small matter . . . to 'legitimate' a legislative measure. The Court's prestige, the spell it casts as a symbol, enable it to entrench and solidify measures that may have been tentative in the conception . . . The Court, regardless of what it intends, can generate consent and may impart permanence." The same is true, albeit to a lesser extent, of lower federal court judgments. Though these decisions may be dictated by overriding factors of expediency, they compromise fundamental values and threaten permanent damage to our constitutional scheme.[15]

In theory such rulings might somehow be segregated from the main body of constitutional law and treated as creatures unique to war. The reality is that isolation is impossible. Rossiter noted that "the Court has had little success in preventing the precedents of war from becoming precedents of peace," resulting in "the permanent peacetime weakening of . . . applicable limits to governmental power." Indeed, because he doubted that the judiciary could ever serve as an effective check against emergency power, Rossiter believed that *Hamilton* and its progeny had "actually backfired on the Court." Justice Brandeis voiced a similar fear concerning the World War I decisions under the Espionage and Sedition Acts, remarking to Felix Frankfurter that it would have been better to have rested them "frankly on [the] war power" rather than on the First Amendment, so that "in peace the protection against restrictions of freedom of speech would be unabated."[16]

The most egregious example of abdication in the form of ritualistic approval occurred during World War II. The 1943 and 1944 rulings in *Hirabayashi, Yasui,* and *Korematsu* upheld the mass evacuation of all Japanese-Americans living in California, Oregon, and Washington. It is now clear that there was no military justification for the internment program, most of whose victims were native-born American citizens. As was true after 1918, the war powers were used to pursue goals unrelated to the emergency but which were otherwise unattainable. The California Joint Immigration Committee (once the Asiatic Exclusion League), the Native Sons and Daughters of the Golden West, the Western Growers Protective Association, and the California Farm Bureau Federation had long sought to rid the Pacific Coast of Orientals. Pearl Harbor provided the opportunity for which they had been waiting. A Joint Immigration Committee spokesman declared early in 1942, "This is our time to get things done that we have been trying to get done for a quarter of a century." Forty years later the federal Commission on Wartime Relocation and Internment of Civilians concluded that the government's treatment of Japanese-Americans had "not [been] justified by military necessity" but was instead the product of "race prejudice, war hysteria and a failure of political leadership."[17]

The judiciary's ability to review these actions was impeded because attorneys for the War and Justice Departments suppressed critical information which would have disclosed the absence of a war justification for the relocation and detention programs. Owing to this governmental misconduct, the convictions of Min Yasui, Fred Korematsu, and Gordon Hirabayashi have since been set aside. Had it been appropriate for the Supreme Court to defer to the military authorities, as it did in these cases, the wartime rulings might have been excused on the basis of the distorted record. A more searching review was called for, however, under which the convictions should not have been sustained in the first place.[18]

Since a war emergency clearly existed when the curfew and exclusion orders were issued, the cases presented no durational challenge. It may also be conceded that these wartime orders were within the broad scope of the government's war powers. Yet because they drastically restricted the civil liberties of a single racial and ancestral group, the measures were highly suspect under the Fifth Amendment. Several years earlier in the *Carolene Products* case Chief Justice Harlan Fiske Stone had observed that as a general rule an enactment will be upheld under the due process clause if it "rests upon some rational basis within the knowledge and experience of the legislators." In the celebrated Footnote Four, however, Stone suggested that "more exacting judicial scrutiny" is required where a law is "directed at particular ... national ... or racial minorities," explaining that "prejudice against discrete and insular minorities may be a special condition, which tends seriously to curtail the operation of those political processes ordinarily to be relied upon to protect minorities." The curfew and evacuation orders fell within this exception, for in addition to the animosity which existed toward Japanese-Americans, there was the fact that few of their number could participate in the political process.[19]

Had this higher standard of review been applied, the government would have been required to demonstrate a military necessity for its actions. As it was, the Justice Department agreed that "the record . . . does not contain any comprehensive account of the facts which gave rise to the exclusion and curfew measures." Instead it asked that judicial notice be taken of various racial characteristics which allegedly distinguished persons of Japanese descent from German- and Italian-Americans. Chief Justice Stone's majority opinion in *Hirabayashi* made no mention of Footnote Four. While he stated that "distinctions between citizens solely because of their ancestry are by their very nature odious to a free people," this did not mandate heightened scrutiny of the curfew imposed only on Japanese-Americans. Rather, "it is enough that circumstances within the knowledge of those charged with the responsibility for maintaining the national defense afforded a *rational basis* for the decision which they made." In a passage omitted from his published opinion, Justice Frank Murphy criticized this capitulation to the military. "If there were substantial evidence that citizens of Japanese ancestry were generally disloyal," he said, "the curfew order and other restrictions imposed on them might be defended . . . But such evidence is lacking."[20]

In *Korematsu* a year and a half later the majority adopted a similar approach to sustain the evacuation of Japanese-Americans from the West Coast. Justice Hugo L. Black's opinion for the Court paid lip service to the premise of Footnote Four, stating that "all legal restrictions which curtail the civil rights of a single racial group are immediately suspect" and subject to "the most rigid scrutiny." Yet the majority then applied "the principles we announced in the *Hirabayashi* case" and deferred to the "military authorities [who], charged with the primary responsibility of defending our shores, concluded that curfew provided inadequate protection and ordered exclusion." The dissenters noted that the record was devoid of any evidence to support the indiscriminate evacuation of all Japanese-Americans.[21]

The Commission on Wartime Relocation and Internment of Civilians observed that in *Hirabayashi, Yasui,* and *Korematsu* the Court "chose not to review the factual basis for military decisions in war-time, accepting without close scrutiny the Government's representation that exclusion and evacuation were militarily necessary." By engaging in what was merely a formal exercise, the justices not only denied relief to the aggrieved individuals but left behind a series of decisions which are still part of our constitutional law. As Justice Jackson declared,

A judicial construction of the due process clause that will sustain this order is a far more subtle blow to liberty than the promulgation of the order itself. A military order, however unconstitutional, is not apt to last longer than the military emergency . . . But once a judicial opinion rationalizes such an order to show that it conforms to the Constitution, or rather rationalizes the Constitution to show that the Constitution sanctions such an order, the court for all time has validated the principle of racial discrimination in criminal procedure and of transplanting American citizens. The principle then lies about like a loaded weapon ready for the hand of any authority that can bring forward a plausible claim of an urgent need.

Such rulings weaken respect for the Court and the Constitution, which, instead of protecting rights, become apologists for their violation. Nor were these cases unique. During World War II there were other occasions when judicial review was, in Rossiter's words, "a shadow play without blood or substance."[22]

Charybdis: The Political Question Doctrine

Perhaps in reaction to the Japanese-American cases courts during the Vietnam War drifted toward the opposite pole of judicial abdication, often treating the constitutional issue as nonjusticiable. The political question doctrine holds that there are situations in which the judiciary must abstain from performing its customary role because the text of the Constitution commits the matter to the political branches, or because of a lack of judicially manageable criteria for resolving the issue, or on account of prudential concerns which counsel against intrusion. The factors that make judges hesitant to interfere in wartime may readily be invoked to label a question political. In *Baker v. Carr* Justice William Brennan listed some of the considerations that might render abstention appropriate, including "the impossibility of a court's undertaking independent resolution without expressing lack of the respect due coordinate branches of government; or an unusual need for unquestioning adherence to a political decision already made; or the potentiality of embarrassment from multifarious pronouncements by various departments on one question." Where the constitutionality of emergency action is challenged, it takes no great ingenuity for a court to invoke the doctrine as a means of abandoning the field.[23]

Such a position constitutes the ultimate in judicial abdication, the end point on a spectrum of deference and avoidance. By adopting a political question stance, courts create a realm in which power may be exercised with impunity. To deem an issue political is, in Bickel's words, to conclude "that there ought to be discretion free of principled rules." Yet, as Fritz Scharpf wrote, the concept comes into play only where there exist constitutional "principles which are relevant to the disposition of the case." The doctrine in effect proclaims that such limitations have no meaning as actual restraints on government but are mere admonitions to be honored or ignored as the political branches choose. This represents an extraordinary retreat from *Hamilton*, a case in which Justice Brandeis specifically rejected the political question approach. It is also at odds with the structural premises of the Constitution, whose checks and balances reflect a profound distrust of the ability of any branch to police itself or even of two branches to control each other. Assuming there are occasions when the political question doctrine may be proper, it should never be employed if the purposes it is intended to serve can be achieved through less drastic means.[24]

Though it is often said that the political question doctrine sees frequent use in the area of foreign policy, *Baker v. Carr* stated "It is error to suppose that every case or controversy which touches foreign relations lies beyond judicial cognizance." Louis Henkin has urged that despite the record of lower federal courts "there is . . . no Supreme Court precedent for extraordinary abstention from judicial review in foreign affairs cases." Significantly, the justices dealt with the Vietnam War challenges not by endorsing the view that the question was a political one but by refusing to hear the appeals. The Court has suggested that the doctrine is particularly inappropriate where a war measure has significant domestic consequences. In *Goldwater v. Carter*, decided in 1979, four justices concluded that the issue of whether the executive could terminate a treaty without consulting Congress was political in nature. They distinguished *The Steel Seizure Case*, which also presented a boundary dispute between Congress and the president, as involving "war powers . . . action of profound and demonstrable domestic impact," whereas in *Goldwater* "the effect . . . is 'entirely external to the United States, and [falls] within the category of foreign affairs.' "[25]

There are sound reasons for this reluctance to employ the political question doctrine in cases concerning war and emergency power. If it is unacceptable that the political branches should be sole judges of their conduct in periods of tranquillity, it is absurd to trust them with such a task in times of national crisis. As the World War I experience showed, it is during and after such upheavals that government officials are most in need of the "sober second thought" afforded by judicial review. Justice Jackson believed the "war power" to be "the most dangerous one . . . in the whole catalogue of powers" because it is "invoked in haste and excitement when calm legislative consideration of constitutional limitation is difficult" and "executed in a time of patriotic fervor that makes moderation unpopular." As Bickel said, "It does not take a lunatic legislature to enact measures that are irrational. It only takes a legislature more than normally whipped up, very intent on the expedient purpose of the moment, acting under severe pressure, rushed, tired, lazy, mistaken, or, forsooth, ignorant." For courts to refrain entirely from reviewing such measures would be a constitutional travesty.[26]

The exercise of emergency power varies in the extent to which it bears the approval of Congress. The president may act pursuant to specific legislation, as was generally true during the World War I era. Under this scenario checks and balances have worked at least insofar as the measure has run the gauntlet of both political branches. Yet, as in the post-1918 period, the nature of the times makes it unlikely that constitutional limitations will have had any effect on the deliberations. Moreover, the role of Congress in approving such measures may amount to little more than ratifying a presidential request. In periods of crisis the executive assumes a dominant role in the legislative process. Though some congressmen may champ at the bit, the majority are typically unwilling to oppose him. As we saw earlier, this was the case with authorization of telephone and telegraph control and with the Lever Act amendment making profiteering a crime. The problem becomes most acute when "the executive branch is supported in the legislature by a solid and disciplined party majority. In such instances it is hardly practicable to look to the legislature for an independent decision that emergency powers be called into action, or for an independent check upon their employment."[27]

A president may seek to invoke emergency power without congressional authorization. In the post–World War I setting this was arguably true of the cable takeover and the use of the Lever Act against strikers, both of which were contrary to the apparent intent of Congress. This was also the case with Truman's seizure of the steel mills and was the primary basis for challenging the Vietnam War. Such unilaterial executive action raises serious separation-of-powers problems. Jesse Choper has urged that all complaints of executive usurpation be treated as political questions. He believes Congress capable of defending itself and argues that if executive conduct threatened individual liberties, those claims would be justiciable. Whatever its merit in ordinary times, history refutes the assumption that the legislature is able to resist the executive in periods of crisis. Indeed, the persistence of the "Imperial Presidency" is evidence that even during peace the executive is able to effect massive redistributions of power at Congress's expense. While Choper concedes that separation of powers was intended as a safeguard against tyranny, he believes that any change in constitutional structure that might result from his proposal would be harmless, since any infringement of the Bill of Rights could be remedied by the courts. Yet there are many abuses of power which are not extreme enough to violate the Constitution. As Thomas M. Cooley and James Bradley Thayer noted a century ago, the judiciary will invalidate a measure only if it is clearly and egregiously unconstitutional. Short of that point, protection against unjust and oppressive laws rests with the political branches. If Congress, for whatever reason, is unwilling or unable to perform its assigned task, rights may be injured in ways that are immune from judicial redress.[28]

To invoke the political question doctrine with respect to emergency power is to abandon judicial review in a setting where checks and balances are already at their weakest. Yet, as between the two forms of judicial abdication, it represents the lesser evil. While in neither case has the judiciary interfered with the challenged action, by treating the matter as nonjusticiable a court avoids conferring its blessing of constitutionality. The effect of such a validation, as Justice Jackson explained in *Korematsu,* is to turn what may have been a "passing incident" into "the doctrine of the Constitution," whereby it gains "generative power of its own." A political question stance recognizes that constitutional principles govern the conduct in issue and places responsibility for honoring them on the coordinate branches. Though this may not have much of a deterrent effect, it is preferable to a situation in which Congress and the president can be certain that any measures they adopt will win approval from the courts.[29]

A Middle Passage: Delaying Review

The pragmatic considerations which may preclude judicial intervention in periods of crisis do not condemn the courts to a choice between Scylla and Charybdis. While there are times when principle must yield to expediency, the judiciary need not totally abdicate, either by ceremonially affirming the executive's action or by labeling the matter a political question. Both routes severely impair the Constitution as an operative check on government. Under exigent circumstances courts should steer a middle course and defer review until the emergency has abated.[30]

This solution acknowledges the political and historical reality that during grave national crises the judiciary is seldom in a position to challenge the executive. After the danger has subsided, the considerations which once made judicial review impossible will have lost much of their force. Information whose release could have endangered national security may now safely be disclosed. The chance that a judgment might interfere with the war effort or be met by noncompliance will also have disappeared. Finally, passions will have cooled to the point where judges are able to evaluate challenges to emergency power with the requisite calm and detachment.[31]

The impact of timing on the integrity of judicial review can be seen by comparing two World War II decisions. In *Korematsu*, decided late in 1944, the justices refused to examine the claim that relocation of Japanese-Americans from the West Coast was compelled by military necessity. After the war had been won, the Court in *Duncan v. Kahanamoku* probed and rejected a government assertion that conditions in Hawaii required the continuation of military rule. Discussing these cases, Rossiter asked: "What would they have decided in [*Duncan*] a year or two years or three years earlier?" Yet one might equally speculate as to the outcome of *Korematsu* had that ruling been deferred by twelve months. In the more recent context of Southeast Asia one federal court explicitly recognized the connection between timing and review. District Judge Orrin Judd had upheld the legality of the Vietnam War in 1970. Three years later, after U.S. troops had been withdrawn from Indochina, he was presented with the *Holtzman* case. Judd noted that "reluctance to jeopardize the safety of American soldiers or prisoners," which might have led him not to intercede, "is no longer a barrier to judicial determination of the constitutionality of a phase of war activity." He then proceeded to hold that the bombing of Cambodia was unlawful.[32]

Bickel suggested that the judiciary's *"raison d'être* [is] to evolve, to defend, and to protect principle." This task often demands compromise and a resort to what he described as "the passive virtues"—devices by which courts may avoid a substantive constitutional decision. He also urged that "the role of principle, when it cannot be the inflexible governing rule, is to affect the tendency of policies of expediency." While Bickel might not have agreed, it would seem to follow that where courts do respond pragmatically, they should choose that path which works the least harm to underlying constitutional values. Delaying review without foregoing it entirely strengthens the Constitution in time of emergency. This "technique of the mediating middle" allows the executive to act unencumbered while the crisis rages, while helping to ensure that its conduct will not become an exercise in tyranny. Those who wield emergency power will act with the knowledge that they may later have to answer for their conduct. If judges defer intervention until they are able to function in an independent manner, courts can play an important role in this process of accountability.[33]

Postponing review presents the obvious drawback of delaying relief for what could be a significant period of time. For a court then to declare the government's conduct unconstitutional may have the appearance of "salvag[ing] a principle at the cost of permitting the practice which it forbids." Yet the vindication of constitutional values, albeit after the fact, is preferable to the likely consequences of attempting to adjudicate at the height of an emergency. As Bickel observed, the judicial function has "often meant the definition of principled goals and the practice of the art of the possible in striving to attain them." That art may entail acceptance of the fact that there are times when half a loaf is better than none.[34]

It might be objected that this approach fails to yield even half a loaf—that "action which comes later is of no use." If this is occasionally true in a remedial sense, a declaration of unconstitutionality nevertheless serves a powerful educational and deterrent function.

Despite the complex relationship between judicial decisions and public opinion, no one seriously doubts that the Court is a significant factor in shaping attitudes on political, social, and moral issues. The importance of the 1954 decision in *Brown v. Board of Education* lay not in the relief the Court granted—which at the time was none—but in its declaration that racial segregation of the public schools was no longer tolerable. Though the case met widespread resistance, it was instrumental in transforming America's conscience on the subject of race. Similarly the 1973 ruling in *Roe v. Wade,* recognizing a woman's freedom of choice concerning abortion, was partly responsible for the fact that a majority of the country today accepts this as a right. A decision invalidating an exercise of emergency power, even if issued after the crisis has passed, serves as a "repressive brake" on official conduct. Notwithstanding his skepticism about the courts, Rossiter could thus agree that "the old cry 'It's unconstitutional!' is no joke."[35]

Mechanisms for Deferral

The federal judiciary has proven adept at avoiding decision in times of crisis, even though this has not been accompanied by an equal willingness to become involved once the emergency is over. There are a number of means available for this purpose which, unlike the political question doctrine, do not forever bar review. The Supreme Court may refuse to hear a case either by denying a petition for certiorari, as was done in many of the Vietnam War suits, or by summarily disposing of an appeal. While its appellate jurisdiction is in theory obligatory, the Court has broad discretion in deciding which appeals to hear. If it agrees with the judgment below, it may issue a one-sentence summary affirmance or dismiss the case for lack of a substantial federal question. These actions muddy the precedential waters, however, for they are treated as being on the merits and bind other courts. The justices may therefore instead elect to dismiss an appeal for want of a properly presented federal question or because the record is allegedly inadequate; these dispositions may be entirely fictitious but they have no precedential effect and thus leave lower courts free to explore the issue.[36]

Other avenues of deferral may be utilized at all levels of the federal system. A trial or appellate court may simply postpone decision of a case. This occurred in *Ex parte Endo,* challenging the government's internment of concededly loyal Japanese-American citizens. After reporting to the Tanforan assembly center in July 1942, Mitsuye Endo filed a habeas corpus petition in the San Francisco district court. A hearing was held a week later before Judge Michael J. Roche, who said that he would rule within fifteen days. Months then went by, during which Endo was transferred to an internment camp. Her lawyer initially acquiesced in this delay, explaining, "We were getting the hell kicked out of us in 1942 and I wanted to let some time pass." In July 1943 Judge Roche issued an order dismissing the petition. Review was sought in the Court of Appeals, which, after eight months, certified the matter to the Supreme Court. *Korematsu* was before the Court at the time, and it was thought that the two appeals might be heard together in the spring of 1944. The justices, however, deferred arguments until the fall. Finally, in December 1944 the Court held that the military lacked authority to detain Mitsuye Endo. But for these delays *Endo* would have been decided at least a year earlier, at a time when the justices might have been unwilling to allow the release of any Japanese-Americans. While such procrastination is a serious matter, especially in a habeas corpus case, there are occasions—as Endo's attorney realized—when it benefits the protection of individual rights.[37]

A court may also avoid review if a case has become moot. At any point in the litigation the government may choose to grant a litigant's demands without abandoning the challenged practice as to others. Since federal courts cannot issue advisory opinions, if there ceases to be a live controversy, the action is subject to dismissal. This device may be employed each time a suit is filed or when it appears that a case is about to reach the Supreme Court. By this route the executive may be able to shield its conduct from judicial scrutiny. The ploy failed in *Endo* but was used to defeat attacks on several other World War II measures, including the wartime use of martial law in Hawaii and the government takeover of Montgomery Ward and Co. facilities during 1944 and 1945. A judge need not go along with these tactics if they fall within an exception to the mootness doctrine. One of these involves issues "capable of repetition, yet evading review." Another is triggered where a defendant has voluntarily but not necessarily permanently acquiesced, and so remains "free to return to his old ways." These doctrines are quite flexible and leave courts with considerable discretion in their application. Yet mootness is of limited use as a device for evading decision since it depends largely on the strategy employed by the government.[38]

Of far greater potential, and the mechanism seemingly best suited for delaying decision in time of crisis, is dismissal for lack of ripeness. This prudential doctrine is tailor-made for the war powers context. It looks to the future and asks whether postponing involvement to a later date would contribute to better resolution of the issues. The factors that render courts ineffective in periods of national crisis—inadequate information, the risk of executive defiance, and fear of jeopardizing successful handling of the emergency—all diminish with the passage of time. The Court has emphasized that invocation of the doctrine is proper where delay will result in "a better factual record."[39]

Ripeness is particularly appropriate in a separation of powers dispute as a means of encouraging the political branches to take responsible action. In the late stages of the Vietnam War some courts intimated that if Congress directly challenged the president's continuation of hostilities, the judiciary might then intercede. Justice Lewis F. Powell adopted this position in *Goldwater v. Carter,* concluding that the boundary dispute over the power to terminate a treaty was not ripe inasmuch as Congress had not yet formally opposed the executive. Such confrontation is not an absolute prerequisite for judicial intervention, however. Since the separation of powers is designed to protect individual rights, even if one branch is willing to tolerate incursions into its domain, its assent cannot waive the rights of others. In *The Steel Seizure Case* the Court struck down an executive usurpation of legislative power in an emergency setting even though Congress had declined to take issue with Truman's action. More recently the justices invalidated the legislative veto, in part as an invasion of the executive sphere, despite the fact that presidents had frequently approved the device. Once Congress has been given an opportunity to oppose an exercise of emergency power, its failure to act should not preclude judicial review.[40]

If suits challenging war measures are dismissed on ripeness grounds in a period of crisis, the litigants should be free to return to court later. Neither the statute of limitations nor the doctrine of mootness should operate as a bar. Courts often toll or stay the running of the statute of limitations where a timely action was dismissed on procedural grounds. This was done after the Civil War to save claims which could not be filed in Confederate states during the rebellion. As to possible mootness, the exception for issues capable of repetition yet evading review would be directly applicable if the judiciary's practice was to stay rather than dismiss unripe cases. Since refiling is treated as a continuation of the original action for limitations purposes, the same principle might govern mootness. Moreover, the Court has recognized that exceptions to mootness are especially warranted if there is "a public interest in having the legality of the practices settled," a condition which is surely met where the aim is to preserve the Constitution in time of emergency.[41]

The determination of when a crisis has sufficiently abated to permit review will depend on several factors, including the nature and status of the emergency, its relationship to the challenged measure, the legal arguments raised, and the type of relief sought. The exigency need not be completely over before a court may intervene. The inquiry should be a functional one, turning on whether necessary information is likely to be available, whether the danger of defiance has passed, and whether the climate is such as will allow judicious resolution of the issues. Justice Brennan suggested that war measures are most susceptible to judicial review when they do not "seriously implicate considerations of finality—e.g., a public program of importance (rent control) yet not central to the emergency effort." Justice Jackson likewise noted that "when the war power is invoked to do things to the liberties of people, or their property or economy that only indirectly affect conduct of the war and do not relate to the management of the war itself, the constitutional basis should be scrutinized with care." The Court's willingness to review President Truman's wartime seizure of the steel industry is partly explainable on this basis. By contrast, the relocation of Japanese-Americans appeared on its face to be closely related to the defense of the West Coast and was thus less suited to adjudication during the period of crisis.[42]

Whether an emergency is such as to preclude review may also hinge on the nature of the legal challenge. To the extent that a ruling will leave the government alternative means of protecting its interests, the risks of judicial intervention are reduced. This is the case where the president has allegedly exceeded his delegated authority or acted without legislative sanction. It was on this ground that the Court freed Mitsuye Endo, struck down martial law in Hawaii, and ordered the return of the steel mills. This was also the basis on which a federal judge enjoined the bombing of Cambodia. If the court's statutory construction is erroneous, Congress is free to rectify the situation. The same is true if a law is found to be impermissibly vague, as was the Lever Act in 1919. These bases of attack not only increase the likelihood of judicial review but also enhance the political process. Without holding a program to be beyond the government's reach, a court can encourage Congress to examine specific executive action—perhaps for the first time—to determine whether it constitutes a proper implementation of the law. If it is feared that serious harm might result in the interim, a judge may stay injunctive relief until the executive has had an opportunity to seek redress from Congress, much as court orders are often stayed pending appeal.[43]

The length of time that review will be deferred might also depend on the type of relief sought. Where personal liberty is directly at stake, as in the case of a criminal defendant facing confinement or an inmate seeking release through habeas corpus, courts are more likely to intercede than in ordinary civil actions. In such instances the price of abstention may be unacceptably high, while the remedy is relatively limited in its impact on the emergency effort. The consequences of discharging a prisoner or dismissing an indictment are of a different order of magnitude than what was sought by New York Congresswoman Elizabeth Holtzman and granted by the district court—declaratory and injunctive relief against continuation of the war in Cambodia. As in the Hawaiian martial law cases a judge might stay a habeas corpus judgment until it can be reviewed on appeal. The judiciary may even be able to safeguard individual rights without having to determine the validity of an emergency measure. As Michael Tigar suggested, if in time of crisis the executive will not supply needed information, a court might "put the government to the option: disclose or dismiss." In this way confidential material remains protected, yet personal liberty does not suffer as a result.[44]

Finally, in a civil action challenging prospective enforcement of a war measure the court might issue a declaratory judgment without an accompanying injunction. The case is in effect treated as being quasiripe: while it is premature to grant coercive relief, the judiciary does impose a moral restraint on the executive. Owen Fiss has noted that "even if the court gave no relief (other than the mere declaration)," still a "right would . . . exist as a standard of criticism, a standard for evaluating present social practices." This limited intervention avoids the danger of hampering an emergency effort; it may be powerful enough, however, to induce abandonment of the infringing practice. In contrast to the political question doctrine, the court has ruled on the constitutional issue, with a possibility that injunctive relief may be forthcoming after the crisis has subsided. For the moment the judiciary functions in its capacity as a teacher, saving for another day any attempt to be a policeman.[45]

In light of the means available for deferring review during times of national emergency the legacy of *Hamilton* need not be lost through judicial abdication. By acknowledging the practical limitations which operate in periods of crisis, judges will be in a better position to protect the Constitution when its existence is most imperiled. Justice Jackson rightly cautioned, "If the people ever let command of the war power fall into irresponsible and unscrupulous hands, the courts wield no power equal to its restraint." Yet the judiciary can help forestall such a day by not hesitating to remind and educate the country, when the occasion demands, that the Constitution applies even to action taken in the name of war.[46]

Abbreviations
Notes
Index

Abbreviations

AMP	Alexander Mitchell Palmer
ASB	Albert Sidney Burleson
ASB MSS	Albert Sidney Burleson Papers, Library of Congress, Washington, D.C.
JPT	Joseph Patrick Tumulty
JPT MSS	Joseph P. Tumulty Papers, Library of Congress, Washington, D.C.
NA DOJ	National Archives, Records of the Department of Justice, Record Group 60, Washington, D.C.
NA POD	National Archives, Records of the Post Office Department, Record Group 28, Washington, D.C.
N.Y. Times	*New York Times*
N. Y. World	*New York World*
OUSB	U.S. Committee on Public Information, *Official U.S. Bulletin*
WW	Woodrow Wilson
WW MSS	Woodrow Wilson Papers, Library of Congress, Washington, D.C.
WWP	*The Papers of Woodrow Wilson,* ed. Arthur S. Link, 58 vols. to date (Princeton, 1966–)
WWPP	*The Public Papers of Woodrow Wilson,* ed. Ray Stannard Baker and William E. Dodd, 6 vols. (New York, 1925–1927)

Notes

Citations to newspapers are to page and column number (e.g., 1:6 refers to page one, column six); unless otherwise indicated, all references are to part one.

1. The War Powers at the Armistice

1. Joint Resolution of July 2, 1921, ch. 40, 42 Stat. 105; ibid., 1939, 1946; Charles K. Burdick, *The Law of the American Constitution*, 255–257 (New York, 1922); Manley O. Hudson, "The Duration of the War between the United States and Germany," 39 *Harvard Law Review* 1020 (1926); Note, "Judicial Determination of the End of the War," 47 *Columbia Law Review* 255 (1947).

2. See Richard Hofstadter, *The Age of Reform: From Bryan to F.D.R.* (New York, 1955); Richard Hofstadter, *The Progressive Movement: 1900–1915*, at 1–15 (Englewood Cliffs, N.J., 1963); Eric F. Goldman, *Rendezvous with Destiny: A History of Modern American Reform* (New York, 1952); Harold U. Faulkner, *The Quest for Social Justice: 1898–1914* (New York, 1931).

3. Goldman, *Rendezvous with Destiny*, 80–81, 193–198, 201, 306; Hofstadter, *Age of Reform*, 231–236; Paul L. Haworth, *The United States in Our Own Times, 1865–1924*, at 355–359 (New York, 1924); *Encyclopedia Americana* (1979), s.v. "The Progressive Movement"; Elizabeth Brandeis, "Labor Legislation," in 3 John R. Commons, *History of Labor in the United States*, 397 et seq. (New York, 1937).

4. Herbert Croly, *The Promise of American Life* (New York, 1909); Charles Forcey, *The Crossroads of Liberalism: Croly, Weyl, Lippmann, and the Progressive Era, 1900–1925*, at xxviii, 117, 145, 258–259 (New York, 1961); Goldman, *Rendezvous with Destiny*, 10–28, 39–40, 188–232; Arthur S. Link, *Woodrow Wilson and the Progressive Era, 1910–1917*, at 18–21, 223–230 (New York, 1954); George C. Osborn, *Woodrow Wilson: The Early Years*, 282–286 (Baton Rouge, 1968); William E. Leuchtenburg,

Introduction, in WW, *The New Freedom,* 12–14 (reprint, Englewood Cliffs, N.J., 1961); John Milton Cooper, Jr., *The Warrior and the Priest: Woodrow Wilson and Theodore Roosevelt,* 120–129, 135–136, 211–217 (Cambridge, Mass., 1983).

5. Goldman, *Rendezvous with Destiny,* 79–81, 163, 192–198, 201; Forcey, *Crossroads of Liberalism,* 38–42, 113–115; Croly, *Promise of American Life,* 446–449.

6. Hofstadter, *Age of Reform,* 236; Forcey, *Crossroads of Liberalism,* xxiii–xxiv, 116, 158, 160–163; James H. Timberlake, *Prohibition and the Progressive Movement, 1900–1920,* at 101, 123–124 (Cambridge, Mass., 1963); Cooper, *Warrior and Priest,* 258–259, 262; WW, *The New Freedom,* 28–30, 36 (New York, 1913); Alpheus T. Mason, *Brandeis: A Free Man's Life,* 130, 160, 167, 535 (New York, 1946).

7. S. Doc. No. 92–82, 92d Cong., 2d Scss., *Constitution of the United States,* 1597–1609, 1623–1670 (1973); Charles G. Haines, "Judicial Review of Acts of Congress and the Need for Constitutional Reform," 45 *Yale Law Journal* 816, 820 n.14 (1936).

8. Oliver P. Field, *Judicial Review of Legislation in Ten Selected States,* 14, 45 (Bloomington, Ind., 1943), analyzing Colo., Ill., Ind., Mass., Minn., N.H., N.Y., N.D., S.D., and Wis.; the study identifies the date each law was enacted rather than the date it was held unconstitutional; from figures for the average delay between passage and invalidation the number of laws overturned in a given range of years can be computed; see also Jackson H. Ralston, *Study and Report for American Federation of Labor upon Judicial Control over Legislatures as to Constitutional Questions,* 55, 91 (2d ed., Washington, D.C., 1923), estimating that between 1820 and 1916 state courts held 3,771 laws invalid; Edward S. Corwin, "The Extension of Judicial Review in New York: 1783–1905," 15 *Michigan Law Review* 281, 285 (1917); Corwin's figures include cases giving state laws a narrowing construction to save their constitutionality; Charles G. Haines, *The American Doctrine of Judicial Supremacy,* 426 n.73 (2d ed., New York, 1932), summarizing study by New York Library; of the 400 cases 55 involved violation of state constitutional requirements that laws have a clear title and deal with a single subject, defects easily cured; the remaining 345 measures were invalidated on grounds placing them beyond legislative redress.

9. Charles Warren, "The Progressiveness of the United States Supreme Court," 13 *Columbia Law Review* 294, 295, 308–309 & n.38 (1913); Brandeis, "Labor Legislation," 667–685; Lochner v. New York, 198 U.S. 45 (1905); Adair v. United States, 208 U.S. 161 (1908); Coppage v. Kansas, 236 U.S. 1 (1915); Hammer v. Dagenhart, 247 U.S. 251 (1918).

10. Lindley D. Clark, "Labor Laws That Have Been Declared Unconstitutional," U.S. Bureau of Labor Statistics, Dept. of Labor, Bull. No. 321, at 8, 85–90 (1922); Roscoe Pound, "Liberty of Contract," 18 *Yale Law Jour-*

nal 454, 470–482 (1909); Roscoe Pound, "Do We Need a Philosophy of Law?" 5 *Columbia Law Review* 339, 344–345 (1905); Henry Schofield, "Unreviewable, Wrong, or Doubtful State Decisions of Questions of Federal Constitutional Law—Their Effect on Private Interests and on the Reserved Power of the States," 3 *Illinois Law Review* 303 (1908); Warren, "Progressiveness of Supreme Court," 295–296.

11. Edward S. Corwin, *Liberty against Government: The Rise, Flowering, and Decline of a Famous Juridical Concept* (Baton Rouge, 1948); Corwin, "Judicial Review in New York," 292–296; Pound, "Liberty of Contract"; Haines, *Judicial Supremacy,* 2d ed., 426 n.73; Fred V. Cahill, Jr., *Judicial Legislation: A Study in American Legal Theory,* 48–52 (New York, 1952).

12. Robert S. Summers, *Instrumentalism and American Legal Theory,* 28, 83–84, 137–147, 255 (Ithaca, N.Y., 1982); Morton J. Horowitz, *The Transformation of American Law, 1780–1860,* at 253–266 (Cambridge, Mass., 1977); Cahill, *Judicial Legislation,* 22–26; Goldman, *Rendezvous with Destiny,* 90–93; Lochner v. New York, 198 U.S. 45, 75–76 (1905) (Holmes, J., dissenting).

13. Charles G. Haines, *American Doctrine of Judicial Supremacy,* 339 (1st ed., New York, 1914), quoting William Allen White.

14. Cahill, *Judicial Legislation,* 8–18; Goldman, *Rendezvous with Destiny,* 85–160; Morton G. White, *Social Thought in America: The Revolt against Formalism* (New York, 1949); Summers, *Instrumentalism,* 153; Southern Pacific v. Jensen, 244 U.S. 205, 222 (1917) (Holmes, J., dissenting); Roscoe Pound, "Law in Books and Law in Action," 44 *American Law Review* 12, 28 (1910).

15. Goldman, *Rendezvous with Destiny,* 93–97, 158–160; Cahill, *Judicial Legislation,* 26–30; White, *Social Thought,* 107.

16. William James, *Pragmatism: A New Name for Some Old Ways of Thinking,* 97–98 (1907) (reprint, Cambridge, Mass., 1978) (emphasis in original); Lord Lloyd and M. D. A. Freeman, *Introduction to Jurisprudence,* 679–680 (London, 1985).

17. Summers, *Instrumentalism,* 20–26; Pound, "Law in Books," 25; Roscoe Pound, "Mechanical Jurisprudence," 8 *Columbia Law Review* 605, 608–610 (1908); Oliver W. Holmes, Jr., *The Common Law,* 1 (Boston, 1881).

18. Summers, *Instrumentalism,* 28, 153–154; Cahill, *Judicial Legislation,* 42–43; Lochner v. New York, 198 U.S. 45, 75–76 (1905) (Holmes, J., dissenting).

19. Cahill, *Judicial Legislation,* 58–69; Walter F. Dodd, "The Growth of Judicial Power," 24 *Political Science Quarterly* 193, 194 (1909); Ernst Freund, "Limitation of Hours of Labor and the Federal Supreme Court," 17 *Green Bag* 411, 416 (1905); Frank J. Goodnow, *Social Reform and the*

Constitution, 4, 15–16 (New York, 1911); Pound, "Law in Books," 15–16, 27; Pound, "Do We Need a Philosophy of Law?" 343.

20. Summers, *Instrumentalism,* 21, 27, 29, 32, 43–49, 53, 60–61, 83–86, 142–143, 151, 157, 201, 239; Oliver W. Holmes, Jr., "Law in Science and Science in Law," 12 *Harvard Law Review* 443, 460 (1899); Pound, "Mechanical Jurisprudence," 608–610; J. Allen Smith, *The Spirit of American Government, A Study of the Constitution: Its Origin, Influence, and Relation to Democracy,* 400–401 (New York, 1907); Walter Lippmann, *Drift and Mastery: An Attempt to Diagnose the Current Unrest,* 157–158 (New York, 1914); Forcey, *Crossroads of Liberalism,* 17–21, 77–78, 96–101, 145–146; Goldman, *Rendezvous with Destiny,* 158–160, 222–223.

21. Lochner v. New York, 198 U.S. 45, 75–76 (1905) (Holmes, J., dissenting), recognizing an exception if "a rational and fair man necessarily would admit that the statute proposed would infringe fundamental principles as they have been understood by the traditions of our people and our law"; Summers, *Instrumentalism,* 153–154; Goodnow, *Social Reform,* 16; WW, *New Freedom,* 48.

22. Summers, *Instrumentalism,* 28, 51–52, 85, 98–99, 250–252; Oliver Wendell Holmes to Learned Hand, June 24, 1918, in Gerald Gunther, "Learned Hand and the Origins of Modern First Amendment Doctrine: Some Fragments of History," 27 *Stanford Law Review* 719, 735, 756–757 (1975).

23. Goodnow, *Social Reform,* 9–10; Goldman, *Rendezvous with Destiny,* 87–88, 143–149; Smith, *Spirit of American Government,* 31–32, 78, 103–105, 186.

24. Charles A. Beard, *An Economic Interpretation of the Constitution of the United States,* v–ix, 324 (1913) (reprint, New York, 1935); White, *Social Thought,* 114–115, 125–127; Goldman, *Rendezvous with Destiny,* 149–155.

25. Marbury v. Madison, 5 U.S. (1 Cranch) 137 (1803); Alan F. Westin, "Charles Beard and the American Debate over Judicial Review, 1790–1961," in Charles A. Beard, *The Supreme Court and the Constitution,* 12–24, 134–139 (1912; reprint, Englewood Cliffs, N.J., 1962), noting that between 1901 and 1920 over ninety scholarly books and articles were published in the judicial usurpation debate; Haines, *Judicial Supremacy,* 2d ed., 132–135; Edward S. Corwin, 7 *American Political Science Review* 330 (May 1913); Horace A. Davis, *The Judicial Veto* (New York, 1914).

26. Pound, "Do We Need a Philosophy of Law?" 344; Jane Addams, 13 *American Journal of Sociology* 770–773 (May 1908), discussing John R. Commons, "Is Class Conflict in America Growing and Is It Inevitable?"; Haines, *Judicial Supremacy,* 1st ed., 32.

27. Pound, "Liberty of Contract," 487; Pound, "Do We Need a Philosophy of Law?" 349–352; Pound, "Mechanical Jurisprudence," 606.

28. Pound, "Do We Need a Philosophy of Law?" 352; Cahill, *Judicial Legislation*, 40, 71–83; Goodnow, *Social Reform*, 357–358; James B. Thayer, "The Origin and Scope of the American Doctrine of Constitutional Law," in *Legal Essays*, 1, 21 (Boston, 1908), originally in 7 *Harvard Law Review* 129 (1893).

29. Maurice S. Culp, "A Survey of the Proposals to Limit or Deny the Power of Judicial Review by the Supreme Court," 4 *Indiana Law Journal* 486–487 (1929); Katherine B. Fite and Louis B. Rubinstein, "Curbing the Supreme Court—State Experiences and Federal Proposals," 35 *Michigan Law Review* 762, 763–767 (1937); Charles C. Tansill, *Proposed Amendments to the Constitution of the United States, 1889–1926*, S. Doc. No. 93, 69th Cong., 1st Sess. (1926); American Federation of Labor, *Report of 39th Annual Convention*, 97–100, 361–362 (Washington, D.C., 1919).

30. Donald B. Johnson and Kirk H. Porter, *National Party Platforms: 1840–1972*, at 176, 252–254 (Urbana, Ill., 1973); Haines, *Judicial Supremacy*, 2d ed., 484–487; Fite, "Curbing the Supreme Court," 763, 772–773; 2 *Congressional Digest* 272 (June 1923).

31. Haines, *Judicial Supremacy*, 2d ed., 469–475; Fite, "Curbing the Supreme Court," 766–767; AFL, *39th Annual Convention*, 97–100, 361–362.

32. Johnson, *National Party Platforms*, 106, 118, 136, 254; Tansill, *Proposed Amendments*, 56 et seq.; Culp, "Survey of Proposals," 479–480; Cahill, *Judicial Legislation*, 62; Haines, *Judicial Supremacy*, 2d ed., 482, 498; AFL, *39th Annual Convention*, 361–362 (emphasis added).

33. Johnson, *National Party Platforms*, 156, 176; Act of Dec. 23, 1914, ch. 2, 38 Stat. 790, 28 U.S.C. § 1257(3) (1982).

34. Johnson, *National Party Platforms*, 176; Haines, *Judicial Supremacy*, lst ed., 345, and 2d ed., 485–486; Tansill, *Proposed Amendments*, 55–56; under Article V of the Constitution an amendment may be proposed by a two-thirds vote of both houses of Congress or by application from two-thirds of the state legislatures; ratification requires approval by three-quarters of the states.

35. Haines, *Judicial Supremacy*, 1st ed., 352.

36. Goldman, *Rendezvous with Destiny*, 254; Hofstadter, *Age of Reform*, 273; Will Durant, "The War within the War," 65 *Dial* 5 (June 20, 1918); Will and Ariel Durant, *A Dual Autobiography*, 76–79 (New York, 1977); Burl Noggle, *Into the Twenties: The United States from Armistice to Normalcy*, 7–8, 31–45 (Urbana, Ill., 1974); Stanley Shapiro, "The Great War and Reform: Liberals and Labor, 1917–19," 12 *Labor History* 324, 325–329 (1971).

37. Noggle, *Into the Twenties*, 48–52; Hofstadter, *Age of Reform*, 273–280; Robert K. Murray, *Red Scare: A Study in National Hysteria, 1919–1920* (Minneapolis, 1955); Shapiro, "War and Reform," 343.

38. William F. Willoughby, *Government Organization in War Time and After: A Survey of the Federal Civil Agencies Created for the Prosecution of the War,* v (New York, 1919); Clarence A. Berdahl, *War Powers of the Executive in the United States,* 167–181, 203–219 (1920; reprint, New York, 1970); Carroll H. Wooddy, *The Growth of the Federal Government, 1915–1932,* at 1, 544, 547–551 (New York, 1934).

39. Goldman, *Rendezvous with Destiny,* 218; Frederick P. Keppel, Introduction, in Willoughby, *Government Organization,* xvii–xviii.

40. WW, Address to Joint Session of Congress, Dec. 2, 1918, 53 *WWP* 274, 286; *Washington Post,* Dec. 3, 1919, at 1:8 and 2:2–3; John R. Bolling, *Chronology of Woodrow Wilson,* 125–136 (New York, 1927); Edwin A. Weinstein, *Woodrow Wilson: A Medical and Psychological Biography,* 349–370 (Princeton, 1981); Edwin A. Weinstein, "Woodrow Wilson's Neurological Illness," 57 *Journal of American History* 324, 347–351 (Sept. 1970); Tom Schactman, *Edith & Woodrow: A Presidential Romance,* 204–264 (New York, 1981).

41. Schactman, *Edith & Woodrow,* 217, 221–222; Noggle, *Into the Twenties,* 122; O. A. Hilton, "Freedom of the Press in Wartime, 1917–1919," 28 *Southwestern Social Science Quarterly* 346, 357 (Mar. 1948); Harry N. Scheiber, *The Wilson Administration and Civil Liberties, 1917–1921,* at 36–39, 56–57 (Ithaca, N.Y., 1960); H.R. Rep. No. 801, 66th Cong., 2d Sess., pt. 2, section 2(II) (1920), 59 Cong. Rec. 6488 (1920), listing war laws remaining in effect until the declaration of peace or a stated period thereafter. Burleson was postmaster general from 1913 to 1921; Palmer was Alien Property Custodian from 1917 until 1919, when he became attorney general.

42. United States v. E. C. Knight Co., 156 U.S. 1 (1895); Hammer v. Dagenhart, 247 U.S. 251 (1918); compare The Employers' Liability Cases, 207 U.S. 463, 498–499 (1908) and Adair v. United States, 208 U.S. 161 (1908), with Southern Ry. Co. v. United States, 222 U.S. 20, 26–27 (1911), Mondou v. New York, N.H., & H.R.R., 223 U.S. 1 (1912), and Houston E. & W. Tex. Ry. v. United States, 234 U.S. 342, 353 (1914); McCray v. United States, 195 U.S. 27 (1904); Bailey v. Drexel Furniture Co., 259 U.S. 20, 43 (1922). For contemporary views on the commerce and taxation clauses see 1 Westel W. Willoughby, *The Constitutional Law of the United States,* 580 (New York, 1910); 2 ibid., chaps. 42–43; Burdick, *American Constitution,* chap. 8; James P. Hall, *Constitutional Law,* §§ 279–284 (Chicago, 1922); Walter Thompson, *Federal Centralization: A Study and Criticism of the Expanding Scope of Congressional Legislation,* 65–69, 292–301 (New York, 1923); Croly, *Promise of American Life,* 351, 357.

43. *The Federalist* No. 26, at 213 (B. F. Wright ed. 1961); 12 Cong. Deb. 4038 (May 25, 1836) (Rep. John Q. Adams); 2 Joseph Story, *Commentaries on the Constitution,* 95, 97 (2d ed., Boston, 1851). The war powers are

shared by Congress and the president, and are found in Article I, § 8, and Article II, § 2 of the Constitution. Lichter v. United States, 334 U.S. 742, 755 n.3 (1948); S. Doc. No. 92–82, *Constitution of United States,* 323–325; Berdahl, *War Powers,* 15–21.

44. The principal cases arising from each war were as follows (those involving an act of Congress are noted by an asterisk): undeclared naval war with France (1798–1800): Little v. Barreme, 6 U.S. (2 Cranch) 170 (1804); War of 1812: Brown v. United States, 12 U.S. (8 Cranch) 110 (1814); McCulloch v. Maryland,* 17 U.S. (4 Wheat.) 316 (1819); Mexican War (1846–1848): Mitchell v. Harmony, 54 U.S. (13 How.) 115 (1852); Jecker v. Montgomery, 54 U.S. (13 How.) 498 (1852); Cross v. Harrison, 57 U.S. (16 How.) 164 (1853); Leitensdorfer v. Webb, 61 U.S. (20 How.) 176 (1857); Civil War (1861–1865): The Prize Cases, 67 U.S. (2 Black) 635 (1863); Ex parte Milligan, 71 U.S. (4 Wall.) 2 (1866); Hepburn v. Griswold,* 75 U.S. (8 Wall.) 603 (1870); The Grapeshot, 76 U.S. (9 Wall.) 129 (1870); McVeigh v. United States, 78 U.S. (11 Wall.) 259 (1871); Miller v. United States,* 78 U.S. (11 Wall.) 268 (1871); Stewart v. Kahn,* 78 U.S. (11 Wall.) 493 (1871); Handlin v. Wickliffe, 79 U.S. (12 Wall.) 173 (1871); The Legal Tender Cases,* 79 U.S. (12 Wall.) 457 (1871); Pennywit v. Eaton, 82 U.S. (15 Wall.) 382 (1873); Hamilton v. Dillin, 88 U.S. (21 Wall.) 73 (1874); Mechanics' and Traders' Bank v. Union Bank, 89 U.S. (22 Wall.) 276 (1874); Raymond v. Thomas, 91 U.S. 712 (1876); United States v. Pacific R.R., 120 U.S. 227 (1887); United States v. Gettysburg Electric Ry.,* 160 U.S. 668 (1896); Spanish-American War (1898): Neely v. Henkel, 180 U.S. 109 (1901); Dooley v. United States, 182 U.S. 222 (1901). The government was found to have acted unconstitutionally in Little v. Barreme, Brown v. United States, Mitchell v. Harmony, Jecker v. Montgomery, Ex parte Milligan, Raymond v. Thomas, Dooley v. United States, and Hepburn v. Griswold (overruled by The Legal Tender Cases).

45. See, e.g., Little v. Barreme, 6 U.S. (2 Cranch) 170, 177–179 (1804), affirming $8,504 award against naval captain who, under presidential orders, seized a Danish ship; the Court ruled that the president had exceeded his authority as commander in chief by acting contrary to the Non-Intercourse Act and implied that the seizure would have been legal if sanctioned by statute; Brown v. United States, 12 U.S. (8 Cranch) 110, 128 (1814), invalidating wartime seizure of enemy property on the basis that Congress alone could authorize this use of the war powers; Jecker v. Montgomery, 54 U.S. (13 How.) 498, 515 (1852), nullifying condemnation proceeding of prize court established by U.S. military commander in territory captured from Mexico on the ground that only Congress may establish such a tribunal; Dooley v. United States, 182 U.S. 222, 235 (1901), ruling that Congress but the not president could authorize imposition of duties on goods shipped from New York to San Juan after the Spanish-American War.

46. Presidential actions were invalidated on durational grounds in Raymond v. Thomas, 91 U.S. 712 (1876), and Dooley v. United States, 182 U.S. 222 (1901); such challenges were rejected in Cross v. Harrison, 57 U.S. (16 How.) 164 (1853), Leitensdorfer v. Webb, 61 U.S. (20 How.) 176 (1857), and Neely v. Henkel, 180 U.S. 109 (1901). War statutes were upheld without discussion of the latent durational issue in McCulloch v. Maryland, 17 U.S. (4 Wheat.) 316, 407 (1819), The Legal Tender Cases, 79 U.S. (12 Wall.) 457 (1871), and United States v. Gettysburg Electric Ry., 160 U.S. 668 (1896). Martin v. Mott, 25 U.S. (12 Wheat.) 19, 29–32 (1827) hinted that the Court would not determine whether there was a sufficient emergency to trigger Congress's war powers. In Stewart v. Kahn, 78 U.S. (11 Wall.) 493, 506–507 (1871), and Raymond v. Thomas, 91 U.S. 712, 714–715 (1876), Justice Swayne distinguished between "measures to be taken in carrying on war" and those "to suppress insurrection," stating that in the "latter case the power is not limited to victories in the field." If this implied that Congress could not exercise its war power once hostilities had ceased, the distinction was ignored in Hamilton v. Kentucky Distilleries Co., 251 U.S. 146, 161 (1919), where the Court cited *Stewart* to support Congress's post–World War I use of the war powers. After the Civil War President Andrew Johnson vetoed or refused to enforce several measures on the ground that Congress could no longer exercise its war powers. Kenneth M. Stampp, *The Era of Reconstruction, 1865–1877,* at 69 (reprint, New York, 1965); 1 Henry S. Commager, *Documents in American History,* 462–464, 481–485 (7th ed., New York, 1963).

47. Mitchell v. Harmony, 54 U.S. (13 How.) 115, 134–135 (1852). After the trial court entered judgment against Col. David Mitchell for $104,562.23, Congress provided that the attorney general should handle his appeal to the Supreme Court, and that any final judgment against him should be paid from the Treasury. Act of Mar. 11, 1852, ch. 14, 10 Stat. 727; S. Rep. No. 53, 32d Cong., 1st Sess. (1852). And see Ex parte Milligan, 71 U.S. (4 Wall.) 2, 127 (1866), rejecting martial law on the basis that to justify its use, "the necessity must be actual and present; the invasion real, such as effectually closes the courts and deposes the civil administration."

48. McCulloch v. Maryland, 17 U.S. (4 Wheat.) 316, 407, 421 (1819); Brown v. United States, 12 U.S. (8 Cranch) 110, 128–129 (1814).

49. Hepburn v. Griswold, 75 U.S. (8 Wall.) 603, 617 (1870); The Legal Tender Cases, 79 U.S. (12 Wall.) 457, 542–543 (1871). See also The Chinese Exclusion Case, 130 U.S. 581, 606 (1889), and United States v. Gettysburg Electric Ry., 160 U.S. 668, 681 (1896).

50. Brief for the United States, Ex parte Milligan, 71 U.S. (4 Wall.) 2, 18–19 (1866); Ex parte Milligan, 71 U.S. (4 Wall.) 2, 120–124, 139–140 (1866). And see United States v. Russell, 80 U.S. (13 Wall.) 623, 627–629 (1871); but cf. United States v. Pacific R.R., 120 U.S. 227, 239 (1887).

51. Ex parte Milligan, 71 U.S. (4 Wall.) 2, 122, 125, 138–139 (1866). Chase agreed, however, that separation of powers might bar Congress from seeking to "direct the conduct of campaigns."

52. Miller v. United States, 78 U.S. (11 Wall.) 268, 304–305, 315 (1871). Ochoa v. Hernandez, 230 U.S. 139, 153–154 (1913), invalidated an order issued by the military governor of Puerto Rico during the Spanish-American War; though the case was decided on nonconstitutional grounds, the opinion stated that "the court below held . . . that, assuming General Henry possessed all the legislative power that is possessed by Congress . . . he was still necessarily subject (as Congress would be) to the 'due process of law' clause of the Fifth Amendment." This language passed unnoticed until 1935, when it was cited for the rule that Congress's war powers are subject to the Bill of Rights. Louisville Bank v. Radford, 295 U.S. 555, 589 n.19 (1935).

53. Address by Charles Evans Hughes to American Bar Association, Saratoga, N.Y., Sept. 5, 1917, in 2 *Marquette Law Review* 3, 10, 18 (1917–1918); the ABA distributed copies of the speech throughout the country; 1 Merlo J. Pusey, *Charles Evans Hughes*, 369–370 (New York, 1951); *N.Y. Times*, Sept. 6, 1917, at 1:7; ibid., Sept. 7, 1917, at 5:4; Henry J. Fletcher, "The Civilian and the War Power," 2 *Minnesota Law Review* 110, 113–114, 116, 131 (Jan. 1918), 3 *Virginia Law Register* (n.s.) 730 (1918), and 50 *Chicago Legal News* 241 (1918); Note, "Federal Authority under the War Power," 19 *Columbia Law Review* 489, 491 (Dec. 1919); Ambrose Tighe, "The Legal Theory of the Minnesota 'Safety Commission' Act," 3 *Minnesota Law Review* 1, 9–10 (Dec. 1918); Henry W. Ballantine, "Constitutional Limitations on the War Power," 6 *California Law Review* 134, 141 (Jan. 1918), and 3 *Virginia Law Register* (n.s.) 721, 729 (Feb. 1918); Berdahl, *War Powers*, 15–17; see Zechariah Chafee, Jr., "Freedom of Speech in War Times," 32 *Harvard Law Review* 932, 937, 955–956 (June 1919), reprinted as S. Doc. No. 95, 66th Cong., 1st Sess. (1919), urging that Congress's war powers are limited by the Constitution and rejecting as "extreme" the "view that the Bill of Rights is a peacetime document," but with no supporting authority other than the dictum in *Milligan*.

54. 55 Cong. Rec. 3888 (June 19, 1917) (Rep. Hamlin); ibid., 4459 (June 29, 1917) (Sens. Lewis and Reed); ibid., 4462 (Sen. Hardwick); ibid., 4555–4561 (June 30, 1917) (Sen. Lewis).

55. AMP, Address to Bar Association of the City of New York, Dec. 10, 1918, reprinted as "The Great Work of the Alien Property Custodian," 53 *American Law Review* 43, 51–55 (Jan.-Feb. 1919). The Court's perfunctory decisions during and shortly after World War I suggested no change in its practice of nonintervention. See Selective Draft Law Cases, 245 U.S. 366, 389–390 (Jan. 7, 1918), unanimously upholding military draft law, stating that each argument against it "is refuted by its mere statement"; Cox v. Wood, 247 U.S. 3 (May 6, 1918), unanimously affirming conviction under

Selective Service Law; McKinley v. United States, 249 U.S. 397, 399 (Apr. 14, 1919), unanimously sustaining wartime conviction for operating bawdy house near army base on the ground that the law's validity was so clear as not "to require more than the statement of the proposition."

56. Though the constitutionality of every war powers measure hinged on the specific facts, those who objected in one context were often supportive in another. During the 1918–19 debates fifteen House members spoke against the validity of one or both of the wartime prohibition laws, eleven of whom were in Congress in October 1919 when the war powers were again used to ban profiteering and create a District rent board; ten of the eleven approved these schemes: Reps. Coady (Md.), Gard (Ohio), Hardy (Tex.), Husted (N.Y.), Igoe (Mo.), Kahn (Calif.), Lea (Calif.), Sherwood (Ill.), Tilson (Conn.), and Voigt (Wis.); only Rep. Gallagher (Ill.) voted against the profiteering and rent laws; see Chapter 3; 58 Cong. Rec. 3005, 6759–6760, 7610–7611 (1919). James B. Thayer, *John Marshall,* 103–104 (1901; reprint, New York, 1974); Summers, *Instrumentalism,* 103. In a May 3, 1907, speech at Elmira, N.Y., Hughes declared, "We are under a Constitution, but the Constitution is what the judges say it is." Charles Evans Hughes, *Addresses, 1905–1916,* at 179, 185 (2d ed., New York, 1916).

57. Donald G. Morgan, *Congress and the Constitution: A Study of Responsibility,* 45–98, 332–333 (Cambridge, Mass., 1966); Paul Brest, "The Conscientious Legislator's Guide to Constitutional Interpretation," 27 *Stanford Law Review* 585, 587–588 (1975); Paul Brest, *Processes of Constitutional Decisionmaking,* 70 (Boston, 1975); 1 Story, *Commentaries,* 255; and see Marbury v. Madison, 5 U.S. (1 Cranch.) 137, 179–180 (1803).

58. Morgan, *Congress and Constitution,* 181–183, 332–335. The political question doctrine is discussed in Chapter 9. Despite the tension between legal pragmatism and constitutionalism, most instrumentalists recognized some limits on the majority; they did not claim that Congress and the president could ignore questions of validity on the theory that their conduct, as an embodiment of majority will, was *ipso facto* constitutional.

59. Morgan, *Congress and Constitution,* 11; Brest, "Legislator's Guide," 589.

60. 5 Jonathan Elliott, *Debates on the Adoption of the Federal Constitution,* 344 (Philadelphia, 1901); Cohens v. Virginia, 19 U.S. (6 Wheat.) 264, 404 (1821).

61. Thomas M. Cooley, *Constitutional Limitations,* 56, 78, 192–193 (2d ed., Boston, 1871); the same view was expounded in later editions; the Court has since held that this presumption does not operate if a law burdens a fundamental right or discriminates on the basis of a suspect or quasisuspect classification. See, e.g., United States v. Carolene Products Co., 304 U.S. 144, 152–153 n.4 (1938); John Hart Ely, *Democracy and Distrust: A Theory of Judicial Review* (Cambridge, Mass., 1980).

62. Thayer, "Origin and Scope," 21–22, 31–32, 38–39; Thayer, *John Marshall*, 103–104; largely because of Thayer, the doctrine of judicial self-restraint won considerable support. Alexander M. Bickel, *The Least Dangerous Branch: The Supreme Court at the Bar of Politics*, 35–45 (Indianapolis, 1962); Mark DeWolfe Howe, Introduction, in James B. Thayer et al., *John Marshall*, x–xii (reprint, Chicago, 1967); Wallace Mendelsohn, Introduction, in James B. Thayer, *John Marshall*, ix–x (reprint, New York, 1974).

63. McCulloch v. Maryland, 17 U.S. (4 Wheat.) 316, 423 (1819); see, e.g., Palmer v. Thompson, 403 U.S. 217 (1971); United States v. O'Brien, 391 U.S. 367, 382–386 (1968); United States v. Doremus, 249 U.S. 86, 93 (1919); Wilson v. New, 243 U.S. 332, 358–359 (1917); Weber v. Freed, 239 U.S. 325, 330 (1915); McCray v. United States, 195 U.S. 27, 56 (1904); compare Washington v. Davis, 426 U.S. 229 (1976); Paul Brest, "Palmer v. Thompson: An Approach to the Problem of Unconstitutional Legislative Motive," *1971 Supreme Court Review* 95; John H. Ely, "Legislative and Administrative Motivation in Constitutional Law," 79 *Yale Law Journal* 1205 (1970).

64. United States v. Kahriger, 345 U.S. 22, 38 (1953) (Frankfurter, J., dissenting); McCray v. United States, 195 U.S. 27, 54–55 (1904). Even if deemed a proper exercise of the war powers, the measure might of course violate the Bill of Rights.

65. Thayer, "Origin and Scope," 31–32; see Note, "Legislative Purpose and Federal Constitutional Adjudication," 83 *Harvard Law Review* 1887, 1891 (1970).

2. Experiments in Socialism

1. Carl D. Thompson, *Public Ownership: A Survey of Public Enterprises, Municipal, State, and Federal, in the United States, and Elsewhere* (New York, 1925); Harold U. Faulkner, *The Quest for Social Justice*, 120–121 (New York, 1931); Act of Mar. 12, 1914, ch. 37, § 1, 38 Stat. 305, 306–307; Charles Forcey, *The Crossroads of Liberalism: Croly, Weyl, Lippmann, and the Progressive Era, 1900–1925*, at 84, 211, 247 (New York, 1961); N.Y. *Times*, Apr. 12, 1914, at 14:3.

2. United States v. Gettysburg Elec. Ry., 160 U.S. 668 (1896); John A. Gordon, "Nationalizing the Railroads," 18 *Case and Comment* 530, 535 (1912); Christopher G. Tiedeman, "Government Ownership of Public Utilities," 16 *Harvard Law Review* 476, 487–488 (May 1903); Lindsay Rogers, *The Postal Power of Congress: A Study in Constitutional Expansion*, 150–157 (Baltimore, 1916); James P. Hall, *Constitutional Law*, 321 (Chicago, 1922); U.S. Const. art. I, § 8, cls. 3, 7, 17.

3. Walker D. Hines, *War History of American Railroads*, 1–21 (New

Haven, 1928); K. Austin Kerr, *American Railroad Politics, 1914–1920: Rates, Wages, and Efficiency,* 39–71 (Pittsburgh, 1968); Act of Aug. 29, 1916, ch. 418, 39 Stat. 645; Proclamation of Dec. 26, 1917, 40 Stat. 1733; Act of Mar. 21, 1918, ch. 25, 40 Stat. 451.

4. Act of Mar. 21, 1918, §§ 14, 16, ch. 25, 40 Stat. 451; S. Rep. No. 246, 65th Cong., 2d Sess. 8 (1918).

5. 56 Cong. Rec. 9070 (July 13, 1918) (Sen. Reed); ibid., 9073–9074 (Sen. Wadsworth); Act of Mar. 21, 1918, ch. 25, § 2, 40 Stat. 453–454; Blewett Lee, "Constitutional Objections to the Railway Control Act," 28 *Yale Law Journal* 158 (1918).

6. Vidkunn Ulriksson, *The Telegraphers: Their Craft and Their Unions,* 69–87, 97 (Washington, D.C., 1953); Paul H. Douglas, *Real Wages in the United States, 1890–1926,* at 644–647 (Boston, 1930); S. Doc. No. 725, 60th Cong., 2d Sess. 41, 48 (1909).

7. Ulriksson, *Telegraphers,* 107–108; Harlan B. Phillips, *Felix Frankfurter Reminisces,* 121–127 (New York, 1960); *N.Y. Times,* Nov. 3, 1917, at 18:3; *San Francisco Chronicle:* Nov. 10, 1917, at 1:8; Nov. 16, 1917, at 9:1; Nov. 23, 1917, at 9:1; Nov. 26, 1917, at 1:4; Nov. 27, 1917, at 9:5; Nov. 30, 1917, at 4:4; Dec. 3, 1917, at 3:4; Valerie Jean Conner, *The National War Labor Board: Stablility, Social Justice, and the Voluntary State in World War I* (Chapel Hill, 1983).

8. U.S. Bur. of Lab. Stats., Dept. of Labor, Bull. No. 287, *National War Labor Board,* 24–25 (1921); "Nat'l War Labor Bd. Report on Western Union Telegraph Co. Dispute," *OUSB,* June 4, 1918, at 6–7; *N.Y. Times:* Apr. 29, 1918, at 17:2; May 2, 1918, at 17:4; May 11, 1918, at 6:5; June 3, 1918, at 1:1; June 5, 1918, at 17:1; June 7, 1918, at 9:2; June 12, 1918, at 4:6; June 14, 1918, at 22:2; American Federation of Labor, *Report of 38th Annual Convention,* 202–203 (Washington, D.C., 1918); Conner, *War Labor Board,* 35–49.

9. WW to Clarence Mackay, June 11, 1918, 48 *WWP* 282; WW MSS, ser. 3, vol. 52, at 187–195; Mackay to WW, June 12, 1918, 48 *WWP* 298; Mackay to WW, June 14, 1918, WW MSS, ser. 4, case 4341; Newcomb Carlton to WW, June 17, 1918, 48 *WWP* 337; *N.Y. Times:* June 14, 1918, at 22:2; June 15, 1918, at 7:1; June 16, 1918, at 12:2; June 19, 1918, at 1:1; June 27, 1918, at 11:3; July 1, 1918, at 1:3 and 6:4.

10. Ulriksson, *Telegraphers,* 91–98, 107; H.R.J. Res. 206, 65th Cong., 2d Sess., 56 Cong. Rec. 617 (1918).

11. WW to Thomas W. Gregory, June 17, 1918, WW MSS, ser. 2; *San Francisco Chronicle,* June 19, 1918, at 3:4; 56 Cong. Rec. 8719–8720 (July 5, 1918) (Rep. Aswell); *Hearings on H.R.J. Res. 309 before House Comm. on Interstate and Foreign Commerce,* 65th Cong., 2d Sess. 36 (July 2, 1918).

12. William B. Wilson to WW, June 10, 1918, 48 *WWP* 281.

13. American Federation of Labor, *Report of 26th Annual Convention,* vi, 238–241 (Washington, D.C., 1906); *Dictionary of American Biography,* s.v. "Wilson, William B."; ibid., s.v. "Burleson, Albert S."; *N.Y. Times,* Nov. 27, 1937, at 31:1; S. Doc. No. 399, 63d Cong., 2d Sess. (1914); Post Office Dept., *1913 Annual Report,* 15–16; Post Office Dept., *1914 Annual Report,* 12–14, 62–64; ASB to Thomas R. Marshall, Mar. 4, 1918, 56 Cong. Rec. 2957–2959 (1918).

14. Frederick C. Howe, "Baker: Trained Administrator," 85 *Independent* 415 (Mar. 20, 1916); *Dictionary of American Biography,* s.v. "Baker, Newton D."; ibid., s.v. "Daniels, Josephus"; ibid., s.v. "Lane, Franklin K."; E. David Cronon, *The Cabinet Diaries of Josephus Daniels: 1913–1921,* at 81, 123, 126, 169 & n.38, 243, 598 (Lincoln, Neb., 1963); *House Hearings on H.R.J. Res. 309,* at 21, 27; Josephus Daniels to WW, Nov. 30, 1917, 45 *WWP* 170; John J. Broesamle, *William Gibbs McAdoo: A Passion for Change, 1863–1917,* at 217–221 (Port Washington, N.Y., 1973); Mary Synon, *McAdoo: The Man and His Times, A Panorama in Democracy,* 179–183 (Indianapolis, 1924); Franklin K. Lane to Key Pittman, May 15, 1913, 51 Cong. Rec. 1584–1585 (1914); Dept. of the Interior, *1913 Annual Report,* 10–11.

15. JPT to WW, [ca. Jan. 1918], JPT MSS, Box 48; John M. Blum, *Joe Tumulty and the Wilson Era,* 150 (Boston, 1951); JPT to Alexander Simpson, Jan. 18, 1918, JPT MSS, Box 10; JPT to WW, Feb. 21, 1918, ibid., Box 48; 14 *New Republic* (Feb. 16, 1918), pt. 2.

16. WW, *The State: Elements of Historical and Practical Politics,* 497, 662–663 (Boston, 1890); WW, "Trust Crusading," 16 *American Lawyer* 267–268 (May 1908); WW, "Draft of a Platform for the Democratic Party of Pennsylvania," [ca. Apr. 4, 1910], 20 *WWP* 316; WW to ASB, Apr. 4, 1913, 27 *WWP* 260.

17. WW to ASB, Jan. 19, 1918, 46 *WWP* 37; WW to JPT, May 11, 1918, ASB MSS, vol. 20, items 3211–3218; JPT to E. M. House, May 23, 1918, JPT MSS, Box 44; House to JPT, May 25, 1918, ibid.; JPT to WW, June 18, 1918, 48 *WWP* 347; Indiana Democratic platform, ibid., 318; Blum, *Tumulty,* 151.

18. WW to Morris Sheppard, June 26, 1918, 48 *WWP* 440.

19. *Hearing on H.R.J. Res. 309 before Senate Comm. on Interstate Commerce,* 65th Cong., 2d Sess. 7–8 (July 9, 1918); *N.Y. Times,* July 1, 1918, at 1:3; ibid., July 10, 1918, at 1:2; 56 Cong. Rec. 8969 (July 11, 1918) (Sen. Underwood).

20. Albert B. Paine, *Theodore N. Vail: A Biography,* 318–322 (New York, 1921); *House Hearings on H.R.J. Res. 368,* at 8; *N.Y. Times,* Jan. 21, 1919, at 8:7; Theodore N. Vail to John A. Moon, Dec. 30, 1918, 57 Cong. Rec., appendix, 32–36 (1919); S. Doc. No. 399, 63d Cong., 2d Sess. 10–11 (1914); Theodore N. Vail to WW, July 19, 1918, WW MSS, ser. 4, case

350K; many small companies favored federal control for financial reasons. 56 Cong. Rec. 9064–9065 (1918) (Sen. Harding).

21. *Senate Hearing on H.R.J. Res. 309,* at 4–6; Paine, *Vail,* 249; 106 *Nation* 748 (June 29, 1918); *N.Y. Times,* June 4, 1918, at 14:1; ibid., June 19, 1918, at 9:3; ibid., July 10, 1918, at 1:1; Ulriksson, *Telegraphers,* 109.

22. William Hard, "Mr. Burleson, Unionizer," 18 *New Republic* 299 (Apr. 5, 1919); William Hard, "Mr. Burleson, Junker in Vain," ibid., 369 (Apr. 19, 1919); Post Office Dept., *1917 Annual Report,* 31–35; *N.Y. Times,* June 3, 1918, at 8:3; *House Hearings on H.R.J. Res. 309,* at 41.

23. *N.Y. Times,* July 3, 1918, at 1:1 and 11:4; ibid., July 5, 1918, at 15:1; AFL, *38th Annual Convention,* 203; *House Hearings on H.R.J. Res. 309,* at 40–41, 49.

24. Josephus Daniels to Rep. Thetus W. Sims, June 27, 1918, 56 Cong. Rec. 8718–8719 (1918); ASB to Sims, June 28, 1918, ibid.; Newton D. Baker to Sims, July 1, 1918, ibid.; Sims to WW and WW to Sims, June 28, 1918, 48 *WWP* 457–458; *N.Y. Times,* July 2, 1918, at 1:1 and 6:4.

25. *House Hearings on H.R.J. Res. 309,* at 10–18, 21–30, 35–41, 46; *N.Y. Times,* July 3, 1918, at 1:1 and 11:4.

26. *N.Y. Times,* July 4, 1918, at 12:8; H.R. Rep. No. 741, 65th Cong., 2d Sess. (July 4, 1918); 56 Cong. Rec. 8719–8721 (July 5, 1918); ibid., 8729 (Rep. Sims); ibid., 8717 (Rep. Campbell); ibid., 8727 (Rep. Moore); ibid., 8735.

27. 56 Cong. Rec. 8746 (July 6, 1918) (Sen. Johnson); JPT to WW, July 5, 1918, JPT MSS, Box 48; WW to Thomas S. Martin, July 5, 1918, 48 *WWP* 526; JPT to WW, July 6, 1918, JPT MSS, Box 48; WW to Atlee Pomerene, July 6, 1918, 48 *WWP* 534; ibid., 535 n.1; William B. Wilson to ASB (n.d.), ASB MSS, vol. 21, item 3329; William B. Wilson to Sylvester J. Konenkamp, July 7, 1918, WW MSS, ser. 4, case 4341; William B. Wilson to WW, July 7 1918, 48 *WWP* 546; *N.Y. Times,* July 7, 1918, at 1:4; ibid., July 8, 1918, at 1:1 and 6:1.

28. 56 Cong. Rec. 8742 (July 6, 1918) (Sen. Martin); ibid., 8743 (July 6, 1918) (Sen. Cummins); ibid., 8860–8865 (July 8, 1918) (Sens. Smith, Kellogg, Reed, and Penrose); ibid., 8968–8969 (July 11, 1918) (Sens. Underwood and Smith); ibid., 8986 (July 12, 1918) (Sen. Pomerene).

29. 56 Cong. Rec. 8863 (July 8, 1918) (Sen. Smith); ibid., 8864 (Sen. Reed); ibid., 8982 (July 11, 1918) (Sen. Kellogg); ibid., 9070 (July 13, 1918) (Sen. Reed); ibid., 9076 (Sen. Lenroot).

30. 56 Cong. Rec. 8969–8971 (July 11, 1918) (Sen. Underwood); ibid., 8989 (July 12, 1918) (Sen. Gore); ibid., 8997 (Sens. Lewis and Knox); ibid., 9070 (July 13, 1918) (Sen. Smith); ibid., 9076–9077 (Sen. Lenroot); *N.Y. Times,* July 12, 1918, at 1:2.

31. 56 Cong. Rec. 8744 (July 11, 1918) (Sen. Borah); ibid., 8981–8982 (Sen. Kellogg); ibid., 8994 (July 12, 1918) (Sen. Sherman); ibid., 9070 (July

13, 1918) (Sen. Reed); ibid., 9073–9075 (Sen. Wadsworth); ibid., 9076 (Sen. Lenroot); ibid., 9082 (Sen. Watson).

32. *56 Cong. Rec.* 8747 (July 6, 1918) (Sen. Vardaman); ibid., 8863, 9007, 9070 (July 8, 12, 13, 1918) (Sen. Reed); ibid., 8969 (July 11, 1918) (Sen. Underwood); ibid., 9001 (July 12, 1918) (Sen. Lewis); ibid., 9064 (July 13, 1918) (Sen. Harding); ibid., 9085–9086 (Sen. Thomas); ibid, 9094.

33. *N.Y. Times:* July 16, 1918, at 14:2; July 17, 1918, at 10:7; July 18, 1918, at 6:5; July 20, 1918, at 7:4; July 24, 1918, at 1:3; John W. Tevis to WW, July 18, 1918, WW MSS, ser. 4, case 350K; Proclamation of July 22, 1918, 40 Stat. 1807; ASB to WW, July 17, 1918, WW MSS, ser. 4, case 350K; ASB to WW, with memo from W. H. Lamar to ASB, July 19, 1918, ibid.

34. *N.Y. Times,* July 24, 1918, at 8:3; ibid., July 25, 1918, at 9:1 and 17:3; William J. Bryan to ASB, July 23, 1918, ASB MSS, vol. 21, items 3324–3325.

35. *N.Y. Times:* July 24, 1918, at 1:3 and 8:2; Aug. 1, 1918, at 1:1; Aug. 22, 1918, at 6:2; Aug. 30, 1918, at 9:2; *OUSB,* July 24, 1918, at 2; ibid., Aug. 1, 1918, at 1; ibid., Aug. 19, 1918, at 16; Post Office Dept., *Government Control and Operation of Telegraph, Telephone, and Marine Cable Systems, August 1, 1918, to July 31, 1919,* at 59–92 (1921), hereinafter cited as *Government Control.*

36. *Report of the Postmaster General on the Supervision and Operation of the Telegraph, Telephone, and Cable Properties,* S. Doc. No. 152, 66th Cong., 1st Sess. 6, 8, 22 (1919), hereinafter cited as *Report of Postmaster; N.Y. Times,* July 24, 1918, at 1:3 and 8:2; ibid., Aug. 20, 1918, at 13:2; ibid., Sept. 14, 1918, at 15:5; *OUSB,* Aug. 7, 1918, at 2; ibid., Aug. 19, 1918, at 16; ASB MSS, vol. 21, items 3333, 3340, 3365; S. Doc. No. 399, 63d Cong., 2d Sess. (1914).

37. *Report of Postmaster,* 6–9.

38. Proclamation of Nov. 2, 1918, 40 Stat. 1872; *OUSB,* Nov. 16, 1918, at 4; *N.Y. Times,* Nov. 17, 1918, at 1:3; ibid., Apr. 30, 1919, at 10:1; Post Office News Release, Dec. 30, 1918, ASB MSS, vol. 22, item 3467.

39. ASB, penciled notes (n.d.), ASB MSS, vol. 25, items 3957–3959; ASB to WW, Nov. 2, 1918, WW MSS, ser. 4, case 22.

40. Robert Lansing to WW, Nov. 6, 1918, WW MSS, ser. 4, case 350K; and see Lansing to WW, July 15, 1918, ibid. McAdoo's resignation as treasury secretary was possibly influenced by his not having been consulted on the cable seizure. See Herman H. Kohlsaat, *From McKinley to Harding: Personal Recollections of Our Presidents,* 212–215 (New York, 1923); John Milton Cooper, Jr., *The Warrior and the Priest: Woodrow Wilson and Theodore Roosevelt,* 240–241 (Cambridge, Mass., 1983).

41. ASB to WW, Nov. 12, 1918, enclosing ASB to WW, Nov. 11, 1918, WW MSS, ser. 4, case 350K; Gilbert F. Close to Rudolph Forster, Nov. 13,

1918, ibid. Lansing may have delayed the cable seizure in hopes of sabotaging it. See Arthur S. Link, *Wilson: Campaigns for Progressivism and Peace*, 221–225 (Princeton, 1965); Cooper, *Warrior and Priest*, 292.

42. *N.Y. Times,* Nov. 16, 1918, at 4:2; ibid., Nov. 20, 1919, at 1:2 and 24:2; *OUSB*, Nov. 20, 1918, at 1–2. The proclamation relaxing war prohibition was signed in Paris on Jan. 30, 1919 (40 Stat. 1930); the administration announced that it could not take effect until the official seal was affixed by the State Department in Washington. *N.Y. Times,* Feb. 21, 1919, at 1:3.

43. H. H. Kohlsaat to WW, Nov. 20, 1918, 53 *WWP* 148; WW to Kohlsaat, Nov. 22, 1918, ibid., 164; Kohlsaat, *McKinley to Harding*, 212–215; *N.Y. Times,* Oct. 18, 1924, at 15:1; WW to AMP, Nov. 22, 1918, WW MSS, ser. 14, file 55. And see WW to AMP, Nov. 27, 1918, ibid.

44. *St. Louis Post-Dispatch,* Nov. 23, 1918, at 12:2; *Springfield Republican,* Nov. 21, 1918, at 6:2; ibid., Nov. 25, 1918, at 6:2; *N.Y. Times,* Nov. 21, 1918, at 14:2; ibid., Nov. 24, 1918, pt. 3, at 1:1; ibid., Apr. 30, 1919, at 10:1; William F. Willoughby, *Government Organization in War Time and After,* 198 (New York, 1919).

45. 56 Cong. Rec. 11602–11603 (Nov. 21, 1918) (Sen. Kellogg); ibid., 11614–11615 (Sen. Watson); ibid., 11616–11619 (Sen. Sherman); *N.Y. Times,* Nov. 22, 1918, at 12:2; ibid., Dec. 1, 1918, at 1:4 and 19:1; Charles Evans Hughes, "Our After-War Dangers: In Saving the World Have We Lost Our Republic?" 61 *Forum* 237 (Feb. 1919).

46. WW, Message to Congress, Dec. 2, 1919, 53 *WWP* 274, 285; *N.Y. Times,* Dec. 3, 1918, at 2:2; ibid., Dec. 6, 1918, at 9:1; ibid., Dec. 7, 1918, at 1:6; *Washington Post,* Dec. 5, 1918, at 3:5; 57 Cong. Rec. 130–131 (Dec. 5, 1918); *OUSB*, Dec. 3, 1918, at 4.

47. 57 Cong. Rec. 788 (Dec. 23, 1918) (Sen. Hitchcock); *N.Y. Times,* Dec. 24, 1918, at 5:1.

48. Elisha M. Friedman, *American Problems of Reconstruction: A National Symposium on the Economic and Financial Aspects,* 35 (New York, 1918); 41 *Survey* 224–225 (Nov. 23, 1918); Harold Stearns, "Why Reconstruction?" 65 *Dial* 249, 252 (Oct. 5, 1918); Walter E. Weyl, *The End of the War,* 307 (New York, 1918); Federal Trade Commission, *Report on the Meat-Packing Industry,* pt. 1, at 25–26 (1919); 48 *WWP* 507; Public Ownership League of America, *Conference Proceedings,* 17, 22, 237–246, 278–288 (Chicago, 1919); James Weinstein, *The Decline of Socialism in America, 1912–1925,* at 229–230 (New Brunswick, N.J., 1984); 66 *Current Opinion* 72–75 (Feb. 1919); *N.Y. Times,* Nov. 24, 1918, pt. 3, at 1:1; ibid., Nov. 25, 1918, at 12:1; ibid., Nov. 27, 1918, at 12:1; ibid., Nov. 28, 1919, at 16:4; on the Hearst newspapers, see, e.g., 25 *American Federationist* 1055 (Dec. 1918).

49. *OUSB:* Nov. 20, 1918, at 5; Nov. 25, 1918, at 1; Nov. 27, 1918, at

5; Dec. 9, 1918, at 1, 3; ibid., Dec. 14, 1918, at 2–3; Dec. 16, 1918, at 1–2; Jan. 2, 1919, at 6; *N.Y. Times:* Nov. 24, 1918, at 1:4; Nov. 26, 1918, at 3:5; Dec. 9, 1918, at 1:1 and 13:3; Dec. 14, 1918, at 1:3; Dec. 27, 1918, at 20:6; Jan. 1, 1919, at 22:1; Theodore N. Vail to ASB, Dec. 6, 1918, ASB MSS, vol. 22, items 3441–3450; 58 Cong. Rec. 915–917 (June 10, 1919); *Report of Postmaster,* 8, 10–11.

50. *Government Control,* 59–92.

51. JPT to WW, Dec. 1, 1918, JPT MSS, Box 48; WW, Message to Congress, Dec. 2, 1918, 53 *WWP* 274, 282–284; a few weeks earlier Wilson had told the War Council that the United States should retain ownership of the ships it operated during the war. Cronon, *Cabinet Diaries,* 349.

52. H.R.J. Res. 368, 65th Cong., 3d Sess. (1918); *N.Y. Times,* Dec. 14, 1918, at 1:3 and 7:3; ibid., Dec. 17, 1918, at 15:1; *Hearings on H.R.J. Res. 368,* at 3, 393, 401; ASB, "Telegraph and Telephones in Government Hands," 58 *American Review of Reviews* 619 (Dec. 1918); *N.Y. Journal of Commerce and Commercial Bulletin,* Jan. 2, 1919, pt. 2, at 5:5; ASB, "Why We Should Keep the Wires: A Question of National Defense and Economic Efficiency, Not a Partisan Question," 61 *Forum* 152 (Feb. 1919).

53. William G. McAdoo to WW, Nov. 24, 1918, Library of Congress, William Gibbs McAdoo Papers, Box 525; McAdoo to WW, Feb. 25, 1919, 55 *WWP* 258; McAdoo to Thetus W. Sims, Dec. 11, 1918, 57 Cong. Rec. 363–364 (1918); McAdoo to Ellison D. Smith, Dec. 11, 1918, ibid., 337–338; *N.Y. Times,* Dec. 12, 1918, at 1:1 and 4:2; ibid., Dec. 13, 1918, at 16:3–5; 57 Cong. Rec. 338 (Dec. 12, 1918) (Sen. Kellogg); Kerr, *Railroad Politics,* 135–143.

54. Address by Walker D. Hines to Railroad Committee of U.S. Chamber of Commerce, Dec. 12, 1918, UCLA Library, William Gibbs McAdoo Papers, Box 12; *N.Y. Times,* Dec. 13, 1918, at 1:1 and 14:1–2; ibid., Dec. 18, 1918, at 17:4; 17 *New Republic* 207 (Dec. 21, 1918); *Springfield Republican,* Dec. 13, 1918, at 8:2; 57 Cong. Rec. 339 (Dec. 12, 1918) (Sen. Kellogg); ibid., 464–465 (Dec. 14, 1918) (Rep. Black); ibid., 1460 (Jan. 15, 1919) (Rep. Denison).

55. *Hearings on H.R.J. Res. 368,* at 3–4, 402; H.R. Rep. No. 1012, 65th Cong., 3d Sess. 1–5 (1919); *N.Y. Times:* Jan. 5, 1919, pt. 7, at 3; Jan. 8, 1919, at 1:3; Jan. 13, 1919, at 14:4; Jan. 28, 1919, at 8:6; Jan. 29, 1919, at 1:1; Feb. 8, 1919, at 14:8; Feb. 18, 1919, at 17:4; Feb. 21, 1919, at 6:2; Mar. 1, 1919, at 3:5; Mar. 2, 1919, at 1:4 and 7:3; Mar. 5, 1919, at 3:4; 57 Cong. Rec. 1460, 3892–3893 (1919) (Sen. Denison); addresses by Walker D. Hines, UCLA Library, William Gibbs McAdoo Papers, Box 12; JPT to WW, Jan. 7, 1919, JPT MSS, Box 49; *Hearings on Extension of Time for Relinquishment by Gov't of Railroads to Corporate Ownership and Control before House Comm. on Interstate and Foreign Commerce,* 65th Cong., 3d Sess. (1919); *Hearings on Extension of Time for Relinquishment by Gov't of*

Railroads to Corporate Ownership and Control before Sen. Comm. on Interstate Commerce, 65th Cong., 3d Sess. (1919).

56. 56 Cong. Rec. 11601 (Nov. 21, 1918); 58 Cong. Rec. 857 (June 9, 1919) (Sen. Cummins); ibid., 917–918 (June 10, 1919); ibid., 1341–1342 (June 18, 1919); *OUSB,* Mar. 31, 1919, at 1; *N.Y. Times:* Jan. 18, 1919, at 14:1; Jan. 21, 1919 at 1:2; Jan. 22, 1919, at 1:1 and 4:5; Jan. 23, 1919, at 7:1–3; Jan. 30, 1919, at 10:8; Feb. 6, 1919, at 13:2; Feb. 10, 1919, at 15:4–5; Feb. 24, 1919, at 16:2–5; Mar. 30, 1919, at 1:4; June 3, 1919, at 4:2; *San Francisco Chronicle,* Apr. 3, 1919, at 8:4; "Mr. Burleson on the Grill," 61 *Literary Digest* (Apr. 19, 1919), at 14–15; Norman S. Richards to WW, Nov. 26, 1918, WW MSS, ser. 4, case 350K; Motion of United States to Advance, Dakota Cent. Tel. Co. v. South Dakota, 250 U.S. 153 (1919), noting that decisions had been issued against rate order in Fla., Ill., Ind., Mich., Minn., Mo., Neb., Ohio, Pa., and S.D.

57. "Mr. Burleson on the Grill," 61 *Literary Digest* (Apr. 19, 1919), at 14–15; "Mr. Aswell Apologizes," *N.Y. World,* Apr. 7, 1919, at 1:1 and 12:2; "Samuel" to JPT, Apr. 6, 1919, JPT MSS, Box 11; Blum, *Tumulty,* 192–193.

58. Ulriksson, *Telegraphers,* 1–14, 140–141; *Senate Hearing on H.R.J. Res. 309,* at 4, 6, 9; *Telegraph, Telephone, and Cable Properties,* S. Doc. No. 152, 66th Cong., 1st Sess. 14–15 (1919); "Memorandum of the Mackay System of Telegraphs and Cables," Aug. 19, 1918, ASB MSS, vol. 21, items 3346–3349; *N.Y. Times,* Nov. 13, 1938, at 1:3 and 46:1; 57 Cong. Rec. 5009–5014 (Mar. 4, 1919) (Sen. Sherman).

59. Clarence Mackay to ASB, Nov. 11, 1918, 56 Cong. Rec. 11602 (1918); *OUSB,* Dec. 5, 1918, at 5; ibid., Dec. 14, 1918, at 3; *N.Y. Times:* Aug. 20, 1918, at 13:2; Nov. 16, 1918, at 12:8; Nov. 21, 1918, at 4:3–5; Nov. 24, 1918, at 1:4 and 20:3; Nov. 26, 1918, at 3:5; Dec. 5, 1918, at 1:1; Dec. 9, 1918, at 1:1 and 13:3; Dec. 28, 1918, at 5:1; Theodore N. Vail to John A. Moon, December 30, 1918, in 57 Cong. Rec., App., 34 (Jan. 7, 1919). AT&T had earlier sought to gain control of the Mackay interests. 57 Cong. Rec. 5010–5011 (Mar. 4, 1919) (Sen. Sherman). Four of the seven cable companies seized were Mackay's. *N.Y. Times,* Dec. 14, 1918, at 7:5; *Telegraph, Telephone, and Cable Properties,* 5; *Poor's Manual of Public Utilities,* 848–849 (New York, 1914). The seizure was later upheld in Commercial Cable Co. v. Burleson, 255 F. 99 (S.D.N.Y.), *rev'd on grounds of mootness,* 250 U.S. 360 (1919).

60. *OUSB,* Nov. 21, 1918, at 5, 7; ibid., Dec. 5, 1918, at 5; ibid., Dec. 14, 1918, at 3; *N.Y. Times:* Oct. 7, 1918, at 12:6; Nov. 21, 1918, at 1:1; Dec. 5, 1918, at 13:4; Dec. 7, 1918, at 20:4; Dec. 14, 1918, at 7:6; Mar. 23, 1919, at 1:1 and 18:3–4; Apr. 2, 1919, at 20:1; 57 Cong. Rec. 314 (Dec. 11, 1918); Clarence Mackay to JPT, May 7, 1919, JPT MSS, Box 11; *Government Control,* 33–34, 84–85; *Telephone, Telegraph, and Cable Properties,*

14–20; Post Office News Release, Apr. 12, 1919, ASB MSS, vol. 23, items 3577–3581. Burleson sued Postal-Telegraph to collect its "excess" earnings, but the Harding administration later dropped the suit. S. Doc. No. 415, 66th Cong., 3d Sess. 3 (1921); *N.Y. Times*, Feb. 22, 1921, at 27:1; ibid., Apr. 27, 1922, at 12:1; Charles E. Hughes to Clarence Mackay, May 2, 1919, WW MSS, ser. 4; Mackay to JPT, May 19, 1919, ibid.

61. Clarence Mackay to JPT, May 7, 1919, JPT MSS, Box 11; *N.Y. Times*, Dec. 30, 1918, at 8:6; ibid., Mar. 23, 1919, at 18:2; *N.Y. World*, Mar. 24, 1919, at 12:2; ibid., Mar. 31, 1919, at 10:2; ibid., Apr. 7, 1919, at 6:4; 57 Cong. Rec. 5012–5013 (Mar. 4, 1919) (Sen. Sherman); *Newark Evening News*, Mar. 24, 1919, at 8:1.

62. JPT to James B. Regan, May 2, 1919, JPT MSS, Box 84, Letter Book 10, at 320; Clarence Mackay to JPT, May 7, 1919, ibid., Box 11; JPT to WW, May 8, 1919, ibid., Box 49; JPT to Mackay, May 8, 1919, ibid., Box 11.

63. *N.Y. Times*, July 17, 1918, at 10:4; Phillips, *Frankfurter*, 122.

64. Alexander M. Bing, *War-Time Strikes and Their Adjustment*, 109–111 (New York, 1921); *Hearings on H.R.J. Res. 368*, at 114–115; ASB to William B. Wilson, March 15, 1919, WW MSS, ser. 4, case 22; *OUSB*, Sept. 16, 1918, at 3; ibid., Jan. 2, 1919, at 6; *Minneapolis Journal*, Nov. 15, 1918, at 1:4; "Mr. Burleson on the Grill," 61 *Literary Digest* (Apr. 19, 1919), at 14; *N.Y. Times:* Jan. 1, 1919, at 22:1; Jan. 12, 1919, at 15:1; Jan. 31, 1919, at 3:6; Feb. 6, 1919, at 9:1. In 1918 the average annual income of full-time telephone workers was 14 percent less than in 1902. Douglas, *Real Wages*, 646–647.

65. *N.Y. Times:* Aug. 2, 1918, at 1:4; Aug. 4, 1918, at 14:2; Aug. 5, 1918, at 1:2 and 7:3–4; Aug. 6, 1918, at 24:7; Aug. 7, 1918, at 12:2; Aug. 8, 1918, at 11:3; Aug. 22, 1918, at 6:2; Jan. 31, 1919, at 3:16; Mar. 21, 1919, at 11:1; June 1, 1919, at 18:5; *OUSB*, Oct. 4, 1918, at 4; Ulriksson, *Telegraphers*, 109–110, 121–122; ASB to William B. Wilson, Mar. 15, 1919, WW MSS, ser. 4, case 22; Bing, *War-Time Strikes*, 110–111; *Government Control*, 66; Blum, *Tumulty*, 195–196; Conner, *War Labor Board*, 163–165.

66. William Hard, "Mr. Burleson, Back from Boston," 19 *New Republic* 15 (May 3, 1919); Anne Worthington, "The Telephone Strike," 42 *Survey* 146 (Apr. 26, 1919); Bing, *War-Time Strikes*, 112–115, 160 n.2; *N.Y. Times*, Jan. 31, 1919, at 3:6; ibid., March 9, 1919, at 8:2; Julia O'Connor and J. P. Noonan to JPT, March 26, 1919, JPT MSS, Box 49.

67. JPT to WW, Mar. 27, 1919, 56 *WWP* 340–341, using "telegraphers" to include telephone operators; JPT to WW, Mar. 28, 1919, JPT MSS, Box 49; ASB to JPT, Mar. 28, 1919, ibid, enclosing ASB to WW, Mar. 28, 1919, 56 *WWP* 403–404; ASB to JPT, Mar. 29, 1919, JPT MSS, Box 44.

68. WW to JPT, Mar. 28, 1919, JPT MSS, Box 49; JPT to WW, Mar. 28,

1919, ibid.; *N.Y. Times,* Apr. 19, 1919, at 6:1; ibid., Apr. 21, 1919, at 1:2; ibid., Apr. 22, 1919, at 24:2; *Springfield Republican,* Apr. 18, 1919, at 1:8; ibid., Apr. 19, 1919, at 1:7; ibid., Apr. 24, 1919, at 8:2; *N.Y. World,* Apr. 17, 1919, at 1:3; *Baltimore Sun,* Apr. 17, 1919, at 6:1; William Hard, "Mr. Burleson, Back from Boston," 19 *New Republic* 15 (May 3, 1919); Skeffington to H. L. Kerwin, Apr. 17, 1919, JPT MSS, Box 11; Robert W. Woolley to JPT, Apr. 19, 1919, WW MSS, ser. 4, case 4967.

69. Bing, *War-Time Strikes,* 110; *N.Y. Times:* Mar. 3, 1919, at 24:1; Apr. 11, 1919, at 2:6; Apr. 18, 1919, at 6:3; Apr. 27, 1919, at 3:6; "Mr. Burleson on the Grill," 61 *Literary Digest* (Apr. 19, 1919), at 14; "Burleson Dropping the Wires," ibid. (May 10, 1919), at 17; American Federation of Labor, *Report of 39th Annual Convention,* 345, 429–430 (Washington, D.C., 1919).

70. "Burleson Dropping the Wires," 61 *Literary Digest* (May 10, 1919), at 16–17; *N.Y. World,* Apr. 21, 1919, at 1:1–2 and 6:1–7; ibid., Apr. 23, 1919, at 1:1–2; *St. Louis Post-Dispatch,* Apr. 23, 1919, at 24:2; *N.Y. Times,* Apr. 24, 1919, at 1:2 and 3:5–6; ibid., Apr. 26, 1919, at 13:2. The incident was reported widely; see, e.g., *San Francisco Chronicle,* Apr. 24, 1919, at 3:1; *Los Angeles Times,* Apr. 24, 1919, at 5:1; *St. Louis Post-Dispatch,* Apr. 23, 1919, at 1:5 and at 2:2–4; *Minneapolis Journal,* Apr. 23, 1919, at 1:4; ibid., Apr. 24, 1919, at 1:1.

71. *Los Angeles Times,* Apr. 24, 1919, at 5:1; Arthur S. Link, *Woodrow Wilson and the Progressive Era, 1910–1917,* at 288 (New York, 1954); *N.Y. Times,* Mar. 23, 1919, at 18:2; ibid., Apr. 1, 1919, at 5:2–4; *Baltimore Sun,* Apr. 10, 1919, at 6:2; *Washington Star,* Apr. 20, 1919, at 1:6–7; *N.Y. World,* Apr. 21, 1919, at 16:2; ibid., Apr. 22, 1919, at 12; *St. Louis Post-Dispatch,* Apr. 23, 1919, at 24:2; "Mr. Burleson on the Grill," 61 *Literary Digest* (Apr. 19, 1919), at 14; "Burleson Dropping the Wires," ibid. (May 10, 1919), at 16; "Samuel" to JPT, Apr. 7, 1919, JPT MSS, Box 11; C. A. Minnis to JPT, Apr. 12, 1919, WW MSS, ser. 4, case 22; Blum, *Tumulty,* 196; AMP to JPT, Apr. 25, 1919, enclosing Samuel M. Wolfe, Atty. Gen. of S.C., to AMP, Apr. 18, 1919, JPT MSS, Box 49.

72. 57 Cong. Rec. 5014 (Mar. 4, 1919) (Sen. Sherman); *N.Y. Times,* Apr. 29, 1919, at 6:2; ibid., Apr. 30, 1919, at 10:1; *N.Y. World,* Mar. 23, 1919, pt. 3, at 1:1–2; JPT to WW, April 24, 1919 (message from ASB), 58 *WWP* 106; JPT to WW, April 27, 1919 (message from ASB), ibid, 176.

73. JPT to WW, Apr. 25, 1919, JPT MSS, Box 49 (two cables); WW to JPT, Apr. 28, 1919, ibid., ASB MSS, vol. 23, item 3623.

74. Post Office News Release, Apr. 28, 1919, ASB MSS, vol. 23, item 3622; Post Office News Release and Order, ibid., items 3624–3625; *N.Y. Times,* Apr. 29, 1919, at 1:1; ibid., Apr. 30, 1919, at 1:3, 5:5 and 10:1; *Washington Evening Star,* Apr. 28, 1919, at 1:6; ibid., Apr. 29, 1919, at 1:6; Draft Press Release, Apr. 28, 1919, ibid., JPT MSS, Box 11; Gilbert Close to

JPT, Apr. 29, 1919, ibid., Box 44; "Burleson Dropping the Wires," 61 *Literary Digest* (May 10, 1919), at 16–17; "The Tie That Binds," 19 *New Republic* 8 (May 3, 1919).

75. Act of July 11, 1919, ch. 10, 41 Stat. 157; *Government Control,* 92; 58 Cong. Rec. 917–918 (June 10, 1919); ASB to A. Wardman, July 9, 1919, WW MSS, ser. 4, case 350K; JPT to WW, May 5, 1919, JPT MSS, Box 49; WW to JPT, May 7, 1919, ibid.; ASB to JPT, May 7, 1919, ibid., Box 44; F. B. MacKinnon to WW, July 1, 1919, WW MSS, ser. 4, case 22.

76. *N.Y. Times:* Apr. 7, 1919, at 13:1; Apr. 18, 1919, at 6:2; Apr. 23, 1919, at 19:1; May 5, 1919, at 7:2; May 11, 1919, at 7:3; May 24, 1919, at 15:2; June 1, 1919, at 18:5; June 2, 1919, at 7:3–4 and 17:8; June 3, 1919, at 7:3–4; June 6, 1919, at 2:1; June 13, 1919, at 1:2; June 14, 1919, at 3:2; *N.Y. World,* Apr. 17, 1919, at 1:3; *Springfield Republican,* Apr. 24, 1919, at 8:2; Bing, *War-Time Strikes,* 114; Ulriksson, *Telegraphers,* 110–112; ASB to JPT, Mar. 28, 1919, JPT MSS, Box 49.

77. *N.Y. Times,* June 6, 1919, at 1:7–8 and 2:1; ibid., June 7, 1919, at 1:4, 14:2 and 18:1–2; ibid., June 8, 1919, at 1:3; JPT to WW, June 6, 1919, JPT MSS, Box 50; "Mr. Burleson Returns the Wires," 61 *Literary Digest* (June 21, 1919), at 17.

78. *N.Y. Times:* July 3, 1919, at 15:4; June 7, 1919, at 14:3–4; June 10, 1919, at 1:2; June 15, 1919, at 1:4; June 17, 1919, at 1:4 and 8:4; June 27, 1919, at 17:1; AFL, *39th Annual Convention,* 280, 306–309, 444, 474; Post Office Dept., Order No. 3209, June 14, 1919, ASB MSS, vol. 24, item 3735; Ulriksson, *Telegraphers,* 110–115; Bing, *War-Time Strikes,* 111–112; "Mr. Burleson Returns the Wires," 61 *Literary Digest* (June 21, 1919), at 17.

79. ASB to JPT (n.d.), JPT MSS, Box 44; JPT to ASB, June 2, 1919, ibid., Box 84, Letter Book 10, at 423; *St. Louis Post-Dispatch,* July 8, 1919, at 1:2; *Springfield Republican,* July 13, 1919, at 1:4; ibid., July 15, 1919, at 1:3; ibid., July 16, 1919, at 2:3 and 6:2; ASB to WW (draft, n.d.), ASB MSS, vol. 25, items 3955–3956; *N.Y. Times,* Nov. 25, 1937, at 31:1; *National Cyclopedia of American Biography,* s.v. "Burleson, Albert S."

80. *N.Y. Times,* Apr. 22, 1919, at 24:2; ibid., Apr. 30, 1919, at 10:1–2; ibid., June 2, 1919, at 14:3; *N.Y. World,* Apr. 7, 1919, at 1:1; ibid., Apr. 21, 1919, at 16:2; *Springfield Republican,* Apr. 8, 1919, at 8:2; ibid., Apr. 18, 1919, at 10:3; "Burleson Dropping the Wires," 61 *Literary Digest* (May 10, 1919), at 17; S. Rep. No. 304, 66th Cong., 1st Sess., pt. 2, at 2–3 (1919); Kerr, *Railroad Politics,* 179–186; I. Leo Sharfman, *The American Railroad Problem: A Study in War and Reconstruction,* 124–156, 183 (New York, 1921); Frank H. Dixon, *Railroads and Government: Their Relations in the United States, 1910–1921,* at 206–209 (New York, 1922); WW, Message to Congress, May 20, 1919, 5 *WWPP* 485, 494. The railroads were not actually returned until March 1, 1920. Proclamation of Dec. 24, 1919, 41 Stat. 1782; Act of Feb. 28, 1920, ch. 91, 41 Stat. 456.

81. State ex rel. Langer v. Northern Pac. Ry., 43 N.D. 556, 172 N.W. 324 (1919), *rev'd,* Northern Pac. Ry. v. North Dakota, 250 U.S. 135 (1919) (suit to bar rates on intrastate trips other than as set by state; the federal rates were 20 to 25 percent higher than the state's); State ex rel. Payne v. Dakota Cent. Tel. Co., 41 S.D. 460, 171 N.W. 277 (1919), *rev'd,* Dakota Cent. Tel. Co. v. South Dakota, 250 U.S. 163 (1919) (suit to bar use of federal rate schedule for intrastate long-distance calls). The telephone schedule was also upheld in three companion cases decided the same day: Kansas v. Burleson, 250 U.S. 188 (1919); Burleson v. Dempcy, 250 U.S. 191 (1919); MacLeod v. New England Tel. Co., 250 U.S. 195 (1919).

82. State ex rel. Langer v. Northern Pac. Ry., 43 N.D. at 565, 172 N.W. at 327–328; ibid., 43 N.D. at 619, 172 N.W. at 351–352 (Bronson, J., dissenting); ibid., 43 N.D. at 581, 172 N.W. at 335 (Robinson, J., concurring); Brief for Nat'l Ass'n of Ry. and Util. Comm'rs as Amicus Curiae at 29; Brief for North Dakota at 10, 14.

83. State ex rel. Payne v. Dakota Cent. Tel. Co., 41 S.D. at 466, 171 N.W. at 278; ibid., 41 S.D. at 471–473, 171 N.W. at 280 (McCoy and Smith, JJ., dissenting); Brief for South Dakota at 28–29, 33. In a companion case Massachusetts argued that "the determination of the amount to be charged . . . had no relation whatever to the conduct of the war . . . Such action seems to go beyond the scope even of the far-reaching war powers." Brief for Mass. Pub. Serv. Comm'n, MacLeod v. New England Tel. Co., 250 U.S. 195, 196 (1919).

84. Northern Pac. Ry. v. North Dakota, 250 U.S. at 149–150; Dakota Cent. Tel. Co. v. South Dakota, 250 U.S. at 183–184; the latter decision effectively overturned rulings in the eleven states where Burleson's rate order was held invalid as to intrastate calls. *N.Y. Times,* June 3, 1919, at 4:2.

85. *N.Y. Times:* Jan. 18, 1919, at 9:3; Feb. 9, 1919, pt. 2, at 5:5; May 20, 1919, at 4:2; May 21, 1919, at 1:1; Nov. 1, 1919, at 2:1; *OUSB,* Feb. 1, 1919, at 2; ibid., Feb. 7, 1919, at 6; William C. Mullendore, *History of the United States Food Administration, 1917–1919,* at 350–353 (Stanford, 1941); H.R. 277 and H.R.J. Res. 22, 66th Cong., 1st Sess., 58 Cong. Rec. 18, 22 (May 19, 1919); WW, Message to Congress, May 20, 1919, 5 *WWPP* 485, 495–496. The defendant companies wished to implement the higher federal rates and thus did not contest them; Wisconsin argued that the telephone order took a caller's property in violation of the Fifth Amendment but agreed that the Bill of Rights did not apply if the order were within the scope of the war powers. Brief for Wisconsin as Amicus Curiae at 81–85, Dakota Cent. Tel. Co. v. South Dakota, 250 U.S. 163 (1919).

86. 58 Cong. Rec. 918 (June 10, 1919); Post Office Dept., Order No. 3237 (June 21, 1919), in *Government Control,* 91.

87. Act of July 11, 1919, ch. 10, § 1, 41 Stat. 157; 58 Cong. Rec. 857–859 (June 9, 1919) (Sen. Cummins); ibid., 1343–1344 (June 18, 1919) (Memo from U.S. Independent Telephone Ass'n, June 9, 1919); H.R. Rep. No. 45, 66th Cong., 1st Sess. 2–4 (1919). The extension did not apply to telegraph rates, for though Western Union wished to retain the 20 percent increase, Postal-Telegraph promised to roll back its rates at the first opportunity. 58 Cong Rec. 858 (June 9, 1919) (Sen. Cummins); ibid., 919–920 (June 10, 1919) (Sen. Pomerene).

88. H.R. Rep. No. 45, 66th Cong., 1st Sess. 3, 9–12 (June 16, 1919); 58 Cong. Rec. 1338–1339 (June 18, 1919) (Rep. Esch); ibid., 1345 (Rep. Barkley).

89. 58 Cong. Rec. 1349–1350 (June 18, 1919) (Rep. Denison), also citing McCulloch v. Maryland, 17 U.S. (11 Wheat.) 316 (1819), United States v. Gettysburg Elec. Ry., 160 U.S. 668 (1896), and Stewart v. Kahn, 78 U.S. (11 Wall.) 493 (1871); Frederick C. Stevens, "Constitutional Authority of Congress, under Its War Power, to Temporarily Authorize Extension of Federal Telephone Rates beyond the Period of the War" (June 9, 1919), 58 Cong. Rec. 1343–1344 (June 18, 1919).

3. Wartime Prohibition

1. E. H. Cherrington, *History of the Anti-Saloon League* (Westerville, Ohio, 1913); E. H. Cherrington, *The Evolution of Prohibition in the United States* (Montclair, N.J., 1969); D. L. Colvin, *Prohibition in the United States* (New York, 1926); Peter H. Odegard, *Pressure Politics: The Story of the Anti-Saloon League* (New York, 1928); James H. Timberlake, *Prohibition and the Progressive Movement, 1900–1920* (Cambridge, Mass., 1963).

2. Cherrington, *Anti-Saloon League*, 255, 284, 319–320; Odegard, *Pressure Politics*, 21, 87–94; Timberlake, *Prohibition*, 20–21, 134, 138, 140–141, 146–150.

3. Cherrington, *Anti-Saloon League*, 141–157, 253, 277–278; Cherrington, *Prohibition*, 304; Charles Merz, *The Dry Decade*, 11–14 (Garden City, N.Y., 1931); Odegard, *Pressure Politics*, 130–146, 161–162; Timberlake, *Prohibition*, 145–146, 158–166, 173; Colvin, *Prohibition*, 394, 430–442; Act of Mar. 1, 1913, ch. 90, 37 Stat. 699, as amended by Act of Mar. 3, 1917, ch. 162, 39 Stat. 1069.

4. Cherrington, *Prohibition*, 317–321; *Anti-Saloon League Yearbook, 1914*, at 4–5, 8–10 (Westerville, Ohio, 1914); Anti-Saloon League, *Proceedings of 15th National Convention*, 213–215 (Westerville, Ohio, 1914); Andrew Sinclair, *Prohibition: The Era of Excess*, 154 (Boston, 1962); Anti-Saloon League, *Proceedings of 16th National Convention*, 77, 117 (Westerville, Ohio, 1916); S. Rep. No. 1563, 49th Cong., 1st Sess. (1886); S. Rep. No. 1584, 51st Cong., 1st Sess. (1890); S. Rep. No. 52, 65th Cong., 1st

Sess. 4 (1917); J. R. Long, "Tinkering with the Constitution," 24 *Yale Law Journal* 573, 584 (1915).

5. Anti-Saloon League, *15th National Convention,* 65; Anti-Saloon League, *16th National Convention,* 34, 49, 90; Wayne B. Wheeler, "The Inside Story of Prohibition's Adoption," *N.Y. Times,* Mar. 29, 1926, at 21:3–6; ibid., Mar. 30, 1926, at 27:3; Colvin, *Prohibition,* 443; Timberlake, *Prohibition,* 164–165; Merz, *Dry Decade,* 27.

6. Timberlake, *Prohibition,* 174; Colvin, *Prohibition,* 442–443, 448; Richard Hofstadter, *The Age of Reform: From Bryan to F.D.R.,* 287–290 (New York, 1955); Merz, *Dry Decade,* 32–36; S.J. Res. 17, 65th Cong., 1st Sess., 55 Cong. Rec. 197–198 (Apr. 4, 1917); H.R.J. Res. 44, 65th Cong., 1st Sess., ibid., 611 (Apr. 11, 1917); Wheeler, "Inside Story," *N.Y. Times,* Mar. 30, 1926, at 27:3–4; ibid., Mar. 31, 1926, at 25:6; H.R. Rep. No. 211, 65th Cong., 2d Sess. 1–2 (Dec. 14, 1917); 40 Stat. 1050; 56 Cong. Rec. 424 (Dec. 17, 1917) (Rep. Webb); Odegard, *Pressure Politics,* 140.

7. Colvin, *Prohibition,* 448–451; Merz, *Dry Decade,* 42–44; H. L. Mencken, *Prejudices: Fourth Series,* 162–163 (New York, 1924); *Washington Times,* Dec. 14, 1917, in Odegard, *Pressure Politics,* 173; H. L. Mencken, "Anti-Saloon League Lobby Has Congress Badly Scared," *N.Y. Evening Mail,* Aug. 21, 1917, in B. Adler, *H.L.M.: The Mencken Bibliography,* 55 (Baltimore, 1961).

8. William H. Anderson, "Prohibition or War? The Views of the Anti-Saloon League," 117 *Outlook* 46 (Sept. 12, 1917) (emphasis in original). Anderson was also league superintendent for New York. *Anti-Saloon League Year Book, 1918,* at 422, 425 (Westerville, Ohio, 1918).

9. Wheeler, "Inside Story," *N.Y. Times,* Mar. 28, 1926, pt. 2, at 1:4-5; ibid., Mar. 30, 1926, at 27:3; John M. Blum, *Joe Tumulty and the Wilson Era,* 148–149 (Boston, 1951); Arthur S. Link, *Wilson: The Road to the White House,* 151–152, 389 n.179 (Princeton, 1947); Arthur S. Link, *Wilson: The New Freedom,* 259 (Princeton, 1956); Timberlake, *Prohibition,* 152–154, 168; and see Sinclair, *Prohibition,* 147–150.

10. 55 Cong. Rec. 4161–4163, 4169, 4180–4181, 4190 (June 23, 1917); Odegard, *Pressure Politics,* 166–171; Justin Steuart, *Wayne Wheeler, Dry Boss,* 103–105 (New York, 1928); Wheeler, "Inside Story," *N.Y. Times,* Mar. 30, 1926, at 27:4–7; WW to Rev. James Cannon, Jr., June 29, 1917, 43 *WWP* 42–43; Cannon to WW, June 29, 1917, ibid., 52; Cannon to WW, June 30, 1917, ibid., 64–65; WW to Cannon, July 3, 1917, ibid., 84; *N.Y. Times,* July 1, 1917, at 1:1.

11. Act of Aug. 10, 1917, ch. 53, § 15, 40 Stat. 282; 56 Cong. Rec. 4165–4166 (June 23, 1917) (Rep. Lea); *Cincinnati Enquirer,* July 10, 1917, in Odegard, *Pressure Politics,* 171.

12. Herbert Hoover to WW, Nov. 19, 1917, 45 *WWP* 83; WW to Hoover,

Nov. 20, 1917, ibid., 91; Proclamation of Dec. 8, 1917, 40 Stat. 1728. The alcoholic content of most beer at this time was 4.75 to 5 percent.

13. Rev. James Cannon, Jr. to WW, June 30, 1917, 43 *WWP* 64; Cannon to WW, Apr. 1, 1918, *Anti-Saloon League Year Book, 1918,* at 48–49; 58 Cong. Rec. 4771 (Apr. 8, 1918) (Sen. Sherman); Wheeler, "Inside Story," *N.Y. Times,* Mar. 30, 1926, at 27:6.

14. *Anti-Saloon League Year Book, 1918,* at 45–48; Wheeler, "Inside Story," *N.Y. Times,* Mar. 30, 1926, at 27:6; 56 Cong. Rec. 9627 (Aug. 29, 1918); *N.Y. Times,* June 6, 1918, at 12:8; ibid., Aug. 30, 1918, at 1:2 and 11:4–5; Anti-Saloon League to Morris Sheppard, Aug. 27, 1918, 56 Cong. Rec. 9627 (Aug. 29, 1918); WW to Sheppard, March 22, 1918, 47 *WWP* 106–107; Herbert Hoover to JPT, May 27, 1918, 48 *WWP* 166; WW to Sheppard, May 28, 1918, ibid., 175; 2 Herbert Hoover, *An American Epic,* 117 (Chicago, 1960).

15. *N.Y. Times,* Aug. 30, 1918, at 1:2; ibid., Sept. 7, 1918, at 1:1 and 5:3–4; ibid., Sept. 8, 1918, at 7:2; 56 Cong. Rec. 9628, 9631 (Aug. 30, 1918) (Sens. Sheppard and Phelan); ibid., 10085–10086 (Sept. 6, 1918); ibid., 10686–10687, 10693, 10694 (Sept. 23, 1918); Herbert Hoover to WW, Sept. 13, 1918, 49 *WWP* 550; Proclamation of Sept. 16, 1918, 40 Stat. 1848; Act of Nov. 21, 1918, ch. 212, 40 Stat. 1046; Louis Siebold, "The Workings of Prohibition," *N.Y. World,* May 1919, in Odegard, *Pressure Politics,* 128.

16. S. Rep. No. 52, 65th Cong., 1st Sess. 2, 4–5 (1917); 56 Cong. Rec. 6975 (May 23, 1918) (Rep. Lea); ibid., 9627 (Aug. 29, 1918) (Sen. Sheppard); ibid., 9783 (Aug. 31, 1918) (Sen. Phelan); ibid., 10691 (Sept. 23, 1918) (Rep. Igoe); ibid., App. 633 (Rep. Voigt).

17. 56 Cong. Rec. 9365 (Aug. 29, 1918) (Sen. Jones); ibid., 9641 (Sen. Wadsworth); ibid., 9645 (Sen. Norris); ibid., 9647 (Sen. Thomas); ibid., 10682 (Sept. 23, 1918) (Rep. Gallagher).

18. 56 Cong. Rec. 10685 (Sept. 23, 1918) (Rep. Stafford); ibid., 10672 (Rep. Kahn); ibid., 9632 (Aug. 29, 1918) (Sen. Phelan).

19. Act of May 18, 1917, ch. 15, §12, 40 Stat. 76, 82–83; Timberlake, *Prohibition,* 174; George J. Anderson, "Making the Camps Safe for the Army," 79 *Annals of the American Academy of Political and Social Science* 143, 145 (Sept. 1918); Act of Nov. 21, 1918, ch. 212, 40 Stat. 1047; Joint Res. of Sept. 12, 1918, ch. 170, 40 Stat. 958; 56 Cong. Rec. 9628 (Aug. 29, 1918) (Sen. Sheppard); ibid., 9635 (Sen. Jones); 56 Cong. Rec. 9641 (Sen. Wadsworth); ibid., 9650 (Sen. Lenroot); ibid., 10682 (Sept. 23, 1918) (Rep. Gallagher).

20. H.R. Rep. No. 801, pt. 2, 66th Cong., 2d Sess. (1920), 59 Cong. Rec. 6487 (1920); 56 Cong. Rec. 9641 (Aug. 29, 1918) (Sen. Sheppard); ibid., 9645–9646 (Sen. Norris); ibid., 10685 (Sept. 23, 1918) (Rep. Stafford); ibid., App. 633 (Rep. Voigt); ibid., 10691 (Rep. Igoe).

21. *56 Cong. Rec.* 6973 (May 23, 1918) (Rep. Lea); ibid., 9641–9642 (Aug. 29, 1918) (Sen. Wadsworth); ibid., 9650 (Sen. Shafroth); ibid., 9783 (Aug. 31, 1918) (Sen. Phelan); ibid., 10681 (Sept. 23, 1918) (Rep. Slayden); ibid., 10682 (Rep. Gallagher); ibid., App., 633 (Rep. Voigt).

22. *56 Cong. Rec.* 9631 (Aug. 29, 1918) (Sen. Phelan); ibid., 9647 (Sen. Thomas); ibid, 10081–10082 (Sept. 6, 1918) (Sen. Bankhead); ibid., 10083 (Sen. Lodge); ibid., 10679 (Sept. 23, 1918) (Rep. Gordon); ibid., 10681 (Rep. Slayden); ibid., App., 633 (Rep. Voigt).

23. Donald G. Morgan, *Congress and the Constitution: A Study of Responsibility,* 150 (Cambridge, Mass., 1966); 56 Cong. Rec. 10675–10676 (Sept. 23, 1918) (Rep. Sherwood); ibid., 10679 (Rep. Gordon); as to Lever's presence, see ibid., 10671, 10678, 10680.

24. Mencken, *Prejudices,* 161; 56 Cong. Rec. 10676 (Sept. 23, 1918) (Rep. Meeker); ibid., 10679 (Rep. Gordon); ibid., 10681 (Rep. Slayden); ibid., 10685 (Rep. Stafford).

25. S. Rep. No. 499, 60th Cong., 1st Sess. (1908); 42 Cong. Rec., App. 176 (1908); Anti-Saloon League, *Proceedings of 14th National Convention,* 33–34 (Westerville, Ohio, 1911); Odegard, *Pressure Politics,* 132–137.

26. Steuart, *Wheeler,* 81; Morgan, *Congress and Constitution,* 158–159; William H. Taft, Message to Senate, 49 Cong. Rec. 4291–4292 (Feb. 28, 1913); William H. Taft, *Our Chief Magistrate and His Powers,* 19-23 (New York, May 1916); Clark Distilling Co. v. Western Maryland R.R., 242 U.S. 311 (1917).

27. "War Measures for War Times," 208 *North American Review* 180–183 (Aug. 1918); "Nation-Wide Drought in Sight," 58 *Literary Digest* (Sept. 21, 1918), at 17-18; JPT to WW, Sept. 7, 1918, 49 *WWP* 476; and see Walter Thompson, *Federal Centralization: A Study and Criticism of the Expanding Scope of Congressional Legislation,* 184, 186 (New York, 1923); *N.Y. World,* April 22, 1919, at 12:2; ibid., Oct. 28, 1919, at 10:2; *Washington Post,* Dec.17, 1919, at 6:3; *Chicago Tribune,* Dec. 17, 1919, at 8:1; *San Francisco Chronicle,* Dec. 17, 1919, at 18:1-2; *St. Louis Post-Dispatch,* Dec. 16, 1919, at 28:2.

28. Shaemas O'Sheel to WW, Sept. 24, 1918, WW MSS, ser. 4, case 4409; JPT to WW, Sept. 7, 1918, 49 *WWP* 476; ASB to WW, Sept. 12, 1918, JPT MSS, Box 48, noting that ASB's letter was drafted by JPT; Diary of Colonel Edward M. House, Sept. 24, 1918, Edward M. House Papers, Yale University Library, and 51 *WWP* 105, noting that Attorney General Gregory and Secretary McAdoo also opposed a veto.

29. " 'War-Time' Prohibition," *N.Y. World,* Nov. 19, 1918, at 10:3; " 'War' Prohibition," *N.Y. Times,* Nov. 20, 1918, at 14:3–4; "War Powers after a War," *St. Louis Post-Dispatch,* Nov. 19, 1918, at 18:2.

30. Joseph P. Tumulty, *Woodrow Wilson as I Know Him,* 413 (Garden City, N.Y., 1921); 56 Cong. Rec. 10086 (Sept. 6, 1918); ibid., 10694 (Sept.

23, 1918); Seward H. Livermore, *Politics Is Adjourned: Woodrow Wilson and the War Congress, 1916–1918,* at 206–247 (Middletown, Conn., 1966).

31. *N.Y. Times,* Dec. 1, 1918, at 13:1; JPT to WW, Dec. 17, 1918, 53 *WWP* 413; Herbert Hoover to WW, Dec. 19, 1918, ibid., 443; WW to JPT, Dec. 20, 1918, ibid., 450; WW to JPT, Jan. 17, 1919, JPT MSS, Box 49, ASB MSS, vol. 22, item 3528.

32. JPT to WW, Jan. 21, 1919, 54 *WWP* 193; Herbert Hoover to WW, Jan. 22, 1919, ibid., 216; WW to JPT, Jan. 23, 1919, ibid., 227; Gilbert Close to Herbert Hoover, Jan. 24, 1919, ibid., 262; Proclamation of Jan. 30, 1919, 40 Stat. 1930; *N.Y. Times,* Jan. 29, 1919, at 8:1; ibid., Feb. 21, 1919, at 1:3 and 24:3; ibid., Mar. 9, 1919, pt. 4, at 1:1; Proclamation of Mar. 4, 1919, 40 Stat. 1937.

33. *N.Y. Times:* Jan. 29, 1919, at 8:1; Feb. 21, 1919, at 24:3; Feb. 22, 1919, at 1:1; Mar. 16, 1919, at 16:2; Mar. 18, 1919, at 1:1; Daniel C. Roper, *Fifty Years of Public Life,* 53–55, 190–191 (Durham, S.C., 1941); 31 *National Cyclopedia of American Biography,* s.v. "Roper, Daniel C."; *Encylopedia Britannica* (1954), s.v. "beer"; Proclamation of Dec. 8, 1917, 40 Stat. 1729.

34. *N.Y. Times:* Mar. 16, 1919, at 16:2; Mar. 18, 1919, at 1:1 and 4:3–4; Mar. 19, 1919, at 1:3 and 4:3; Mar. 20, 1919, at 3:5–6; Apr. 12, 1919, at 13:2; Apr. 13, 1919, at 18:2; Apr. 21, 1919, at 4:2; Apr. 23, 1919, at 18:3; Apr. 28, 1919, at 8:5–8; May 18, 1919, at 18:4; May 24, 1919, at 3:6; May 25, 1919, pt. 2, at 1:8.

35. E. L. Whitney, "Strikes and Lockouts in the United States, 1916–1919," 10 *Monthly Labor Review* 1505 (1920); Robert K. Murray, *Red Scare: A Study in National Hysteria, 1919–1920,* at 9, 111–112 (Minneapolis, 1955); *N.Y. Times,* Feb. 21, 1919, at 1:3; ibid., Mar. 3, 1919, at 13:1.

36. *N.Y. Times:* Feb. 8, 1919, at 1:3; Feb. 12, 1919, at 1:2; Feb. 13, 1919, at 9:1 and 14:3; Feb. 15, 1919, at 6:2; Feb. 22, 1919, at 1:1; Feb. 23, 1919, at 16:3; Mar. 1, 1919, at 8:2–3; Mar. 8, 1919, at 4:3; June 15, 1919, at 1:3 and 15:3–6; July 21, 1919, at 1:4; *Newark Evening News,* Mar. 17, 1919, at 8:2; 26 *American Federationist* 243–244 (Mar. 1919); ibid., 316–318 (Apr. 1919); American Federation of Labor, *Report of 39th Annual Convention,* 263–266 (Washington, D.C., 1919).

37. *N.Y. World,* Apr. 22, 1919, at 12:2; Louis Siebold, "The Workings of Prohibition," ibid., May 1919, in Odegard, *Pressure Politics,* 128–129; *N.Y. Times,* Apr. 13, 1919, at 1:2; ibid., Apr. 21, 1919, at 4:2; ibid., May 8, 1919, at 27:2; Wheeler, "Inside Story," ibid., Mar. 28, 1926, pt. 2, at 1:4; Diary of Colonel Edward M. House, Sept. 24, 1918, Edward M. House Papers, Yale University Library, and 51 *WWP* 105.

38. Cary T. Grayson to JPT, May 9, 1919, JPT MSS, Box 44; JPT to Grayson, May 9, 1919, ibid.; JPT to WW, May 9, 1919, ibid., Box 49; JPT to WW, May 10, 1919, ibid.; JPT to WW, May 12, 1919, ibid.

39. WW to JPT, May 12, 1919, JPT MSS, Box 49; AMP to JPT, May 12, 1919 (emphasis added), ibid., Box 46; JPT to WW, May 12, 1919, ibid., Box 49. AMP did not specify what would constitute a conclusion to the war.

40. WW to JPT, May 16, 1919, JPT MSS, Box 49; JPT to WW, May 16, 1919, ibid.; WW to JPT, May 17, 1919, ibid.; WW, Message to Congress, May 20, 1919, 5 *WWPP* 485, 495–496; 61 *Literary Digest* (May 31, 1919), at 18; *N.Y. Times:* May 21, 1919, at 1:1; May 23, 1919, at 4:4; May 24, 1919, at 3:6; June 7, 1919, at 3:5; June 16, 1919, at 1:4; June 18, 1919, at 7:2; June 19, 1919, at 15:6; June 22, 1919, at 4:5–7; June 29, 1919, at 1:1.

41. *N.Y. Times:* June 19, 1919, at 15:6; June 22, 1919, at 4:5–7; June 26, 1919, at 3:1; June 28, 1919, at 1:1 and 4:5; June 29, 1919, at 1:1 and 11:1; JPT to WW, June 25, 1919, JPT MSS, Box 50; JPT to WW, June 27, 1919, ibid.; WW to JPT, June 27, 1919, ibid.; JPT to WW, June 28, 1919, ibid.; WW to JPT, June 28, 1919, ibid.

42. JPT to WW, July 1, 1919, cabling letter from AMP, JPT MSS, Box 50; *St. Louis Post-Dispatch,* July 1, 1919, at 1:4; Cary T. Grayson to JPT, July 4, 1919, JPT MSS, Box 44; WW, Press Conference, July 10, 1919, 50 *WWP* 792–793; *N.Y. Times,* July 11, 1919, at 2:7.

43. Trading with the Enemy Act, Act of Oct. 6, 1917, ch. 106, § 2, 40 Stat. 412, defining "end of the war" flexibly; *N.Y. Times:* Apr. 13, 1919, at 1:2; Apr. 21, 1919, at 4:2; Apr. 26, 1919, at 8:2; Apr. 28, 1919, at 8:5–8; Stanley Coben, *A. Mitchell Palmer: Politician,* 111 (New York, 1963).

44. Coben, *Palmer,* 127–154; AMP, Address at Washington, D.C., *OUSB,* Oct. 9, 1918, at 8; AMP, Address to Boston Chamber of Commerce, *N.Y. Times,* Dec. 31, 1918, at 10:6; see also AMP, Address at Philadelphia, *OUSB,* Nov. 12, 1918, at 24. The *Nation* noted that by Palmer's own account German investment amounted to only 0.2 percent of America's capital wealth, and found his "discovery of a 'German industrial menace' . . . difficult to reconcile with a normal mind." 110 *Nation* 824 (1920).

45. AMP, Address at Harrisburg, Pa., *N.Y. Times,* Sept. 15, 1918, at 18:1–2; Act of Oct. 6, 1917, ch. 106, § 2, 40 Stat. 411; AMP to Thomas W. Gregory, Oct. 15, 1918, WW MSS, ser. 4, file 4879; Alien Property Custodian, *Report, 1918–1919,* at 150–151 (1919); *Report of the Alien Property Custodian, 1917–1922,* S. Doc. No. 181, 67th Cong., 2d Sess. 118, 195, 332, 399, 454, 509–511, 569, 574 (1922).

46. August A. Busch to W. C. McConaughey, May 31, 1918, in *St. Louis Globe-Democrat,* June 1, 1918, at 9:7–8; *St. Louis Post-Dispatch:* Oct. 11, 1913, at 3:1–6; Oct. 12, 1913, at 1:3, 3:1–8, and 4:1–4; Mar. 1, 1918, at 2:8; June 17, 1918, at 3:6; July 10, 1918, at 3:4; *N.Y. Times,* Mar. 2, 1918, at 3:3; ibid., June 18, at 1:2; ibid., July 9, 1918, at 24:3; Alien Property Custodian, *Report,* 476; William J. Vollmar, Anheuser Busch Cos., to Christopher N. May, Oct. 19, 1984, Loyola Law School Library, Los Angeles; *Dictionary of American Biography,* s.v. "Busch, Adolphus"; Roland Krebs,

Making Friends Is Our Business: 100 Years of Anheuser-Busch (St. Louis, 1953).

47. AMP to Thomas W. Gregory, Oct. 15, 1918, WW MSS, ser. 4, case 4879; *St. Louis Globe-Democrat,* June 1, 1918, at 9:7–8.

48. WW to AMP, Oct. 21, 1918, 51 *WWP* 395; AMP to WW, Oct. 25, 1918, ibid., 445; AMP to Thomas W. Gregory, Oct. 25, 1918, WW MSS, ser. 4, case 4879; WW to AMP, Nov. 20, 1918, 53 *WWP* 141; Act of Oct. 6, 1917, ch. 106, §12, 40 Stat. 423, as amended by Act of Mar. 28, 1918, ch. 28, 40 Stat. 460; *OUSB,* Dec. 14, 1918, at 2; S. Doc. No. 181, 67 Cong., 2d Sess. 675, 682 (1922); *Report of the Alien Property Custodian,* 8, 237–238; *St. Louis Post-Dispatch,* Dec. 13, 1918, at 3:8; ibid., Dec. 14, 1918, at 3:8; *N.Y. Times,* Dec. 14, 1918, at 20:6.

49. Steuart, *Wheeler,* 122, 131–132; S. Doc. No. 62, 66th Cong., 1st Sess. iii–vi, ix (1919); *N.Y. Times,* June 15, 1919, at 20:1–2.

50. Coben, *Palmer,* 57–63, 67–72; Josephus Daniels, *The Wilson Era, Years of Peace: 1910–1917,* at 61 (Chapel Hill, 1944); *N.Y. Times,* May 28, 1919, at 17:2; ibid., June 16, 1919, at 5:2.

51. Wayne B. Wheeler to AMP, May 3, 1918, in Steuart, *Wheeler,* 121–122; Wheeler to AMP, Feb. 28, 1919, ibid., 135–136; Wheeler to AMP, March 17, 1919, ibid., 136–137; ibid., 137–139.

52. 5 Ida H. Harper, *History of Woman Suffrage,* 643 (New York, 1969); Eleanor Flexner, *Century of Struggle: The Woman's Rights Movement in the United States,* 231, 286, 306–309, 337 (rev. ed., Cambridge, Mass., 1975); David Morgan, *Suffragists and Democrats: The Politics of Woman Suffrage in America,* 120–121, 139, 157–165 (East Lansing, Mich., 1972); "The American Woman Voter Arrives," 66 *Literary Digest* (Aug. 28, 1920), at 9–11; *N.Y. Times,* Aug. 19, 1920, at 2:3–5; William F. Ogburn and Inez Goltra, "How Women Vote: A Study of an Election in Portland, Oregon," 34 *Political Science Quarterly* 413 (Sept. 1919); Arthur Capper, "What She Will Do With the Vote," 101 *Independent* 15 (Jan. 2, 1920); Timberlake, *Prohibition,* 122–123, 127, 140; Odegard, *Pressure Politics,* 79–87.

53. Coben, *Palmer,* 110–111, 171–172; Murray, *Red Scare,* 67–81; *N.Y. Times,* May 1, 1919, at 1:1; ibid., June 3, 1919, at 1:1–8.

54. Jacob Hoffman Brewing Co. v. McElligot, 259 F. 321 (S.D. N.Y., May 17, 1919), *rev'd,* 259 F. 525 (2d Cir., June 28, 1919); *N.Y. Times:* Apr. 21, 1919, at 4:2; May 18, 1919, at 18:2–4; May 24, 1919, at 1:1 and 3:6; May 25, 1919, pt. 2, at 1:8; May 28, 1919, at 16:1–3; June 27, 1919, at 16:1.

55. *N.Y. Times:* July 2, 1919, at 1:1 and 10:2–3; July 3, 1919, at 4:5; July 16, 1919, at 4:3; July 17, 1919, at 17:8; Aug. 28, 1919, at 1:2 and 4:3; Sept. 26, 1919, at 6:3; Oct. 14, 1919, at 19:5; United States v. Standard Brewery, Inc., 260 F. 486 (D. Md., July 1, 1919), *aff'd,* 251 U.S.

210 (1920); ibid., record at 1–2, 13; on the nonappealability of the *Jacob Hoffman* case, see City of New Orleans v. Emsheimer, 181 U.S. 153 (1901); Corning v. Troy Iron and Nail Factory, 56 U.S. (15 How.) 451 (1854).

56. *N.Y. Times,* July 1, 1919, at 1:6–8; ibid., July 2, 1919, at 1:1; ibid., July 4, 1919, at 4:4; 31 *Attorney General Opinions* 498 (July 3, 1919). *Standard Brewery* was not decided until Jan. 5, 1920, when the Court held that the War-Time Prohibition Act applied only to intoxicating beer and wine. 251 U.S. 210.

57. *N.Y. Times,* July 1, 1919, at 2:1–2; ibid., July 2, 1919, at 1:2; ibid., July 4, 1919, at 4:4; *St. Louis Post-Dispatch,* July 1, 1919, at 1:8.

58. "2.75 Per Cent. Alcohol," 62 *Literary Digest* (July 12, 1919), at 12–13. Boston: United States v. Petts, 260 F. 663 (D.Mass., July 15, 1919); *N.Y. Times,* July 16, 1919, at 4:4; Chicago: United States v. Stenson Brewing Co. (N.D. Ill., July 25, 1919); *N.Y. Times,* July 26, 1919, at 2:8; ibid., Aug. 4, 1919, at 10:8; Los Angeles: United States v. Baumgartner, 259 F. 722 (S.D. Calif., Aug. 8, 1919); *Los Angeles Times,* Aug. 9, 1919, pt. 2, at 5:1; Madison: United States v. Mohr (W.D. Wis., Aug. 22, 1919); New Haven: United States v. Schmauder, 258 F. 251 (D. Conn., July 23, 1919); *N.Y. Times,* July 25, 1919, at 15:8; New Orleans: United States v. American Brewing Co. (E.D. La., July 15, 1919), *aff'd,* 251 U.S. 210 (1920); *N.Y. Times,* July 4, 1919, at 4:4, ibid., July 16, 1919, at 4:4; Philadelphia: United States v. Bergner & Engel Brewing Co., 260 F. 764 (E.D. Pa., July 17, 1919) (case allowed to proceed on basis that issue must be resolved at trial, not on demurrer); *N.Y. Times,* July 3, 1919, at 4:3; ibid., Aug. 4, 1919, at 10:8; Pittsburgh: United States v. Pittsburgh Brewing Co., 260 F. 762 (W.D. Pa., July 15, 1919); *N.Y. Times,* July 10, 1919, at 36:2; ibid., July 16, 1919, at 4:3–4; Providence: United States v. James Hanley Brewing Co. (D.R.I., July 23, 1919); *N.Y. Times,* Aug. 4, 1919, at 10:8; San Francisco: United States v. Ranier Brewing Co., 259 F. 359 (N.D. Calif., July 28, 1919); *San Francisco Chronicle,* July 29, 1919, at 3:1; *N.Y. Times,* July 2, 1919, at 10:4; ibid., July 29, 1919, at 24:2; Trenton: *N.Y. Times,* Aug. 3, 1919, at 5:4 (test case filed against the Feigenspan Brewing Co. of Newark, but unclear whether action allowed to proceed); Puerto Rico: United States v. Porto Rico Brewing Co. (D.P.R., Aug. 23, 1919). A ruling was later issued against the government in Milwaukee: United States v. Valentine Blatz Brewing Co. (E.D. Wis., Oct. 14, 1919). The unreported cases noted above are discussed in Brief for Standard Brewery at 7–8, Brief for American Brewing Co. at 46–62, Brief for United States at 5–8, United States v. Standard Brewery, Inc., 251 U.S. 210 (1920); and see 64 L.Ed. at 230, 232. For a survey of the cases decided through the end of July, see *N.Y. Times,* Aug. 4, 1919, at 10:8; ibid., Aug. 7, 1919, at 6:7.

59. Jacob Hoffman Brewing Co. v. McElligott, 259 F. 321 (S.D. N.Y., May 17, 1919); United States v. Ranier Brewing Co., 259 F. 359 (N.D. Calif., July 28, 1919); Scatena v. Caffey, 260 F. 756 (S.D. N.Y., Aug. 20, 1919), holding act constitutional as applied to wine; *N.Y. Times,* July 2, 1919, at 10:2; ibid., July 17, 1919, at 17:8; ibid., Aug. 28, 1919, at 4:3; 58 Cong. Rec. 4906–4907 (1919).

60. *N.Y. Times:* June 6, 1918, at 12:8; Apr. 7, 1919, at 12:2–3; Apr. 23, 1919, at 18:3; Apr. 28, 1919, at 8:3–8; May 24, 1919, at 3:4–6; May 25, 1919, at 1:8; June 2, 1919, at 14:3–4; June 17, 1919, at 12:1; 58 Cong. Rec. 2436–2438 (July 10, 1919) (Rep. Newton); "Futile Efforts at Intoxication on 2.75 Beer," 62 *Literary Digest* (Aug. 16, 1919), 60–62.

61. *N.Y. Times:* July 3, 1919, at 4:2–3; July 4, 1919, at 4:4; July 16, 1919, at 4:4; July 20, 1919, at 4:7; Aug. 4, 1919, at 10:8; *St. Louis Post-Dispatch:* July 6, 1919, editorial section, at 9:3; July 8, 1919, at 14:4; July 9, 1919, at 1:2; July 28, 1919, at 9:1; *San Francisco Chronicle,* Aug. 2, 1919, at 5:1; ibid., Aug. 8, 1919, pt. 2, at 1:8; Act of Oct. 28, 1919, ch. 85, title I, § 1, 41 Stat. 305.

62. *N.Y. Times,* Mar. 9, 1919, pt. 4 , at 1:1; ibid., May 24, 1919, at 3:6; H.R. Rep. No. 1143, 65th Cong., 3d Sess. (1919); H.R. 6810, 66th Cong., 1st Sess., 58 Cong. Rec. 1944 (June 27, 1919); ibid., 2288–2292 (July 8, 1919); ibid., 2301 (Rep. Gallivan); ibid., 2446 (July 11, 1919) (Rep. Volstead); H.R. Rep. No. 91, 66th Cong., 1st Sess. (1919); Wheeler, "Inside Story," *N.Y. Times,* Apr. 2, 1926, at 21:3; J. Kobler, *Ardent Spirits: The Rise and Fall of Prohibition,* 213–214 (New York, 1973).

63. Act of Oct. 28, 1919, ch. 85, title I, §§ 1–4, 41 Stat. 305–307.

64. 58 Cong. Rec. 2286 (July 8, 1919) (Rep. Walsh); ibid., 2778 (July 17, 1919) (Rep. Tilson); ibid., 4907 (Sept. 5, 1919) (Sen. Wadsworth); *N.Y. Times,* Oct. 19, 1919, at 1:4; ibid., Nov. 18, 1919, at 5:3; E. Jay Howenstine, "Demobilization after the First World War," 58 *Quarterly Journal of Economics* 91, 103 (1943).

65. H.R. Rep. No. 1143, 65th Cong., 3d Sess. 3–4 (Feb. 26, 1919); ibid., 6 (Rep. Steele for minority).

66. H.R. Rep. No. 91, 66th Cong., 1st Sess. 3 (June 30, 1919), referring, though not by name, to Jacob Hoffman Brewing Co. v. McElligott, 259 F. 525 (2d Cir., June 28, 1919); *N.Y. Times,* June 29, 1919, at 1:1 and 11:1; S. Rep. No. 151, 66th Cong., 1st Sess. 2, 8, 11 (Aug. 18, 1919).

67. 58 Cong. Rec. 2283 (July 8, 1919) (Rep. Cantrill); ibid., 2297 (Rep. Volstead); ibid., 2429 (July 10, 1919) (Rep. Steele); ibid., 2433 (Rep. Currie); ibid., 2442–2443 (Rep. Vaile); ibid., 2452–2453 (July 11, 1919) (Rep. Hersey); ibid., 2458 (Rep. Lea); ibid., 2506 (July 12, 1919) (Rep. Hardy); ibid., 4905 (Sept. 5, 1919) (Sen. Sterling).

68. 58 Cong. Rec. 2561 (July 14, 1919) (Rep. Luce); ibid., 4905 (Sept. 5, 1919) (Sens. Sterling and Shields); ibid., 4907 (Sen. Wadsworth).

69. 58 Cong. Rec. 4907 (Sept. 5, 1919) (Sen. Sterling); H.R. Rep. No. 91, 66th Cong., 1st Sess., pt. 2, at 1–2 (June 30, 1919).

70. 58 Cong. Rec. 2448 (July 11, 1919) (Rep. Gard); ibid., 2458 (Rep. Lea); ibid., 2482 (Rep. Sherwood); ibid., 2497 (July 12, 1919) (Rep. Coady); ibid., 2500 (Rep. Husted); ibid., 2563 (July 14, 1919) (Rep. Igoe); ibid., 2778 (July 17, 1919) (Rep. Tilson); ibid., 2781 (Rep. Gallagher).

71. 58 Cong. Rec. 2512 (July 12, 1919) (Rep. Volstead); ibid., 2506–2507 (Rep. Hardy); ibid., 3005 (July 22, 1919); ibid., 4908 (Sept. 5, 1919); *N.Y. Times*, Sept. 6, 1919, at 1:2. Congressional challengers from wet districts were: Reps. Coady (Baltimore), Gallagher (Chicago), Husted (Peekskill, N.Y.), Igoe (St. Louis), and Tilson (New Haven); challengers from dry states or districts were: Sens. Borah (Idaho), Shields (Tenn.), and Thomas (Colo.), and Reps. Gard (Hamilton, Ohio, wet until May 1919), Hardy (Corsicana, Tex.), and Sherwood (Toledo, wet until May 1919); Rep. Lea's (Santa Rosa, Calif.) district was roughly two-thirds dry. See *Anti-Saloon League Yearbook, 1919*, at 95–99, 165, 171, 175–227 (Westerville, Ohio, 1919); *Official Congressional Directory*, 67th Cong., 2d Sess. 475–522 (1921).

72. WW, Veto Message of Oct. 27, 1919, 6 *WWPP* 424–425; 58 Cong. Rec. 7607 (1919); *N.Y. Times*, Oct. 28, 1919, at 1:1 and 3:3; Draft veto message, JPT MSS, Box 50; Blum, *Tumulty*, 217.

73. *N.Y. World*, Oct. 28, 1919, at 10:2; John L. Heaton, *Cobb of 'The World': A Leader in Liberalism*, 209–210 (New York, 1924); 58 Cong. Rec. 7610 (Oct. 27, 1919) (Rep. Volstead); ibid., 7611 (House passes bill 175 to 55).

74. 58 Cong. Rec. 7621, 7629 (Oct. 28, 1919) (Sen. Borah); ibid., 7625 (Sen. Thomas); ibid., 7621–7622 (Sen. Underwood); ibid., 7633–7634 (Senate passes bill 65 to 20). Title I became effective immediately. Act of Oct. 28, 1919, ch. 85, title III, § 21, 41 Stat. 322.

75. 58 Cong. Rec. 2432–2433 (July 10, 1919) (Rep. Currie); ibid., 7633 (Oct. 28, 1919) (Sen. Lodge); Whitney, "Strikes and Lockouts," 1505; *N.Y. Times*, Oct. 1, 1919, at 16:8; ibid., Oct. 28, 1919, at 3:3; ibid., Oct. 29, 1919, at 1:1–8 and 3:1.

76. WW, Statement to coal miners, 58 Cong. Rec. 7583 (Oct. 27, 1919); ibid., 7621 (Oct. 28, 1919) (Sen. Borah); "The Coal War," 109 *Nation* 577 (Nov. 8, 1919); Lincoln Colcord, "The Administration Adrift," ibid., 636 (Nov. 15, 1919). The coal strike message was written by Tumulty and Walker Hines, Director General of Railroads, while the veto was drafted by Tumulty and Agriculture Secretary David Houston. JPT MSS, Boxes 12 and 50; Blum, *Tumulty*, 217. See *N. Y. Times*, Nov. 1, 1919, at 2:1 (Justice Department attempt to reconcile messages on basis that one involved existing law and the other new legislation).

77. 58 Cong. Rec. 7630 (Oct. 28, 1919) (Sens. Spencer, Smoot, and Phelan); ibid., 7631–7632 (Sen. Fall); ibid., 7633 (Sen. Lodge); Edwin A. Weinstein, *Woodrow Wilson: A Medical and Psychological Biography,* 358–363 (Princeton, 1981); John Milton Cooper, Jr., *The Warrior and the Priest: Woodrow Wilson and Theodore Roosevelt,* 172, 265, 341–342 (Cambridge, Mass., 1983).

78. *N.Y. Times:* Oct. 28, 1919, at 3:1; Oct. 29, 1919, at 1:1; Nov. 3, 1919, at 4:2; Nov. 4, 1919, at 17:1; Nov. 11, 1919, at 9:4; Nov. 21, 1919, at 10:8; Dec. 20, 1919, at 6:1.

4. The High Cost of Living

1. Paul H. Douglas, *Real Wages in the United States, 1890–1926,* at 60, 391 (Boston, 1930); Harold U. Faulkner, *The Decline of Laissez Faire, 1897–1917,* at 251–255 (New York, 1951); Frank H. Streightoff, *The Standard of Living among the Industrial People in America,* 121 (Boston, 1911); Scott Nearing, *Financing the Wage-Earner's Family,* 106–107 (New York, 1914); Walter E. Weyl, *The New Democracy,* 221, 244–251 (New York, 1912); Walter Lippmann, *Drift and Mastery: An Attempt to Diagnose the Current Unrest,* 71, 74–75 (New York, 1914).

2. Charles Forcey, *The Crossroads of Liberalism: Croly, Weyl, Lippmann, and the Progressive Era, 1900–1925,* at xix (New York, 1961); Donald B. Johnson and Kirk H. Porter, *National Party Platforms, 1840–1972,* at 169, 177–178, 185 (Urbana, Ill., 1973); Arthur S. Link, *Woodrow Wilson and the Progressive Era, 1910–1917,* at 66–74 (New York, 1954); Harold U. Faulkner, *The Quest for Social Justice, 1898–1914,* at 119–124 (New York, 1931); Diary of Colonel Edward M. House, Oct. 2, 1914, Edward M. House Papers, Yale University Library, and 31 WWP 122.

3. Scott Nearing, *Reducing the Cost of Living,* 19–29, 300–301 (Philadelphia, 1914); Lippmann, *Drift and Mastery,* 72–73; Frederic C. Howe, *The High Cost of Living,* 155–156 (New York, 1917); 55 Cong. Rec. 3811–3812 (June 18, 1917) (Reps. Anderson, Gordon, Green, and Madden); Munn v. Illinois, 94 U.S. 113 (1876); German Alliance Ins. Co. v. Lewis, 233 U.S. 389 (1914); Note, "Regulation of Rates—Business Affected with a Public Interest," 14 *Columbia Law Review* 534 (1914); James P. Hall, *Constitutional Law,* 148–150 (Chicago, 1922); Charles K. Burdick, *The Law of the American Constitution,* 568–570 (New York, 1922); Charles C. Black, *American Constitutional Law,* 412–414 (3d ed., St. Paul, 1910); Faulkner, *Social Justice,* 124; Act of June 29, 1906, ch. 3591, §§ 1, 4, 34 Stat. 584, 589; Paul W. Garrett, *Government Control over Prices,* 25–29 (Washington, D.C., 1920); Douglas, *Real Wages,* 60.

4. Garrett, *Government Control,* 37–38, 40–59, 145–148; George P. Adams, Jr., *Wartime Price Control,* 28–30, 55–56 (Washington, D.C.,

1942); Act of Aug. 10, 1917, ch. 53, 40 Stat. 276; William C. Mullendore, *History of the United States Food Administration, 1917–1919*, at 195–225, 334–335 (Stanford, 1941); Charles O. Hardy, *Wartime Control of Prices*, 162–163 (Washington, D.C., 1940).

5. Act of Aug. 10, 1917, ch. 53, § 25, 40 Stat. 284; Garrett, *Government Control*, 160–194, 642–657; Hardy, *Wartime Control*, 187–194; Adams, *Price Control*, 43–54; U.S. Fuel Administration, *Final Report of the Fuel Administrator, 1917–1919* (Washington, D.C., 1921).

6. Douglas, *Real Wages*, 60, 198–203, 364, 391; Adams, *Price Control*, 57–58, 104–109; Garrett, *Government Control*, 27, 35, 504, 550–552; David Friday, *Profits, Wages, and Prices*, 14–30 (New York, 1920); George Soule, *Prosperity Decade, from War to Depression: 1917–1929*, at 78–80 (New York, 1947); John M. Clark, *The Costs of the World War to the American People*, 130–132 (New Haven, 1931).

7. William A. White to Mark Sullivan, Jan. 28, 1918, in Walter Johnson, *Selected Letters of William Allen White, 1899–1943*, at 185 (New York, 1947); Elisha M. Friedman, *American Problems of Reconstruction*, 8–9 (New York, 1918); H.R. Rep. No. 75, 65th Cong., 1st Sess. 1 (1917); 55 Cong. Rec. 3794–3795 (June 18, 1917) (Rep. Lever); ibid., 3809–3812 (Rep. Anderson); ibid., 3816–3818 (Rep. Towne); ibid., 3822 (Rep. Overmyer); ibid., 3822–3827 (Memo by Solicitor to Dept. of Agriculture on constitutionality of Lever bill); ibid., 3887–3890 (June 19, 1917) (Rep. Hamlin); ibid., 4016 (June 21, 1917) (Rep. La Guardia); H.R.J. Res. 107, 65th Cong., 1st Sess., ibid., 4055; ibid., 4413–4414 (June 28, 1917) (Sen. Kellogg).

8. Mullendore, *Food Administration*, 350–354; Fuel Administration, *Final Report*, 10–13, 24–25; *OUSB*, Feb. 1, 1919, at 2; ibid., Feb. 7, 1919, at 6; *N.Y. Times*, Jan. 18, 1919, at 9:3; ibid., Feb. 9, 1919, pt. 2, at 5:5; Garrett, *Government Control*, 411; "Prices and Cost of Living," 11 *Monthly Labor Review* 67, 72–73, 84 (1920); E. L. Whitney, "Strikes and Lockouts in the United States, 1916–1919," 10 *Monthly Labor Review* 1505–1513 (1920); Robert K. Murray, *Red Scare: A Study in National Hysteria, 1919–1920*, at 111–112 (Minneapolis, 1955); "Labor, Its Grievances, Protests, and Demands," 27 *American Federationist* 33, 37 (Jan. 1920).

9. "Labor's Duty to the Public," 62 *Literary Digest* (Sept. 6, 1919), at 13–15; Forcey, *Crossroads of Liberalism*, xix–xx; WW, Address at Pittsburgh, Pa., Apr. 16, 1910, 20 *WWP* 363, 366, 368; WW, *New Freedom*, 28–30, 36 (New York, 1913); John Milton Cooper, Jr., *The Warrior and the Priest: Woodrow Wilson and Theodore Roosevelt*, 145–146, 151, 258–259, 262–264 (Cambridge, Mass., 1983); but cf. ibid., 172, 219.

10. Herbert Croly, *The Promise of American Life*, 128 (New York, 1909); *N.Y. Times*, May 4, 1919, at 3:4–5; ibid., Aug. 1, 1919, at 2:7; Irving Fisher, "High Prices; and a Remedy," 60 *American Review of Reviews* 268, 271

(Sept. 1919); 58 Cong. Rec. 3395–3396 (July 31, 1919) (Sen. Myers); *San Francisco Chronicle,* Aug. 1, 1919, at 1:8 and 2:1.

11. *N.Y. Times:* July 31, 1919, at 1:6 and 2:4; Aug. 1, 1919, at 1:1 and 2:6; Aug. 2, 1919, at 1:3 and 2:4–5; Aug. 3, 1919, at 2:2; Aug. 4, 1919, at 2:7; *San Francisco Chronicle,* Aug. 1, 1919, at 1:7 and 2:1; Edward Berman, *Labor Disputes and the President of the United States,* 154–157 (New York, 1924); Walker D. Hines to WW, July 30, 1919, 58 Cong. Rec. 3545 (Aug. 1, 1919); Whitney, "Strikes and Lockouts," 1506; Alexander M. Bing, *War-Time Strikes and Their Adjustment,* 213 (New York, 1921).

12. *N.Y. Times:* Aug. 3, 1919, at 1:5–8 and 2:1; Aug. 5, 1919, at 1:5–7; Aug. 7, 1919, at 1:6; Aug. 8, 1919, at 1:4; H.R. 8157, 66th Cong., 1st Sess., 58 Cong. Rec. 3586 (Aug. 2, 1919); American Federation of Labor, *Report of 40th Annual Convention,* 318–325 (Washington, D.C., 1920); K. Austin Kerr, *American Railroad Politics, 1914–1920: Rates, Wages, and Efficiency,* 161–178 (Pittsburgh, 1968).

13. *N.Y. Times:* Aug. 1, 1919, at 1:1; Aug. 2, 1919, at 1:8; Aug. 4, 1919, at 1:2 and 2:5; Aug. 6, 1919, at 1:8 and 2:1; Aug. 7, 1919, at 1:2; JPT to WW, Aug. 6, 1919, JPT MSS, Box 50; JPT to WW, Aug. 7, 1919 (two letters), ibid.; WW, Address to Congress, Aug. 8, 1919, 5 *WWPP* 558–571.

14. *N.Y. Times:* Aug. 8, 1919, at 1:1; Aug. 10, 1919, at 1:3 and 3:4; Aug. 18, 1919, at 14:4; Aug. 19, 1919, at 16:6; Aug. 24, 1919, at 2:5; Aug. 26, 1919, at 1:8; Aug. 27, 1919, at 1:3; Aug. 29, 1919, at 1:5; Sept. 22, 1919, at 1:6.

15. AMP to Gilbert Haugen, Aug. 12, 1919, H.R. Rep. No. 247, 66th Cong., 1st Sess. 2 (Aug. 21, 1919); H.R. 8624, 66th Cong., 1st Sess., 58 Cong. Rec. 4140 (Aug. 21, 1919); *N.Y. Times,* Aug. 23, 1919, at 1:5; Act of Oct. 22, 1919, ch. 80, 41 Stat. 297. Other section 4 conduct for which no penalty existed included limiting facilities for transporting, producing, or dealing in necessaries; restricting their supply or distribution; and interfering with production of necessaries to enhance their price. Act of Aug. 10, 1917, ch. 53, § 4, 40 Stat. 276, 277.

16. Stanley Coben, *A. Mitchell Palmer: Politician,* 155–170 (New York, 1963); *N.Y. Times,* Aug. 21, 1919, at 1:5; ibid., Aug. 25, 1919, at 5:1.

17. *N.Y. Times:* July 31, 1919, at 2:5; Aug. 1, 1919, at 1:1; Aug. 2, 1919, at 1:8; Aug. 4, 1919, at 1:2 and 2:5; Aug. 6, 1919, at 1:8 and 2:1; Aug. 7, 1919, at 1:1 and 2:2; *San Francisco Chronicle,* Dec. 17, 1919, at 3:6; Act of Aug. 10, 1917, ch. 53, §§ 6, 7, 40 Stat. 276, 278–279.

18. *N.Y. Times:* Aug. 11, 1919, at 1:6–8; Aug. 13, 1919, at 1:7; Aug. 14, 1919, at 2:1; Aug. 15, 1919, at 10:5–6; Aug. 19, 1919, at 4:2; Aug. 23, 1919, at 2:2–3; Dec. 23, 1919, at 1:1 and 4:3–4; Dept. of Justice, *Annual Report of the Attorney General, 1919,* at 17–19.

19. *N.Y. Times:* Aug. 4, 1919, at 2:5; Aug. 11, 1919, at 1:8; Aug. 15, 1919, at 1:8; Aug. 16, 1919, at 1:5–7; Aug. 19, 1919, at 4:2; Aug. 21, 1919,

at 3:4; Sept. 11, 1919, at 17:5; *Hearings before House Committee on Agriculture on Amendments Proposed to Food Control Act,* 66th Cong., 1st Sess. 63 (Aug. 15 and 20, 1919) (testimony of AMP).

20. *N.Y. Times:* Aug. 7, 1919, at 15:8; Aug. 9, 1919, at 3:5; Aug. 14, 1919, at 1:6–7; Aug. 15, 1919, at 1:8; Aug. 17, 1919, at 3:4; Aug. 19, 1919, at 4:2; Aug. 23, 1919, at 2:2–3; *Hearing before Senate Committee on Agriculture & Forestry on Proposed Amendments to Public No. 241,* 66th Cong., 1st Sess. 9 (Aug. 14, 1919) (testimony of AMP); Mossew v. United States, 266 F. 18, 20, 22 (2d Cir. 1920).

21. *N.Y. Times,* Aug. 9, 1919, at 3:5; ibid., Aug. 19, 1919, at 4:2; ibid., Sept. 11, 1919, at 17:5; Act of Aug. 10, 1917, ch. 53, § 9, 40 Stat. 279; U.S Const. art. I, § 9. Palmer and his assistant, C. B. Ames, admitted to Congress that the act did not prohibit conspiracies to raise prices. *Hearings before House Comm. on Agric.,* 8–10; *Hearing before Senate Comm. on Agric. & For.,* 44.

22. Joshua Bernhardt, *Government Control of the Sugar Industry in the United States,* 160–188 (New York, 1920); Mullendore, *Food Administration,* 182–183; Garrett, *Government Control,* 53 n.1, 79–83; Adams, *Price Control,* 33–35; *N.Y. Times,* Aug. 15, 1919, at 2:2; ibid., Aug. 22, 1919, at 3:5–6; Proclamation of Oct. 30, 1920, 41 Stat. 1807.

23. Dept. of Justice, *Annual Report of the Attorney General, 1919,* at 18–19; *N.Y. Times,* Sept. 21, 1919, pt. 2, at 8:1–5. The cost of living in fact rose between August and December 1919. Douglas, *Real Wages,* 57.

24. *N.Y. Times,* Aug. 15, 1919, at 1:8; ibid., Aug. 20, 1919, at 17:6; ibid., Aug. 25, 1919, at 1:6; 58 Cong. Rec. 4197, 4227 (Aug. 22, 1919); ibid., 5163–5164 (Sept. 10, 1919); ibid., 5237 (Sept. 11, 1919).

25. Act of Aug. 10, 1917, ch. 53, § 1, 40 Stat. 276; 58 Cong. Rec. 5161 (Sept. 10, 1919) (Sen. Kenyon); ibid., 5164–5165 (Sens. Owen and Harrison); ibid., 5167 (Sen. Dial); ibid., 5227 (Sept. 11, 1919) (Sens. McKellar and Dial).

26. 58 Cong. Rec. 4198, 4206 (Aug. 22, 1919) (Rep. Huddleston); ibid., 5724 (Sept. 22, 1919) (Rep. Mason); WW, Address to Congress, Aug. 8, 1919, 5 *WWPP* 558–571.

27. Soule, *Prosperity Decade,* 81–95; Robert A. Gordon, *Business Fluctuations,* 402–403 (2d ed., New York, 1961); Fisher, "High Prices," 268–271; *Hearings before House Comm. on Agric.,* 47–48 (C. B. Ames, Assistant Attorney General, says war powers cannot be used to deal with cost of living).

28. H.R. Rep. No. 247, at 2; Act of Oct. 22, 1919, ch. 80, title I, § 2, 41 Stat. 298; United States v. Reese, 92 U.S. 214, 220 (1866); International Harvester Co. v. Kentucky, 234 U.S. 216, 221–223 (1914).

29. *Hearing before Senate Comm. on Agric. & For.,* 8; *N.Y. Times,* Aug. 15, 1919, at 2:3; *Hearings before House Comm. on Agric.,* 79–80, 89–90

(apparently referring to Tozer v. United States, 52 F. 917, 919 (C.C.E.D. Mo. 1892)); Dept of Justice, *Annual Report of the Attorney General, 1919*, at 17.

30. S. Rep. No. 162, 66th Cong., 1st Sess. 1–2 (Aug. 23, 1919); 58 Cong. Rec. 5166 (Sept. 10, 1919); ibid., 5167 (Sens. Kellogg and Dial); ibid., 5297–5298 (Sept. 12, 1919) (Sen. Smith); ibid., 5296–5304.

31. 58 Cong. Rec. 5166–5167 (Sept. 10, 1919) (Sen. Harrison); ibid., 5298–5299 (Sept. 12, 1919) (Sens. Kenyon and Smoot).

32. *Hearing before Senate Comm. on Agric. & For.*, 4–5; WW, Address to Congress, Aug. 8, 1919, 5 *WWPP* 558–571.

33. Hardy, *Wartime Control*, 198; 56 Cong. Rec. 6101 (May 6, 1918) (Sens. Pomerene and Saulsbury); ibid., 6249–6250 (May 9, 1918); WW to ASB, Jan. 19, 1918, 46 *WWP* 37; Act of May 31, 1918, ch. 90, 40 Stat. 593–594; Edward L. Schaub, "The Regulation of Rentals during the War Period," 28 *Journal of Political Economy* 1, 20–25 (1920); 58 Cong. Rec. 1301 (June 18, 1919) (Sen. Pomerene); ibid., 1849 (June 26, 1919) (Rep. Davis); Act of July 11, 1919, ch. 7, § 13, 41 Stat. 104.

34. 58 Cong. Rec. 4206 (Aug. 22, 1919) (Rep. Huddleston); ibid., 4207, 4228; S. Rep. No. 162, at 1; S. 2992, 66th Cong., 1st Sess., 58 Cong. Rec. 5213; S. Rep. No. 179, 66th Cong., 1st Sess. (1919).

35. Act of Oct. 22, 1919, ch. 80, title II, 40 Stat. 298–304.

36. U.S. Const. art. I, § 8, cl. 17; ibid., art. I, §10; 56 Cong. Rec. 7120 (May 27, 1918) (Sen. Brandegee); Burdick, *American Constitution*, 305, 413–414 (quote); 2 Westel W. Willoughby, *Constitutional Law of the United States*, 874–876 (New York, 1910); Hall, *Constitutional Law*, 219–220; James P. Hall, *Cases on Constitutional Law*, 788 n.1 (St. Paul, 1913); Act of Oct. 22, 1919, ch. 80, title II, § 106, 40 Stat. 300; 58 Cong. Rec. 6325 (Oct. 3, 1919) (Sen. Sherman).

37. Schaub, "Regulation of Rentals," 11–17; Note, "Rent Legislation," 20 *Columbia Law Review* 109 (1920); Westel W. Willoughby, *Principles of the Constitutional Law of the United States*, 500 (New York, 1912); 2 Willoughby, *Constitutional Law*, 1212–1213; Burdick, *American Constitution*, 268.

38. 56 Cong. Rec. 6103–6105 (May 6, 1918) (Sen Reed); ibid., 6555 (May 15, 1918) (Rep. Johnson); ibid., 6824 (May 21, 1918) (Sen. Saulsbury); ibid., 6825 (Sen. Kellogg); ibid., 7117–7120 (May 27, 1918) (Sens. Hardwick, Cummins, and Pomerene); ibid., 7122 (Sen. Brandegee); Willard Saulsbury to WW, May 28, 1918, 46 *WWP* 192–193; WW to Saulsbury, May 29, 1918, ibid.; WW to Thomas W. Gregory, May 29, 1918, ibid.

39. S. Rep. No. 179, at 1–2; 58 Cong. Rec. 5300–5301 (Sept. 12, 1919); ibid., 6322 (Oct. 3, 1919) (Sen. Norris); ibid., 6325–6326 (Sen. Sherman); ibid., 6372 (Oct. 4, 1919) (Rep. Haugen); ibid., 6758 (Oct. 11, 1919) (Rep. McLaughlin); H.R. Rep. No. 349, 66th Cong., 1st Sess. 8, 13 (Oct. 2, 1919); Act of Oct. 22, 1919, ch. 80, title II, § 122, 41 Stat. 304.

40. *58 Cong. Rec.* 6320 (Oct. 3, 1919) (Sen. Kellogg); ibid., 6322 (Sen. King); ibid., 6375 (Oct. 4, 1919) (Rep. Moon); ibid., 6755 (Oct. 11, 1919) (Rep. Begg); ibid., 6757 (Rep. Hersey); ibid., 6758 (Reps. Begg and McLaughlin).

41. *58 Cong. Rec.* 6325 (Oct. 3, 1919) (Sen. Sherman); ibid., 6375 (Oct. 4, 1919) (Rep. Mapes). As Sherman implied, the law contained a severability clause. Act of Oct. 22, 1919, ch. 80, title II, § 121, 40 Stat. 304.

42. *58 Cong. Rec.* 6755 (Oct. 11, 1919) (Rep. Begg); ibid., 6759–6760.

43. Act of Oct. 22, 1919, ch. 80, title II, § 119, 41 Stat. 304; JPT to WW, Nov. 7, 1919, JPT MSS, Box 50; JPT to WW, Dec. 11, 1919, ibid.; Wilson v. McDonnell, 265 F. 432 (D.C. Cir., 1919) (see Chapter 8); *Washington Post,* Dec. 7, 1919, pt. 3, at 1:1; *59 Cong. Rec.* 1109 (Jan. 6, 1920); ibid., 1537 (Jan. 14, 1920).

44. JPT to AMP, Sept. 29, 1919, JPT MSS, Box 84; *N.Y. Times,* Sept. 12, 1919, at 24:5; "Prices and Cost of Living," 12 *Monthly Labor Review* 268–269, 309 (1921); Douglas, *Real Wages,* 57; American Legion Post No. 1, Memphis, Tenn., to AMP, Nov. 15, 1919, NA DOJ, file 186701–74–12; AMP to Memphis Post No. 1, Nov. 20, 1919, ibid.

45. AMP, "How to Bring Down Prices," 100 *Independent* 167, 203 (Dec. 13, 1919); Dept. of Justice, *Annual Report of the Attorney General, 1920,* at 180–182; *N.Y. Times,* Dec. 23, 1919, at 4:3–4; ibid., July 13, 1920, at 7:1.

46. *N.Y. Times:* Apr. 1, 1920, at 11:5; Apr. 7, 1920, at 7:1; May 5, 1920, at 3:1; May 23, 1920, at 20:1; May 28, 1920, at 17:2; July 28, 1920, at 20:2; July 29, 1920, at 21:4; Aug. 23, 1920, at 2:2–3; Sept. 21, 1920, at 16:3; Dept. of Justice, *Annual Report of the Attorney General, 1920,* at 180.

47. *San Francisco Chronicle,* Dec. 17, 1919, at 18:1–2; *N.Y. Times,* May 5, 1920, at 3:1.

48. *N.Y. Times:* Oct. 26, 1919, at 5:1; Nov. 4, 1919, at 17:1; Nov. 15, 1919, at 8:2; Dec. 13, 1919, at 14:2; Dec. 23, 1919, at 4:3–4; Jan. 4, 1920, at 6:7 (Willard case dropped); Dept. of Justice, *Annual Report of the Attorney General, 1919,* at 18–19; NA DOJ file 24–363; Mullendore, *Food Administration,* 60–61, 333–337; Garrett, *Government Control,* 145 n.1.

49. Dept. of Justice, *Annual Report of the Attorney General, 1920,* at 183; "Prices and Cost of Living," 11 *Monthly Labor Review* 67, 69 (1920); 12 ibid., 260, 262–263 (1921); S. Rep. No. 286, 66th Cong., 1st Sess. 2–4 (1919); Mullendore, *Food Administration,* 186–193; Bernhardt, *Government Control of Sugar Industry,* 85–91, 109–116, 233–235; 59 Cong. Rec. 360–361 (1919) (Sen. McNary); *N.Y. Times,* Oct. 17, 1919, at 19:7; ibid., Oct. 19, 1919, pt. 2, at 1:1–2; Joshua Bernhardt, *The Sugar Industry and the Federal Government: A Thirty-Year Record,* 77 n.1, 109–111, 217 (Washington, D.C., 1948).

50. Bernhardt, *Sugar Industry,* 83; *N.Y. Times:* Oct. 28, 1919, at 16:1; Nov. 4, 1919, at 17:8; Nov. 8, 1919, at 15:2; Nov. 22, 1919, at 1:3, 3:2, and

9:2; Nov. 25, 1919, at 24:4; Nov. 30, 1919, pt. 2, at 1:4; Dec. 10, 1919, at 4:2; July 29, 1920, at 21:4; Jan. 1, 1921, at 20:3; Dept. of Justice, *Annual Report of the Attorney General, 1920,* at 183; Proclamation of Nov. 21, 1919, 41 Stat. 1774; Act of Aug. 10, 1917, ch. 53, § 5, 40 Stat. 277–278; United States v. Mulligan, 268 F. 983 (N.D. N.Y. 1920); NA DOJ, High Cost of Living Division ("HCL Div."), Box 9, file "Attorney General" (sugar license revocations).

51. Act of Dec. 31, 1919, ch. 33, 41 Stat. 386; 59 Cong. Rec. 404 (Dec. 11, 1919) (Sen. Smith); ibid., 443 (Dec. 12, 1919) (Sen. Gay); ibid., 708 (Dec. 16, 1919) (Rep. Bee); ibid., 787 (Dec. 18, 1919) (Sen. Ransdell); ibid., 945–947 (Dec. 20, 1919) (Sen. Gay); Bernhardt, *Government Control of Sugar Industry,* 119–123; *N.Y. Times,* Jan. 2, 1919, at 1:4; Bernhardt, *Sugar Industry,* 80–85.

52. Dept. of Justice, *Annual Report of the Attorney General, 1920,* at 182; *N.Y. Times:* Apr. 15, 1920, at 17:5; Apr. 18, 1920, at 7:1; Apr. 25, 1920, at 22:1; May 14, 1920, at 2:7.

53. Dept. of Justice, *Annual Report of the Attorney General, 1920,* at 183; *N.Y. Times:* Nov. 7, 1919, at 17:4; Nov. 15, 1919, at 19:2; Nov. 29, 1919, at 8:2; Jan. 16, 1920, at 4:5; Jan. 27, 1920, at 8:3; April 11, 1920, at 9:2; April 12, 1920, at 1:4; *N.Y. World,* April 11, 1920, at 13:1; ibid., April 12, 1920, at 1:4.

54. U.S. Bituminous Coal Commission, *Award and Recommendations Accepted by the President,* v–vi, x, 39, 44 (Washington, D.C., 1920).

55. *N.Y. Times:* Apr. 4, 1920, at 18:3; June 24, 1920, at 21:2; July 18, 1920, at 6:6; July 29, 1920, at 10:3; July 31, 1920, at 11:2; Aug. 2, 1920, at 1:2; Sept. 11, 1920, at 5:1; Oct. 5, 1920, at 1:4; Oct. 31, 1920, pt 2, at 1:2; Nov. 18, 1920, at 5:2; Nov. 19, 1920, at 4:2; Dec. 3, 1920, at 4:2; Dec. 30, 1920, at 5:3; Dept. of Justice, *Annual Report of the Attorney General, 1920,* at 48–50, 183; "Prosecutions under Food Control Act," May 12, 1920, NA DOJ, HCL Div., Box 10.

56. *N.Y. Times:* Oct. 16, 1920, at 23:3; Oct. 31, 1920, at 12:3; Jan. 1, 1921, at 3:4 and 20:3; Jan. 26, 1921, at 2:4; Feb. 1, 1921, at 6:3; United States v. L. Cohen Grocery Co., 255 U.S. 81 (1921) (see Chapter 7); Dept. of Justice, *Annual Report of the Attorney General, 1920,* at 183. Some accounts give higher figures; e.g., *N.Y. Times,* Apr. 4, 1920, at 1:4; ibid., Aug. 8, 1920, pt. 2, at 8:4; these may include the war years and/or record individuals rather than suits, for many cases involved multiple defendants.

57. Memo from Howard Figg to Charles B. Ames, Sept. 19, 1919, NA DOJ, HCL Div., Box 9; *St. Louis Post-Dispatch,* Dec. 15, 1919, at 24:3; *N.Y. Times,* Apr. 19, 1920, at 14:5; ibid., Apr. 25, 1920, at 5:1; ibid., May 24, 1920, at 1:5; 59 Cong. Rec. 7285 (May 19, 1920) (Sen. Kenyon); Samuel Gompers, "Labor's Protest against a Rampant Tragedy," 27 *American Federationist* 521 (June, 1920).

58. *N.Y. Times:* Apr. 17, 1920, at 3:1; Apr. 18, 1920, at 16:3; Apr. 24, 1920, at 21:3; May 27, 1920, at 1:1; June 12, 1920, at 17:8 and 24:6; June 20, 1920, at 7:1; June 24, 1920, at 23:3; July 8, 1920, at 23:5; July 20, 1920, at 2:8; Aug. 22, 1920, pt. 2, at 1:7; Mar. 20, 1921, pt. 2, at 1:3; Mar. 23, 1921, at 19:1; Dept. of Justice, *Annual Report of the Attorney General, 1920,* at 184–185; but see Coben, *Palmer,* 169 (defending Palmer on the basis that while corporate prices increased in 1919 and 1920, rates of profit declined; small businesses, however, also faced rising costs and declining profit margins, but they were not immune from prosecution).

59. WW, Speech to businessmen, Columbus, Ohio, Sept. 20, 1912, 25 *WWP* 201; WW, *New Freedom,* 80, 169–170, 263, 270; William E. Leuchtenberg, Introduction, in WW, *New Freedom,* 9–10 (reprint, Englewood Cliffs, N.J., 1961); WW, Interview in *N.Y. Times,* Nov. 24, 1907, 17 *WWP* 513, 518; WW, Address to American Bankers' Association, Denver, Colo., Sept. 30, 1908, 18 *WWP* 424, 433; Cooper, *Warrior and Priest,* 215–220; Edwin A. Weinstein, *Woodrow Wilson: A Medical and Psychological Biography,* 217–225 (Princeton, 1981).

60. David Morgan, *Suffragists and Democrats: The Politics of Woman Suffrage in America,* 110–114 (East Lansing, Mich., 1972); Eleanor Flexner, *Century of Struggle: The Woman's Rights Movement in the United States,* 325–328, 334–336, 392 n.32 (rev. ed., Cambridge, Mass., 1975); 5 Ida H. Harper, *History of Woman Suffrage,* 649–652 (New York, 1969); Carrie C. Catt and Nettie R. Shuler, *Woman Suffrage and Politics: The Inner Story of the Suffrage Movement,* 374, 388, 426–427, 465 (Seattle, 1969); Coben, *Palmer,* 84–86; *N.Y. Times,* June 25, 1919, at 3:2–3.

61. *Hearings before House Comm. on Agric.,* 63–65, 67–68, 76; H.R. Rep. No. 247, at 3.

62. Dept. of Justice, *Annual Report of the Attorney General, 1920,* at 180–182.

63. *N.Y. Times,* Nov. 26, 1919, at 3:6; ibid., Jan. 18, 1920, pt. 4, at 1:1–2 and 2:1–4; Memo of Conference with Retail Clothiers' Committee, Jan. 20, 1920, NA DOJ, HCL Div., Box 9; 64 *Literary Digest* (Mar. 27, 1920), at 51; *Pittsburgh Dispatch,* May 28, 1920, at 6:2.

64. 59 Cong. Rec. 7285 (May 19, 1920) (Sen. Kenyon); S. Res. 357, 66th Cong., 2d Sess., ibid., 7326–7327 (May 20, 1920). Though Palmer ran a low-budget campaign, he spent more than twice as much as any of his Democratic rivals. S. Rep. No. 823, 66th Cong., 3d Sess. 3 (1921).

65. Harper, *Woman Suffrage,* 643; *Hearings Pursuant to S. Res. 357 before Sen. Subcomm. on Privileges and Elections to Investigate Campaign Expenses of Various Presidential Candidates in All Political Parties,* 66th Cong., 2d Sess., vol. 1, at 1022–1039 (1921).

66. *N.Y. Times,* July 10, 1920, at 2:2; ibid., July 11, 1920, at 2:6; *San*

Francisco Chronicle, July 10, 1920, at 1:3; ibid., July 11, 1920, at 1:5; *Hearings Pursuant to S. Res. 357,* at 1040–1048 (Mary S. Scott); ibid., 1048–1055 (Mrs. John R. Leighty); ibid., 1060–1062 (Annie L. Meehan).

67. *San Francisco Chronicle,* July 3, 1920, at 1:1–5; ibid., July 4, 1920, at 1:1–6; Douglas, *Real Wages,* 57; "Prices and Cost of Living," 12 *Monthly Labor Review* 260, 270, 300–309 (1921); Gordon, *Business Fluctuations,* 403–404; *N.Y. Times,* Apr. 20, 1920, at 1:4; Dept. of Justice, *Annual Report of the Attorney General, 1920,* at 185.

68. Croly, *Promise of American Life,* 128; Weyl, *New Democracy,* 253, 293 n.1; Stanley Shapiro, "The Great War and Reform: Liberals and Labor, 1917–1919," 12 *Labor History* 324, 337 (1971); Richard Hofstadter, *The Age of Reform: From Bryan to F.D.R.,* 239–240 (New York, 1955); Forcey, *Crossroads of Liberalism,* xx.

69. WW, "A Credo," Aug. 6, 1907, 17 *WWP* 337; Arthur S. Link, *Wilson: The Road to the White House,* 112, 127, 183, 509 (Princeton, 1947); Cooper, *Warrior and Priest,* 251–262; Valerie Jean Conner, *The National War Labor Board: Stability, Social Justice, and the Voluntary State in World War I* (Chapel Hill, 1983); JPT to WW, Aug. 7, 1917, JPT MSS, Box 50.

70. "Public Opinion Defeated the Strikes," 63 *Literary Digest* (Nov. 22, 1919), at 12; Friday, *Profits, Wages, and Prices,* 3, 6; Douglas, *Real Wages,* 391.

71. *N.Y. Times:* Aug. 19, 1919, at 16:6; Aug. 24, 1919, at 22:4; Aug. 25, 1919, at 1:2; Aug. 26, 1919, at 1:6–7; Aug. 27, 1919, at 2:5; Aug. 29, 1919, at 1:8 and 2:1; Aug. 30, 1919, at 2:1–2; Aug. 31, 1919, at 5:7; Berman, *Labor Disputes,* 164–169; JPT to WW, Aug. 22, 1919, JPT MSS, Box 50; JPT to Walker D. Hines, Aug. 27, 1919, ibid., Box 12; WW, Statement, Aug. 25, 1919, 5 *WWPP* 584–587.

72. Act of Oct. 15, 1914, ch. 323, § 20, 38 Stat. 738; *N.Y. Times,* Sept. 21, 1919, at 15:1. In the eyes of many contemporaries § 20 did not entirely shield unions from suit under the antitrust laws. Link, *Wilson and Progressive Era,* 73 n. 46.

73. Douglas, *Real Wages,* 352–354; Melvyn Dubofsky and Warren Van-Tine, *John L. Lewis: A Biography,* 43–50, 57–58 (New York, 1977); Bituminous Coal Commission, *Award and Recommendations,* 20–21; C. F. Stoddard, "The Bituminous Coal Strike," 9 *Monthly Labor Review* 1725–1730 (1919); Berman, *Labor Disputes,* 177 n.1; William L. Chenery, "The Coal Strike," 43 *Survey* 150–152 (Nov. 22, 1919).

74. Berman, *Labor Disputes,* 177–179; Stoddard, "Bituminous Strike," 1730–1731; JPT to Walker Hines, and Walker Hines to JPT, Oct. 24, 1919, JPT MSS, Box 12; Act of Aug. 10, 1917, ch. 53, § 9, 40 Stat. 279; Act of Oct. 22, 1919, ch. 80, § 2, 41 Stat. 298; E. David Cronon, *The Cabinet Diaries*

of Josephus Daniels, 1913–1921, at 452–453 (Lincoln, Neb., 1963); WW, Statement, Oct. 25, 1919, 6 *WWPP* 420–423.

75. Fuel Admin., *Final Report,* 12–13, 16, 26; *N.Y. Times:* Oct. 30, 1919, at 1:8; Nov. 1, 1919, at 1:5 and 2:1–2; Nov. 8, 1919, at 22:4; Dec. 1, 1919, at 1:2; Dec. 2, 1919, at 1:1; Dec. 9, 1919, at 1:1; Dec. 13, 1919, at 1:7–8; Dec. 14, 1919, at 1:6; Bituminous Coal Commission, *Award and Recommendations,* v–vi, x, 36–40; Stoddard, "Bituminous Strike," 1725, 1733–1734; Dubofsky, *Lewis,* 55–57; Berman, *Labor Disputes,* 182–193; Zechariah Chafee, Jr., *The Inquiring Mind,* 198–207 (New York, 1928); Whitney, "Strikes and Lockouts," 1506–1507; War Dept., *1920 Annual Report,* 68–70; Abraham Glasser, "Records Relating to a Study of the Use of Force in Internal Disturbances by the Federal Government," NA DOJ, Box 3.

76. Stoddard, "Bituminous Strike," 1733; Coben, *Palmer,* 171–177; Donald Wilhelm, "If He Were President," 102 *Independent* 46, 63–64 (Apr. 10, 1920); *N.Y. Times:* Nov. 27, 1919, at 1:6; Nov. 28, 1919, at 11:1–2; Nov. 29, 1919, at 2:8; Dec, 4, 1919, at 1:1; *U.M.W. Journal,* Dec. 15, 1919, at 8–9; *Minneapolis Journal,* Dec. 17, 1919, at 1:3; Cronon, *Cabinet Diaries,* 459, 467; *Washington Post,* Nov. 27, 1919, at 1:6–7.

77. Willis J. Abbot, "A. Mitchell Palmer, 'Fighting Quaker,' " 64 *Literary Digest* (Mar. 27, 1920), at 51, 55; William T. Ellis, "The 'Fighting Quaker' of the Cabinet," 61 *American Review of Reviews* 35 (Jan. 1920); *N.Y. Times:* Nov. 24, 1919, at 1:4; Nov. 25, 1919, at 1:1; Nov. 29, 1919, at 1:1; Dec. 5, 1919, at 1:1; Dec. 7, 1919, at 1:2; Dec. 8, 1919, at 2:1; Dec. 9, 1919, at 1:4; Dec. 13, 1919, at 2:2; *Minneapolis Journal,* Dec. 17, 1919, at 1:3; AFL, *40th Annual Convention,* 187–188; Lincoln Colcord, "The Administration Adrift," 109 *Nation* 635–636 (Nov. 15, 1919).

78. 55 Cong. Rec. 4084 (June 22, 1917) (Rep. Lever); ibid., 4084, 4186 (June 22–23, 1917); ibid., 5834–5837 (Aug. 6, 1917) (Sens. Chamberlain et al.); ibid., 5904 (Aug. 8, 1917) (Sen. Husting); Samuel Gompers, Address at Washington, D.C., Nov. 22, 1919, 59 Cong. Rec. 40–44 (Dec. 2, 1919); Sen. Chamberlain to Samuel Gompers, Nov. 24, 1919, ibid., 1020 (Jan. 5, 1920); Samuel Gompers, "The Broken Pledge," 27 *American Federationist* 41 (1920); *N.Y. Times,* Nov. 12, 1919, at 2:3; ibid., Nov. 23, 1919, at 12:1; AFL, *40th Annual Convention,* 190–193; Berman, *Labor Disputes,* 190–192; Coben, *Palmer,* 178.

79. John M. Blum, *Joe Tumulty and the Wilson Era,* 219–221 (Boston, 1951); Tom Schachtman, *Edith & Woodrow, A Presidential Romance,* 223–224 (New York, 1981); Edwin A. Weinstein, "Woodrow Wilson's Neurological Illness," 57 *Journal of American History* 324, 339–345 (1970); Weinstein, *Wilson,* 252, 344–345, 359; Arthur S. Link, *Wilson: The New Freedom,* 265–269, 427–433 (Princeton, 1956).

80. *N.Y. Times,* Jan. 18, 1920, pt. 4, at 2:1–4; Mark Sullivan, "Your

Move, Democracy," 65 *Collier's* (June 19, 1920), at 3, noting AMP's decline among party leaders after January 1920.

81. AFL, *40th Annual Convention,* 187; S. Con. Res. 15, 66th Cong., 1st Sess., 58 Cong. Rec. 7761, 7821 (1919); Stoddard, "Coal Strike," 73–74; "The Surrender at Indianapolis," 109 *Nation* 630 (Nov. 15, 1919); Zechariah Chafee, Jr., "The Progress of the Law, 1919–1920," 34 *Harvard Law Review* 388, 401–407 (1921); Berman, *Labor Disputes,* 192–193; Blum, *Tumulty,* 221. Compare In re Debs, 158 U.S. 564, 598 (1895), upholding strike injunction limited to activities (interstate movement of trains and carrying of mails) over which government had plenary legislative power under Article I. On mining as a local activity, see Hammer v. Dagenhart, 247 U.S. 251, 272 (1918); United Mine Workers v. Coronado Coal Co., 259 U.S. 344, 407–408 (1922). The Clayton Act's provision for jury trial in contempt cases did not apply to suits filed by the government. Act of Oct. 15, 1914, ch. 323, §§ 22, 24, 38 Stat. 738–740.

82. WW, Statement, Oct. 25, 1919, 6 *WWPP* 420–423; WW, Veto message, Oct. 27, 1919, 58 Cong. Rec. 7607 (Oct. 27, 1919); "The Coal War," 109 *Nation* 577–578 (Nov. 8, 1919); 58 Cong. Rec. 7718 (Oct. 29, 1919) (Rep. Bland); ibid., 7749 (Oct. 30, 1919) (Sen. Borah); Cronon, *Cabinet Diaries,* 453; *N.Y. Times,* Nov. 1, 1919, at 2:1; Felix Frankfurter, "Law and Order," 9 *Yale Review* n.s. 225, 227 (Jan. 1920).

83. *N.Y. Times:* Nov. 18, 1919, at 1:3, 4:4, and 5:5; Nov. 20, 1919, at 5:2; Nov. 21, 1919, at 4:2; Nov. 23, 1919, at 20:3–4; Nov. 24, 1919, at 17:8; Nov. 25, 1919, at 3:2; Nov. 28, 1919, at 11:2; Nov. 29, 1919, at 1:2; Nov. 30, 1919, at 1:7; Dec. 1, 1919, at 1:6–7 and 16:2; Dec. 2, 1919, at 1:2; Dec. 3, 1919, at 1:7 and 8:4; Dec. 4, 1919, at 1:2 and 3:4; Dec. 5, 1919, at 1:2; Dec. 6, 1919, at 1:2 and 3:4–5; Dec. 7, 1919, at 1:4 and 3:4; Dec. 10, 1919, at 2:3; Henry J. Allen, *The Party of the Third Part: The Story of the Kansas Industrial Relations Court,* 48–61 (New York, 1921); John H. Bowers, *The Kansas Court of Industrial Relations,* 28–38 (Chicago, 1922).

84. Coben, *Palmer,* 204; *St. Louis Post-Dispatch,* Dec. 13, 1919, at 3:4; Memo of Conference with Retail Clothiers' Committee, Jan. 20, 1920, NA DOJ, HCL Div., Box 9. There is no evidence of such action being taken against the garment workers.

85. *Minneapolis Journal,* Dec. 17, 1919, at 1:3; *U.M.W. Journal:* Dec. 15, 1919, at 9; Apr. 15, 1920, at 5, 8; May 15, 1920, at 3–5, 9; June 1, 1920, at 3–5, 8–9; "Public Opinion Defeating Strikes," 63 *Literary Digest* (Nov. 22, 1919), at 11; *N.Y. Times:* Mar. 12, 1920, at 1:4; Mar. 13, 1920, at 6:5; Mar. 28, 1920, at 2:2; Apr. 8, 1920, at 25:5; May 9, 1920, at 12:3; May 26, 1920, at 17:3; May 27, 1920, at 1:2 and 3:2; May 28, 1920, at 1:6; Oct. 14, 1920, at 26:1; Oct. 15, 1920, at 21:3; Nov. 9, 1920, at 23:2; Jan.

5, 1921, at 3:3; S. Doc. No. 159, 67th Cong., 2d Sess. 37 (1922); United States v. Armstrong, 265 F. 683 (D.Ind. 1920); 1 Merlo J. Pusey, *Charles Evans Hughes*, 388 (New York, 1936); D. J. Danelski and J. S. Tulchin, *Autobiographical Notes of Charles Evans Hughes*, 194 n.28 (Cambridge, Mass., 1973); Dept. of Labor, *1920 Annual Report*, at 109–111; Berman, *Labor Disputes*, 199–203.

86. *Pittsburgh Daily Dispatch*, May 27, 1920, at 1:7; *N.Y. Times:* Feb. 11, 1920, at 1:1 and 9:3; Feb. 13, 1920, at 1:5; Feb. 14, 1920, at 1:1; Feb. 15, 1920, at 1:1 and 3:6; Apr. 9, 1920, at 2:5; Apr. 10, 1920, at 1:6; May 27, 1920, at 3:3; "Strikes and Lockouts in the United States, 1916 to 1920," 12 *Monthly Labor Review* 1280 (1921); Berman, *Labor Disputes*, 193–199; Coben, *Palmer*, 184–188; Walker Hines to WW, Apr. 10, 1920, WW MSS, ser. 4, case 645A.

87. AMP, "Three Strikes—And Out," 102 *Independent* 243, 268 (May 22, 1920); *N.Y. Times:* Apr. 11, 1920, at 1:5; Apr. 12, 1920, at 3:2; Apr. 13, 1920, at 3:1; Apr. 14, 1920, at 1:5; Apr. 15, 1920, at 1:5; Cronon, *Cabinet Diaries*, 518.

88. Cronon, *Cabinet Diaries*, 517–518; Josephus Daniels, *The Wilson Era, Years of Peace: 1910–1917*, at 546 (Chapel Hill, 1946); 2 David F. Houston, *Eight Years with Wilson's Cabinet*, 69–70 (New York, 1926); *N.Y. Times:* Apr. 12, 1920, at 1:4; Apr. 15, 1920, at 1:5 and 2:5; Apr. 16, 1920, at 1:5 and 3:1; Apr. 17, 1920, at 2:2; Apr. 20, 1920, at 2:2; Apr. 21, 1920, at 2:4; Apr. 23, 1920, at 2:1–2; Apr. 24, 1920, at 2:3; Apr. 29, 1920, at 2:4; May 12, 1920, at 17:6; May 27, 1920, at 3:3; June 20, 1920, at 20:6; July 24, 1920, at 6:5; July 29, 1920, at 11:3; Aug. 5, 1920, at 1:5; Aug. 6, 1920, at 14:5; *San Francisco Chronicle:* Apr. 14, 1920, at 1:1; June 27, 1920, at 12:7; June 29, 1920, at 14:1; July 4, 1920, at 6:2; July 16, 1920, at 4:8; *Los Angeles Times:* Apr. 18, 1920, at 1:6; Apr. 20, 1920, at 1:7; June 20, 1920, pt. 2, at 2:1; Oct. 15, 1920, at 16:3; Oct. 6, 1921, at 7:3; *Pittsburgh Daily Dispatch*, Apr. 23, 1920, at 1:5; ibid., May 27, 1920, at 1:7; NA DOJ, file 16–145–23; S. Doc. No. 190, 67th Cong., 2d Sess. 2 (1922); Fannon v. United States, 276 F. 109 (9th Cir. 1921); National Industrial Conference Board, *The Kansas Court of Industrial Relations*, 61 (New York, 1924).

89. *N.Y. Times:* Apr. 17, 1920, at 4:2; Apr. 24, 1920, at 32:4; Apr. 27, 1920, at 3:1; Apr. 29, 1920, at 3:1; Florence Peterson, "Strikes in the United States, 1880–1936," U.S. Bureau of Labor Statistics, Dept. of Labor, Bulletin No. 651, at 35 (1937); "Strikes and Lockouts," 1278.

90. Dept. of Labor, *1920 Annual Report*, 106–113; Berman, *Labor Disputes*, 202–204; JPT to WW, July 12, 1920, JPT MSS, Box 50; JPT to WW, July 26, 1920, ibid.; *San Francisco Chronicle*, July 10, 1920, at 5:4; ibid., July 19, 1920, at 1:6–7; ibid., July 28, 1920, at 5:4; *N.Y. Times*, July 19, 1920, at 1:6 and 2:2.

5. The War on Radicalism

1. *N.Y. Times,* Nov. 23, 1919, pt. 9, at 1:1–8.

2. Act of June 15, 1917, ch. 30, title I, § 3, 40 Stat. 217, 219; title I, § 4 punished conspiracies to violate § 3. Ibid., 219–220.

3. Ibid., title 12, § 1, 40 Stat. 230; § 3 made it a crime to use the mails to transmit nonmailable material. Ibid., 230–231. On the reviewability of the postmaster general's rulings, see Public Clearing House v. Coyne, 194 U.S. 497 (1904); Ex parte Jackson, 96 U.S. 727 (1877); 2 Westel W. Willoughby, *The Constitutional Law of the United States,* 1283, 1285 (New York, 1910); Thomas F. Carroll, "Freedom of Speech and of the Press in War Time: The Espionage Act," 17 *Michigan Law Review* 621, 634 (1919).

4. Harry N. Scheiber, *The Wilson Administration and Civil Liberties, 1917–1921,* at 19, 61–63 (Ithaca, N.Y., 1960); National Civil Liberties Bureau, *War-Time Prosecutions and Mob Violence,* 4 (New York, Mar. 1919).

5. Robert K. Murray, *Red Scare: A Study in National Hysteria, 1919–1920,* at 28–32, 52, 62 (Minneapolis, 1955); William Preston, Jr., *Aliens and Dissenters, 1903–1933,* at 91–151 (Cambridge, Mass., 1963); Robert L. Tyler, *Rebels of the Woods: The I.W.W. in the Pacific Northwest,* 116–126 (Eugene, Ore., 1967) (quote); Horace C. Peterson and Gilbert C. Fite, *Opponents of the War, 1917–1918,* at 43–60, 167–180, 235–247 (Madison, 1957); Scheiber, *Wilson and Civil Liberties,* 48.

6. James Weinstein, *The Decline of Socialism in America, 1912–1925,* at 84–102, 119–127, 144 (New Brunswick, N.J., 1984); Murray, *Red Scare,* 20; O. A. Hilton, "Freedom of the Press in Wartime, 1917–1919," 28 *Southwestern Social Science Quarterly* 346, 353 (Mar. 1948); James O'Neal, "The Socialists in the War," 10 *American Mercury* 418, 423 (Apr. 1927); Lindsay Rogers, "Freedom of Press in the United States," 298 *Living Age* 769, 770 (Sept. 28, 1918).

7. 55 Cong. Rec. 4645 (1918) (Sen. Hardwick); James R. Mock, *Censorship 1917,* at 145 (Princeton, 1941); Murray, *Red Scare,* 30–39; Peterson, *Opponents of War,* 55–56, 179, 235.

8. United States v. Hall, 248 F. 150 (D.Mont. 1918); 56 Cong. Rec. 4559–4560 (Apr. 4, 1918); Preston, *Aliens and Dissenters,* 111. Bourquin's strict interpretation of wartime laws led to calls for his impeachment.

9. Act of May 16, 1918, ch. 75, 40 Stat. 553 (Sedition Act); Act of Oct. 6, 1917, ch. 106, § 19, 40 Stat. 411, 426 (Trading with the Enemy Act). The mail termination provision was aimed at depriving radical groups of monetary contributions. 56 Cong. Rec. 6174 (1918) (Rep. Webb); J. Bond Smith, "Memorandum in re Proposed Amendment to Espionage Act," Mar. 27, 1918, NA DOJ, file 187415–1.

10. 56 Cong. Rec. 4830 (1918) (Sen. Myers, Mont.); ibid., 4764, 4766–

4767 (Sen. Nelson, Minn.); ibid., 4639 (Sen. King, Utah); 56 Cong. Rec. 6181 (Rep. Green, Iowa); ibid., 4638–4639 (Sen. Hardwick, Ga.). For the comparable state provisions, see Zechariah Chafee, Jr., *Free Speech in the United States,* 575–597 (Cambridge, Mass., 1941); Murray, *Red Scare,* 223–238.

11. Memorandum for Mr. [John Lord] O'Brian, Apr. 15, 1918, at 5–6, NA DOJ, file 187415–3–11; "Memorandum on Pending Amendment of Espionage Act," Apr. 25, 1918, 56 Cong. Rec. 6051–6052 (1918). And see Dept. of Justice, *Annual Report of the Attorney General, 1918,* at 18; Chafee, *Free Speech,* 41.

12. 56 Cong. Rec. 4645 (1918) (Sen. Lodge); ibid., 4692 (Sen. Overman); ibid., 4714 (Sen. Myers); ibid., 4764 (Sen. Nelson); ibid., 4768–4771 (Sen. Sherman). And see ibid., 4568, 4633 (Sen. Borah); ibid., 4646 (Sen. Shields); ibid., 4782 (Sen. Fall); ibid., 4846 (Sen. Jones). On Myers's authorship of the act, see ibid., 4694–4696, 4712, 4784 (Sen. Myers).

13. John L. O'Brian to Robert Bell, June 26, 1918, NA DOJ, file 187415–3–7 (and see files 187415–101, 187415–127, 187415–137); U.S. Constitution amend. I; Prudential Ins. Co. v. Cheek, 259 U.S. 530, 543 (1922) ("Neither the Fourteenth Amendment nor any other provision of the Constitution . . . imposes upon the States any restrictions about 'freedom of speech' "). The states became subject to First Amendment restrictions in 1925. Gitlow v. New York, 268 U.S. 652 (1925).

14. 56 Cong. Rec. 4715 (1918) (Sen. Shields); ibid., 4845 (Sen. Cummins); and see ibid., 4768, 4770 (Sen. Sherman).

15. 56 Cong. Rec. 5989 (1918) (Sen. Sherman); ibid., 4835–4839 (Sen. Reed); ibid., 4566 (Sen. Johnson); ibid., 4712 (Sen. Vardaman); ibid., 4895 (Sen. King); ibid., 6173 (Rep. Gordon); ibid., 4636–4637, 4645, 4779, 4898 (Sen. Hardwick); ibid., 6172, 6179 (Rep. London). On the France Amendment, see ibid., 4826, 4897, 5541 (Sen. Overman); ibid., 6047, 6173 (Rep. Gordon); John L. O'Brian to Edwin Y. Webb, Apr. 16, 1918, ibid., 5542; O'Brian to Lee S. Overman, Apr. 26, 1918, ibid., 6051–6053; Dept. of Justice, *Annual Report of the Attorney General, 1918,* at 18.

16. 56 Cong. Rec. 4567 (1918) (Sen. Watson); ibid., 4637, 4835 (Sen. Overman); ibid., 5543–5544 (Sen. Fall); ibid., 6183 (Rep. Fess); ibid., 4772, 5984, 5989 (Sen. Sherman); ibid., 4631 (Sen. Gore); ibid., 4894–4895 (Sen. King); ibid., 5544 (Sen. Johnson); ibid., 4631, 4637, 4894 (Sen. Poindexter); ibid., 4637, 4779 (Sen. Hardwick); ibid., 4837 (Sens. Reed and Lewis); ibid., 4850 (Sen. Williams); ibid., 6180 (Rep. Gard); ibid., 6182 (Rep. Caraway); ibid., 6184 (Rep. Morgan). The Court had suggested that the First Amendment bars exclusions from the mail if other means of distribution are unavailable; since the Trading with the Enemy Act barred distribution of matter made nonmailable by the Espionage Act, the postal power (U.S. Const. art. I, § 8, cl. 7), which was clearly subject to the Bill of Rights, was of dubious

utility. Ex parte Jackson, 96 U.S. 727, 735 (1877); In re Rapier, 143 U.S. 110, 134 (1892); Champion v. Ames, 188 U.S. 321 (1903); 2 Willoughby, *Constitutional Law*, 786–789; R. E. Cushman, "National Police Power under the Postal Clause of the Constitution," 4 *Minnesota Law Review* 402 (1920); Morris E. Cohn, "The Censorship of Radical Materials by the Post Office," 17 *St. Louis Law Review* 95 (1932); E. P. Deutsch, "Freedom of the Press and of the Mails," 36 *Michigan Law Review* 703 (1938); Note, "The Expanding Postal Power," 38 *Columbia Law Review* 474 (1938).

17. 56 Cong. Rec. 4835 (1918) (Sen. Fall); and see ibid., 4835 (Sen. Overman), agreeing that the First Amendment "has about as much to do with this bill as the Lord's Prayer"; Dept. of Justice, "Memorandum on the Proposed Amendment to Section 3, Title I, of the Espionage Law" (n.d.), ibid., 6052–6053.

18. 56 Cong. Rec. 6181 (1918) (Rep. Green); ibid., 6173 (Rep. Clark).

19. 56 Cong. Rec. 4832 (1918) (Sen. Myers); U.S. Const. art. I, § 6; 56 Cong. Rec. 4846 (1918) (Sen. Jones); Henry C. Black, "Sedition, Its Definition and Punishment," 2 *Constitutional Review* 242, 245 (Oct. 1918). On the fact that one could be convicted under the act without an intent to obstruct the war, see Chafee, *Free Speech*, 50; Preston, *Aliens and Dissenters*, 121.

20. Act of May 16, 1918, ch. 75, 40 Stat. 553–554; 56 Cong. Rec. 6051 (1918) (Sen. Overman).

21. Weinstein, *Decline of Socialism*, 177–215; Stanley Coben, *A. Mitchell Palmer: Politician*, 196–216 (New York, 1963); Murray, *Red Scare*, 31–32, 55–57.

22. See Act of Oct. 16, 1916, ch. 186, §§ 1–2, 40 Stat. 1012 (Act to Exclude and Expel from the United States Aliens Who Are Members of the Anarchistic and Similar Classes); Fong Yue Ting v. United States, 149 U.S. 698, 711 (1893); 1 Willoughby, *Constitutional Law*, §§ 124, 125, 190; Preston, *Aliens and Dissenters*, 11–12, 180–237; Murray, *Red Scare*, 190–222, 251; Chafee, *Free Speech*, 196–240; Coben, *Palmer*, 217–245.

23. Richard Hofstadter, *The Age of Reform: From Bryan to F.D.R.*, 278–281 (New York, 1955); Eric F. Goldman, *Rendezvous with Destiny: A History of Modern American Reform*, 261–283 (New York, 1952); Burl Noggle, *Into the Twenties: The United States From Armistice to Normalcy*, 84–92 (Urbana, Ill., 1974).

24. NA DOJ, Box 758, file 187415, section 2; Scheiber, *Wilson and Civil Liberties*, 59–60.

25. Dept. of Justice, *Annual Report of the Attorney General, 1918*, at 674; John L. O'Brian, "Civil Liberty in War Time," 42 *Reports of the New York State Bar Association* 275, 304–309 (1919); John L. O'Brian to John W. Preston, Aug. 29, 1918, NA DOJ, file 187415–148; O'Brian to Preston, Oct. 23, 1918, ibid., file 187415–161.

26. NA DOJ, files 187415–171, 187415–172, 187415–178, 187415–182, 187415 (section 5); Alfred Bettman to John L. O'Brian, Dec. 9, 1918, ibid., file 187415–183; Dept. of Justice, Circular No. 923, Dec. 12, 1918, ibid.; *N.Y. Times,* Nov. 22, 1918, at 3:7; Peterson, *Opponents of War,* 286.

27. John M. Blum, *Joe Tumulty and the Wilson Era,* 187–188 (Boston, 1951); Murray, *Red Scare,* 191–192; T. S. Allen to the Attorney General, Mar. 14, 1919, NA DOJ, file 187415–430; John L. O'Brian to Allen, Mar. 18, 1919, ibid.; *N.Y. Times,* Apr. 5, 1919, at 24:3–4.

28. *N.Y. Times,* Apr. 1, 1919, at 10:7; ibid., Apr. 2, 1919, at 10:4; Coben, *Palmer,* 199–200; AMP to WW, Apr. 19, 1920, WW MSS, ser. 2.

29. "Charges of Illegal Practices of Department of Justice," *Hearings before a Subcomm. of the Senate Comm. on the Judiciary,* 66th Cong., 3d Sess. 579–580 (1921).

30. Coben, *Palmer,* 196–216; "Minutes of a Conference between the Attorney General and Committee Elected by the National Convention of the Socialist Party," May 14, 1920, at 18, NA DOJ, file 77175, quoted ibid., 202–203.

31. Coben, *Palmer,* 211; WW to JPT, June 28, 1919, JPT MSS, Box 50; JPT to WW, June 28, 1919, ibid.

32. *N.Y. Times,* Nov. 23, 1919, pt. 9, at 1:2; Murray, *Red Scare,* 81; "Investigation Activities of the Department of Justice," S. Doc. No. 153, 66th Cong., 1st Sess. 6, 8 (Nov. 14, 1919), filed in response to S. Res. 213, 66th Cong., 1st Sess. (Oct. 17, 1919), criticizing Palmer for insufficient action against the radicals; AMP, "The Case Against the 'Reds,'" 63 *Forum* 173 (Feb. 1920).

33. Dept. of Justice, *Annual Report of the Attorney General, 1919,* at 22, 120; Dept. of Justice, *Annual Report of the Attorney General, 1920,* at 126, 201; Dept. of Justice, *Annual Report of the Attorney General, 1921,* at 98, 151; *N.Y. Times,* Jan. 20, 1921, at 3:1. Between 1917 and 1921 a total of 2,168 criminal actions were brought under the Espionage and Sedition Acts, of which nearly half resulted in convictions. Scheiber, *Wilson and Civil Liberties,* 61–63.

34. Chafee, *Free Speech,* 52 n.30; Coben, *Palmer,* 241–244; *N.Y. Times,* Mar. 29, 1919, at 9:1; ibid., May 3, 1919, at 1:1; 111 *Nation* 365 (Oct. 6, 1920); "Investigation Activities," 6. Some cases were summarized in Justice Department bulletins entitled *Interpretation of War Statutes,* numbers 174–204 of which appeared after the armistice; from the information given it cannot be established that any of the cases dealt with postarmistice conduct; it has been suggested that the department omitted decisions with which it disagreed. Carroll, "Freedom of Speech," 641 n.43.

35. *N.Y. Times,* Nov. 30, 1918, at 3:8; *N.Y. World,* Nov. 30, 1918, at 3:3; 111 *Nation* 365 (Oct. 6, 1920).

36. NA DOJ, files 9–19–20, 187415, and 201931–1 (United States v. Itzickson (aka Isaacson)); 111 *Nation* 365 (Oct. 6, 1920).

37. Harry Weinberger to AMP, Jan. 28, 1920, NA DOJ, file 9-19-20-10; Robert P. Stewart (for AMP) to Albert DeSilver, Director, National Civil Liberties Bureau, Sept. 18, 1919, ibid., file 9-19-20-5.

38. United States v. Steene, 263 F. 130, 132–133 (N.D. N.Y., Jan. 12, 1920), *rev'd*, 255 U.S. 580 (1921); NA DOJ, file 211562; *N.Y. Times*, Mar. 22, 1921, at 3:3; Peterson, *Opponents of War*, 272.

39. *N.Y. Times*, Nov. 13, 1919, at 1:5; State v. Smith, 115 Wash. 405, 197 P. 770 (1921); Murray, *Red Scare*, 181–189; Tyler, *Rebels*, 164–176; Ralph Chaplin, *The Centralia Conspiracy* (Chicago, 1924).

40. S. Res. 213, 66th Cong., 1st Sess. (Oct. 17, 1919); "Investigation Activities," 13.

41. Clarance B. Blethen to AMP, Nov. 12, 1919, NA DOJ, file 186701-74-1; Blethen sent a copy of this wire to JPT; ibid., file 186701-74-14; *Cyclopedia of American Biography*, s.v., "Blethen, Clarance B." For other telegrams urging Palmer to act, see NA DOJ, file 186701–74, items 2, 4, 8, 9, 12, and 57.

42. AMP to Robert C. Saunders, Nov. 13, 1919, NA DOJ, file 186701-74-1; Tyler, *Rebels*, 165; Chafee, *Free Speech*, 104.

43. 109 *Nation* 421 (Sept. 27, 1919).

44. Clarance B. Blethen to AMP, Nov. 13, 1919, NA DOJ, file 186701-74-3; AMP to Robert C. Saunders, Nov. 14, 1919, ibid., file 186701-74-4; Saunders to AMP, Nov. 14, 1919, ibid., file 186701-74-10; Boyle, U.S. Marshal, to AMP, Nov. 14, 1919, ibid., file 186701-74-15; Saunders to AMP, Nov. 17, 1919, ibid., file 186701-74-20; Saunders to AMP, Nov. 25, 1919, ibid., file 186701-74-60; *N.Y. Times*, Nov. 14, 1919, at 1:1; ibid., Nov. 15, 1919, at 2:7; *San Francisco Chronicle*, Nov. 15, 1919, at 4:2; Tyler, *Rebels*, 165; Murray, *Red Scare*, 313 n.34; American Civil Liberties Union, *The Issues in the Centralia Murder Trial*, 4 (New York, 1920).

45. Robert C. Saunders to AMP, Oct. 15, 1920, NA DOJ, file 187415-section 6; Saunders to AMP, Nov. 14, 1919, ibid., file 186701-74-10; Saunders to AMP, Nov. 19, 1919, ibid., file 186701-74-29; AMP to Saunders, Nov. 20, 1919, ibid.; Saunders to AMP, Nov. 26, 1919, ibid., file 186701-74-54; Saunders to AMP, Dec. 4, 1919, ibid., file 186701-74-70; *N.Y. Times*, Nov. 14, 1919, at 1:1; ibid., Dec. 4, 1919, at 1:4; Tyler, *Rebels*, 193.

46. NA DOJ, file 186701-74, passim.

47. See United States v. Strong, 263 F. 789, 794–795 (W.D. Wash. 1920); United States v. Listman, 263 F. 798 (W.D. Wash. 1920); United States v. Ault, 263 F. 800, 801, 804 (W.D. Wash. 1920); Murray, *Red Scare*, 60.

48. *Seattle Union Record*, June 30, 1919, at 10; United States v. Strong, 263 F. at 789–791 (reprinting poem with slight inaccuracies); United States v. Ault, 263 F. at 801, 804.

49. United States v. Listman, 263 F. at 798–799; United States v. Ault, 263 U.S. at 801–808. "Plute" was a reference to plutocrat.

50. Robert C. Saunders to AMP, Mar. 8, 1920, NA DOJ, file 186701-74-95 (the beginning date of Saunders's search fell two days after the Sedition Act was adopted); Rev. Sydney Strong to AMP, ca. Dec. 1919, ibid., file 186701-74-82; Anna Louise Strong to Paul Kellogg, Dec. 4, 1919, ibid., file 186701-74-71; Paul Kellogg to AMP, Dec. 12, 1919, ibid.; Anna Louise Strong, *I Change Worlds: The Remaking of an American,* 84 (New York, 1935); her biographers repeat Strong's account of the case. Tracy B. Strong and Helene Keyssar, *Right in Her Soul: The Life of Anna Louise Strong,* 79 (New York, 1983). Strong enjoyed the rare distinction of having been charged with espionage by both the United States and the Soviet Union; the United States was unable to prove its case against her, and she was later exonerated by the Soviets. *N.Y. Times,* Mar. 30, 1970, at 1:8 and 43:2.

51. United States v. Strong, 263 F. at 792–794, 796–797; United States v. Ault, 263 F. at 809–811; Robert C. Saunders to AMP, Jan. 13, 1920, NA DOJ, file 186701-74-90; Saunders to AMP, Jan. 24, 1920, ibid., file 186701-74-93.

52. Robert C. Saunders to AMP, Mar. 6, 1920, NA DOJ, file 186701-74-94; Saunders to AMP, Mar. 8, 1920, ibid., file 186701-74-95; Alex C. King to Saunders, Mar. 9, 1920, ibid., file 186701-74-94. Saunders had earlier doubts as to whether the acts remained enforceable but proceeded with the suits anyway. Saunders to AMP, Nov. 17, 1919, ibid., file 186701-74-43.

53. United States v. Ault, 263 F. at 801.

54. Robert C. Saunders to AMP, Nov. 17, 1919, NA DOJ, file 186701-74-43; Saunders to AMP, Mar. 8, 1920, ibid., file 186701-74-95.

55. Robert C. Saunders to AMP, Nov. 13, 1919, NA DOJ, file 186701-74-27.

56. Robert C. Saunders to AMP, Nov. 17, 1919, NA DOJ, file 186701-74-43; Saunders to AMP, Nov. 24, 1919, ibid., file 186701-74-62. Owing to extensive legal and extralegal attacks on the IWW during and after the war, the organization went underground. Many Wobblies became "two-card" men, joining an AFL union for protective purposes. The February 1919 Seattle general strike was blamed on the IWW but was in fact inspired by the AFL unions, some of whose leaders were former or clandestine Wobblies. Tyler, *Rebels,* 185–194; Weinstein, *Decline of Socialism,* 227.

57. Tyler, *Rebels,* 185–187; Murray, *Red Scare,* 30–31, 52.

58. *N.Y. Times,* Nov. 15, 1919, at 2:3; ibid., Nov. 21, 1919, at 17:2; ibid., Dec. 9, 1919, at 19:6; *Minneapolis Journal,* Nov. 16, 1919, at 1:6; *San Francisco Chronicle,* Nov. 16, 1919, at 3:1; Lindsay L. Thompson to AMP, Nov. 18, 1919, NA DOJ, file 186701-74-26; AMP to Thompson, Nov. 20, 1919, ibid.

59. Robert C. Saunders to AMP, Oct. 15, 1920, NA DOJ, file 187415-section 6; *N.Y. Times*, Dec. 25, 1919, at 15:2; ibid., Jan. 22, 1920, at 33:3; *Tacoma Daily Ledger*, Dec. 25, 1919, at 4:5; ibid., Jan. 22, 1920, at 1:6.

60. U.S. Attorney, Phoenix, to AMP, Mar. 24, 1919, NA DOJ, file 187415-482; John Lord O'Brian to U.S. Attorney, Phoenix, Mar. 31, 1919, ibid., approving request to prosecute Robert L. Morton and W. F. Burleson; while the date of their offense is uncertain, of interest here is the rationale for prosecution. Many other cases in this file were begun after the armistice, but it is unclear when most violations occurred. On November 15, 1919, twelve Wobblies were arrested by federal agents in Morgantown, West Virginia, but it is not known what charges were brought against them. *N.Y. Call*, Nov. 16, 1919, at 2:8.

61. *Minneapolis Journal*, Oct. 8, 1920, at 1:7; ibid., Oct. 29, 1920, at 14:6; S. Doc. No. 190, 67th Cong., 2d Sess. 2–3 (1922); *American Labor Yearbook, 1921–1922*, at 26.

62. Weinstein, *Decline of Socialism*, 229-230; *N.Y. Times*, Aug. 15, 1919, at 13:2; ibid., Aug. 18, 1919, at 7:3-4; ibid., Sept. 22, 1919, at 7:4; *St. Louis Post-Dispatch*, Dec. 8, 1919, at 1:1.

63. *St. Louis Post-Dispatch*, Dec. 8, 1919, at 1:1; ibid., Dec. 14, 1919, at 1:1; *N.Y. Times*, Dec. 11, 1919, at 2:8; ibid., Dec. 22, 1919, at 5:1.

64. Dept. of Justice, *Annual Report of the Attorney General, 1919*, at 120; Dept. of Justice, *Annual Report of the Attorney General, 1920*, at 201; Dept. of Justice, *Annual Report of the Attorney General, 1921*, at 151; *N.Y. Times*, Mar. 11, 1919, at 3:3; Kirchner v. United States, 255 F. 301 (4th Cir. 1918), *cert. dismissed*, 250 U.S. 678 (1919). See also *N.Y. Times*, Dec. 2, 1919, at 3:2, and Dec. 19, 1919, at 1:3, reporting conviction of thirty Wobblies under the Espionage Act and other laws, without noting that case involved prearmistice conduct. And see 111 *Nation* 365 (Oct. 6, 1920), reporting Sedition Act prosecution of J. E. Snyder, editor of the *Oakland World*, for an editorial criticizing the Constitution; Justice Department files contain no record of this case, which appears merely to have involved state law. NA POD, Box 69, file B-404; *San Francisco Chronicle*, Nov. 20, 1919, at 7:3.

6. Censorship and the "Cowed Mind"

1. Act of June 15, 1917, ch. 30, title XII, § 1, 40 Stat. 230; Act of Oct. 6, 1917, ch. 106, § 19, 40 Stat. 426; Act of May 16, 1918, ch. 75, § 2, 40 Stat. 554. These powers were in addition to the censorship authority possessed as a result of the Post Office's control of the telegraph lines used by the press to send and receive stories. See Chapter 2.

2. Zechariah Chafee, Jr., *Free Speech in the United States*, 98 (Cam-

bridge, Mass., 1941). Attorney General Gregory had advised President Wilson that the breadth of the Sedition Act's postal provisions might render it unconstitutional. Thomas W. Gregory to WW, May 14, 1918, 48 *WWP* 12–14.

3. Alfred Bettman to John Lord O'Brian, May 28, 1918, NA DOJ, file 187415-121.

4. James R. Mock, *Censorship 1917,* at 55–72 (Princeton, 1941); WW to ASB, Nov. 27, 1918, 53 *WWP* 214; WW to ASB, Dec. 2, 1918, ibid., 289; E. David Cronon, *The Cabinet Diaries of Josephus Daniels, 1913–1921,* at 348, 354 (Lincoln, Neb., 1963); JPT to WW, Feb. 7, 1919, 54 *WWP* 555; JPT to WW, Mar. 25, 1919, JPT MSS, Box 49; WW to ASB, Feb. 28, 1919, 55 *WWP* 327; Executive Order No. 3132, July 30, 1919, dissolving Censorship Board.

5. ASB, "Why We Should Keep the Wires: A Question of National Defense and Economic Efficiency—Not a Partisan Question," 61 *Forum* 152, 154 (Feb. 1919); R. E. Cushman, "National Police Power under the Postal Clause of the Constitution," 4 *Minnesota Law Review* 402, 415–416 (1920); Lindsay Rogers, "Freedom of the Press in the United States," 298 *Living Age* 769, 770–771 (1918); Mock, *Censorship,* 138–139; O. A. Hilton, "Freedom of Press in Wartime, 1917–1919," 28 *Southwestern Social Science Quarterly* 346, 353–354 (Mar. 1948).

6. 9 *Masses,* no. 3, at 2 (Jan. 1917); Masses Publishing Co. v. Patten, 246 F. 24, 34 (2d Cir. 1917). For the magazine's early years, see Leslie Fishbein, *Rebels in Bohemia: The Radicals of* The Masses, *1911–1917,* at 15–29 (Chapel Hill, 1982).

7. N.Y. *Times,* July 17, 1917, at 7:3; ibid., July 22, 1917, at 7:1; "What Happened to the August Masses," 9 *Masses,* no. 11, at 3 (Sept. 1917); Max Eastman, *Love and Revolution: My Journey through an Epoch,* 58–59 (New York, 1964); Masses Publishing Co. v. Patten, 246 F. at 26.

8. Max Eastman, Amos Pinchot, and John Reed to WW, July 12, 1917, 43 *WWP* 164–165; WW to Pinchot, July 13, 1917, ibid.; WW to ASB, July 13, 1917, ibid.; 7 Ray S. Baker, *Woodrow Wilson: Life and Letters,* 165 and n. 1 (New York, 1939).

9. N.Y. *Times:* July 22, 1917, at 7:1; July 25, 1917, at 11:1; July 27, 1917, at 4:2; Aug. 7, 1917, at 8:7; Eastman, *Love and Revolution,* 59–61; Masses Publishing Co. v. Patten, 244 F. 535 (S.D. N.Y., July 24, 1917), 245 F. 102 (2d Cir. 1917).

10. Eastman, *Love and Revolution,* 61; Act of Mar. 3, 1879, ch. 180, § 14, 20 Stat. 355, 359.

11. Eastman, *Love and Revolution,* 61-62; N.Y. *Times,* Aug. 23, 1917, at 3:5.

12. Masses Publishing Co. v. Patten (S.D. N.Y. 1917) (unreported), in Dept. of Justice, *Interpretation of War Statutes,* Bulletin No. 26, at 1–4;

Hilton, "Freedom of the Press," 349–350; Chafee, *Free Speech*, 78–79; *N.Y. Times*, Sept. 15, 1917, at 7:3.

13. WW to Max Eastman, Sept. 18, 1917, 44 *WWP* 210–211; *N.Y. Times*, Sept. 28, 1917, at 1:4; 10 *Masses*, nos. 1 & 2, at 21, 24 (Nov.–Dec. 1917); Eastman, *Love and Revolution*, 63; Act of Mar. 3, 1879, ch. 180, §§ 11, 17, 20 Stat. 359–360; Chafee, *Free Speech*, 302.

14. 10 *Masses*, nos. 1 & 2, at 44 (Nov.–Dec. 1917).

15. *N.Y. Times*, Oct. 25, 1917, at 15:2; ibid., Oct. 27, 1917, at 8:6.

16. Masses Publishing Co. v. Patten, 246 F. 24, 33, 38 (2d Cir. 1917); 246 F. at 39 (Ward, J., concurring). In rejecting petitioner's First Amendment claim the court declared that the Espionage Act "does not undertake to say that certain matter . . . shall not be transmitted in interstate commerce. It simply declares that such matter shall not be carried in the United States mails." While technically correct, the court was seemingly unaware that the Trading with the Enemy Act recently had made it illegal to ship or distribute such material.

17. *N.Y. Times*, Nov. 3, 1917, at 10:3; ibid., Nov. 6, 1917, at 8:3.

18. *N.Y. Times*, Nov. 4, 1917, at 17:5; ibid., Nov. 6, 1917, at 8:3; ibid., Nov. 7, 1917, at 20:6; Eastman, *Love and Revolution*, 64.

19. Masses Publishing Co. v. Patten, 246 F. at 37; 9 *Masses*, no. 10 (Aug. 1917); *N.Y. Times*, Nov. 4, 1917, at 17:5; ibid., Nov. 20, 1917, at 4:5. Defendants Arthur Young and Henry Glintenkamp were indicted based on cartoons appearing in the September 1917 and October 1917 issues; business manager Merrill Rogers's indictment was not based on any specific article or drawing.

20. William L. O'Neill, *The Last Romantic: A Life of Max Eastman*, 75-77 (New York, 1978); Eastman, *Love and Revolution*, 85–99, 104–105, 118–124; 1 *Liberator*, no. 4, at 5–18, 22–23, 35 (June 1918); Upton Sinclair to WW, May 18, 1918, 48 *WWP* 59; William Kent to WW, May 20, 1918, ibid., 93; Kent to WW, June 3, 1918, ibid., 235; Amos Pinchot to WW, May 24, 1918, ibid., 146–147; Edward P. Costigan to WW, May 29, 1918, ibid., 197–198; JPT to WW, May 27, 1918, JPT MSS, Box 48; WW to Kent, May 22, 1918, ibid., 116; Max Eastman to Kent, May 31, 1918, ibid., 235; Thomas W. Gregory to WW, June 6, 1918, ibid., 251; *N.Y. Times*, Oct. 1, 1918, at 18:4; ibid., Oct. 6, 1918, at 9:6; ibid., Jan. 11, 1919, at 22:2.

21. Eastman, *Love and Revolution*, 70; O'Neill, *Last Romantic*, 75; 1 *Liberator*, no. 5, at 5 (July 1918).

22. William H. Lamar to Postmaster, Bridgeport, Connecticut, Apr. 11, 1918, NA POD, Box 209, file 50606.

23. Ibid.; William H. Lamar to Postmaster, New York City, Oct. 23, 1918, ibid. The September 1918 issue was approved only after Eastman blacked in advertisements for two books that had been declared nonmailable.

24. William H. Lamar to 3d Assistant Postmaster General, Jan. 21, 1918, NA POD, Box 209, file 50606; Lamar to 3d Assistant Postmaster General, Oct. 29, 1918, ibid.; Memorandum from Post Office Solicitor's Office, July 2, 1919, ibid.; Dulany and Shepard, Attorneys at Law, to ASB, Sept. 3, 1920, ibid.

25. Post Office Dept., *1921 Annual Report*, 88–90; William H. Lamar to ASB, Sept. 3, 1920, and ASB to WW, ca. Sept. 4, 1920, in Hilton, "Freedom of Press," 355–357.

26. Eastman, *Love and Revolution*, 246; 4 *Liberator*, no. 7, at 5 (July 1921); *N.Y. Times*, May 26, 1921, at 17:1.

27. Eastman, *Love and Revolution*, 63, 69–78; 1 *Liberator*, no. 3, back cover (May 1918); 2 *Liberator*, no. 1, at 48 (Jan. 1919). The Wells Fargo Express Company was initially reluctant to handle *The Liberator* and asked the Post Office for assurance that it was mailable. William H. Lamar to Wells Fargo & Co., May 1, 1918, NA POD, Box 209, file 50606. Beginning in late 1918 the journal handled its own newsstand distribution after the nation's largest magazine distributor took offense at its contents and canceled its contract. 1 *Liberator*, no. 10, at 49 (Dec. 1918).

28. Post Office Dept., *1919 Annual Report*, 22, 112.

29. "Investigation Activities of the Department of Justice," S. Doc. No. 153, 66th Cong., 1st Sess. 11–13 (1919); Post Office Dept., *1920 Annual Report*, 125–126.

30. 59 Cong. Rec. 981 (Dec. 20, 1919) (Rep. Byrnes); Hilton, "Freedom of Press," 355–357.

31. William H. Lamar to Postmaster, Chicago, Jan. 9, 1919, NA POD, Box 278, file 51361; Lamar to Postmaster, Youngstown, Jan. 13, 1919, ibid., file 51362; ibid., Box 26, file B-38; *Minneapolis Journal*, Feb. 8, 1920, at 2:7. On the Post Office's selective use of censorship to split the Socialist party, see James Weinstein, *The Decline of Socialism in America, 1912–1925*, at 231–232 (New Brunswick, N.J., 1984).

32. "List of Publications Declared Nonmailable under Espionage Act after May 16, 1918," NA POD, file 50994; Paul F. Brissenden, *The I.W.W.: A Study of American Syndicalism*, 395–399 (New York, 1920); NA POD, Box 278, file 51365; "Protracted Censorship," 108 *Nation* 283 (Feb. 22, 1919). It is estimated that during the entire World War I period four hundred issues of domestic publications were barred from the mails. Mock, *Censorship*, 48. The postarmistice exclusions thus represented a significant portion of the whole. For other cases, see NA POD, Box 278, files 51367, 51370, 51373; ibid., Box 279, file 51389.

33. William H. Lamar to Edgar C. Battle, Apr. 8, 1919, NA POD, Box 26, file B-35; Robert C. Saunders to AMP, Nov. 17, 1919, NA DOJ, file 186701-74-20; AMP to Saunders, Nov. 18, 1919, ibid.; Saunders to AMP, Nov. 25, 1919, ibid., file 186701-51 and file 186701-60; Battle to Lamar, Nov. 26,

1919, NA POD, Box 26, file B-35; Lamar to Battle, Nov. 29, 1919, ibid.; Seattle Union Record Publishing Co. v. Edgar C. Battle, Postmaster at Seattle, Equity No. 175 (W.D. Wash., Nov. 25, 1919).

34. Burleson v. U.S. ex rel. Workingmen's Co-op. Publishing Ass'n, 274 F. 749 (D.C. Cir. 1921), *appeal dismissed,* 260 U.S. 757 (1923); "Burleson and the Call," 21 *New Republic* 157 (Jan. 7, 1920); U.S. ex rel. Milwaukee Social Democratic Publishing Co. v. Burleson, 258 F. 282 (D.C. Cir. 1919), *aff'd,* 255 U.S. 407 (1921); *N.Y. Times:* Dec. 4, 1919, at 2:5; Dec. 23, 1919, at 15:8; Aug. 26, 1920, at 32:6; Oct. 13, 1920, at 2:4; May 26, 1921, at 19:4; June 1, 1921, at 19:4; *N.Y. World,* May 26, 1921, at 1:2–3; Mock, *Censorship,* 148.

35. Weinstein, *Decline of Socialism,* 231–232; Thomas W. Gregory to WW, May 14, 1918, 48 *WWP* 12–14; NA POD, Box 171, file 49841, and Box 77, file B-576, containing letters from postmasters to Lamar noting that *The Leader* was using other addresses; Postmaster, Cheyenne, Wyo., to William H. Lamar, Aug. 14, 1920, ibid.; H. J. Donnelly, Acting Solicitor, to Theodore T. Frankenberg, Nov. 27, 1920, ibid., noting mail was still not being delivered to *The Leader.*

36. Chafee, *Free Speech,* 247–269; Weinstein, *Decline of Socialism, 5–9;* Robert K. Murray, *Red Scare: A Study in National Hysteria, 1919–1920,* at 21–22, 226–229 (Minneapolis, 1955); Berger v. United States, 255 U.S. 22 (1921).

37. Eastman, *Love and Revolution,* 70; O'Neill, *Last Romantic,* 75; Robert C. Saunders to AMP, Mar. 8, 1920, NA DOJ, file 186701-74-95.

38. 57 Cong. Rec. 2936–2937 (Feb. 8, 1919) (Sen. Borah); *N.Y. Times,* Feb. 9, 1919, at 1:2; William Hard, "Mr. Burleson, Espionagent," 19 *New Republic* 42, 44 (May 10, 1919).

39. Address by Frank I. Cobb to Women's City Club of New York, Dec. 11, 1919, 59 Cong. Rec. 1025-1028 (Jan. 5, 1920).

40. "The Raiding of the Reds," *Baltimore Sun,* Jan. 4, 1920, at 10:1–2; *N.Y. Times,* Jan. 23, 1920, at 8:2; Walter Nelles, *Seeing Red: Civil Liberty and Law in the Period Following the War,* 3 (New York, Aug. 1920), reprinted as "In the Wake of the Espionage Act," 111 *Nation* 684 (Dec. 15, 1920).

41. P. H. O'Brien to WW, Feb. 21, 1919, NA DOJ, Box 758, file 187415-258; for similar petitions sent in May 1919, see ibid., files 187415-511, 187415-512, 187415-513.

42. *N.Y. Times,* Feb. 17, 1919, at 3:4; ibid., Mar. 2, 1919, at 8:1; ibid., Apr. 6, 1919, at 15:1; Albert DeSilver to AMP, Sept. 15, 1919, NA DOJ, file 9-19-20-5; Robert P. Stewart (for AMP) to DeSilver, Sept. 18, 1919, ibid.

43. Charles E. Hughes, Address at Wellesley College, June 14, 1920, *N.Y. Times,* June 15, 1920, at 8:2; ibid., June 16, 1920, at 10:2.

44. "Again the Censor," *Baltimore Sun,* July 26, 1919, at 6:1–2; "The

Tyranny of the Majority," *N.Y. World,* Dec. 28, 1919, Section E, at 2:1; 108 *Nation* 241 (Feb. 15, 1919); 111 *Nation* 365 (Oct. 6, 1920); *N.Y. Times,* Nov. 3, 1919, at 1:7.

45. *N.Y. Times:* Feb. 13, 1919, at 8:3; Mar. 4, 1919, at 3:1; Nov. 4, 1919, at 17:2; Nov. 23, 1919, pt. 9, at 1:5; S. 5070, 65th Cong., 3d Sess. (1918); S. 5314, 65th Cong., 3d Sess. (1919); H.R. 238, 66th Cong., 1st Sess. (1919); S. 81, 66th Cong., 1st Sess. (1919); H.R. 1697, 66th Cong., 1st Sess. (1919); S. 1233, 66th Cong., 1st Sess. (1919); S. 3090, 66th Cong., 1st Sess. (1919); Act of Mar. 3, 1921, ch. 136, 41 Stat. 1359. The Espionage Act was not repealed. See 18 U.S.C. §§ 1717, 2388 (1982).

46. "Investigation Activities," 8–9, 14–15; AMP to Philip P. Campbell, Jan. 21, 1920, at 59 Cong. Rec. 2208 (1920); WW, State of the Union Message, Dec. 2, 1919, 6 *WWPP* 428, 434–435; 59 Cong. Rec. 2207 (1920) (Rep. Blanton); Murray, *Red Scare,* 230–231, 244–246.

47. *N.Y. Times,* Nov. 4, 1919, at 17:2; Act of June 15, 1917, ch. 30, title IX, 40 Stat. 217, 228–230.

48. 57 Cong. Rec. 1171 (Jan. 9, 1919) (Sen. France); ibid., 4867 (Mar. 3, 1919) (Sen. Sherman); *N.Y. Times,* Mar. 4, 1919, at 3:1.

49. *N.Y. Times,* July 30, 1919, at 2:1; 58 Cong. Rec. 3323–3324 (July 29, 1919) (Sen. France); "Again the Censor," *Baltimore Sun,* July 26, 1919, at 6:1–2; "Censorship Indeed!" *Baltimore News,* July 26, 1919, at 6:2. Though the Justice Department may have threatened the publisher, there is no evidence that the book was actually suppressed.

50. 57 Cong. Rec. 2938 (Feb. 8, 1919) (Sen. Overman); ibid., 2943 (Sen. Nelson); ibid., 3230, 3232 (Feb. 12, 1919) (Rep. London); 59 Cong. Rec. 980–981 (Dec. 20, 1919) (Reps. Byrnes and Fess); *N.Y. Times,* Feb. 13, 1919, at 8:3.

51. Act of May 16, 1918, ch. 75, § 1, 40 Stat. 553; 59 Cong. Rec. 1265–1268 (Jan. 9, 1920) (Sen. France); Penn. Federation of Labor to Joseph I. France, Nov. 10, 1919, ibid., 1329 (1920); ibid., 1771 (Jan. 20, 1920) (statement of Samuel Gompers); Samuel Gompers, "The Graham-Rice 'Sedition Bill' Would Manufacture Law-Breakers," 27 *American Federationist* 138 (Feb. 1920).

52. Francis G. Caffey to Thomas W. Gregory, Feb. 20, 1919, in Stephen J. Whitfield, *Scott Nearing: Apostle of American Revolution,* 118 (New York, 1974); United States v. American Socialist Society, 260 F. 885 (S.D. N.Y. 1919), *aff'd,* 266 F. 212 (2d Cir.), *cert. denied,* 254 U.S. 637 (1920); *N.Y. Times,* Mar. 30, 1919, pt. 3, at 1:4; ibid., Apr. 6, 1919, at 15:1. Of the twenty-five jury convictions in sedition cases during the 1919–20 fiscal year, only two were in the East. Dept. of Justice, *Annual Report of the Attorney General, 1920,* at 202–375.

53. *N.Y. Times,* May 3, 1919, at 1:1; ibid., Nov. 23, 1919, pt. 9, at 1:1; "What Is Attorney General Palmer Doing?" 110 *Nation* 190 (Feb. 14, 1920). The same problem occurred at the state level. Selig Perlman and Philip Taft,

History of Labor in the United States, 1896–1932, at 427 (New York, 1935). The ratio of federal jury convictions to acquittals remained at about 2 to 1 between 1918 and 1920. Dept. of Justice, *Annual Report of the Attorney General, 1919*, at 22, 120, 170–173; Dept. of Justice, *Annual Report of the Attorney General, 1920*, at 201, 300–307. The ratio fell slightly in 1920–21. Dept. of Justice, *Annual Report of the Attorney General, 1921*, at 98, 151.

54. James Alexander, *A Brief Narrative of the Case and Trial of John Peter Zenger* (Cambridge, Mass., 1963); 2 John Fiske, *The Dutch and Quaker Colonies in America*, 290–300 (Boston, 1902); Edmund S. Morgan and Helen M. Morgan, *The Stamp Act Crisis: Prologue to Revolution*, 40 (revised paper ed., New York, 1962); Robert M. Cover, *Justice Accused: Antislavery and the Judicial Process*, 191 (New Haven, 1975); *N.Y. Times*, Apr. 5, 1919, at 24:3–4.

55. NA DOJ, file 9-19-20-17.

56. Robert C. Saunders to AMP, Mar. 8, 1920, NA DOJ, file 186701-74-95; Donald Wilhelm, "If He Were President," 102 *Independent* 46, 47 (Apr. 10, 1920); Dept. of Justice, *Annual Report of the Attorney General, 1921*, at 151.

57. Carroll, "Freedom of Speech," 665 n.113; Wilhelm, "If He Were President," 47.

58. JPT to WW, Mar. 23, 1920, JPT MSS, Box 50; JPT to WW, Apr. 15, 1920, ibid.

59. AMP to WW, Apr. 19, 1920, WW MSS, ser. 2.

60. William G. McAdoo to WW, May 15, 1920, Library of Congress, William Gibbs McAdoo Papers, Box 526.

61. WW to AMP, Oct. 4, 1920, WW MSS, ser. 14; Dept. of Justice, *Annual Report of the Attorney General, 1921*, at 151.

62. On the 1798 Act, see John C. Miller, *Crisis in Freedom: The Alien and Sedition Acts* (Boston, 1952); James M. Smith, *Freedom's Fetters: The Alien and Sedition Laws and American Civil Liberties* (Ithaca, N.Y., 1956).

63. Thomas Jefferson, Inaugural Address, Mar. 4, 1801, 8 Paul L. Ford, *The Writings of Thomas Jefferson*, 3 (New York, 1897); Thomas Jefferson to Abigail Adams, July 22, 1804, in 11 Andrew A. Lipscomb, *The Writings of Thomas Jefferson*, 43–44 (Washington, D.C., 1905); Smith, *Freedom's Fetters*, 268–269 & n.67, 358 n.84.

64. *N.Y. Times*: Jan. 20, 1921, at 3:1; Nov. 19, 1921, at 9:1; Dec. 24, 1921, at 1:5 and 4:6; July 20, 1922, at 8:1–3; Oct. 17, 1922, at 7:2; Dec. 31, 1922, at 1:5; June 21, 1923, at 3:3; Nov. 17, 1923, at 13:1; Dec. 16, 1923, at 1:6; William Preston, Jr., *Aliens and Dissenters: Federal Suppression of Radicals, 1903–1933*, at 258–259 (Cambridge, Mass., 1963).

65. Smith, *Freedom's Fetters*, 221–417.

66. Smith, *Freedom's Fetters,* 148–150; Josephus Daniels, "Jefferson's Contribution to a Free Press," 18 Lipscomb, *Jefferson,* xxii–xxviii; but cf. Cover, *Justice Accused,* 9–28.

67. *N.Y. Times,* Dec. 16, 1923, at 2:3; 56 Cong. Rec. 4568, 4633 (1918); Oliver W. Holmes, Jr., to Learned Hand, June 24, 1918, in Gerald Gunther, "Learned Hand and the Origins of Modern First Amendment Doctrine: Some Fragments of History," 27 *Stanford Law Review* 719, 756–757 (1975).

7. Judicial Review

1. *N.Y. Times,* Oct. 28, 1919, at 3:4; Dryfoos v. Edwards, 284 F. 596 (S.D. N.Y., Nov. 14, 1919); Hamilton v. Kentucky Distilleries Co., 251 U.S. 146 (Dec. 15, 1919); Ruppert v. Caffey, 284 F. 596 (S.D. N.Y., Nov. 14, 1919), *aff'd,* 251 U.S. 264 (Jan. 5, 1920).

2. United States v. L. Cohen Grocery Co., 255 U.S. 81 (1921).

3. Northern Pac. Ry. Co. v. North Dakota, 250 U.S. 135 (1919); Dakota Cent. Tel. Co. v. South Dakota, 250 U.S. 163, 184 (1919); Brief for South Dakota, ibid., 177. See Chapter 2.

4. Schenck v. United States, 249 U.S. 47 (Mar. 3, 1919); Sugarman v. United States, 249 U.S. 182 (Mar. 3, 1919); Frohwerk v. United States, 249 U.S. 204 (Mar. 10, 1919); Debs v. United States, 249 U.S. 211 (Mar. 10, 1919); Stilson v. United States, 250 U.S. 583 (Nov. 10, 1919); Abrams v. United States, 250 U.S. 616 (Nov. 10, 1919); Schaefer v. United States, 251 U.S. 466 (Mar. 1, 1920); Pierce v. United States, 252 U.S. 239 (Mar. 8, 1920). In only two of these cases did the government identify the source of Congress's power to adopt the statutes: in *Sugarman* the Espionage Act was said to rest on the "power to make war and to raise armies" (Brief for United States at 35); in *Abrams* the Sedition Act was said to stem from the "inherent . . . power of self-preservation" (Brief for United States at 10); the change in strategy may have reflected Palmer's desire to establish the legitimacy of a peacetime sedition law, for which he was then lobbying.

5. Brief for United States, Frohwerk v. United States, 63 L.Ed. at 563; Brief for United States, Debs v. United States, 63 L.Ed. at 568; Brief for United States at 35, 37, Sugarman v. United States; Brief for United States at 20, Schenck v. United States; Brief for United States at 20, 23, Abrams v. United States. Only four of the eight justices who joined Holmes's opinion in Patterson v. Colorado, 205 U.S. 454, 462 (1907), were still on the Court in 1919.

6. Schenck v. United States, 249 U.S. at 51–52; Fred D. Ragan, "Justice Oliver Wendell Holmes, Jr., Zechariah Chafee, Jr., and the Clear and Present Danger Test for Free Speech: The First Year, 1919," 58 *Journal of American History* 24 (1971); and see Robert M. Cover, "The Left, the Right and the First Amendment: 1918–1928," 40 *Maryland Law Review* 349, 382 (1981).

7. Schenck v. United States, 249 U.S. at 52; Edward S. Corwin, "Bowing Out 'Clear and Present Danger,'" 27 *Notre Dame Lawyer* 325, 329–331 (1952); Samuel J. Konefsky, *The Legacy of Holmes and Brandeis: A Study in the Influence of Ideas,* 181–201, 220–221 (New York, 1974); Frohwerk v. United States, 249 U.S. at 208 (emphasis added).

8. Cover, "Left, Right and First Amendment," 372; Oliver W. Holmes, Jr., to Learned Hand, June 24, 1918, in Gerald Gunther, "Learned Hand and the Origins of Modern First Amendment Doctrine: Some Fragments of History," 27 *Stanford Law Review* 719, 735, 756–757 (1975); Hand to Holmes, June 22, 1918, ibid., 755–756.

9. Stilson v. United States, 250 U.S. at 585; Abrams v. United States, 250 U.S. at 618–619; Pierce v. United States, 252 U.S. at 242; Schaefer v. United States, 251 U.S. at 477. Holmes's transformation has been attributed to the influence of Zechariah Chafee (Ragan, "Justice Oliver Wendell Holmes"), Louis Brandeis (Konefsky, *Legacy of Holmes and Brandeis,* 202), and Learned Hand (Gunther, "Learned Hand").

10. Henry C. Black, "Constitutional Government in War and Peace," 3 *Constitutional Review* 222, 232 (Oct. 1919).

11. Front-page stories concerning the Lever Act and the coal strike appeared in the *N.Y. Times* on Nov. 20–30, 1919, and Dec. 1–5, 7–14, 1919, and in the *Washington Post* on Nov. 20–23, 25, 27–30, 1919, and Dec. 1–5, 7–9, 11–13, 1919.

12. Articles concerning the Lever Act and profiteering appeared in the *N.Y. Times* on Nov. 21, 22, 26, 27, 29, 30, 1919, and Dec. 3, 5, 7, 9–14, 1919; stories appeared in the *Washington Post* on Nov. 21 and 30, 1919, and Dec. 1, 2, 7, 9–13, 1919.

13. Articles on the Espionage and Sedition Acts appeared in the *N.Y. Times* on Nov. 23, 1919, and Dec. 4, 9, and 14, 1919.

14. *N.Y. Times:* Nov. 20, 1919, at 1:1 and 1:5; Nov. 21, 1919, at 1:5; Nov. 22, 1919, at 2:1; Nov. 23, 1919, at 1:8; Nov. 24, 1919, at 1:8; Dec. 2, 1919, at 1:5; Dec. 6, 1919, at 1:6; Dec. 7, 1919, at 1:7; Dec. 9, 1919, at 1:7; Dec. 11, 1919, at 1:2; Dec. 12, 1919, at 1:1; Dec. 14, 1919, at 1:8.

15. *Washington Post,* Dec. 17, 1919, at 6:3; *San Francisco Chronicle,* Dec. 17, 1919, at 18:1; *St. Louis Post-Dispatch,* Dec. 16, 1919, at 28:2; *Chicago Tribune,* Dec. 17, 1919, at 8:1; Bailey v. Drexel Furniture Co., 259 U.S. 20, 37 (1922).

16. "Brandeis-Frankfurter Conversations," Louis D. Brandeis Papers, Harvard Law School Library, Box 114, folders 7-8, and Melvin I. Urofsky, "The Brandeis-Frankfurter Conversations," *1985 Supreme Court Review* 320, 324. Chief Justice White assigned the opinion to Brandeis believing that he had the best chance of winning Holmes's vote to sustain the act. Ibid.

17. Hamilton v. Kentucky Distilleries Co., 251 U.S. at 163–168.

18. Ibid., 251 U.S. at 156–158, 161. Ex parte Milligan, 71 U.S. (4 Wall.)

2, 121–127 (1866), held unilateral wartime conduct of the president to be unconstitutional; a dictum stated that the result would have been the same even with congressional authorization. See Chapter 1.

19. The drafts of Brandeis's *Hamilton* opinion appear in Louis D. Brandeis Papers, Harvard Law School Library, Box 2, folder 7.

20. Ibid. The Indian cases, Perrin v. United States, 232 U.S. 478 (1914), and Johnson v. Gearlds, 234 U.S. 422 (1914), were cited in Brief for Appellant, Ruppert v. Caffey, 251 U.S. at 271. The government urged the Court to take a political question approach in reviewing war power legislation. See Brief for United States at 29, Hamilton v. Kentucky Distilleries Co.; Ruppert v. Caffey, 251 U.S. at 269–270, 273.

21. Hamilton v. Kentucky Distilleries Co., 251 U.S. at 158–163.

22. Ibid., 251 U.S. at 157, 163.

23. "Brandeis-Frankfurter Conversations," Louis D. Brandeis Papers, Harvard Law School Library, Box 114, folders 7-8, and Urofsky, "Brandeis-Frankfurter Conversations," 324. On the attitudes of Pitney, McReynolds, Day and Van Devanter toward federal regulation, see Wilson v. New, 243 U.S. 332 (1917) (eight-hour day for railroad workers); Hammer v. Dagenhart, 247 U.S. 251 (1918) (child labor law); United States v. Doremus, 249 U.S. 86 (1919) (federal tax on narcotics); Newberry v. United States, 256 U.S. 232 (1921) (regulation of primary elections for members of Congress); 3 Leon Friedman and Fred L. Israel, *The Justices of the Supreme Court of the United States, 1789–1969,* at 1784, s.v. "William R. Day"; ibid., 2001, s.v. "Mahlon Pitney" (New York, 1969); Joseph E. McLean, *William Rufus Day: Supreme Court Justice from Ohio,* 65, 157 (Baltimore, 1946).

24. *N.Y. Times,* Dec. 16, 1919, at 12:1. Acceptance of the decision was also aided by the fact that the Court spoke through a justice known to oppose prohibition. Brandeis had once represented liquor dealers in the fight against prohibition, and the Anti-Saloon League therefore strongly opposed his appointment to the Supreme Court. Alpheus T. Mason, *Brandeis: A Free Man's Life,* 89–90, 479 (New York, 1946); Louis D. Brandeis to George W. Anderson, Mar. 6, 1916, 4 Melvin I. Urofsky and David W. Levy, *Letters of Louis D. Brandeis,* 104 (Albany, N.Y., 1975).

25. Abrams v. United States, 250 U.S. at 624 (Nov. 10, 1919); Schaefer v. United States, 251 U.S. at 482 (argued Oct. 21, 1919; decided Mar. 1, 1920); Pierce v. United States, 252 U.S. at 253 (argued Nov. 18–19, 1919; decided Mar. 8, 1920).

26. Eric F. Goldman, *Rendezvous with Destiny: A History of Modern American Reform,* 188–207, 214–215 (New York, 1952); Dean Acheson, *Morning and Noon,* 101 (Boston, 1965). Brandeis returned often to this theme in later years. See, e.g., Louis D. Brandeis to Paul Kellogg, Nov. 7, 1920, 4 Urofsky, *Letters of Brandeis,* 497–498; Brandeis to Felix Frank-

furter, Dec. 30, 1920, ibid., 520; Brandeis to WW, Apr. 15, 1923, 5 ibid., 91; Brandeis to Norman Hapgood, June 1, 1922, Mason, *Brandeis,* 558. He opposed the New Deal for the same reason. Ibid., 614–622.

27. Northern Securities Co. v. United States, 193 U.S. 197, 402–403 (1904); Mark DeWolfe Howe, *Holmes-Laski Letters: The Correspondence of Mr. Justice Holmes and Harold J. Laski, 1916–1935,* at 117, 120, 130, 140, 146 (Cambridge, Mass., 1953); while these letters written between December 1917 and March 1918 were Laski's, he spoke of "our feeling of the danger involved in over-centralised administration." Ibid., 130; Harold J. Laski, *Studies in the Problem of Sovereignty,* 281–285 (New Haven, 1917); Oliver W. Holmes, Jr., to Herbert Croly, May 12, 1919 (draft), Howe, *Holmes-Laski Letters,* 203–204.

28. "Brandeis-Frankfurter Conversations," Louis D. Brandeis Papers, Harvard Law School Library, Box 114, folders 7–8, and Urofsky, "Brandeis-Frankfurter Conversations," 324. Brandeis noted that in contrast to Holmes' opinions in *Schenck* and *Debs, Hamilton* was "put frankly on [the] war power," thereby limiting its precedential impact. Ibid.

29. Brief for Appellants at 38, *Ruppert v. Caffey* (emphasis in original); 251 U.S. at 281–282; ibid., 305, 310 (McReynolds, J., dissenting). The other issues raised by appellants and rejected by the Court were that the act had expired by its own terms; that the ban on war beer was precluded by the Eighteenth Amendment; and that the act effected a taking of property without just compensation. 251 U.S. at 265–278.

30. Brief for Appellants, 251 U.S. at 276–277; 251 U.S. at 282, 298–299, 303.

31. Ruppert v. Caffey, 251 U.S. at 308; Hamilton v. Kentucky Distilleries Co., 251 U.S. at 161. McReynolds's dissent was joined by Day and Van Devanter; Clarke dissented without opinion.

32. 251 U.S. at 309–310. This disagreement over the breadth of Congress's authority to implement the war powers mirrored a similar debate as to the scope of the federal commerce power. See Hammer v. Dagenhart, 247 U.S. 251 (1918), ruling 5 to 4 that Congress could not bar the interstate shipment of goods produced by child labor.

33. 251 U.S. at 163.

34. *N.Y. Times,* Dec. 16, 1919, at 12:1; ibid., Jan. 6, 1920, at 14:1; *Chicago Tribune,* Dec. 16, 1919, at 1:8; ibid., Dec. 17, 1919, at 8:1; *San Francisco Chronicle,* Dec. 17, 1919, at 18:1; *St. Louis Post-Dispatch,* Dec. 16, 1919, at 28:2.

35. Thomas Reed Powell, "The Supreme Court and the Constitution, 1919–1920," 35 *Political Science Quarterly* 411, 418 (Sept. 1920); Note, "Prohibition and the War Power," 33 *Harvard Law Review* 585–587 (Feb. 1920). And see Comment, "Do Constitutional Limitations Control Reformers?" 29 *Yale Law Journal* 437 (Feb. 1920), criticizing failure to find a

"taking"; "War Time Prohibition," 5 *Virginia Law Register* (n.s.) 874 (Mar. 1920), objecting to result in *Ruppert* and reprinting dissent in full; Note, "Constitutionality of War Time Prohibition," 90 *Central Law Journal* 2 (Jan. 2, 1920), stating that the significance of *Hamilton* was its requirement that only a formal declaration by the president can end a war. No other law journals reported on either *Hamilton* or *Ruppert*.

36. *San Francisco Chronicle,* Dec. 17, 1919, at 18:1; Charles E. Hughes, Address at Wellesley College, June 14, 1920, *N.Y. Times,* June 15, 1920, at 8:2; *San Francisco Chronicle,* June 15, 1920, at 2:5; Charles E. Hughes, Address at Harvard Law School, June 21, 1920, *N. Y. Times,* June 22, 1920, at 6:1; *San Francisco Chronicle,* June 22, 1920, at 6:1. Hughes's displeasure with the postarmistice use of the war powers may explain the narrower view he took of federal power after being reappointed to the Supreme Court in 1930. Compare Houston E. & W. Ry. Co. v. United States, 234 U.S. 342 (1914) and Eckman's Alternative v. United States, 239 U.S. 510 (1916), with Schechter Poultry Corp. v. United States, 295 U.S. 495 (1935) and Carter v. Carter Coal Co., 298 U.S. 238, 317 (1936). But see 2 Merlo J. Pusey, *Charles Evans Hughes,* 739–740 (New York, 1963).

37. Joint Resolution of Mar. 3, 1921, ch. 136, 41 Stat. 1359.

38. H.R.J. Res. 327, 66th Cong., 2d Sess., 59 Cong. Rec. 5129, 6485–6486 (1920); *N.Y. Times:* Mar. 27, 1920, at 1:4; Apr. 1, 1920, at 1:1; Apr. 2, 1920, at 1:7; Apr. 3, 1920, at 3:6; Apr. 5, 1920, at 1:4. For the statutes affected, see H.R. Rep. No. 801, 66th Cong., 2d Sess., pt. 2, at 5–13 (1920); laws which were to continue for a stated period after the end of the war would not terminate until the expiration of that period.

39. Cary T. Grayson, *Woodrow Wilson: An Intimate Memoir,* 114–115 (New York, 1960); *N.Y. Times,* Apr. 5, 1920, at 3:2; ibid., Apr. 10, 1920, at 1:3; H.R. Rep. No. 801, 66th Cong., 2d Sess. 3 (1920); ibid., pt. 2, at 5.

40. 59 Cong. Rec. 5480–5481 (Apr. 9, 1920); ibid., 9373–9374 (Rep. Kitchin); *N.Y. Times,* Apr. 9, 1920, at 1:6; ibid., Apr. 10, 1920, at 1:3 and 9:2.

41. H.R. 13827, 66th Cong., 2d Sess (1920); H.R.J. Res. 347, 66th Cong., 2d Sess. (1920); S. 4315, 66th Cong., 2d Sess. (1920); *N.Y. Times:* May 3, 1920, at 1:6; May 10, 1920, at 1:1; May 12, 1920, at 1:1; May 13, 1920, at 1:1; May 15, 1920, at 1:1; E. David Cronon, *The Cabinet Diaries of Josephus Daniels, 1913–1921,* at 525–526 (Lincoln, Neb., 1963).

42. 59 Cong. Rec. 7102 (May 15, 1920) (Sen. Walsh); *N.Y. Times,* May 16, 1920, at 1:1. One Republican opposed the measure.

43. 59 Cong. Rec. 7424 (May 21, 1920) (Rep. Porter); ibid., 7426 (Rep. Huddleston); ibid., 7427 (Rep. Longworth); ibid., 7429; *N.Y. Times,* May 22, 1920, at 1:8.

44. 59 Cong. Rec. 7747 (May 27, 1920); ibid., 7808–7809 (May 28, 1920); *N.Y. Times,* May 28, 1920, at 1:8; ibid., May 29, 1920, at 3:1;

N.Y. World, May 28, 1920, at 10:1; *Washington Post,* May 28, 1920, at 1:1.

45. H.R.J. Res. 373, 66th Cong., 2d Sess., 59 Cong. Rec. 8157 (June 1, 1920); ibid., 8412–8415 (June 3, 1920); *N.Y. Times,* May 30, 1920, at 9:7; ibid., June 4, 1920, at 1:2.

46. H.R. Rep. No. 1087, 66th Cong., 2d Sess. 1 (June 2, 1920); Act of June 5, 1920, ch. 235, 41 Stat. 874, 921–922; 59 Cong. Rec. 6829–6835 (May 10, 1920); ibid., 7284 (May 19, 1920) (Sen. Kenyon).

47. 59 Cong. Rec. 8413, 8416 (June 3, 1920); ibid., 8414 (Rep. Goody-koontz); ibid., 8415 (Rep. Connally); ibid., 8493, 8614 (June 4, 1920); ibid., 8678 (June 5, 1920); *N.Y. Times,* June 3, 1920, at 22:1; ibid., June 5, 1920, at 16:4.

48. *N.Y. Times,* June 6, 1920, at 1:2; *Washington Post,* June 6, 1920, at 16:1; *Los Angeles Times,* June 6, 1920, at 9:6; Lindsay Rogers, "The Power of the President to Sign Bills after Congress Has Adjourned," 30 *Yale Law Journal* 1 (1920).

49. H.R. 3184, 66th Cong., 1st Sess. (1919); 59 Cong. Rec. 8048 (May 31, 1920); *San Francisco Chronicle,* June 8, 1920, at 2:6; *N.Y. Times,* June 11, 1920, at 17:7; *Washington Post,* June 11, 1920, at 9:4; AMP to WW, June 19, 1920, WW MSS, ser. 4, case 20; 32 *Attorney General Opinions* 225 (1921). See Edwards v. United States, 286 U.S. 482 (1932), upholding practice suggested by Palmer.

50. *Washington Post,* June 18, 1920, at 2:2; ibid., June 19, 1920, at 3:2. The measures signed were the Federal Water Power Act, 41 Stat. 1063, ch. 285 (June 10, 1920); 41 Stat. 1077, ch. 286 (June 14, 1920), allowing non-English speakers to enlist in army; 41 Stat. 1077–1079, chs. 287–291 (June 14, 1920), extending time to complete bridges; 41 Stat. 1522, ch. 292 (June 14, 1920), for the relief of Michael MacGarvey.

51. Woodrow Wilson, interview by Louis Siebold, June 15, 1920, *N.Y. Times,* June 18, 1920, at 1:7.

52. 59 Cong. Rec. 7806 (May 28, 1920) (Rep. Porter); Edwin A. Weinstein, *Woodrow Wilson: A Medical and Psychological Biography,* 359–363 (Princeton, 1981).

53. Kirk H. Porter and Donald B. Johnson, *National Party Platforms, 1840–1960,* at 213–214, 233–234 (Urbana, Ill., 1961).

54. H.R.J. Res. 382, 66th Cong., 3d Sess., 60 Cong. Rec. 11 (Dec. 6, 1920); H.R. Rep. No. 1111, 66th Cong., 3d Sess. 1 (1920); 60 Cong. Rec. 290–291 (Dec. 13, 1920); ibid., 292, 302 (Rep. Volstead); ibid., 298 (Rep. Bland).

55. 60 Cong. Rec. 302–303 (Dec. 13, 1920); ibid., 4062 (Feb. 28, 1921); ibid., 4209–4210 (Mar. 1, 1921); *N.Y. Times,* Dec. 14, 1920, at 1:4.

56. Joint Resolution of Mar. 3, 1921, ch. 136, 41 Stat. 1359. In addition to the handful of exempted laws, acts which were to continue for a set time

after the war would remain operative until that period expired. See H.R. Rep. No. 801, 66th Cong., 2d Sess., pt. 2, at 5–13 (1920).

57. Hamilton v. Kentucky Distilleries Co., 251 U.S. at 161; Vincenti v. United States, 272 F. 114 (4th Cir.), *cert. denied,* 256 U.S. 700, 257 U.S. 634 (1921); United States v. Russel, 265 F. 414 (E.D. La. 1920); United States v. Milligan, 268 F. 893, 895 (N.D. N.Y. 1920); United States v. L. Cohen Grocer Co., 264 F. 218, 219–220 (E.D. Mo. 1920), *aff'd,* 255 U.S. 81 (1921); United States v. Swedlow, 264 F. 1016, 1018 (D.Colo. 1920); C. A. Weed & Co. v. Lockwood, 264 F. 453 (W.D. N.Y.), *aff'd,* 266 F. 785 (2d Cir. 1920), *rev'd,* 255 U.S. 104 (1921); Corneli v. Moore, 268 F. 993, 996 (E.D. Mo. 1920), *aff'd,* 257 U.S. 491 (1922); United States v. Oglesby Grocery Co., 264 F. 691 (N.D. Ga. 1920), *rev'd,* 255 U.S. 108 (1921).

58. Ex parte Sichofsky, 273 F. 694, 695–696 (S.D. Cal. 1921), *aff'd* sub nom. Sichofsky v. United States, 277 F. 762, 764 (9th Cir. 1922).

59. United States v. People's Fuel and Feed Co., 271 F. 790, 790–791 (D.Ariz., Mar. 30, 1920), writ of error dismissed, 255 U.S. 581 (1921). While the judge did not specify the basis of his ruling, it presumably rested on the Fifth Amendment due process clause or the Sixth Amendment right of an accused "to be informed of the nature and cause of the accusation."

60. United States v. L. Cohen Grocer Co., 264 F. 218, 219–220 (E.D. Mo., Apr. 8, 1920), *aff'd,* 255 U.S. 81 (1921); *N.Y. World,* Apr. 11, 1920, at 13:1; ibid., Apr. 12, 1920, at 1:4.

61. Detroit Creamery Co. v. Kinnane, 264 F. 845, 850–851 (E.D. Mich., Apr. 23, 1920), *aff'd,* 255 U.S. 102, 103–104 (1921); A. T. Lewis & Son Dry Goods Co. v. Tedrow (D.Colo. 1920) (unreported), *aff'd,* 255 U.S. 98 (1921); *N.Y. Times,* May 27, 1920, at 3:3; United States v. Bernstein, 267 F. 295, 296 (D.Neb., June 8, 1920); Lamborn v. McAvoy, 265 F. 944 (E.D. Pa., June 9, 1920); Brief for United States at 40, United States v. L. Cohen Grocery Co., 255 U.S. 81 (1921); "Prosecutions in Districts where Judges Have Held Food Control Act Unconstitutional," NA DOJ, High Cost of Living Division, Box 10.

62. Act of Aug. 10, 1917, ch. 53, § 22, 40 Stat. 283; Act of Oct. 22, 1919, ch. 80, title I, § 2, 41 Stat. 298, amending Act of Aug. 10, 1917, ch. 53, § 4, 40 Stat. 277; United States v. Armstrong, 265 F. 683, 693 (D.Ind., May 26, 1920).

63. United States v. Rosenblum, 264 F. 578 (W.D. Pa., May 1, 1920); United States v. Yount, 267 F. 861, 865 (W.D. Pa., Oct. 21, 1920); *N.Y. Times,* Oct. 22, 1920, at 14:7; *Pittsburgh Daily Dispatch,* Oct. 22, 1920, at 1:5 and 2:6; Lamborn v. McAvoy, 265 F. 944 (E.D. Pa., June 9, 1920). In New York, after section 4 was upheld by the U.S. Court of Appeals in C. A. Weed & Co. v. Lockwood, 266 F. 785 (2d Cir. 1920), District Judge Augustus N. Hand, though bound by that ruling, heard Charles Evans Hughes argue that section 4 was unconstitutional. According to Hand, "Just before

the Hughes argument, I had fined some people $10,000 for charging too much for some potatoes. But Hughes presented his argument against the absence in the statute of any definite standards . . . with such tremendous force that I at once deferred decision until the Supreme Court had spoken in a pending appeal, and later . . . quashed the indictment." Address by Augustus N. Hand, Dec. 12, 1948, *Proceedings of the Bar and Officers of the Supreme Court in Memory of Charles Evans Hughes,* 136–137 (Washington, D.C., 1950); and see 1 Pusey, *Hughes,* 386.

64. United States v. Spokane Dry Goods Co., 264 F. 209, 211–212 (E.D. Wash., Mar. 13, 1920). Section 4 of the Lever Act was also upheld in United States v. Myatt, 264 F. 442 (E.D. N.C., Mar. 3, 1920); C. A. Weed & Co. v. Lockwood, 264 F. 453 (W.D. N.Y., May 1, 1920), *aff'd,* 266 F. 785 (2d Cir., May 26, 1920), *rev'd,* 255 U.S. 104 (1921); United States v. Oglesby Grocery Co., 264 F. 691 (N.D. Ga., May 6, 1920), *rev'd,* 255 U.S. 108 (1921); United States v. Fannon (C.D. Calif., May 10, 1920), *aff'd,* 276 F. 109 (9th Cir. 1921); United States v. Weeds, Inc. (N.D. N.Y., May 28, 1920), *rev'd,* 255 U.S. 109 (1921); United States v. Russel, 265 F. 414 (E.D. La., May 29, 1920). The following unreported decisions upholding section 4 are noted in Brief for United States at 39, United States v. L. Cohen Grocery Co., 255 U.S. 81 (1921): United States v. Blumenthal (S.D. Calif.); United States v. Goldsmith (D.R.I.); United States v. Taylor (E.D. or M.D. Tenn.); United States v. Diamond Shoe and Garment Co. (D.W.Va.); United States v. Paris (D.Vt.); United States v. Roth (S.D. N.Y.); United States v. Fabian (D.Mont.); and an unnamed decision by Judge Westenhaver (N.D. Ohio). Two other rulings sustaining section 4 were noted in the press: decision by Judge Holmes (S.D. Miss.), *N.Y. Times,* May 7, 1920, at 10:7; United States v. Mueller (W.D. Mich., Sept. 14, 1920), ibid., Sept. 15, 1920, at 8:7. The following cases rejected constitutional challenges to other sections of the Lever Act: United States v. Milligan, 268 F. 893 (N.D. N.Y., Sept. 25, 1920) (§ 5, punishing refusal to allow federal inspection of business premises); Hillsboro Coal Co. v. United States, 273 F. 221 (S.D. Ill., Nov. 8, 1920) (§ 9, punishing certain conspiracies with respect to necessaries); Merritt v. United States, 264 F. 870 (9th Cir., May 3, 1920), *reh. denied,* July 6, 1920, *rev'd* on confession of error, 255 U.S. 579 (1921) (§ 6, punishing hoarding; the case involved a Pasadena millionaire who was fined $5,000 and sentenced to five months in prison for hoarding sugar; see *San Francisco Chronicle,* July 7, 1920, at 4:2). See also Howard Figg to Fair Price Commissioners, Apr. 12, 1920, NA DOJ, High Cost of Living Division, Box 13.

65. Motion of the United States to Advance at 2 (May 17, 1920), United States v. L. Cohen Grocery Co., 255 U.S. 81 (1921); *N.Y. Times,* Oct. 31, 1920, at 12:3.

66. Dept. of Justice, *Annual Report of the Attorney General, 1920,* at

48–51; *N.Y. Times:* Jan. 1, 1921, at 3:4; Jan. 18, 1921, at 7:2; Mar. 1, 1921, at 2:3; Apr. 8, 1921, at 16:2.

67. In five of the appeals lower courts had held section 4 unconstitutionally vague: United States v. L. Cohen Grocery Co., 255 U.S. 81, 87–88 (1921); Tedrow v. A. T. Lewis & Son Dry Goods Co., 255 U.S. 98, 99 (1921); Kinnane v. Detroit Creamery, United States v. Swartz, and United States v. Smith, 255 U.S. 102, 103–104 (1921). In three suits lower courts had upheld the Act: C. A. Weed & Co. v. Lockwood, 255 U.S. 104, 105–106 (1921); Oglesby Grocery Co. v. United States, 255 U.S. 108 (1921); Weeds, Inc. v. United States, 255 U.S. 109, 110 (1921). Two appeals were from decisions denying relief without reaching the constitutional question: Kennington v. Palmer, 255 U.S. 100, 101 (1921); G. S. Willard Co. v. Palmer, 255 U.S. 106, 107 (1921). Hughes represented parties in *Tedrow, Detroit Creamery, Swartz, Smith,* and *Weeds, Inc.* The durational argument is quoted from Brief for Lake and Export Coal Co. as Amicus Curiae at 36, *L. Cohen Grocery Co.* The durational argument was also made in *Tedrow, C. A. Weed & Co., Oglesby Grocery Co.,* and *Weeds, Inc.* For the statutory argument, see *L. Cohen Grocery Co.,* 255 U.S. at 88, and Brief of Utah-Idaho Sugar Company as Amicus Curiae, *L. Cohen Grocery Co.,* 65 L.Ed. at 518–519.

68. Brief for the United States at 11–16, *L. Cohen Grocery Co.* (emphasis added).

69. Brief for L. Cohen Grocery Co. at 54; Brief for Lake and Export Coal Co. as Amicus Curiae at 37–38, *L. Cohen Grocery Co.*

70. United States v. L. Cohen Grocery Co., 255 U.S. 81, 88–89, 93 (Feb. 28, 1921); ibid., 93–97 (Pitney and Brandeis, JJ., concurring); the companion cases were disposed of on the same ground in brief opinions by the chief justice. 255 U.S. at 98–113. In Weeds, Inc. v. United States, 255 U.S. 109, 111–113 (1921), Pitney and Brandeis reached the constitutional issue and concluded that section 4 was not unduly vague; they concurred in the reversal because defendant had not been given a chance to prove its prices were reasonable. In 1917 Brandeis had advised Herbert Hoover on how to secure passage of the Lever Act; this may partly explain his reluctance to find the act unconstitutional. But see Bruce Allen Murphy, *The Brandeis/Frankfurter Connection,* 50–51, 54–55 (New York, 1982), mistakenly asserting that Brandeis agreed with the Court's decision to invalidate section 4 and that he gave no account of his reasoning. Justice William Day did not participate in the cases because his son appeared on behalf of appellants in G. S. Willard Co. v. Palmer, 255 U.S. 106 (1921). The younger Day was a six-foot former football player, in contrast to his frail and diminutive father. It was perhaps during oral argument in this case that Justice Holmes passed a note to his colleagues remarking, "He's a block off the old chip." McClean, *William Rufus Day,* 62; Silas Bent, *Justice Oliver Wendell Holmes: A Biography,* 270 (New York, 1932).

71. *N.Y. Times:* Mar. 1, 1921, at 2:3; Mar. 3, 1921, at 17:3; Mar. 13, 1921, pt. 2, at 1:5; Mar. 20, 1921, pt. 2, at 1:3; Mar. 23, 1921, at 19:1; Apr. 8, 1921, at 16:2.

72. Hepburn v. Griswold, 75 U.S. (8 Wall.) 603 (1870), overruled by The Legal Tender Cases, 79 U.S. (12 Wall.) 457 (1871).

8. *The Tug-of-War over Rent Control*

1. Wilson v. McDonnell, 265 F. 432 (D.C. Cir., Dec. 1, 1919; opinion on motion for reargument, Dec. 24, 1919), *error dismissed,* 257 U.S. 665 (1921). See Chapter 4.

2. Hirsh v. Block, 267 F. 614, 621 (D.C. Cir., June 2, 1920), *rev'd,* 256 U.S. 135 (1921); United States ex rel. McCathran v. Doyle, 267 F. 631, 632 (D.C. Cir., June 2, 1920); *Washington Post,* June 10, 1920, at 2:1; ibid., June 12, 1920, at 2:6.

3. *Washington Post,* June 15, 1920, at 2:6; ibid., June 18, 1920, at 2:3; D.C. Rent Commission, *Report of the Rent Comm'n of the District of Columbia to the President of the United States of America,* 21 (May 22, 1925) (hereafter, *Rent Comm'n Report*).

4. Brief for Plaintiff in Error at 29–30, 33, Block v. Hirsh, 256 U.S. 135 (1921); Brief for United States as Amicus Curiae at 16, 39; Brief for Defendant in Error at 33; 256 U.S. at 137–138, 145, 147–153.

5. Block v. Hirsh, 256 U.S. 135, 153, 155 (1921).

6. Act of Oct. 22, 1919, ch. 80, title II, §§ 106, 122, 41 Stat. 300, 304; Brief for United States as Amicus Curiae at 14; Block v. Hirsh, 256 U.S. at 154–155.

7. Block v. Hirsh, 256 U.S. at 156–157; Marcus Brown Holding Co. v. Feldman, 256 U.S. 170, 198 (Apr. 18, 1921). The dissenters in both cases were Justices McKenna, Van Devanter, and McReynolds and Chief Justice White.

8. *Washington Post,* Apr. 19, 1921, at 1:1; ibid., Apr. 20, 1921, at 2:1; ibid., Apr. 22, 1921, at 16:3.

9. Block v. Hirsh, 256 U.S. at 157; S. 2131, 67th Cong., 1st Sess., 61 Cong. Rec. 2883 (June 22, 1921); Act of Aug. 24, 1921, ch. 91, 42 Stat. 200.

10. H.R. Rep. No. 358, 67th Cong., 1st Sess. 1 (Aug. 20, 1921); Joint Resolution of July 2, 1921, ch. 40, 42 Stat. 105; 61 Cong. Rec. 5588 (Aug. 23, 1921) (Rep. Husted); ibid., 5585 (Rep. Blanton); ibid., 5588 (Rep. Mann); ibid., 5053 (Aug. 16, 1921) (Sen. Pomerene); ibid., 5054 (Sen. Ball).

11. 61 Cong. Rec. 4753–4754 (Aug. 9, 1921) (Sen. Brandegee); ibid., 4754, 4759 (Sen. Shortridge); ibid., 4772 (Sen. Ball); ibid., 4867 (Aug. 11, 1921) (quoting Sen. Ball); ibid., 5578 (Aug. 23, 1921) (Rep. Rhodes); ibid., 5588 (Rep. Husted); H.R. Rep. No. 358, at 3.

12. 61 Cong. Rec. 4754–4755 (Aug. 9, 1921) (Sen. Fletcher); ibid., 4872 (Aug. 11, 1921) (Sen. Gooding); ibid., 4869 (Sen. Fletcher); ibid., 5054 (Aug. 16, 1921) (Sen. Brandegee).

13. 61 Cong. Rec. 4755-4756 (August 9, 1921) (Sen. Fletcher); ibid. 4773 (Sen. Ball); ibid., 4867 (Aug. 11, 1921) (Sen. Ball); ibid., 4871 (Sen. Poindexter); H.R. Rep. No. 358, at 1.

14. "Changes in the Cost of Living in the United States," 20 *Monthly Labor Review* 293, 301, 306 (Feb. 1925); Charles O. Hardy, *Wartime Control of Prices*, 196–201 (Washington, D.C., 1940).

15. Paul H. Douglas, *Real Wages in the United States, 1890–1926*, at 376–377 (Boston, 1920).

16. Congressional Quarterly, *Guide to the Congress of the United States*, 353–360 (Washington, D.C., 1971); 61 Cong. Rec. 4873 (Aug. 11, 1921) (Sen. Poindexter). Poindexter later proposed giving the District representation in Congress. See S. Rep. Nos. 507 and 508, 67th Cong., 2d Sess. (Feb. 20, 1922).

17. 61 Cong. Rec. 4773 (Aug. 9, 1921) (Sen. Ball); ibid., 4866 (Aug. 11, 1921) (Sen Lenroot); ibid., 5053 (Aug. 16, 1921) (Sen. Pomerene); ibid., 5575 (Aug. 23, 1921) (Rep. Woodruff); ibid., 5577-5578 (Rep. Rhodes); ibid., 5578 (Rep. Blanton); ibid., 5584 (Rep. Begg).

18. 61 Cong. Rec. 4874 (Aug. 11, 1921) (Sen. Poindexter); ibid., 5055; ibid., 5587 (Aug. 23, 1921) (Rep. Goodykoontz); ibid., 5576 (Rep. Layton); ibid., 5590.

19. 61 Cong. Rec. 4772 (Aug. 9, 1921) (Sen. Ball); ibid., 4867 (Aug. 11, 1921) (Sen. Ball); S. 2919, 67th Cong., 2d Sess., 62 Cong. Rec. 748 (Jan. 4, 1922); Act of May 22, 1922, ch. 197, 42 Stat. 543; *N.Y. Times*, May 23, 1922, at 3:6.

20. H.R. Rep. No. 1006, 67th Cong., 2d Sess. 2 (May 12, 1922); 62 Cong. Rec. 5520 (Apr. 14, 1922) (Sen. Pomerene); ibid., 7391 (May 22, 1922) (Sen. Williams); ibid., 13740 (Rep. Reed, W.Va.); Act of May 22, 1922, ch. 187, § 1, 42 Stat. 543–544; S. Rep. No. 523, 67th Cong., 2d Sess. 6 (Feb. 23, 1922).

21. H.R. Rep. No. 1006, at 2; Edgar A. Levy Leasing Co. v. Siegel, 258 U.S. 242, 245–247 (Mar. 20, 1922); Justices McKenna, Van Devanter, and McReynolds dissented without opinion. Clarke's expansive language in *Siegel* contrasted with Holmes's cautious approach in *Block;* this may reflect the Court's greater discomfort with peacetime use of the federal war powers as compared with state exercises of the police power.

22. S. Rep. No. 523, 67th Cong., 2d Sess. 6 (Feb. 23, 1922); H.R. Rep. No. 1006, at 2; ibid., pt. 2, at 1–2 (views of the minority); 62 Cong. Rec. 7389 (May 22, 1922) (Sen. Ball); ibid., 7414 (Rep. Hammer); William E. Shannon, "The Effect of Two and One-Half Years of Rent-Control Legislation at Washington," ibid., 7390–7391; *N.Y. Times*, May 23, 1922, at 3:6.

23. 62 Cong. Rec. 5512 (Apr. 14, 1922) (Sen. McCormick); ibid., 5513–5514 (Sen. Poindexter); ibid., 7390 (May 22, 1922) (Sen. Myers).

24. *Washington Post,* Apr. 22, 1921, at 16:3; ibid., Apr. 28, 1922, at 20:4; ibid., Apr. 29, 1922, at 2:1; *Washington Evening Star,* Dec. 30, 1921, at 1:5; 62 Cong. Rec. 5514 (Apr. 14, 1922) (Sen. Moses); 67th Cong., 2d Sess., *Official Congressional Directory,* 385, 388, 463–473 (Dec. 1921); the Meridian Mansion was located at 2400 Sixteenth Street.

25. 67th Cong., 2d Sess., *Hearings before the House Comm. on the District of Columbia on S. 2919,* at 5–11, 34–101 (1922); *Washington Evening Star,* Dec. 30, 1921, at 1:5 and 2:5; ibid., Apr. 27, 1922, at 1:6. The Meridian Mansion ruling was affirmed by the District of Columbia Court of Appeals; it is unclear whether Judge Smyth, whose rent was reduced, participated in the decision. Kennedy Bros. v. Sinclair, 287 F. 972, 52 App. D.C. 398 (D.C. Cir. 1923); 51 *Washington Law Reporter* 226 (Apr. 13, 1923).

26. 62 Cong. Rec. 7392 (May 22, 1922); ibid., 7425–7426; Act of May 22, 1922, ch. 197, § 4, 42 Stat. 544–545. Wilson did not name new commissioners for more than a year; they included two of the three original appointees. 65 Cong. Rec. 162 (1923); ibid., 786 (1924); *Rent Comm'n Report,* 23.

27. Edgar A. Levy Leasing Co. v. Siegel, 258 U.S. 242, 246 (1922); Chastleton Corp. v. Sinclair, 290 F. 348, 53 App. D.C. 373 (D.C. Cir. 1923). Chief Justice Smyth also voted to uphold the District rent law in an earlier case decided before he received any benefit from the commission. Block v. Hirsh, 267 F. 614, 623, 631, 50 App. D.C. 56, 65, 73 (D.C. Cir. 1920).

28. Chastleton Corp. v. Sinclair, 290 F. 348, 53 App. D.C. 373 (D.C. Cir., June 4, 1923), *rev'd,* 264 U.S. 543, 546 (1924).

29. Block v. Hirsh, 256 U.S. 135 (1921); Marcus Brown Holding Co. v. Feldman, 256 U.S. 170 (1921); Edgar A. Levy Leasing Co. v. Siegel, 258 U.S. 242 (1922).

30. While Taft had voted to uphold the New York rent law in Levy Leasing Co. v. Siegel, this did not mean that he would do likewise in *Chastleton.* The question in *Siegel* was virtually identical to that decided a year earlier in *Feldman,* upholding the same New York law. Even if Taft disagreed with *Feldman,* his vote could not have altered the outcome in *Siegel* but only changed the decision from 6–3 to 5–4. Taft believed firmly in adherence to precedent and also favored "massing the Court" by minimizing dissents. A negative vote in *Siegel* would have violated both of these principles. See Alpheus T. Mason, *William Howard Taft: Chief Justice,* 198–204, 264 (London, 1965); 2 Henry F. Pringle, *The Life and Times of William Howard Taft,* 968–971, 1049 (Hamden, Conn., 1964).

31. Robert G. McCloskey, *The American Supreme Court,* 153 (Chicago, 1960); Wilson v. New, 243 U.S. 332 (1916); Block v. Hirsh, 256 U.S. 135 (1921); Marcus Brown Holding Co. v. Feldman, 256 U.S. 170 (1921); Munn

v. Illinois, 94 U.S. 113 (1877); Mason, *Taft,* 158, 164; 2 Pringle, *Taft,* 967.

32. Adkins v. Children's Hospital, 261 U.S. 525, 546–552 (Apr. 9, 1923); ibid., 562, 566 (Taft, C. J., dissenting).

33. Charles Wolff Packing Co. v. Court of Industrial Relations, 262 U.S. 522, 534–536, 542 (June 11, 1923).

34. Pennsylvania Coal Co. v. Mahon, 260 U.S. 393, 416 (Dec. 11, 1922); Adkins v. Children's Hospital, 261 U.S. 525, 551–552 (Apr. 9, 1923).

35. Donald B. Johnson and Kirk H. Porter, *National Party Platforms, 1840–1972,* at 252–254 (Urbana, Ill., 1973); Allan E. Ragan, *Chief Justice Taft,* 95–103 (Columbus, Ohio, 1938); "The Red Terror of Judicial Reform," 40 *New Republic* 110 (Oct. 1, 1924).

36. Mason, *Taft,* 92–93; Ragan, *Chief Justice Taft,* 100; 2 Pringle, *Taft,* 1041; William H. Taft to Thomas W. Shelton, Mar. 12, 1924, Library of Congress, William Howard Taft Papers, reel 262; Taft to Charles Warren, Apr. 2, 1924, ibid., reel 263.

37. Felix Frankfurter and James M. Landis, *The Business of the Supreme Court: A Study in the Federal Judicial System,* 255–280 (New York, 1928); Mason, *Taft,* 107–114; Charles A. Wright, *The Law of the Federal Courts,* 7 (4th ed., St. Paul, 1983); S. 2060 and H.R. 8206, 68th Cong., 1st Sess. (1924); *Hearings before a Subcomm. of the Sen. Comm. on the Judiciary,* 68th Cong., 1st Sess. 25–48 (Feb. 2, 1924); S. Rep. No. 362, 68th Cong., 1st Sess. 1 (1924); 65 Cong. Rec. 5831 (Apr. 8, 1924); Act of Feb. 13, 1925, ch. 229, 43 Stat. 936; Washington v. Dawson & Co., 264 U.S. 219, 222 (Feb. 25, 1924), invalidating, on the basis of a nearly identical 1920 Supreme Court ruling, a federal statute permitting state workers' compensation laws to govern injuries within the exclusive admiralty jurisdiction of the United States.

38. H.R. 23, 68th Cong., 1st Sess., 65 Cong. Rec. 26 (Dec. 5, 1923); S. 2110, 68th Cong., 1st Sess., ibid., 1192 (Jan. 21, 1924); H.R. 7962, 68th Cong., 1st Sess., ibid., 4308 (Mar. 15, 1924); *Hearings on H.R. 23 before a Subcomm. of the House Comm. on the District of Columbia,* 68th Cong., 1st Sess. (Feb. 1924); *Washington Post,* Mar. 14, 1924, at 2:4; ibid., Mar. 15, 1924, at 2:1; ibid., Mar. 27, 1924, at 5:4.

39. H.R. Rep. No. 467, 68th Cong., 1st Sess. 1–4 (Apr. 7, 1924); see *Rent Comm'n Report,* 9–14.

40. Alfred B. Moore, "Survey of Housing and Rental Conditions in the District of Columbia," Apr. 3, 1924, S. Rep. No. 530, 68th Cong., 1st Sess. (1924), Library of Congress, Calvin Coolidge Papers, reel 51, case 63; *Washington Post,* Mar. 22, 1924, at 8:4; ibid., Mar. 27, 1924, at 1:2–3; H.R. Rep. No. 467, pt. 3, at 15; and see 65 Cong. Rec. 7402–7417 (Apr. 28, 1924) (Rep. Blanton), reprinting advertisements of available rentals from *Washington Star,* Apr. 27, 1924.

41. H.R. Rep. No. 467, at 2; ibid., pt. 2, at 1–2 (Apr. 11, 1924) (minority

report of Rep. Underhill and Rep. Jost); 65 Cong. Rec. 6340 (Apr. 14, 1924) (Rep. Jost).

42. Chastleton Corp. v. Sinclair, 264 U.S. 543, 546–548 (1924).

43. 264 U.S. at 548.

44. 264 U.S. at 548–549.

45. Louis D. Brandeis to Felix Frankfurter, Apr. 23, 1924, 5 Melvin I. Urofsky and David W. Levy, *Letters of Louis D. Brandeis,* 126 (Albany, N.Y., 1978); *Washington Post:* Apr. 15, 1924, at 1:6; Apr. 16, 1924, at 3:4–5; Apr. 17, 1924, at 2:5; Apr. 18, 1924, at 2:1; Apr. 20, 1924, at 2:1.

46. Brandeis's note to Holmes appears in Oliver Wendell Holmes, Jr., Papers, Harvard Law School Library, Bound Opinions, Oct. Term, 1923; 264 U.S. at 549–551 (Brandeis, J., concurring in part).

47. 264 U.S. at 546–547; Louis D. Brandeis to Felix Frankfurter, Sept. 19, 1922, 5 Urofsky, *Brandeis Letters,* 63–64; and see Ashwander v. Tennessee Valley Authority, 297 U.S. 288, 345–348 (1936) (Brandeis, J., concurring).

48. Louis D. Brandeis to Felix Frankfurter, Sept. 19, 1922, 5 Urofsky, *Brandeis Letters,* 63–64; three drafts of Holmes's *Chastleton* opinion are found in the Louis D. Brandeis Papers, Harvard Law School Library, Box 21, folder 3; the justices' responses to Holmes's drafts are in the Oliver Wendell Homes, Jr., Papers, Harvard Law School Library, Bound Opinions, Oct. Term, 1923.

49. McKenna objected to the emphasized portion of the following sentence: "*Without assuming to know judicially all that a man with his eyes open can see,* we can say at least that the plaintiffs' allegations [as to the lack of a housing emergency] cannot be declared offhand to be unmaintainable." Oliver Wendell Holmes, Jr., Papers, Harvard Law School Library, Bound Opinions, Oct. Term, 1923. Holmes changed the phrase to read: "Without going beyond the limits of judicial knowledge." 264 U.S. at 548.

50. Louis D. Brandeis Papers, Harvard Law School Library, Box 21, folder 3; 264 U.S. at 548–549.

51. Mason, *Taft,* 198–204; 2 Pringle, *Taft,* 968–971, 1049; 264 U.S. at 549.

52. 65 Cong. Rec. 7394–7395 (Apr. 28, 1924) (Rep. Hersey); ibid., 8357–8358 (May 12, 1924) (Sen. King).

53. 65 Cong. Rec. 8654 (May 15, 1924) (Rep. Underhill); ibid., 7378 (Apr. 28, 1924) (Rep. Tincher); for similar views, see ibid., 7378 (Rep. Sanders); ibid., 7390 (Rep. Blanton); ibid., 7391 (Rep. Jost); ibid., 7394 (Rep. Gilbert); ibid., 7400 (Rep. Luce); ibid., 7401 (Rep. Rogers).

54. 65 Cong. Rec. 7378 (Apr. 28, 1924) (Rep. Begg); ibid., 7393–7394 (Rep. Moore); ibid., 7393 (Rep. La Guardia); ibid., 7396 (Rep. Hammer); ibid., 7421 (Rep. Raker); *Washington Post,* May 11, 1924, at 2:1.

55. Block v. Hirsh, 256 U.S. at 154; Chastleton Corp. v. Sinclair, 264 U.S. at 548.

56. 65 Cong. Rec. 7107, 7396–7397 (Apr. 28, 1924) (Rep. Hammer); ibid., 7400 (Rep. Luce); Commercial Trust Co. v. Miller, 262 U.S. 51, 57 (Apr. 23, 1923) (unanimous decision). Since Congress's authority to deal with alien property is not dependent on the war power but stems from the treaty power and/or the government's plenary power over aliens (Geofroy v. Riggs, 133 U.S. 258, 266–268 [1890]; Fong Yue Ting v. United States, 149 U.S. 698, 731 [1893]), the presence of a war emergency was relevant in *Miller* only to the statutory question of whether the Trading with the Enemy Act should be deemed terminated; the emergency did not affect the act's compatibility with the Bill of Rights, for the Court had previously held its procedures to satisfy due process. Central Trust Co. v. Garvan, 254 U.S. 554 (1921); Stoehr v. Wallace, 255 U.S. 239 (1921).

57. *Washington Post,* Apr. 22, 1924, at 2:3; 65 Cong. Rec. 7392–7393 (Apr. 28, 1924) (Rep. La Guardia).

58. *Washington Post,* Apr. 23, 1924, at 6:1; Act of May 17, 1924, ch. 156, 43 Stat. 120. The House had approved a two-year extension but concurred in a Senate amendment reducing it to one year. 65 Cong. Rec. 7426, 8352–8359, 8655 (1924). The president promptly extended the terms of the incumbent commissioners. Ibid., 8891, 9195 (1924); *Washington Post,* May 20, 1924, at 1:4; ibid., May 23, 1924, at 4:4.

59. Harry Norment v. Richard S. Whaley, Equity No. 42516 (D.C. Sup. Ct., filed Apr. 26, 1924); Bates Warren v. Richard S. Whaley, Equity No. 42520 (D.C. Sup. Ct., filed Apr. 28, 1924); *Washington Post:* Apr. 27, 1924, at 2:1; Apr. 28, 1924, at 16:6; Apr. 29, 1924, at 5:4 and 18:4; May 10, 1924, at 1:4; *Rent Comm'n Report,* 30–31; George R. Linkins to Calvin Coolidge, May 12, 1924, Library of Congress, Calvin Coolidge Papers, case 51F, reel 50.

60. *Washington Post,* May 10, 1924, at 1:4; ibid., May 20, 1924, at 1:4.

61. *Rent Comm'n Report,* 28, 31; *Washington Post,* May 20, 1924, at 1:4; ibid., Nov. 4, 1924, at 2:3; George W. Linkins v. Richard S. Whaley, Equity No. 42672 (D.C. Sup. Ct.), 52 *Washington Law Reporter* 402 (June 27, 1924). Commission orders issued prior to *Chastleton* were set aside by the District of Columbia courts on a showing that no emergency existed when the order was made. See Gilbert v. Sargent, 19 F.2d 681, 57 App. D.C. 207 (D.C. Ct. App., 1927). No further proceedings appear to have been taken in *Chastleton* itself following the remand.

62. *Washington Post,* May 20, 1924, at 1:4; *Rent Comm'n Report,* 31, 33.

63. *Washington Post,* May 20, 1924, at 1:4; Peck v. Fink, 2 F.2d 912, 913, 55 App. D.C. 110, 111 (D.C. Cir., Nov. 3, 1924), *cert. denied,* 266 U.S.

631 (1925); *Rent Comm'n Report,* 31–33; and see Whaley v. Norment, 6 F.2d 716, 56 App. D.C. 18 (D.C. Cir., June 1, 1925).

64. *Rent Comm'n Report,* 34, 38; *Washington Post,* Nov. 5, 1924, at 10:3; Peck v. Fink, 266 U.S. 631 (1925); Act of Aug. 24, 1921, ch. 91, 42 Stat. 200.

65. *N.Y. Times,* Nov. 16, 1924, pt. 9, at 10:1; "Survey of Rental Conditions in the District, May, 1925," *Rent Comm'n Report,* 41–44.

66. *Washington Post:* Oct. 18, 1924, at 1:8; Oct. 21, 1924, at 2:4; Jan. 8, 1925, at 2:5; Feb. 19, 1925, at 5:6; Feb. 20, 1925, at 2:3; Edward H. Schirmer to Calvin Coolidge, Oct. 17, 1924, Library of Congress, Calvin Coolidge Papers, case 63, reel 52; John W. Weeks to C. Bascom Slemp, Oct. 25, 1924, ibid., enclosing "Informal Memorandum for the Secretary of War," Oct. 20, 1924; S. 3764 and H.R. 11078, 68th Cong., 2d Sess. (1924); 66 Cong. Rec. 1182 (1924); *Rent Comm'n Report,* 34; *N.Y. Times,* Dec. 23, 1924, at 31:4; ibid., Dec. 28, 1924, at 20:8. For a more recent and equally futile attempt by the homeless to use the parks of Washington, see Clark v. Community for Creative Non-Violence, 468 U.S. 288 (1984).

67. John B. Cochran to C. Bascom Slemp, Dec. 31, 1924, Library of Congress, Calvin Coolidge Papers, case 63, reel 52; 66 Cong. Rec. 3148 (Feb. 6, 1925) (Rep. Blanton).

68. *N.Y. Times,* Aug. 4, 1923, at 4:2; ibid., Aug. 22, 1923, at 1:2–3; Calvin Coolidge, *The Autobiography of Calvin Coolidge,* 158–159 (New York, 1929); William A. White, *A Puritan in Babylon: The Story of Calvin Coolidge,* 221 (New York, 1938).

69. 66 Cong. Rec. 3151–3152 (Feb. 6, 1925) (Rep. Blanton); H.R. Rep. No. 1406, 68th Cong., 2d Sess. 2 (Feb. 6, 1925); S. Rep. No. 1135, 68th Cong., 2d Sess. 2–4, 66 Cong. Rec. 3923 (Feb. 17, 1925).

70. *Washington Post:* Oct. 21, 1924, at 2:4; Jan. 6, 1925, at 3:1; Jan. 7, 1925, at 1:5; Feb. 25, 1925, at 2:6; *Rent Comm'n Report,* 35; Thomas P. Gore to Calvin Coolidge, Feb. 10, 1925, enclosing letter from Frederick M. Corse, Secretary in Charge, N.Y. Life Ins. Co., to Fred Thorpe Nesbit, Jan. 23, 1925, Library of Congress, Calvin Coolidge Papers, case 63, reel 52; 66 Cong Rec. 4488–4491 (Feb. 23, 1925) (Rep. La Guardia).

71. H.R. Rep. No. 467, 68th Cong., 1st Sess. 3 (1924); 65 Cong. Rec. 6515 (Apr. 16, 1924) (Rep. Hill); *Rent Comm'n Report,* 5–8; 66 Cong. Rec. 1183 (Jan. 3, 1925) (Rep. Blanton); *Washington Post:* Feb. 20, 1925, at 2:3; Feb. 22, 1925, at 4:1; Feb. 23, 1925, at 1:4; Feb. 24, 1925, at 1:8; Feb. 25, 1925, at 2:1; Feb. 26, 1925, at 2:6; Feb. 27, 1925, at 2:2. Thomas Blanton would no doubt have suffered the same reaction had he visited New York 270 years earlier. "In 1655 you might have gone from the Penobscot all the way to Harlem River without meeting any other civilized language than English, but in crossing the island of Manhattan, you might have heard a dozen or fifteen European languages spoken. At that early state the place had

already begun to exhibit the cosmopolitan character which has ever since distinguished it." 1 John Fiske, *The Dutch and Quaker Colonies in America*, 267–268 (Boston, 1902).

9. Preserving the Legacy

1. Hamilton v. Kentucky Distilleries Co., 251 U.S. 146 (1919); Senate Committee on Government Operations, 94th Cong., 2d Sess., *The National Emergencies Act*, 1–2, 5, 351–354 (Committee Print 1976); Senate Committee on Termination of the National Emergency, *Summary of Emergency Power Statutes*, iii, 17–46 (Committee Print 1973); International Emergency Economic Powers Act, 50 U.S.C. §§ 1701–1706 (1982).

2. Laurence H. Tribe, *American Constitutional Law*, 305–317 (2d ed., Mineola, N.Y., 1988).

3. Bowsher v. Synar, 106 S.Ct. 3181, 3186 (1986); Arthur M. Schlesinger, Jr., *The Imperial Presidency* (Boston, 1973); Arthur M. Schlesinger, Jr., *The Cycles of American History*, 277–301 (Boston, 1986).

4. Clinton L. Rossiter, *Constitutional Dictatorship: Crisis Government in the Modern Democracies*, 219–220 (reprint, Westport, Conn., 1979); War Powers Resolution, 50 U.S.C. §§ 1541–1548 (1982), as amended (Supp. III, 1985); Allan Ides, "Congress, Constitutional Responsibility and the War Power," 17 *Loyola of Los Angeles Law Review* 599 (1984); National Emergencies Act, 50 U.S.C. §§ 1601–1651 (1982), as amended (Supp. III, 1985); Immigration and Naturalization Service v. Chadha, 462 U.S. 919 (1983).

5. Edward Keynes, *Undeclared War: Twilight Zone of Constitutional Power*, 66–67, 80 (University Park, Pa., 1982); Korematsu v. United States, 323 U.S. 214, 245 (1944) (Jackson, J., dissenting); United States v. Nixon, 418 U.S. 683, 706–711 (1974), quoting from United States v. Reynolds, 345 U.S. 1, 10 (1952).

6. 1 Alexis de Tocqueville, *Democracy in America*, 157 (reprint, New York, 1945); Louis Smith, *American Democracy and Military Power*, 264–267 (Chicago, 1951); Jesse H. Choper, *Judicial Review and the National Political Process: A Functional Reconsideration of the Role of the Supreme Court*, 142–146 (Chicago, 1980); Norman Redlich, "Concluding Observations: The Constitutional Dimension," in *The Tethered Presidency: Congressional Restraints on Executive Power*, ed. Thomas M. Frank, at 289 (New York, 1981).

7. Clinton Rossiter, *The Supreme Court and the Commander in Chief*, 91 (expanded ed., Ithaca, 1976); Learned Hand to Zechariah Chafee, Jr., Jan. 2, 1921, in Gerald Gunther, "Learned Hand and the Origins of Modern First Amendment Doctrine: Some Fragments of History," 27 *Stanford Law Review* 719, 770 (1975); Woods v. Cloyd W. Miller Co., 333 U.S. 138, 146 (1948) (Jackson, J., concurring); Smith, *American Democracy*, 262, 303–

304; and see Alexander M. Bickel, *The Least Dangerous Branch: The Supreme Court at the Bar of Politics,* 184 (Indianapolis, 1962).

8. Smith, *American Democracy,* 262–263; Alexander M. Bickel, *The Morality of Consent,* 88 (New Haven, 1975); Korematsu v. United States, 323 U.S. 214, 244 (1944) (Jackson, J., dissenting).

9. Cases overturning exercise of the war powers, and the war to which they related (with dates of hostilities), are as follows: undeclared naval war with France (1798–1800): Little v. Barreme, 6 U.S. (2 Cranch) 170 (1804); Brown v. United States, 12 U.S. (8 Cranch) 110 (1814); Mexican War (1846–1848): Mitchell v. Harmony, 54 U.S. (13 How.) 115 (1852); Jecker v. Montgomery, 54 U.S. (13 How.) 498 (1852); Civil War (1861–1865): Ex parte Milligan, 71 U.S. (4 Wall.) 2, 109 (1866) (emphasis in original); Hepburn v. Griswold, 75 U.S. (8 Wall.) 603 (1870); Raymond v. Thomas, 91 U.S. 712 (1876); Spanish-American War (1898): Dooley v. United States, 182 U.S. 222 (1901); World War I (1917–1918): United States v. L. Cohen Grocery Co., 255 U.S. 81 (1921); cf. Chastleton Corp. v. Sinclair, 264 U.S. 543 (1924).

10. Ex parte Endo, 323 U.S. 283 (1944); Duncan v. Kahanamoku, 327 U.S. 304 (1946); Rossiter, *Supreme Court and Commander in Chief,* 127. For discussion of the World War II cases, see ibid., 40–120; Alan I. Bigel, *The Supreme Court on Emergency Powers, Foreign Affairs, and Protection of Civil Liberties, 1935–1975* (Lanham, Md., 1986).

11. Dennis v. United States, 341 U.S. 494 (1951); Youngstown Sheet & Tube Co. v. Sawyer, 343 U.S. 579, 587–588 (1952). Any danger that *Youngstown* might interfere with the war effort was further minimized by the fact that the Taft-Hartley Act authorized the president in an emergency to obtain a strike injunction for an eighty-day cooling-off period. Ibid., 343 U.S. at 586; 29 U.S.C. §§ 176–180 (1982); Truman did not invoke this authority.

12. The court-martial cases were: United States ex rel. Toth v. Quarles, 350 U.S. 11 (1955); Reid v. Covert, 354 U.S. 1 (1957); Kinsella v. United States ex rel. Singleton, 361 U.S. 234 (1960); Grisham v. Hagan, 361 U.S. 278 (1960); McElroy v. United States ex rel. Guagliardo, 361 U.S. 281 (1960). The Communist party cases were: Aptheker v. Secretary of State, 378 U.S. 500 (1964); United States v. Robel, 389 U.S. 258, 263–264 (1967), quoting Home Building & Loan Ass'n v. Blaisdell, 290 U.S. 398, 426 (1934).

13. Trop v. Dulles, 356 U.S. 86 (1958); Kennedy v. Mendoza-Martinez, 372 U.S. 144, 185 (1963).

14. Mottola v. Nixon, 318 F.Supp. 538 (N.D. Calif. 1970), *rev'd,* 464 F.2d 178 (9th Cir. 1972); Holtzman v. Schlesinger, 361 F.Supp. 553 (E.D. N.Y.), *rev'd,* 484 F.2d 1307 (2d Cir.), order stayed, 414 U.S. 1321 (1973), *cert. denied,* 416 U.S. 936 (1974). On Vietnam, see Robert P. Sugarman, "Judicial Decisions Concerning the Constitutionality of United States Military Activity in Indo-China: A Bibliography of Court Decisions," 13 *Colum-*

bia Journal of Transnational Law 470 (1974); Anthony A. D'Amato and Robert M. O'Neil, *The Judiciary and Vietnam* (New York, 1972); Keynes, *Undeclared War*, 119–160; Schlesinger, *Imperial Presidency*, 288–295. On Central America, see Crockett v. Reagan, 558 F.Supp. 893 (D.D.C. 1982), *aff'd*, 720 F.2d 1355 (D.C. Cir. 1983), *cert. denied*, 467 U.S. 1251 (1984) (El Salvador); Sanchez-Espinoza v. Reagan, 568 F.Supp. 596 (D.D.C. 1983), *aff'd*, 770 F.2d 202 (D.C. Cir. 1985) (Nicaragua); Chaser Shipping Corp. v. United States, 108 S. Ct. 695 (1988) (Nicaragua); Ramirez de Arellano v. Weinberger, 568 F. Supp. 1236 (D.D.C. 1983), *rev'd*, 745 F.2d 1500 (D.C. Cir. 1984), *vacated*, 471 U.S. 1113 (1985) (Honduras); Francis D. Wormuth and Edwin B. Firmage, *To Chain the Dog of War: The War Power of Congress in History and Law*, 248–254 (Dallas, 1986).

15. Alexander M. Bickel, "Forward: The Passive Virtues," 75 *Harvard Law Review* 40, 48 (1961); and see Bickel, *Least Dangerous Branch*, 29–33, 129.

16. Rossiter, *Supreme Court and Commander in Chief*, 129; "Brandeis Frankfurter Conversations," Louis D. Brandeis Papers, Harvard Law School Library, Box 114, folders 7–8, and Melvin I. Urofsky, "The Brandeis-Frankfurter Conversations," *1985 Supreme Court Review* 299, 323–324.

17. Hirabayashi v. United States, 320 U.S. 81 (1943), upholding conviction for curfew violation in Seattle, Wash.; Yasui v. United States, 320 U.S. 115 (1943), upholding conviction for curfew violation in Portland, Ore.; Korematsu v. United States, 323 U.S. 214 (1944), upholding conviction for violation of exclusion order; Commission on Wartime Relocation and Internment of Civilians, *Personal Justice Denied*, 18, 27–44, 51–63, 69–72, 86–92, 382 n.175 (Washington, D.C., 1982) (hereinafter, *Comm'n on Wartime Relocation*); Carey McWilliams, *Brothers under the Skin*, 140–169 (rev. ed., Boston, 1964); Peter Irons, *Justice at War: The Story of the Japanese American Internment Cases*, 202–208, 280–284 (New York, 1983).

18. Irons, *Justice at War*, 208–212, 285–292; Yasui v. United States (D.Ore., Jan. 26, 1984) (unreported) (granting government's motion to dismiss indictment, vacate conviction, and dismiss petition for writ of coram nobis), *remanded*, 772 F.2d 1496 (9th Cir. 1985); Korematsu v. United States, 584 F.Supp. 1406 (N.D. Calif. 1984) (granting writ of coram nobis to vacate conviction); Hirabayashi v. United States 828 F.2d 591 (9th Cir. 1987) (granting writ of coram nobis to vacate conviction); and see United States v. Hohri, 107 S.Ct. 2246 (1987).

19. Hirabayashi v. United States, 320 U.S. 81, 93 (1943); United States v. Carolene Products Co., 304 U.S. 144, 152 n.4 (1938). Stone also suggested that heightened scrutiny was appropriate where "legislation appears on its face to be within a specific prohibition of the Constitution." The curfew, evacuation, and detention orders qualified for stricter review on this basis as well, for they impinged on the interest in personal liberty protected by the

Fifth Amendment. See Ebel v. Drum, 52 F.Supp. 189, 194–196 & n.5 (D.Mass. 1943), invalidating the evacuation order issued against naturalized citizen of German descent, noting that because it imposed a "drastic restriction of individual liberty," it should be tested under the due process standards applicable to restrictions on speech. Because Japanese immigrants were barred by federal law from acquiring citizenship through naturalization, none of the immigrant-generation Issei were eligible to vote. Few second-generation Nisei, who acquired citizenship by birth in the United States, were old enough to vote in 1942. See *Comm'n on Wartime Relocation,* 28–31, 99.

20. Irons, *Justice at War,* 186–218, 223–226, 242–247; *Comm'n on Wartime Relocation,* 90–92; Hirabayashi v. United States, 320 U.S. 81, 100, 102 (1943) (emphasis added); ibid., 110–111 (Murphy, J., concurring).

21. Korematsu v. United States, 323 U.S. 214, 217–218 (1944).

22. *Comm'n on Wartime Relocation,* 50. See also ibid., 236–238; Eugene V. Rostow, "The Japanese American Cases—A Disaster," 54 *Yale Law Journal* 489, 505–509, 520–523, 531 (1945); Korematsu v. United States, 323 U.S. 214, 245–246 (1944) (Jackson, J., dissenting); Rossiter, *Supreme Court and Commander in Chief,* 116. Several district courts on the East Coast applied a more searching standard in overturning individual evacuation orders against naturalized citizens of German descent. *Comm'n on Wartime Relocation,* 115–116. No racial discrimination was involved in these cases, for the actions were taken under a proclamation applying to all persons, regardless of ancestry, whose presence was deemed dangerous to national defense. Nevertheless, closer scrutiny was called for owing to the orders' severe interference with personal liberty. Schueller v. Drum, 51 F.Supp. 383 (E.D. Pa. 1943); Ebel v. Drum, 52 F.Supp. 189 (D.Mass. 1943).

23. See Bickel, *Least Dangerous Branch,* 183–198; Fritz W. Scharpf, "Judicial Review and the Political Question: A Functional Analysis," 75 *Yale Law Journal* 517 (1966); Michael E. Tigar, "Judicial Power, The 'Political Question Doctrine,' and Foreign Relations," 17 *UCLA Law Review* 1135 (1970); Philippa Strum, *The Supreme Court and "Political Questions": A Study in Judicial Evasion* (University, Alabama, 1975); Louis Henkin, "Is There a 'Political Question' Doctrine?" 85 *Yale Law Journal* 597 (1976); Irwin Chemerinsky, *Interpreting the Constitution,* 95-105 (New York, 1987); Baker v. Carr, 369 U.S. 186, 217 (1962); Goldwater v. Carter, 444 U.S. 996, 998–1001 (1979) (Powell, J., concurring).

24. Bickel, "Passive Virtues," 75; Scharpf, "Political Question," 559.

25. Louis Henkin, *Foreign Affairs and the Constitution,* 214 (Mineola, N.Y., 1972); Baker v. Carr, 369 U.S. 186, 211 (1962); Strum, *Political Questions,* 144; Goldwater v. Carter, 444 U.S. 996, 1004–1005 (1979) (Rehnquist, J., concurring); Wormuth, *Dog of War,* 245. In one Vietnam War case, Atlee v. Laird, 347 F.Supp. 689 (E.D. Pa. 1972), *aff'd* sub nom. Atlee v. Richardson, 411 U.S. 911 (1973), by summarily affirming a dis-

missal which rested entirely on political question grounds, the Court may have endorsed that position; while such an affirmance is binding on the lower courts (Hicks v. Miranda, 422 U.S. 332, 343–345 [1975]), however, it carries little weight with the Supreme Court. Edelman v. Jordan, 415 U.S. 651, 670–671 (1974).

26. Woods v. Cloyd W. Miller Co., 333 U.S. 138, 146 (1948) (Jackson, J., concurring); Bickel, *Least Dangerous Branch*, 39; Rossiter, *Constitutional Dictatorship*, 296–297.

27. Rossiter, *Constitutional Dictatorship*, 242, 249, 257–261, 268–271, 299; Rossiter, *Supreme Court and Commander in Chief*, 89–91.

28. Choper, *Judicial Review*, 260–330; Thomas M. Cooley, *Constitutional Limitations*, 56, 192–193 (2d ed., Boston, 1871); James B. Thayer, "The Origin and Scope of the American Doctrine of Constitutional Law," 7 *Harvard Law Review* 129 (1893), reprinted in James B. Thayer, *Legal Essays*, 1 (Boston, 1908); and see Chemerinsky, *Interpreting the Constitution*, 100–105.

29. Korematsu v. United States, 323 U.S. 214, 246 (1944) (Jackson, J., dissenting); Bickel, "Passive Virtues," 48–49; Scharpf, "Political Question," 559–560. But see Henkin, " 'Political Question' Doctrine," 600–601, suggesting that under a political question approach the Court implicitly affirms the constitutionality of the challenged action.

30. Cf. Smith, *American Democracy*, 302; Scharpf, "Political Question," 583–584; Tigar, "Judicial Review," 1151–1152; Keynes, *Undeclared War*, 82.

31. Keynes, *Undeclared War*, 173–174; Scharpf, "Political Question," 567–568.

32. Korematsu v. United States, 323 U.S. 214 (1944); Duncan v. Kahanamoku, 327 U.S. 304 (1946); Rossiter, *Supreme Court and Commander in Chief*, 59; Holtzman v. Richardson, 361 F.Supp. 544, 551 (E.D. N.Y. 1973); Holtzman v. Schlesinger, 361 F.Supp. 553 (E.D. N.Y. 1973); Keynes, *Undeclared War*, 139–142, 151–152.

33. Bickel, "Passive Virtues," 41, 49, 77.

34. Smith, *American Democracy*, 285; Bickel, "Passive Virtues," 50.

35. Tigar, "Judicial Review," 1148; Brown v. Board of Education, 347 U.S. 483 (1954); Roe v. Wade, 410 U.S. 113 (1973); *Los Angeles Times*, July 11, 1987, at 26:2; Rossiter, *Supreme Court and Commander in Chief*, 212; but see Rossiter, *Constitutional Dictatorship*, 127–128. On the Court's educational function, see Michael Perry, *The Constitution, the Courts, and Human Rights: An Inquiry into the Legitimacy of Constitutional Policymaking by the Judiciary*, 111–119 (New Haven, 1982); Choper, *Judicial Review*, 123–127, 138–139, 151–154.

36. See Edward L. Barrett, Jr., and William Cohen, *Constitutional Law: Cases and Materials*, 58–63 (7th ed., Mineola, N.Y., 1985); Charles Alan

Wright, *Handbook of the Law of Federal Courts*, 755–759 (4th ed., St. Paul, Minn., 1983).

37. On the delays in Ex parte Endo, 323 U.S. 283 (1944), see Irons, *Justice at War*, 102–103, 144–151, 255–257, 265–268. Because of the Sixth Amendment right to a speedy trial, this device cannot be employed at the trial stage in criminal cases.

38. Irons, *Justice at War*, 102–103, 255–258; Rossiter, *Supreme Court and Commander in Chief*, 57 n.49, 61–63, discussing Zimmerman v. Walker, 319 U.S. 744 (1943) and Montgomery Ward & Co. v. United States, 326 U.S. 690 (1945); 13A Wright, Miller, and Cooper, *Federal Practice and Procedure*, §§ 3533.7–3533.8 (St. Paul, Minn., 1984); Roe v. Wade, 410 U.S. 113, 125 (1973); United States v. W. T. Grant Co., 345 U.S. 629, 632–633 (1953).

39. Tribe, *American Constitutional Law*, 77–82; 13A Wright, *Federal Practice*, § 3532.3; see, e.g., Babbitt v. United Farm Workers National Union, 442 U.S. 289, 300 (1979). Additional means of deferring review include dismissal for failure to exhaust other remedies, denial of injunctive relief for want of equity, and, in a suit for declaratory relief, dismissal on the ground that this remedy is discretionary with the court. Tigar, "Judicial Review," 1150–1151.

40. Wormuth, *Dog of War*, 241–244; Keynes, *Undeclared War*, 133–134; Goldwater v. Carter, 444 U.S. 996, 997–998 (Powell, J., concurring); Youngstown Sheet & Tube Co. v. Sawyer, 343 U.S. 579 (1952); Immigration and Naturalization Service v. Chadha, 462 U.S. 919, 942 n.13 (1983); ibid., 462 U.S. at 969 & n.5 (White, J., dissenting); and see National League of Cities v. Usery, 426 U.S. 833, 841–842 n.12 (1976).

41. On the statute of limitations, see Stewart v. Kahn, 78 U.S. (11 Wall.) 493 (1871); American Pipe & Constr. Co. v. Utah, 414 U.S. 538, 552–555 (1974); Burnett v. New York Central R.R., 380 U.S. 424 (1965); and see Johnson v. Railway Express Agency, Inc., 421 U.S. 454, 463–467 (1975). On mootness, see 13A Wright, *Federal Practice*, § 3533.8; United States v. W. T. Grant Co., 345 U.S. 629, 632 (1953).

42. Baker v. Carr, 369 U.S. 186, 213–214 (1962); Woods v. Cloyd W. Miller Co., 333 U.S. 138, 146–147 (1948) (Jackson, J., concurring); Youngstown Sheet & Tube Co. v. Sawyer, 343 U.S. 579, 587 (1952); Keynes, *Undeclared War*, 76–77.

43. Bickel, "Passive Virtues," 58–68; on statutory interpretation as a device for controlling executive policy making, see Paul Gewirtz, "The Courts, Congress, and Executive Policy-Making: Notes on Three Doctrines," 40 *Law and Contemporary Problems* (Summer 1976), at 46.

44. Smith, *American Democracy*, 284; Tigar, "Judicial Review," 1177–1178; 18 U.S.C. App., Classified Information Procedures Act, § 6(e)(2) (1982); Jencks Act, 18 U.S.C. § 3500(d) (1982); Fed. R. Crim. P. 16(d)(2).

Courts have thus been reluctant to invoke the political question doctrine against individual rights claims. See Henkin, *Foreign Affairs,* 215-216, 253 n.; Scharpf, "Political Question," 584.

45. Owen M. Fiss, "Forward: The Forms of Justice," 93 *Harvard Law Review* 1, 52 (1979); on the use of declaratory but not injunctive relief, see, e.g., Steffel v. Thompson, 415 U.S. 452 (1974).

46. Korematsu v. United States, 323 U.S. 214, 248 (1944) (Jackson, J., dissenting).

Index

Abrams v. United States, 195, 199, 202
Acheson, Dean, 202–203
Adams, Abigail, 189
Adams, John Quincy, 16
Addams, Jane, 11
Adkins v. Children's Hospital, 236, 238
Albany Journal, 123
Amalgamated Clothing Workers, 183–184
American Bar Association, 238, 287 n.53
American Federation of Labor (AFL): on judicial review, 11, 12; and public ownership, 29, 30, 33, 37, 50, 99; and telegraph strike, 53; and Prohibition, 75–76; and A. Mitchell Palmer, 82, 126; and cost of living, 97; and coal strike injunction, 126–127; contemplated prosecution of, 158
American Legion, 113, 150, 151, 153, 157, 160–161
American Telephone and Telegraph Co. (AT&T), 32–33, 38, 39, 43, 46, 47. *See also* Vail, Theodore N.
Anderson, Pete, 159
Anderson, William H., 63
Anheuser-Busch Brewing Association, 80–81, 82
Anti-Saloon League of America: influence of, 60–63, 64, 66, 70–71, 73, 76, 89, 90, 91, 92; prewar dry crusade, 60–62; war strategy of, 62–64; and Lever Act, 64, 65, 66; and War-Time Prohibition Act, 66, 77, 79, 84, 93; and constitutional questions, 71–72; and A. Mitchell Palmer, 81–82; and brewers, 81–82; and woman suffrage, 82; and war beer, 86; and Volstead Act, 86, 87; and Louis D. Brandeis, 338 n.24
Aswell, James B., 29, 30, 34, 46
Ault, E. B., 152–153

Baker, Newton D., 30, 34, 186–187
Baker, Rev. Purley, 61–62
Baker v. Carr, 264–265
Ball, Lewis Heisler, 228, 229, 231
Ball Rent Law (1919): terms of, 109, 110–111, 112, 223–224, 226; constitutional questions concerning, 109–112; challenges to, 224–227; extension (1921), 229–230; extension (1922), 231–234, 235, 240–244, 247–248; extension (1924), 239–240, 244–247, 248–249; proposed extension (1925), 249–252
Baltimore News, 182
Baltimore Sun, 50, 178–179, 180, 182, 184
Bankhead, John H., 70
Barkley, Alben W., 58
Battle, Edgar C., 175

Beard, Charles A., *An Economic Interpretation of the Constitution of the United States*, 10
Bee, Carlos, 116
Begg, James T., 112, 231, 245
Bell, Josephine, 170
Berger, Victor L., 177, 187
Bickel, Alexander M., 257, 261, 265, 266, 269
Bill of Rights, 9, 267. *See also* War powers, and Bill of Rights
Black, Henry Campbell, 141, 196
Black, Hugo L., 263
Blackstone, William, 193
Bland, Oscar E., 215
Blanton, Thomas L., 250, 252
Blethen, Clarance B., 151, 152
Block v. Hirsh, 232–233, 235–236, 237, 243; proceedings in, 224–227; significance of, 227, 252–253; Congress's response to, 228–230, 240, 245–246
Borah, William E., 92–93, 178, 190
Bourquin, George M., 136
Brandegee, Frank B., 110
Brandeis, Louis D.: and revolution, 3–4; and Espionage and Sedition Acts, 195, 202, 261; and *Hamilton v. Kentucky Distilleries Co.*, 198–203, 265; on concentration of power, 202–203; on judicial review, 203, 242, 261; and *Ruppert v. Caffey*, 204; and Lever Act, 221–222, 344 n.70; and *Chastleton Corp. v. Sinclair*, 241–242, 244; influence on Oliver W. Holmes, Jr., 337 n.9; and Prohibition, 338 n.24
Brennan, William J., 264–265, 273
Brewing and Liquor Interests and German and Bolshevik Propaganda, 81
British Labour Party, 13, 31
Brown v. Board of Education, 270
Brueggeman, Olivia, 121–122
Bryan, William Jennings, 37, 64
Burke, Edmund, 257
Burleson, Albert S., 15; and labor, 13, 48–50, 52–53, 123; and public ownership, 30, 31, 33–35, 37, 38, 44, 164; and cable seizure, 39–40; and demise of wire control, 45–54; and Prohibition, 64, 72; and censorship

of radical press, 163–164, 173–174, 176–177; and *Masses*, 165–171
Busch, Adolphus, 80
Busch, Lilly Anheuser, 80–81
Butler, Pierce, 235
Byrnes, James F., 174

California Farm Bureau Federation, 262
California Joint Immigration Committee, 262
Campbell, Philip P., 35
Cannon, Joseph G., 71
Cantrill, James C., 89
Capper, Arthur, 197
Carlton, Newcomb, 29, 32, 33, 36, 39, 43, 47, 48–49
Censorship. *See* Espionage Act; Post Office Department; Sedition Act; Trading with the Enemy Act
Central America, intervention in, 254, 255, 260
Centralia, Wash., Armistice Day riot, 150, 158
Chafee, Zechariah, Jr., 147, 287 n.53, 337 n.9
Chamberlain, George E., 126–127
Charles Wolff Packing Co. v. Court of Industrial Relations, 236–237
Chase, Salmon P., 19
Chastleton Corp. v. Sinclair, 235–249, 251, 252–253, 258
Chicago Post, 120
Chicago Socialist, 175
Chicago Tribune, 51, 198, 206
Chicago Yardmen's Association, 130
Choper, Jesse H., 267
Cincinnati Enquirer, 65
Civil War (1861–1865), 17, 18–19, 272, 285 n.44, 353 n.9
Clark, James B. (Champ), 140
Clark, Solomon, 135
Clarke, John H., 204, 232, 233–234, 235
Clayton Act (1914), 95, 124, 126–127
Clifford, Nathan, 19
Coady, Charles P., 90, 288 n.56
Cobb, Frank I., 178
Columbia Law Review, 20
Commentaries on the Constitution (Story), 16, 21–22
Commerce power, 15–16, 27, 95, 104–105, 255, 339 n.32

Commercial Cable Co., 40, 46, 47. *See also* Mackay, Clarence

Commercial Telegraphers Union of America (CTUA), 28–30, 33–34, 35, 48–49, 53

Commercial Trust Co. v. Miller, 246

Commission on Wartime Relocation and Internment of Civilians, 262, 263–264

Committee of Forty-Eight, 42, 160–161, 180–181

Communist Party, 160, 258–259

Congress: interpretation of Constitution by, 21–24, 71–72; and validity of telephone rate extension, 58–59; and validity of War-Time Prohibition Act, 69–71, 72; and validity of Volstead Act, 87–91, 92; and validity of amended Lever Act, 104–108; and validity of District rent control, 110–112, 228–230, 240; self-interest in rent control, 112, 231, 233–235; and validity of McNary Act, 115–116; and validity of Sedition Act, 138–141; independence of in wartime, 266–267

Connally, Thomas T., 212

Constitution: attack on framers of, 9–10; interpretation of by political branches, 21–22, 24, 71–72; judicial construction of, 22–24, 71–72. *See also* Commerce power; Eighteenth Amendment; Postal power; Taxing power; War powers

Cooley, Thomas M., 23, 71, 267

Coolidge, Calvin, 189, 190, 247, 249–252

Corwin, Edward S., 10

Cost of living: prearmistice, 94–95, 96, 123; in 1919–1920, 97, 101, 105–106, 113, 116; and social unrest, 97–100; impact of government on, 122; and repeal of Lever Act, 211–212, 215; and federal employees, 230. *See also* Price control; Profiteering

Cover, Robert M., 194

Cox, James M., 129, 214

Creel, George, 42, 135

Croly, Herbert, 3, 14, 98, 122, 202

Cummins, Albert B., 99, 139

Current Opinion, 43

Currie, Gilbert A., 92

Dakota Central Telephone Co. v. South Dakota, 55–57, 58–59, 89, 192, 200

Daniels, Josephus, 30, 34, 64, 128

Davis, Horace A., 10

Davis, John W., 170

Day, William R., 201–202, 203, 204, 235, 238, 344 n.70

Debs, Eugene V., 154, 187, 189

Debs v. United States, 194, 203

Dell, Floyd, 170

Demobilization: and Prohibition, 74, 76–78, 87, 88, 89–90, 91, 92–93; and 1919 coal strike, 92–93, 128; and War-Time Prohibition Act, 128, 201; and Volstead Act, 205

Democracy and the Eastern Question (Millard), 182

Denison, Edward E., 58–59

Dennis v. United States, 258

DeSilver, Albert, 179–180

Dial, Nathaniel B., 104

District of Columbia: rent control in, 112, 231–232, 233–235, 249; housing shortage in, 226–227, 229, 232–233, 239–240, 247; representation in Congress, 230–231. *See also* Ball Rent Law; Saulsbury Resolution

District of Columbia Rent Commission, 109, 112, 223–224, 233–235, 247–249

Dodd, Walter F., 8

Douglas, Paul H., 230

Duncan v. Kahanamoku, 258, 268, 273, 274

Durant, Will, 13

Dyer, Leonidas C., 64

Eastman, Crystal, 172, 173

Eastman, Max, 164–167, 169–171, 173, 176, 177

Economic Interpretation of the Constitution, An (Beard), 10

Eddy, R. E., 159

Edgar A. Levy Leasing Co. v. Siegel, 232, 233, 234, 237, 240

Eighteenth Amendment, 60, 61–63, 86, 87, 199

Emergency, states of, 254

Emergency power. *See* War powers

Esch, John J., 58

Espionage Act (1917): terms of, 132–133, 162; wartime use of, 134; am-

Espionage Act (1917) (*Cont.*)
nesty for victims of, 144–145, 146,
149, 179, 186–189; and *Masses*,
165–171; and *Liberator,* 171–173;
calls for repeal of, 179–180; retention of, 181–184, 334 n.45; jury opposition to, 184–186, 190; and
judicial review, 192–195. *See also*
Sedition Act
Executive privilege, 256
Ex parte Endo, 258, 270–271, 273
Ex parte Milligan, 19, 20, 199, 258,
286 n.47

Fall, Albert B., 139–140
Federal Control Act (1918), 27–28
Federalist, The, 16
Field, Stephen J., 19
Figg, Howard E., 121, 122, 129
Fiss, Owen M., 274
Fletcher, Duncan U., 229
Fletcher, Henry J., 20
Food Administration, 65, 66, 74, 95–
96, 97, 114, 115. *See also* Hoover,
Herbert
Forcey, Charles, 98
Formalism, legal, 6–9
France, Joseph I., 139, 140, 182, 183, 211
France, undeclared naval war with
(1798–1800), 285 nn.44–45, 353 n.9
Frankfurter, Felix, 24, 48, 128, 203,
241, 242, 261
Freund, Ernst, 8
Friday, David, 123
Frohwerk v. United States, 194
Fuel Administration, 95–96, 97, 117,
125, 196

Gallagher, Thomas, 69, 288 n.56
Gard, Warren, 288 n.56
Garfield, Harry A., 125
Glintenkamp, Henry, 331 n.19
Goldman, Eric F., 2–3
Goldwater v. Carter, 265–266, 272
Gompers, Samuel, 50, 76, 118, 127
Gooding, Frank R., 229
Goodnow, Frank J., *Social Reform and
the Constitution,* 8
Goodykoontz, Wells, 212
Gordon, William, 70
Government ownership. *See* Public
ownership

Grant, A. G., 159
Grayson, Cary T., 209
"Great Madness, The" (Nearing), 184
Green, William R., 140
Gregory, Thomas W.: and return of
cables, 51; and Busch property, 80–
81; and Lever Act as strike weapon,
127; and Sedition Act, 143–144,
148, 176, 330 n.2; and *Masses,* 170;
and War-Time Prohibition Act, 304
n.28
Grenada, invasion of, 255
Griffith, Arthur, "How Ireland Has
Prospered under English Rule and the
Slave Mind," 175, 182
Gross, A., 159

Haines, Charles Grove, 35
Hamilton, Alexander, 16, 20
Hamilton v. Kentucky Distilleries Co.,
222, 225, 227, 253; background of,
191–192, 195–196; Supreme Court
decision in, 196–203; reaction to,
206–207; and lower courts, 216–
220, 224; significance of, 254–256;
application of in wartime, 257–260,
261, 275; and political question doc-
trine, 265
Hamlin, Courtney, 20
Hammer, William C., 246
Hand, Augustus N., 167, 170, 342–343
n.63
Hand, Learned, 166, 168, 170, 191,
194, 257, 337 n.9
Hard, William, 178
Harding, Warren G., 37, 189, 214,
232, 235
Hardwick, Thomas W., 20, 137
Hardy, Rufus, 90–91, 288 n.56
Harrison, Byron P., 104–105
Harvard Law Review, 207
Hawaii, martial law in, 258, 268, 273,
274
Hays, Will H., 173, 176
Henkin, Louis, 265
Hepburn v. Griswold, 18, 222
Hersey, Ira G., 89, 111, 244
Hines, Walker D., 44–45, 124–125,
130, 310 n.76
Hirabayashi v. United States, 261–262,
263–264
Hitchcock, Gilbert M., 42

Hoarding, and Lever Act, 101–102, 103–104, 115, 117

Hofstadter, Richard, 3

Hollis, Henry F., 126

Holmes, Oliver Wendell, Jr.: on judicial opposition to reform, 5; and instrumentalism, 7, 8, 11; and freedom of speech, 9, 190, 193–195; 199–200, 202, 203; and *Hamilton v. Kentucky Distilleries Co.*, 198, 203; and *Block v. Hirsh*, 226–227, 245–246; on rent control, 237; and *Chastleton Corp. v. Sinclair*, 240–244, 245–246

Holtzman v. Schlesinger, 260, 261, 269, 273, 274

Hoover, Herbert, 65, 66, 74, 118, 344 n.70

Hopkins, Ernest, 179

Hotzee, William, 149–150, 160

Hough, Charles M., 166

House, Col. Edward M., 31, 72, 73, 76, 170

Houston, David F., 310 n.76

"How Ireland Has Prospered under English Rule and the Slave Mind" (Griffith), 175, 182

Huddleston, George, 105, 108–109, 210

Hughes, Charles Evans: on war powers, 19–20, 41, 180, 208; on cable seizure, 47; and Lever Act, 218, 220, 342–343 n.63; on constitutional interpretation, 288 n.56

Husted, James W., 90, 288 n.56

Husting, Paul O., 127

Igoe, William L., 212, 288 n.56

Independent, 186

Industrial Workers of the World (IWW), 130; wartime repression of, 134–136, 158, 328 n.56, 329 n.64; and adoption of Sedition Act, 137, 141; postwar prosecution of, 150, 151, 157–160, 183, 189, 197; postal censorship of, 164, 174–175

Instrumentalism, 7–9, 21

Isaacson, Jacob, 148–149, 156, 160, 179, 185

Jackson, Robert H., 257, 264, 266, 267, 273, 275

James, William, 7

Japanese-American internment cases, 258, 261–264, 268, 270–271, 273

Jassinka, John, 160

Jefferson, Thomas, 21, 178, 188–189, 190

Johnson, Andrew, 286 n.46

Johnson, Hiram W., 139

Jones, Andrieus A., 233

Jones, Wesley L., 141, 212

Judd, Orrin, 260, 268–269

Judge's Bill, 238–239

Judicial review: and reform movement, 4–5; attacks on foundation of, 5–10; popular opposition to, 10–11, 13, 238; and rule of clear mistake, 11, 267; efforts to curb, 11–13; and role of political branches, 21–23, 71–72; and legislative motive, 24–25, 199. *See also* Formalism; Instrumentalism —of war powers: pre-1918, 16–21; and rail and wire control, 54–59, 192, 200; and wartime prohibition, 191–192, 195–207; and Espionage and Sedition Acts, 192–195, 199; and Lever Act, 215–222; and rent control, 223–227, 235, 240–244, 247–249; wartime limitations on, 256–258, 268; in World War II era, 258; in Korean War era, 258–259; and Warren Court, 259–260; and Vietnam War, 260, 264–266, 268–269, 272; and Central America, 260; ritualistic exercise of, 261–264, 267–268; and political question doctrine, 264–268; deferral of, 268–275. *See also* Supreme Court; War powers

Juodis, J., 160

Juries: and prohibition, 83, 85, 87; and Espionage and Sedition Acts, 170, 184–186, 190

Justice Department, 137, 139, 140, 174, 248. *See also* Gregory, Thomas W.; Palmer, A. Mitchell; Profiteering

Kahn, Julius, 68, 288 n.56

Kangas, Gus, 159

Kellogg, Frank B., 36, 41, 111

Kellogg, Paul U., 155

Kennedy v. Mendoza-Martinez, 259–260

Kenyon, William S., 105, 107, 120–121

King, William H., 244–245

Kirchner, H. E., 161
Kitchin, Claude, 209–210, 211
Knox, Philander C., 210
Knox-Porter Peace Resolution, 208–211
Kohlsaat, Herman Henry, 40
Konenkamp, Sylvester J., 28–29
Korean War, 254, 258–260
Korematsu v. United States, 261–262, 263–264, 267, 268, 271
Korpi, John, 159

Labor, organized: and Albert S. Burleson, 33, 48–50; and Prohibition, 75–76; and A. Mitchell Palmer, 82–83, 122, 126, 127, 130; and Progressives, 98, 122–123; and cost of living, 98–100, 123. *See also* American Federation of Labor; Strikes
La Follette, Robert M., 11, 12–13, 238, 245, 247
La Follette's Magazine, 10
La Guardia, Fiorello H., 97, 246–247
Lake and Export Coal Co., 221
Lamar, William H., 171–172, 174, 175–176
Lamont, Thomas W., 37
Lampinen, Alfred, 159
Lane, Franklin K., 30
Lansing, Robert, 39
Laski, Harold J., 203
Lea, Clarence F., 90, 288 n.56
League for Amnesty of Political Prisoners, 179
Legal Tender Cases, 18, 222
Legislative motive, and judicial review, 24–25, 199
Lenroot, Irvine L., 36, 118
Lever, Asbury F., 70, 126
Lever Food and Fuel Control Act (1917), 57; and Prohibition, 64–65, 66, 67–68, 73–75, 83; and price controls, 95–96, 100–103; profiteering amendment to, 104–108; and coal strikes, 124–129, 131–132, 196; and railroad strikes, 129, 130–131, 210, 211–212; retention and repeal of, 209–210, 211–212, 214–215; challenges to, 216–222, 273. *See also* Profiteering
Lewis, James H., 20
Liberator, 164, 171–173, 177
Libya, bombing of, 254, 255
Lincoln, Abraham, 19

Lippmann, Walter, 3, 8, 94–95
Listman, George P., 152–153
Literary Digest, 50
Lodge, Henry Cabot, 92, 138, 197–198
London, Meyer, 181, 183
Luce, Robert, 89, 246

Mackay, Clarence, 29, 40, 46–48
Mapes, Carl E., 111
Marbury v. Madison, 10
Marcus Brown Holding Co. v. Feldman, 227, 232, 233, 237, 240
Marshall, John, 10, 18, 21, 23, 24, 71
Masses, 164–171, 173, 184, 185
Masses Publishing Co. v. Patten, 165–166, 167, 168
McAdoo, William Gibbs, 30, 37, 44–45, 64, 187–188, 293 n.40, 304 n.28
McCloskey, Robert G., 236
McCulloch v. Maryland, 18
McKenna, Joseph, 195, 236, 243, 246
McLaughlin, James C., 111
McNary Act (1919), 115–116, 197
McReynolds, James C., 201–202, 203, 204, 205–206, 236, 238, 243
Meeker, Jacob E., 70–71
Mencken, H. L., 62–63, 70
Meridian Mansion rent case, 233–235
Mexican War (1846–1848), 18, 285 n.44, 286 n.47, 353 n.9
Millard, Thomas F., *Democracy and the Eastern Question,* 182
Miller v. United States, 19, 20
Milwaukee Leader, 176–177
Missouri, profiteering campaign in, 121–122
Mitchell v. Harmony, 18
Montgomery Ward and Co., 271
Moon, John A., 58–59
Moore, J. Hampton, 35
Moore, Robert Walton, 245
Mootness doctrine, 271, 272–273
Morgan, Donald G., 22, 70
Mossew, Joseph, 102–103
Mottola v. Nixon, 260, 261
Murphy, Frank, 263
Murray, Robert K., 136
Myers, Henry L., 98, 138, 140–141

Nation, 93, 126, 128, 180, 306 n.44
National Civil Liberties Bureau, 134, 136, 179

National Emergencies Act (1976), 256
National German-American Alliance, 62
Native Sons and Daughters of the Golden West, 262
Nearing, Scott, "The Great Madness," 184, 185, 186
Nelles, Walter, 179
Nelson, Knute, 138, 183
Neterer, Jeremiah, 155, 156
New England Telephone and Telegraph Co., 49–50
New Freedom, The (Wilson), 119
New Jersey Chamber of Commerce, 75
New Republic, 45, 50, 52, 178
New York Call, 176, 197
New York City: enforcement of Espionage Act in, 184–186; rent control in, 227, 232, 237, 252
New York Evening Post, 51
New York Herald, 97
New York Life Insurance Co., 252
New York Merchants' Association, 131
New York Times: and wire control, 39, 41, 48, 52, 54; and public ownership, 43; and rail control, 45; and War-Time Prohibition Act, 73, 202, 206; and cost of living campaign, 102, 116, 118, 120; and war on radicalism, 133, 144, 161, 197; and *Masses*, 168–169; and Sedition Act, 180, 184, 185; and Porter-Knox Resolution, 209
New York World: and wire control, 46, 47, 52; article criticizing Burleson, 50–51; and War-Time Prohibition Act, 73, 76; and Volstead Act veto, 91; and cost of living campaign, 116; and Sedition Act, 180; and Porter-Knox Resolution, 211
Nichthauser, Joseph, 116, 118, 217
Nineteenth Amendment. *See* Woman suffrage
"No Beer, No Work" campaign, 75–76
Norris, George W., 68–69
North American Review, 72
Northern Pacific Railway v. North Dakota, 55–59, 89, 192, 200
Northern Securities Co. v. United States, 203
Nuovo Proletario, Il, 175

O'Brian, John Lord, 143–144, 163
Ogden, Sylvanus, 85
O'Sheel, Shaemas, 72
Overman, Lee S., 183
Owen, Robert L., 105

Palmer, A. Mitchell, 15; as alien property custodian, 20–21, 40, 79–81; on judicial review of war powers, 21, 106–107; and wartime prohibition, 75, 77, 78–86; presidential ambitions, 81–82, 122, 318 n.64; and labor, 82–83, 122, 126, 127, 130; bombing of home, 83; and cost of living campaign, 99–104, 115, 118–122, 196–197, 222; and strikes, 124, 125–126, 127, 129–131; and Espionage and Sedition Acts, 144–150, 181, 185, 186, 187, 336 n.4; and political prisoners, 146, 186–187, 188; and Centralia riot, 150–159; and censorship, 174, 175; and presidential signing of bills, 212–213
Paris peace conference, 15, 41–42, 175, 181–182
Peace: attainment of (1921), 1, 228, 232; prospects for in 1919, 197–198; Porter-Knox Resolution (1920), 208–211; Volstead Resolution (1920), 211–214; and 1920 campaign, 214; Volstead Resolution (1921), 214–215. *See also* Versailles Treaty
Peck v. Fink, 248–249, 251
Pennsylvania State Federation of Labor, 180, 184
Philadelphia Record, 72
Pierce v. United States, 195
Pinchot, Amos, 165
Pitney, Mahlon, 201–202, 203, 221–222, 235
Pittsburgh Dispatch, 120, 218–219
Plumb, Glenn E., 99
Plumb Plan, 99, 100
Poindexter, Miles, 181, 229, 230–231, 233
Political question doctrine, 264–265; and war powers, 18, 19–20, 22, 265–268; and rail and wire control, 55, 192; and Volstead Act, 88; and Espionage and Sedition Acts, 193–195; and War-Time Prohibition Act, 200–201, 207, 265, 338 n.20; and

Political question doctrine (*Cont.*)
Lever Act, 216, 220–221; and Vietnam War, 260, 264, 265
Pomerene, Atlee, 232
Populism, 2, 12, 26
Porter, Stephen G., 210, 213–214
Porter-Knox Peace Resolution, 208–211
Portland Telegram, 46
Postal power, 26, 27, 139, 324–325 n.16
Postal-Telegraph Company, 28–29, 32, 46–48, 51, 301 n.87. *See also* Mackay, Clarence
Post Office Department: censorship powers of, 134, 137, 162, 177; and Socialist Party, 135; and radical press, 164–177, 197. *See also* Burleson, Albert S.; Wire control
Pound, Roscoe, 6, 7, 8–9, 10–11
Powell, Lewis F., 272
Powell, Thomas Reed, 207
Pragmatic instrumentalism, 7–9
Pragmatism, 6–7, 14, 21, 42; and Prohibition, 70, 90; and Lever Act, 107; and rent control, 111–112; and civil liberties, 142, 190
President: interpretation of Constitution by, 21–22, 71–72; and signing of bills, 212–213; exercise of emergency power by, 255–256, 266–267; "Imperial Presidency," 255, 267
Preston, Frank, 149, 160
Price control: power to impose, 95, 97, 100; wartime measures, 95–96; after armistice, 96–97; and sugar, 103. *See also* Food Administration; Fuel Administration; Lever Food and Fuel Control Act; Profiteering
Profiteering: Fair Price Committees, 96, 101–102, 106, 114, 117; and Lever Act (1917), 99–101, 102–103, 117–118, 211; and sugar, 103, 114–116, 197; definition of, 106–107, 113–114, 116; Justice Department Women's Division, 113, 116, 117, 120, 121; Justice Department Flying Squadron, 113–114, 116, 117; and amended Lever Act (1919), 114, 115, 116, 117–118, 196; and clothing, 116; and fuel, 116–117, 196, 219–220, 221; and large corporations,

118, 120–121, 222; and woman suffrage, 119–122; and Missouri campaign, 121–122; challenges to profiteering provisions, 216–222
Progressive Party: of 1912, 3, 12, 95; of 1924, 11–12, 238
Progressivism, 2–3, 14; and revolution, 3–4, 14, 83, 98, 123; judicial opposition to, 4–5; and instrumentalism, 8; and Constitution, 9–10; after armistice, 13–14, 42, 96–97; and public ownership, 26, 95; and Prohibition, 60, 62; and cost of living, 95; and labor, 98, 122–123; waning of, 142
Prohibition: and Progressivism, 60, 62; Webb-Kenyon Act, 61, 71; power to enact, 61; and labor, 65, 66, 72, 73, 75–76, 78, 82–83; Selective Service Act, 68; and woman suffrage, 82. *See also* Anti-Saloon League of America; Eighteenth Amendment; Lever Food and Fuel Control Act; Volstead Act; War-Time Prohibition Act
Public ownership, 26–27, 42–43, 45, 54, 99. *See also* Rail control; Wire control
Public Ownership League of America, 42

Ragan, Fred D., 194
Rail control, 27–28, 44–45, 54. See also *Northern Pacific Railway v. North Dakota*
Randall, William, 159
Reagan, Ronald, 254, 260
Reconstruction, following World War I, 13, 97
Redlich, Norman, 257
Red Scare (1919–1920), 14, 15, 82–83, 141–142; and Prohibition, 83, 92; and cost of living campaign, 98, 99–100; and alien radicals, 142, 146, 148; and Espionage and Sedition Acts, 145, 150–151, 156
Reed, James A., 36, 110, 139
Reed, John, 144, 165, 170, 171, 173, 177, 185
Reform movement. *See* Progressivism
Rent control. *See* District of Columbia, rent control in; New York City, rent control in
Revolutionary Age, 175

Rhodes, Marion E., 231
Ripeness doctrine, 272–273, 274–275
Roche, Michael J., 271
Roe v. Wade, 270
Rogers, Henry W., 168, 170
Rogers, Merrill, 331 n.19
Roosevelt, Theodore, 3, 12
Roper, Daniel C., 74–75, 83
Rossiter, Clinton L., 257, 258, 261, 264, 268, 270
Roth, Charles and Julius, 114
Rudkin, Frank H., 219
Rumpinen, Eva, 159
Ruppert v. Caffey, 191–192, 195, 203–207, 220–221, 227
Russian Revolution (1917), 13, 98, 135–136, 141, 173
Rust, Frank, 152–153

St. Louis Brewing Association, 86
St. Louis Post-Dispatch, 40–41, 42, 51, 73, 118, 198, 207
Sanford, Edward T., 235
San Francisco Chronicle, 198, 206–207, 207–208
San Francisco Yardmen's Association, 131
Saulsbury, Willard, 110
Saulsbury Resolution (1918), 108, 110, 112, 224
Saunders, Robert C., 151–159, 175, 186
Schaefer v. United States, 195
Scharpf, Fritz W., 265
Scheiber, Harry N., 135, 143
Schenck v. United States, 193–195
Scripps, Edward W., 166–167
Seattle Times, 151, 152, 157
Seattle Union Record, 150–157, 160, 175–176, 177, 180, 186, 197
Sedition Act (1798), 139–140, 186, 188–190
Sedition Act (1918): aims and terms of, 136–138, 140–141, 156–158, 162; and strikes, 137, 154, 156, 183–184; validity of, 138–140, 142; and Act of 1798, 139, 188–190; enforcement policy, 143–147, 162–163, 174–175; amnesty for victims of, 144–145, 146, 149, 179, 186–189; postwar prosecutions under, 147–157, 159–161, 197; chilling effect of, 161,

177–179, 180–184, 186; and radical press, 173–177, 182–183, 332 n.32; efforts to repeal, 179–184, 189, 215; and juries, 184–187, 190; and judicial review, 192–195
Selective Service Act (1917), 68, 287–288 n.55
Separation of powers, 255–256, 266–267, 272
Shafroth, John F., 69
Shapiro, Stanley, 14
Sheppard, Morris, 32, 66, 68
Sherman, Lawrence Y., 36, 47, 111–112, 138, 139, 181, 182
Sherwood, Isaac R., 70, 288 n.56
Shields, John K., 89–90, 138–139
Siebold, Louis, 66, 76, 213
Siegel, Isaac, 197
Slayden, James L., 70
Smith, Ellison D., 115–116
Smith, Hoke, 106–107
Smith, J. Allen, *The Spirit of American Government,* 8, 9–10
Smoot, Reed, 107
Smyth, Constantine, 233, 234, 235
Socialism, 11, 13, 231, 236, 250, 252. *See also* Public ownership
Socialist Party: wartime repression of, 134–136; and Sedition Act, 141, 143, 145, 148, 183; and Third International, 141; and Post Office Department, 164, 174–175, 176–177, 332 n.31
Social Reform and the Constitution (Goodnow), 8
South Africa, sanctions against, 254
Spanish-American War (1898), 285 nn.44–45, 287 n.52, 353 n.9
Speech, freedom of. *See* Espionage Act; Post Office Department; Sedition Act; Trading with the Enemy Act
Spencer, Selden P., 93
Spirit of American Government, The (Smith), 8, 9–10
Springfield Republican, 41, 45, 50, 53, 54
Springfield Union, 46
Stafford, Wendell P., 247, 249
Stafford, William H., 67–68, 71
Standard Brewery of Baltimore, 84
State, The (Wilson), 31
States' rights, 15–16, 24–25, 45–46,

States' rights (*Cont.*)
  57, 139, 196, 203, 204, 206, 207,
  255
Stedman, Seymour, 145
Steele, Henry J., 88
Steel Seizure Case, 258–259, 265–266,
  272, 273
Steene, Charles, 149, 152, 160, 180
Sterling, Thomas, 89–90
Stewart v. Kahn, 17
Stilson v. United States, 195
Stone, Harlan Fiske, 262–263
Story, Joseph, *Commentaries on the
  Constitution,* 16, 21–22
Strikes: telegraph, 28–29, 35, 36; tele-
  phone, 48, 49–50; extent of, 1919–
  1920, 75, 92, 131, 215; and
  Prohibition, 75–76, 87–88, 92; bitu-
  minous coal, 92, 117, 124–129,
  131–132, 196, 218; and cost of liv-
  ing, 97; railroad shopmen, 99–100;
  Southwest railroad, 123–124; and
  Lever Act, 124–132, 196, 210, 215;
  Puerto Rico railroad, 129; anthracite
  coal, 129, 131; "outlaw" railroad,
  130–131, 186, 210, 218–219; and
  Sedition Act, 137, 183–184, 186–
  187
Strong, Anna Louise, 152–155, 160
Strong, Rev. Sydney, 155
Strong, William, 19
Summers, Robert S., 7
Supreme Court: and reform movement,
  4–5; and state court rulings, 5, 12;
  attacks on, 5–13, 238; pre-1918 review of war powers, 16–19, 285
  n.44, 353 n.9; and rail and wire control, 55–59, 192, 200; impact on
  Congress's use of war powers, 58–
  59, 88, 89; and Espionage and Sedition Acts, 192–195, 199, 257; and
  wartime prohibition, 198–207; and
  Lever Act, 220–222; and rent control, 225–227, 232, 235–236, 238–
  244; and wage-price controls, 236–
  238; and Judges' Bill, 238–239; and
  Japanese-American internment, 258,
  261–264, 268, 270–271, 273; and
  Vietnam War, 260, 265; educational
  function of, 270
Sutherland, George, 235, 238, 242–243
Swayne, Noah, 17, 286 n.46

Sweigert, William T., 260

Taft, William Howard, 28–29, 61, 71–
  72, 235–239, 243–244, 347 n.30
Taney, Roger B., 18
Taxing power, 16
Telegraph and telephone control. *See*
  Wire control
Telegraphers. *See* Commercial Telegra-
  phers Union of America
Thayer, James Bradley, 11, 23–24, 25,
  71, 267
Thomas, Charles S., 67, 70, 92
Thomson, W. H. Seward, 218
Tigar, Michael E., 274
Tilson, John Q., 87, 288 n.56
Tincher, Jasper N., 245
Tocqueville, Alexis de, 256
Trading with the Enemy Act (1917),
  40, 80–81, 137, 163, 168–170, 173–
  174, 350 n.56
Treaties with Germany and
  Austria-Hungary (1921), 1, 232. *See
  also* Versailles Treaty
Trop v. Dulles, 259
Truman, Harry S., 259, 267, 272, 273
Tumulty, Joseph P.: and public owner-
  ship, 31–32, 43–44; and wire con-
  trol, 47–48, 49, 51–52; and
  Prohibition, 64, 72, 73–74, 76–78,
  91, 310 n.76; and strikes, 99, 123–
  125, 131–132; and profiteering, 113;
  and labor, 123; and censorship, 163;
  and political prisoners, 186–187
Turner, Arthur, 185–186

Underhill, Charles L., 245
Underwood, Oscar W., 36, 92
United Mine Workers Union (UMW),
  124, 125, 128, 129, 131, 196, 218
United States v. Carolene Products Co.,
  262–263
United States v. L. Cohen Grocery Co.,
  217, 220–222, 227, 228, 253, 258
United States v. Nixon, 256
United States v. Standard Brewery, 83–
  84
U.S. Brewers' Association, 75, 79, 81
U.S. Independent Telephone Associa-
  tion, 52, 58
U.S. Sugar Equalization Board, 103,
  115, 197

Vail, Theodore N., 32–33, 39, 43, 47
Van Devanter, Willis, 201–202, 203, 204, 236, 238, 242–243
Versailles Treaty: rejection of, 1, 197–198, 208; and wire control, 41–42, 57; and War-Time Prohibition Act, 73, 77–78; popular reaction to, 142, 153–154; and Sedition Act, 181–182; and Woodrow Wilson, 197, 208, 210, 213–214
Vietnam War, 260, 264, 265, 267, 268–269, 270, 272, 273, 274
Voigt, Edward, 67, 69, 288 n.56
Volstead, Andrew J., 86, 87–88, 89, 90, 91, 211, 214–215
Volstead Act, title I, 86–93, 191–192, 204
Volstead Peace Resolution: of 1920, 211–214; of 1921, 214–215

Wadsworth, James W., 36, 89
Walsh, David I., 210
Walsh, Frank P., 28–29
Walsh, Thomas J., 233–234
War beer (2.75 percent beer), 73–75, 83–86, 204. See also *Ruppert v. Caffey*
War Labor Board, 28–29, 123
War of 1812, 285 nn.44–45, 353 n.9
War powers, 1, 16, 284–285 n.43; traditional view of, 16, 19–21; pre-1918 judicial review of, 16–19, 353 n.9; grounds to challenge, 17, 206, 216; and public ownership, 27; and Prohibition, 63–64, 66–67, 88–90; and price control, 95, 97, 100, 101; and rent control, 109–111, 225, 228; perceived abuse of, 191–192, 196, 198, 206–208, 214; judicial review of in wartime, 256–258, 261–264, 268–275; and *Steel Seizure Case*, 258–259, 265–266, 272; and Communists, 258–259; and court-martial jurisdiction, 259; and loss of citizenship, 259–260; and Japanese-American internment, 261–264, 268, 270–271, 273; and political question doctrine, 264–268. *See also* Separation of powers; States' rights
—duration of, 17, 216–217; and rail and wire control, 55–59, 192, 200;

and wartime prohibition, 68–69, 87, 89–90, 200–201, 204, 206, 216; and amended Lever Act, 104–105, 208, 213, 216, 221; and rent control, 110–111, 225–227, 228–229, 240–241, 244–246, 248–249, 251; and McNary Act, 115–116; and coal strike injunction, 128; criticized, 131–132, 209, 214; and Espionage and Sedition Acts, 155, 178, 184–185, 208
—relation to emergency, 1–2, 18, 22, 24–25; and wartime prohibition, 67–68, 87–88, 89–90, 201, 204–206; and amended Lever Act, 105–106; and coal price controls, 117; and Sedition Act, 138–139, 159–160, 179–180; and wire control, 300 n.83
—and Bill of Rights, 57; traditional view of, 18–21, 22, 106–107, 110; and wartime prohibition, 67, 69–70, 199–200, 204, 206, 339 n.29; and Lever Act, 106–108, 217–219, 220, 221; and rent control, 109–111, 224, 226–227; and Espionage and Sedition Acts, 138–140, 192–195, 199–200, 202; and rail and wire control, 192, 300 n.85; and Japanese-American internment, 262–264
War Powers Resolution (1973), 255
Warren, Earl, 259
War-Time Prohibition Act (1918): adoption of, 66; issues as to validity of, 67–70, 72, 85; and wine, 68, 77; as fake war measure, 69, 72, 73, 198; and "intoxicating" liquor, 74–75, 83–84, 86–87; challenges to, 75, 83–86, 191–192, 198–203, 216; efforts to terminate, 76–79, 93; and war beer, 83–86; amendment of, 85–86. See also *Hamilton v. Kentucky Distilleries Co.*; *Ruppert v. Caffey*; Volstead Act
Washington Post, 15, 112, 198, 247, 248
Watson, James E., 41
Webb, Edwin Y., 62
Webb-Kenyon Act (1913), 61, 71
Weinberger, Harry, 148–149
Weinstein, Edwin A., 127, 214
Western Growers Protective Association, 262

Western Union, 28–29, 32, 33, 39, 40, 43, 46–49, 50–51, 301 n.87. *See also* Carlton, Newcomb
Weyl, Walter E., 3, 94, 122
Wheeler, Wayne B., 62, 71
White, Edward Douglass, 192, 202, 221, 235, 236, 337 n.16
White, William Allen, 97, 281 n.13
Whitman, Charles, 179, 184–185
Willard, Jess, 114, 118
Willoughby, Westel W., 110
Wilson, James, 23
Wilson, William B., 29–30, 127
Wilson, Woodrow: and role of government, 3, 127; and revolution, 3, 14, 98; and instrumentalism, 9; and executive leadership, 14–15; effects of illness, 15, 93, 127, 214; and rail control, 27, 43–44, 54; and wire control, 29, 50, 52; *The State,* 31; and public ownership, 31–32, 34, 43–44; and enemy property, 40, 81; and Anti-Saloon League, 64–65; and wartime prohibition, 65, 66, 72–74, 77–78, 91–93; and coal strikes, 92–93, 125, 127, 128, 131–132; and profiteering, 99–100, 108, 117, 119; and rent control, 108; *The New Freedom,* 119; and small businessmen, 119; and labor, 122–124; and Lever Act as strike weapon, 127; and "outlaw" rail strike, 130; and civil liberties, 142–143, 181; and political prisoners, 144–145, 146, 149, 179, 186–187, 188, 189; and censorship, 163, 174; and *Masses,* 165, 167, 170; and Versailles Treaty, 197, 208, 210, 213–214; and peace resolutions, 209, 210, 211, 212–214, 215; use of war powers by, 255, 267
Wire control: telegraphers' plan for, 28–29; administration's support for, 29–32, 34–35; companies' view of, 32–33; and wages, 33, 43, 48; and nationalization, 34, 35, 37, 38, 42, 43–45; and Congress, 35–37; prearmistice activity, 37–38; cable seizure, 38–42; rate increases, 43, 45–46, 48, 52, 57–58; treatment of Mackay companies, 46–48; challenges to, 46, 47, 54–57, 192; treatment of labor, 48–50, 52–53; *New York World* incident, 50–51; termination of, 51–52. See also *Dakota Central Telephone Co. v. South Dakota*
Wire Control Board, 38, 49
Wire Operating Board, 43, 49
Woman suffrage, 82, 119–122
Woodruff, Roy O., 231
World War I, 1, 13, 14, 62, 258
World War II, 254, 258, 259, 261–264, 268, 270–271

Yasui v. United States, 261–262, 263–264
Young, Arthur, 171, 331 n.19

Zucker, Morris, 148, 160, 187